P9-CMT-644

DISCARDED

5 2125 300823657

FACTS
AND
FEARS

FACTS AND FEARS

HARD TRUTHS
FROM A LIFE IN INTELLIGENCE

JAMES R. CLAPPER

with Trey Brown

VIKING

NEWARK PUBLIC LIBRARY
121 HIGH ST.
NEWARK, NY 14513

VIKING
An imprint of Penguin Random House LLC
375 Hudson Street
New York, New York 10014
penguin.com

Copyright © 2018 by James R. Clapper
Penguin supports copyright. Copyright fuels creativity, encourages diverse voices, promotes free speech, and creates a vibrant culture. Thank you for buying an authorized edition of this book and for complying with copyright laws by not reproducing, scanning, or distributing any part of it in any form without permission. You are supporting writers and allowing Penguin to continue to publish books for every reader.

Photograph credits: Insert page 4 (top right), 5 (middle), 10, 13 (bottom): Alex Wong/Getty Images; 6 (top), 14 (bottom), 16: Courtesy Barack Obama Presidential Library; 6 (middle left), 15 (top): Chip Somodevilla/Getty Images; 8 (top), 8 (bottom): Pete Souza/The White House/MCT via Getty Images; 4 (top left): Getty Images; 4 (middle): Ron Sachs–Pool/Getty Images; 4 (bottom): Thomas Monaster/NY Daily News Archive via Getty Images; 5 (top): Deb Smith/U.S. Air Force/Getty Images; 6 (middle right): Scott J. Ferrell/Congressional Quarterly/Getty Images; 6 (bottom): Everett Collection Inc./Alamy Stock Photo; 7 (top): Tom Williams/Roll Call/Getty Images; 7 (bottom): Win McNamee/Getty Images; 8 (middle): Getty Images/Stringer; 9 (top): STR/AFP/Getty Images; 9 (bottom left): Mahmud Turkia/AFP/Getty Images; 9 (bottom right): Samuel Corum/Anadolu Agency/Getty Images; 11 (top): Carl Court/Getty Images; 11 (bottom): The Guardian via Getty Images; 12 (top): Soner Kilinc/Anadolu Agency/Getty Images; 13 (top): Evy Mages/Stringer/Getty Images; 14 (top): Kevin Dietsch–Pool/Getty Images; 15 (bottom): William B. Plowman/NBC/NBC NewsWire via Getty Images; other photographs courtesy of the author.

ISBN 9780525558644 (hardcover)
ISBN 9780525558651 (ebook)

Printed in the United States of America
1   3   5   7   9   10   8   6   4   2

Set in Minion Pro

This work does not constitute an official release of US government information. All statements of fact, opinion, or analysis expressed are those of the author and do not reflect the official positions or views of the US government, specifically the Office of the Director of National Intelligence and the US Intelligence Community. Nothing in the contents should be construed as asserting or implying US government authentication of information or endorsement of the author's views. This material has been reviewed solely for classification.

Penguin is committed to publishing works of quality and integrity. In that spirit, we are proud to offer this book to our readers; however, the story, the experiences, and the words are the author's alone.

To the men and women of the Intelligence Community,
who keep this nation safe and secure;
to my parents, Anne and Jim Clapper,
who had profound influence on me;
and to Sue, who is always there for me

Contents

Beyond Their Wildest Imagination

As one of more than 40 million Americans who'd already cast an absentee ballot for the 2016 presidential election, I was in Muscat, Oman—on almost certainly my last whirlwind trip to meet with Middle East leaders as US director of national intelligence—when the electorate went to the polls on November 8. Oman is nine hours ahead of Washington, and before I went to bed that night, about 2:00 A.M. in Oman and 5:00 P.M. on the US East Coast, election analysts and pundits were discussing how the Republican candidate for president, Donald Trump, "had a narrow path" to win the election, but only if a long list of specific states improbably broke his way. They predicted that as soon as Florida or Ohio was called for former secretary of state Hillary Clinton, the election would effectively be over. I slept four or five hours, rose, and turned on the TV, discovering that the narrative had flipped: The media analysts had called Ohio for Trump and said Clinton needed massive turnouts in all the left-leaning cities in Florida that hadn't reported yet for her to have a chance of taking the state's twenty-nine Electoral College votes. I was surprised, but didn't really have time to think about it.

I read the overnight intelligence reports and continued getting ready for the day. An hour later, the media called Florida for Trump and laid out a very specific list of states that would now all have to swing to Clinton for her to win. As the morning progressed, I worked through the back-to-back meetings that were typical of foreign trips. In the short breaks between, my staff updated me on how things stood with the election. As we broke for lunch, at 2:31 A.M. on the US East Coast, the Associated Press declared Trump to be the US president-elect.

I was shocked. *Everyone* was shocked, including Mr. Trump, who'd continued on Election Day to cast doubt on whether he would accept the election results as legitimate. Having a few minutes alone, I kept thinking of just how out of touch I was with the people who lived in Middle America. I'd been stationed in heartland states repeatedly during my military career, particularly Texas, and I had traveled extensively as an agency director in the early 2000s and again during the past six and a half years as DNI, meeting with Intelligence Community employees outside of St. Louis, speaking at the University of Texas at Austin and with the Chamber of Commerce in San Antonio, and visiting many other places. I'd joked to audiences about just how out of touch people in Washington were, and I'd never failed to draw a laugh, sometimes applause. Working down in the "engine room" of our national security enterprise—"shoveling intelligence coal," as I liked to say—I never recognized just how much frustration with and resentment toward Washington those communities had, and just how deep the roots of their anger went. But Donald Trump had, and he'd appealed to them more than I'd realized or liked.

I also thought about the warning on Russian interference in the election that Homeland Security Secretary Jeh Johnson and I had issued to the American public a month earlier. We'd agonized over the precise wording of the press release and whether naming Russian president Vladimir Putin as the mastermind and puppeteer of the Russian influence operation would cause an international incident, drawing Jeh's department and the Intelligence Community into the political fray. Reading responses to exit polls, I realized that our release and public statements simply hadn't mattered. I wasn't sure if people were oblivious to the seriousness of the threat we'd described or if they just didn't care what the Russians were doing. Either way, I saw that our efforts ended up having all the impact of another raindrop in a storm at sea.

I wondered what President Obama was thinking and if he regretted his reticence to "put his thumb on the scale" of the election—as he put it—by not publicly calling out the Russian interference while Putin was effectively *standing* on the other end of that scale. At the same time, I was no longer sure it would have mattered to the people in Middle America if the president had presented everything we knew about Russia's massive cyber and propaganda efforts to undermine American democracy, disparage former secretary of state Hillary Clinton, and promote Donald Trump. Despite the public narrative that Edward Snowden had disingenuously started in 2013, alleging we were spying on everyday US citizens, the IC had no authority and no capability to evaluate how Americans were receiving the Russian propaganda or what they were thinking and doing when they entered polling booths. In a lot of ways, our capabilities were like the physical infrastructure at the signals intelligence facilities in Ukraine I'd visited in 1991 after the Iron Curtain fell. Just like the former Soviet antenna arrays had been, our capabilities were oriented outward toward the threat and largely incapable of looking inward, even if we wanted to. It simply wasn't our job. We'd been watching how the Russians were trying to influence US voters, not what impact they may have been having. We had no empirical evidence to assess whether the Russian influence campaign was working, and on Election Day, I was disturbed to recognize it probably had.

I didn't realize it then, but the Russians were just as shocked as we were. They'd succeeded beyond their wildest imagination and were completely unprepared for their own success. The Russian propaganda network in the United States, formerly known as Russia Today and since rebranded as just "RT," was jubilant in calling the election for Mr. Trump: "That's what this is, a defining moment in global history, that America is willing to turn the page and possibly isolate itself from the rest of the world." They declared, "The next speech that Donald Trump gives to the world will be one of the most important speeches in the history of the world." As the anchors reveled in Trump's victory, the crawl at the bottom of the screen continued running lines intended to delegitimize Clinton's win, such as SEVERAL STATES REPORT BROKEN VOTING MACHINES. The Russian internet troll factory scrambled to stop its #DemocracyRIP social media campaign, set to run from its fake accounts on Twitter and Facebook. In the middle of all this, Putin lost the chance to return the favor of challenging Clinton's victory, as she'd challenged the results of the 2011 Russian election when she'd been US secretary of state. I don't believe he minded—at all.

After the election, the CIA and the FBI continued to uncover evidence of preelection Russian propaganda, all intended to undermine Clinton and promote Trump, and the Intelligence Community continued to find indications of Russian cyber operations to interfere with the election. At a National Security Council meeting on Monday, December 5, President Obama gave us more explicit instructions. He wanted the CIA, NSA, and FBI—each agency with the mission-specific tradecraft and capabilities to determine what the Russians had done—to assemble all their findings, encompassing the most sensitive sourcing, into a single report that he could pass on to the next administration and to Congress. He also asked us to produce a paper for public consumption with as much information from the classified version as possible. And critically, he wanted all of this done before he left office.

The highly classified IC assessment that resulted was, I believe, a landmark product—among the most important ever produced by US intelligence. I was proud of our work, but the unclassified version we published ran just a few pages and was written with the clinical sterility of a standard intelligence briefing. I still wanted to more fully capture what it felt like to be on the receiving end of the Russian influence operation in 2015 and 2016. For me, there was no specific moment in that time, no flash of insight when I understood that our primary adversary for nearly all of my half century as a US intelligence professional was—without exaggeration—hacking away at the very roots of our democracy. That realization slowly washed over me in 2016 in a tide that continued to rise after the election, and even after I'd left government and the new administration had transitioned into power. My concern about what I saw taking place in America—and my apprehension that we were losing focus on what the Russians had done to us—is ultimately what persuaded me to write this book, to use what we had learned in our IC assessment to frame my experience and our collective experience as Americans.

My hope is to capture and share the experience of more than fifty years in the intelligence profession, to impart the pride that intelligence officers take in their work, the care with which they consider the ethical implications of surveillance and espionage, and the patriotism and willingness to sacrifice that they bring to the job. And finally, I intend to show that what Russia did to the United States during the 2016 election was far worse than just another post–Cold War jab at an old adversary. What happened to us was a sustained assault on our traditional values and institutions of governance, from external as well as internal pressures. In the wake of that experience, my fear is that many Americans are questioning if facts are even knowable, as foreign adversaries and our national leaders continue to deny objective reality while advancing their own "alternative facts." America possesses great strength and resilience, but how we rise to this challenge—with clear-eyed recognition of the unbiased facts and by setting aside our doubts—is entirely up to us. I believe the destiny of the American ideal is at stake.

CHAPTER ONE

Born into the Intelligence Business

When I accepted President Obama's offer to be the director of national intelligence, I was pushing seventy years old. Today, of course, I'm dragging it closer and closer to eighty. One reason that's significant is that both the earliest notions of a US Intelligence Community and the menace of the Soviet threat to the West were born about the same time as I was. My father was drafted into the Army in 1944, when I was three years old. As a signals intelligence officer during the war, he supported intercepting Japanese and German communications used to help the Allies win the war. He became deeply committed to the mission and respected the people he worked with, and before the ink was dry on the Japanese instrument of unconditional surrender, he'd decided to stay in the Army while most everyone else was demobilizing and shedding the uniform. Growing up and moving around from one signals intelligence site to another, I learned from a very early age to never—*never*—talk about what my dad did. I think my parents would be shocked, and my mother also mildly amused, that after retiring from the intelligence profession in 2017, I'd try to publicly explain what the Intelligence Community—the "IC"—is, what it does, and what it should stand for.

For me, this seven-decade-and-more journey started with a bang, and not a good one. My earliest vivid memory is of my mother and me entering the port of Leghorn (Livorno), Italy, in 1946, on our way to meet my dad in Eritrea, on the Horn of Africa. We were among the first US dependents to cross the Atlantic after the war, a trip my mother portrayed as a big adventure—I'm sure to calm her own apprehensions as much as mine. US forces had liberated the city of Leghorn from the Germans in 1944 and still occupied it and controlled the harbor, but postwar Italy wasn't precisely safe for US dependents, or really for anyone. As our troopship, the USS *Fred T. Berry,* entered the harbor, I heard and felt an explosion, and the ship went dead in the water. Its alarm bells started ringing, three rings and a pause, and then repeated—I can still hear the shrill sound—and we rushed topside. Huddling on the deck, I felt my mother gripping the back of my far-too-big life preserver and watched as lifeboats were lowered over the side. She told me years later that the crew had barely kept the ship from sinking. As we were towed into port, the mast tops of sunken ships slowly passed to either side, looking every bit like crosses in a graveyard for vessels not as fortunate as ours.

We spent a couple of weeks in Leghorn while the rudder was repaired and then continued on our voyage to Africa. In Alexandria, my dad bribed the harbor pilot with a carton of cigarettes to take him out to meet us as our ship made its way into port. I don't recall arriving in Egypt, but my second vivid childhood memory is of leaving, my mother shaking me from sleep in a hotel in Cairo while my dad quickly packed our bags. She told me, calmly but urgently, that we had to go to Payne Field, Cairo's airport, and leave the country immediately. I was barely awake as we raced to board an airplane. The family legend is that King Farouk had met them that night in the hotel bar, which must have seemed like amazing luck, at least until the king made a pass at my mother, my dad tried to punch him, and we all had to depart in a hurry. It's not good to take a swing at the king.

It took eight weeks for my mother and me to travel from Fort Wayne, Indiana, to the primitive but very pretty city of Asmara, Eritrea, which sat atop a 7,500-foot-high plateau. Today Eritrea is a small, independent, and largely forgotten nation on the Red Sea, bordering the African powerhouses of Ethiopia and Sudan. Before the war, it had been in the Italian colony of Abyssinia, but when I arrived in 1946 it was part of Ethiopia, and the long war resulting in Eritrean independence was still a few years off. The locals viewed Americans with reverence; in their eyes we were rich and powerful, even though we lived in a converted barracks building on a former Italian Navy communications station. I made friends, both with the local kids and a few other Army brats, and learned Italian to fluency, but, of course, have forgotten it all since.

One day a friend and I were playing in the Army salvage dump, which was off-limits, but there was so much cool military equipment left over from the war, it was hard to stay away. I picked up a glass vial and dumped out what appeared to be rainwater but was in fact sulfuric acid, which ran down my left leg. I knew I was in trouble when part of my pants began to disappear and my leg started steaming. I ran home, scared to death. The Asmara doctor—one of only seven officers on the post—had just stopped by our quarters, and he and my mother dumped me in the bathtub, emptying a ten-pound bag of baking soda my mother had just bought at the commissary onto me, which was exactly the right emergency procedure. My recovery took months and involved a lot of painful skin grafts, and my dad never forgave himself, since he was the logistics officer responsible for the dump. My accident convinced them that remote stations might not have adequate medical care for small children prone to self-inflicted disasters, and so, in 1948, when I was seven and my parents learned my mother was pregnant, they decided it was time to return to the States.

Some forty-three years later, when I was director of the Defense Intelligence Agency, I visited Asmara and walked around the compound, which was by then an abandoned Eritrean Army post. I was amazed how dinky it seemed compared to the huge complex I remembered, but it was unmistakably the same place. I found the foundation footings of what had been our quarters, and the original Italian Navy communications towers were still there.

My memories of the trip back to the United States are as vivid as those of the trip to Eritrea. We flew out on Ethiopian Airlines, which consisted of a few olive drab B-17s with "EAL" printed on their tails. Our pilot, "Bail Out" Wicker, told us he got his name because he'd parachuted out of more than one B-17 during the war. That did not inspire confidence in seven-year-old Jimmy Clapper, but thankfully we encountered no emergencies on our flight. I will never forget sitting in the nose bubble, which still had its machine-gun mount, and flying into Payne Field, where planes abandoned after the war were parked in the desert as far as the eye could see: fighters, bombers, transport planes, all baking in the sun. From Cairo, we flew to Dhahran, Saudi Arabia, and stayed five days, waiting for a plane to Germany. I remember standing outside our motel in short pants as the blowing sand stung my legs. We flew on a big, slow C-54 (a redesignated DC-4) from Dhahran to Frankfurt, which was still in rubble, with people everywhere begging for handouts. We stayed overnight in Bad Soden, outside the city, with no potable water, and I recall being very thirsty. From Frankfurt, we spent a day and a half on a train to Bremerhaven, single-tracking the whole way and passing mile after mile of abandoned or destroyed rolling stock: locomotives, tankers, passenger cars, and freight cars. In retrospect, Germany's recovery from the war is a remarkable achievement. Finally, we sailed back to the United States on another converted troopship.

My dad was assigned to Vint Hill Farms Station in Virginia, which was at the time an Army signals intelligence post outside Washington. I was a huge fan of Superman and Batman, and I had a large collection of their comics, which I kept in strict chronological order and took very good care of. They'd be worth a fortune today. But when we had to relocate again, there were strict weight limits for transporting household goods and my parents didn't want to use up their allowance with a lot of comic books. I was told we had to leave them behind, and so, with much regret, I handed over my entire pristine-condition collection to a bratty four-year-old girl named Sue. Seventeen years later, after many more moves for both of us, I married Sue, despite the fact that she no longer had my comics.

I wasn't aware of it, but that was a tough move for my parents, too, as we were forced to separate for a while. In 1950, after the North Koreans invaded South Korea, my dad was sent to Chitose, Japan, as the second-in-command of a small Army signals intelligence unit supporting the war effort. Chitose is on Hokkaido, the second largest and northernmost of Japan's four main islands. It's just across the Sea of Japan and on about the same latitude as Vladivostok, Russia. Because we couldn't join him until suitable facilities for dependents were built, my mother, sister, and I returned to Fort Wayne, living with my grandparents on their 160 acres while I was in fourth grade and part of fifth, before we joined my dad near the end of 1951.

Regular Army soldiers viewed the signals intelligence guys in the Army Security Agency as having more brains than brawn and more of an affinity for electronics than shooting, fighting, and sleeping on the ground. But in Chitose, every now and then the commanding officer and my dad wanted to remind the troops that they were part of the Army, and so they'd take the signals intelligence unit to the field and practice putting up tents, operating a field mess, and doing weapons proficiency training. My dad took me along on one of these summer encampments, equipped with cut-down fatigues, a web belt, a canteen, the smallest helmet liner my dad could find, and even a small backpack. The first sergeant, the senior enlisted man in the unit, took a shine to me and let me carry his (unloaded) M1 rifle, or maybe he saw me as a convenient way to get out of having to carry it himself. Either way, it was a cool experience for an eleven-year-old, and undoubtedly something that can't be done in today's Army, even on Bring Your Child to Work Day.

I was enamored with the little I knew of my dad's work, and I was learning a lot about soldiering from watching him, but it was something my mother did in Chitose in 1952 that had a lifelong impact on how I viewed the world. This was before the Supreme Court's 1954 *Brown v. Board of Education of Topeka* ruling that desegregated schools in the States, but it was four years after President Truman signed Executive Order 9981, banning racial discrimination in the military. The executive order may have desegregated the armed forces institutionally, but not socially.

Much of the social life on military bases, particularly overseas, and certainly on the remote base in Chitose, was centered on the Officers' Club. On Sundays the club always served a fancy brunch, putting out its best linen and china and hiring a Japanese band to play and sing its amusing interpretations of popular American songs. The officers, including my dad, who was then a captain, wore dress uniforms, while their wives were in their Sunday best, complete with hats and white gloves. Even the kids dressed up, which for me was torture.

At my age, I didn't know and didn't care about who the senior officers in the club were; I didn't know the colonels and lieutenant colonels. But one Sunday, I recognized my dentist, who was a first lieutenant, a junior Army officer like my dad, and one of the very few black Army officers on the base. On that day my family had a prime table near the band, but when my dentist came in, he took a seat by himself on the perimeter of the room. I noticed him there but didn't think much of it. When the music stopped, my mother—and I'm sure she picked this timing on purpose—stood up and rather ostentatiously walked over to my dentist's table. Many of the officers and their wives in the room noticed and pointedly watched her. She talked with him for a minute or two, invited him to sit with us, took him by the hand, and led him through the center of the room to our table. As she did, all the senior officers began staring at my dad, their faces projecting their unspoken questions—*What is your wife doing? Can't you get her under control?* I'll never forget my dad's expression—a mixture of amusement, admiration, and fear. But to his great credit, he made my sister and me shift our chairs to make room at the table for our guest.

There may have been consequences for my parents, although if there were, they never mentioned them. In fact, my mother never said a word about what she'd done, even though she spoke to me about a lot of other things, sometimes incessantly. That may be why I remember that Sunday brunch so vividly, even though it was more than sixty-five years ago. When I was at a very impressionable age, my mother showed me that the color of someone's skin doesn't determine the human dignity they deserve. That lesson stayed with me and influenced decisions I've made in both my personal and professional lives.

When my family left Japan in 1953, en route to Littleton, Massachusetts, my sister and I were parked with my mother's parents in Philadelphia. This was a good deal for me, because my grandparents let me stay up as late as I wanted to watch TV. Television was a great novelty, since we didn't have one in Japan. On Friday nights, the old movies would end about 12:30, and one night I did the 1950s equivalent of channel surfing, which required actually walking up to the set and manually turning the selector dial. There were only four channels, and one night I stopped between channels four and five—I'll never forget this—because I heard voices speaking in a clipped cadence. There was no picture, just voices. I listened for maybe fifteen minutes as they batted words and numbers back and forth in speech patterns bordering on the nonsensical. Finally I figured out that I'd stumbled onto the broadcast frequency of the Philadelphia Police Department dispatcher. I wanted to hear more, but my arm was getting tired, so I went to the kitchen, found some toothpicks, and stuck them in the dial to secure it. That's right, I "hacked" the Philadelphia Police Department, using my grandparents' black-and-white TV set and some toothpicks.

The next night I was prepared with a map of the city of Philadelphia and began plotting the addresses where the police cruisers were dispatched. After a few nighttime surveillance sessions, I figured out where the police district boundaries were, based on which cruisers responded to specific locations. I wrote down anything they said that I didn't understand, and kept listening until I had figured out what all the "10" codes (10-4, 10-5, etc.) were, the system for call signs, and the personal identifiers for lieutenants and above. I got a pack of index cards to keep track of all the facts I was collecting. Soon I was staying up every night to build my "database." About a month later, when my parents came to Philadelphia to retrieve my sister and me, my dad asked, "So what've you been up to this summer?" I showed him my map and my card files, and I gave him a thorough briefing on how police operations worked in the city. I'll never forget the expression on his face as he exclaimed, "My God, I've raised my own replacement!"

One evening in the fall of 2015, when I was the director of national intelligence, I was shooting the breeze with my staff and recounted this story. A few weeks later, my speechwriter put it into the script for a speech I was scheduled to give for a CIA-sponsored event at George Washington University on "The Ethos and the Profession of Intelligence." I hadn't seriously considered it before, but this vignette from my childhood illustrates what we do in the intelligence profession in simple terms. Intelligence involves research, determination, persistence, patience, continuity, drawing inferences in the absence of complete information, and taking advantage of vulnerabilities and what you overhear in others' conversations, no matter how cryptic and jargon-filled they are. Obviously, the Philadelphia Police Department hadn't foreseen that a twelve-year-old kid would listen in on its radio transmissions, let alone map out its operations. I didn't realize it at the time, but that little avocation, more than sixty years ago, started me down the path to service in the intelligence business.

My family spent most of my seventh-grade year in Littleton while my dad completed the Army Security Agency Officers Career Course at Fort Devens. We lived in an old farmhouse on eighty-five acres with lots of berries to pick. By 1953, when my sister was old enough to start elementary school and I was getting close to starting high school, my parents made plans to settle down in Virginia, near the Army Security Agency headquarters in Arlington. It was going to be a struggle on an Army captain's salary, but they decided to buy a small house in the expensive Washington suburb of Falls Church, Virginia, which would enable me to attend the new Annandale High School. I finished the seventh grade being bused to a dilapidated wreck of an elementary school near Bailey's Crossroads, called the Woodburn Annex. My only distinct memory of that spring was our seventh-grade field trip to New York, when we got to fly on a Lockheed Super Constellation. For me, that plane was the pinnacle of speed and luxury, and the only thing it was missing was a nose bubble with a machine-gun mount.

As planned, I enrolled at Annandale High School as an eighth grader when its doors first opened to students in the fall of 1954—the year of the US Supreme Court decision to desegregate schools, an unpopular ruling in Virginia. When our neighboring Arlington County attempted to observe the ruling, the state government fired its school board and took direct control of enrollments statewide. I don't know what would have happened if Fairfax County, where we lived, had been left to its own devices, but with the state in control, Annandale High remained segregated throughout my four years there. I wasn't involved in segregation protests or anything radical, but I often thought about what my mother had done for my dentist in Chitose.

Meanwhile, things weren't going quite as planned for my dad. After a series of reorganizations involving the three service cryptologic commands—the Army Security Agency, the Air Force Security Service, and the Naval Security Group—he found himself attached to the headquarters unit of a new intelligence organization—the National Security Agency—and when in 1955 NSA began its move from Arlington Hall to Fort Meade, south of Baltimore, Maryland, he was among the first reassigned. My parents decided to stay in Falls Church, and my dad had to spend several hours on the road every day, all so I could remain in my high school. This had to be particularly frustrating, because my brother, Mike, had just joined our family. Mike was born at Fort Belvoir seven years after my sister, Ruth Anne, was born at Walter Reed, seven years after I came into the world.

When I was old enough to drive, my dad bought me a 1947 Cadillac convertible. I think he intentionally picked a car that weighed over two tons and got nine miles to the gallon so I couldn't go very far with it. It was broken most of the time anyway, and we spent many weekends together working on it and "bonding." I still keep a model of that car, and it always reminds me of dad and our grease-monkey Saturday afternoons together.

By my junior year, I was working as a janitor at our church, and over the summer as a lifeguard at our neighborhood pool. And I was terribly in love, as only a seventeen-year-old can be. Then, in early 1958, my dad was unexpectedly reassigned to Germany. I'm sure this was stressful for my parents, but for me it was a Shakespearean tragedy. I announced that I wasn't going and that I had made arrangements to live in a friend's basement for the summer and my senior year. My mother then did a brave thing—she sold our house and traveled to Germany with my sister and brother to join my dad without me. I lasted about six weeks before I wrote a letter asking them to "send my orders" so that I could rejoin the family in Germany. That was a hugely disappointing moment for me, to admit I couldn't manage life by myself and to leave Virginia.

Life can sometimes loop back on itself, and in 2013, when I was the DNI, Annandale High asked me to be its graduation speaker, fifty-nine years after I first enrolled there. The ceremony fell on June 13, and when I accepted the invitation, I had no idea how difficult that week would be for me. It was two and a half months after damaging mandatory budget cuts went into effect for the Intelligence Community, and I was fighting the Defense Department to keep intelligence professionals from being furloughed. It was three weeks after Edward Snowden had fled to Hong Kong, and stolen documents were leaking out through press outlets, cutting into intelligence capabilities on a daily basis. I thought about canceling, but was glad I didn't. The students were in high spirits, and they also made me laugh when I arrived. Rather than my donning the gown commensurate with my master's degree, the students asked me to wear the same one they were wearing, to indicate that, like them, I had yet to graduate from Annandale High. I was game, and I did.

I took about two minutes of my commencement speech to vent, before talking about the graduating class, their accomplishments, and what lay ahead for them. I closed my speech that night by telling them:

> If you take care of yourself, if you have a vision of what you want for the future, if you're kind, and attentive, and responsible, I can pretty much guarantee that you'll live an interesting and successful life. That doesn't necessarily mean you'll reach every goal you set out to achieve. Fifty-nine years ago, I set out to graduate from Annandale High, and I didn't reach

that goal. I never got the chance to wear a red Annandale robe and mortarboard until tonight.

And it's okay to fall short of some of your goals. Even if it feels like a disaster at the time, you'll most likely do some pretty cool other things, as long as you do your best to stay on the right path. I'm proud of how things have turned out in my life. And I've never, ever, been bored. Although these days, I'd like a little boredom. Sometimes, by some circuitous route, you eventually reach those goals you thought had long passed you by. So tonight, I get to wear Annandale red. And you know, it feels pretty sweet.

Back in the summer of 1958, leaving Virginia for Germany with my tail tucked between my legs, the feeling was not pretty sweet. I took a ship to Bremerhaven and a train to Nuremberg, where my parents met me and drove me the last few miles to Herzo Base—less than fifty miles from the East German border—where my dad was the operations officer of an Army signals intelligence battalion. His group was part of an enormous effort to intercept communications among the newly formed Warsaw Pact nations: the Soviet Union and seven satellite countries in Eastern Europe. My dad had a knack for being posted in places just in time for a flash point, and I had just barely arrived when Nikita Khrushchev delivered his November speech, with an ultimatum to remove all Western forces from West Berlin in six months or risk war. President Eisenhower maintained American troops in West Berlin, and he kept the number of service members stationed in West Germany at a quarter million, plus their dependents.

I fell into an easy routine with all the other Army brats at Nuremberg American High School. We were a tiny school and had just enough male bodies to form a football team to play against other dependent-American high schools. I played guard on both offense and defense, not a natural position for me at 160 pounds, and I soon got over leaving my love interest behind in Virginia. The recent history of Nuremberg was intensely omnipresent, and I remember touring the courtroom where the International Military Tribunal had been held just thirteen years before. Here, the Holocaust was not something you just read about in a textbook, and discussions of the atrocities humans are capable of committing were not academic. I think that for all of us, it put the work our parents were doing to counter the Soviets in a sobering light.

That year I befriended two soldiers stationed at Herzo Base—ostensibly working for my dad—who were licensed amateur ham radio operators. Because high-frequency radio carried over great distances, the military in those days sanctioned hams as an alternative way of communicating with family and friends back in the States. Cooperating hams in America could connect the overseas radio operators via phone and save them a ton of money in overseas phone charges. It was all fascinating to me, so I hung out with these two soldiers, both of whom had college degrees and were really good guys. They taught me about communications theory and practice and about the propagation effects of weather, time of day, and seasons of the year, especially in the high-frequency band of the radio frequency spectrum. That primer was a good foundation years later, since HF was the communications mainstay for the Soviets and Chinese during the Cold War. More important to me at the time was the fact that I had a chance to encounter the caliber of people who were in the same profession as my dad. They were not at all interested in the Army as a career, but they were conscientious and professional about their duties, and they stressed that if I was going to join the military, I should do so as a commissioned officer. I was impressed, and the idea of service was growing on me.

By the summer of 1959, I was ready to venture out on my own. I graduated from the American School as covaledictorian and enrolled at the University of Maryland in Munich, a small college campus for dependent sons and daughters on the McGraw Kaserne military installation, with enough course offerings for two years of college. My roommate there was a guy named Mike Leonard, who'd been a classmate in Nuremberg. We both wanted to be Army officers and thought Munich gave us the best chance to secure appointments to one of the service academies the following year. It was a great place to be a college student. I drank a lot of beer and, riding the trolley to the clubs and beer sinks in Schwabing, learned enough Gasthaus German to take advantage of what the city had to offer. Mike and I were studying Russian, and that fall we got the bright idea to take the train to Berlin to spend part of our Christmas holiday trying to find Soviet soldiers to talk to, though I honestly don't know if we were going to try to befriend them, harass them, spy on them, or recruit them. We stayed in West Berlin for a few days, and because it was two years before the Berlin Wall was constructed, we could walk freely into East Berlin. I remember approaching a couple of uniformed Russians on the street and getting about as far as "Hello. How are you?" before they laughed at us.

At the end of our year in Munich, Mike received an appointment to the US Military Academy in West Point, but I failed to secure my own placement. So, in the summer of 1960, I transferred to the University of Maryland's main campus in College Park, where I enrolled in the Air Force ROTC program. Because the university is a federal land-grant college, the government required all male students to participate in ROTC during their freshman and sophomore years. Because I actually wanted to become a military officer, I also joined the Cadet Leadership Academy, the program to train cadet officers. I reapplied to all of the service academies, and that fall I finally received an alternate appointment to the US Naval Academy. I took a bus from College Park to Annapolis for the physical exam, the last requirement for admission. To my profound shock, I failed the exam, in the process learning that the vision in my left eye wasn't within the standards for commissioning as an officer in *any* of the military services. I was devastated.

I wrote my parents to let them know my plans for my life would have to change. A few days later, I received a letter back from my dad. A Marine Corps colonel who was a friend and colleague of his could pull some strings to get me into the Marine Corps Platoon Leaders Course (PLC), a commissioning program for which my deficient eye wouldn't necessarily disqualify me, and on February 2, 1961, I enlisted in the Marine Corps Reserve.

I have vivid memories of the following rather unpleasant summer in Quantico, Virginia. My drill instructors, Gunny Fowler and Sergeant Stiborski, were two tough, squared-away Marines who physically and emotionally scared me. None of us "college boys" had a name other than "maggot." I spent seemingly endless hours on the drill "grinder"—the expanse of asphalt I thought might melt the soles of my boots. I can still recall the serial number of my vintage M1 rifle—1954622—and silently pleading with it to please—*please*—do what Sergeant Stiborski kept telling us our weapons were supposed to do. One day Gunny Fowler said he was fed up with our drill and ceremony proficiency and was going to show us how it was supposed to be done. We were all loaded into what, aptly, were called "cattle cars," small semitrailer trucks with no seats, and driven, standing, to the Marine Barracks at Eighth and I streets in Southeast Washington, to witness a Friday evening Sunset Parade—the ultimate in military pageantry and ceremony.

I remember the first time the Marines went from the commands of "port arms" to "attention," and when their three hundred rifles hit the deck in response, there was just a single sharp crack of butt plates on concrete, rather than the flurry of clanks produced when my training platoon in Quantico executed the same drill. Their precision gave me goose bumps—all those rifles, just one sound. Half a century later it's still thrilling to me, and I still try to attend Sunset Parades at the Marine Barracks at least once each year.

Our training platoon had started with fifty-two "maggots." On the final day of the course, we were down to just thirty-five, and we still needed to pass our final grueling physical test to graduate. All thirty-five of us were successful, and ours was the only platoon that didn't leave someone behind. As we went back to our Quonset hut barracks to shower and change into our clean utility uniforms, Fowler and Stiborski addressed us for the first time as "Marines." I still feel the tingle of pride from that memory, and despite spending thirty-two years in an Air Force uniform, I continue to have a deep spiritual connection to the Corps. I wanted nothing so much as to be a Marine intelligence officer, but the Marine Corps of the sixties didn't have a viable path for an intelligence career. So I returned to College Park and Air Force ROTC for my junior year of college in the fall of 1961, and I transferred my enlistment from the Marine Corps to the Air Force Reserve.

That summer my dad had been reassigned to NSA headquarters in Maryland, and my family had returned to the States. To save money I moved into the basement of their quarters at Fort Meade and commuted to College Park. After a summer with Gunny Fowler and Sergeant Stiborski, I was suddenly a rock star at close-order drill and professional courses, and I quickly moved up the Air Force ROTC cadet ranks.

But the most momentous life event of my junior year was when my parents became reacquainted with the Terrys, a couple they'd been friends with at Vint Hill Farms Station more than a decade earlier, and my mother pressed me to reintroduce myself to their daughter, Sue, who was then a high school senior. Any recommendation on girls from my mother was an immediate turnoff for me, and my lack of interest was only compounded when I realized who she was and that she no longer had my comic books. But my mother bugged me and bugged me, and finally I agreed to call Sue. I brought her down to the university campus on a Sunday afternoon to show her around. She liked it and immediately decided she was going to apply for the following fall. That was the start of a three-and-a-half-year, stormy, on-again, off-again dating relationship.

In the summer of 1962 I attended ROTC summer training for rising seniors at Otis Air Force Base in Massachusetts. After the PLC training in Quantico, Otis felt more like a Boy Scout jamboree than military training. I consider that a testament to the PLC program, rather than a slight to Air Force ROTC, and with the Marine Corps experience behind me, the Air Force officer in charge simply wrote in my evaluation that I acted as if I were "already commissioned." None of the training exercises at Otis was particularly memorable, but one afternoon we were quickly loaded onto buses and driven to the airfield. On the way there we were told that President Kennedy was landing at the base en route to a family vacation at his residence in Hyannis Port, and we were to make him feel welcome when he got off Air Force One. Somehow I ended up with eight or ten other cadets in the front row against the rope as the president shook hands with each of us. When he got to me, I gave him my name, and he asked me what plane I wanted to fly. I told him that I didn't want to fly; I wanted to be an intelligence officer. He stopped and looked at me, a bit askance. There was just a brief pause, and then he said, "Good. We need more like you," and moved on. I'm sure the president never gave that little exchange another thought. I'll never forget it.

I received my commission to be an Air Force second lieutenant as a distinguished military graduate in June 1963. My academic and military grades had been stellar, and I'd been commandant of the Cadet Leadership Academy for the first semester of my senior year and then cadet wing commander the second semester, which meant that I was able to select the profession of intelligence officer, and I had my pick of first assignment. I selected the Signals Intelligence Officers Course at Goodfellow Air Force Base in San Angelo, Texas, the Air Force "SIGINT college of knowledge." Well west of the Houston/Dallas/San Antonio triangle, San Angelo was four hours from any major city. There was very little to do besides studying signals intelligence, and most of us couldn't even do that right away.

That summer the Air Force didn't plan well for how to manage sixty brand-new second lieutenants all showing up at Goodfellow at the same time, most of us lacking the security clearance required to take classes. Background investigations require some time, particularly for people who've lived overseas, so most of us spent our first few months cycling through busy-work assignments like "assistant Officers' Club manager." We played a lot of cards and flag football and drank a lot of beer. Bored, and looking for something professionally useful to do, I found the Air Force major who was in charge of base security and asked if I could ride along with the enlisted air police on their rounds. He looked me over. I was in my Air Force uniform, but still had the starched shirt, shiny shoes, and buzz cut of a Marine. He agreed, and so I spent the next few months working with enlisted security forces.

Meanwhile, Sue was on the opposite work curve. She'd majored in partying during her freshman year at the University of Maryland and, after deciding that college wasn't for her, applied for work at NSA. She first worked as an editor of technical publications and then landed a job as a secretary in the Soviet Air division—the gatekeeper and office manager for a group of analysts tasked with keeping tabs on Soviet Air Defense forces, right in the center of some of the most important intelligence work taking place at the time.

Many of the prominent code crackers of World War II had been women who'd stayed with the agency after the war, and NSA in the 1960s was appreciative of their contributions and more open to having them in leadership positions than the rest of government or corporate America. My dad had worked for several of these women in the 1950s, including Juanita Moody and Ann Caracristi, who in 1980 would shatter the glass ceiling as deputy director of NSA. Hearing him talk about these individuals as smart, capable leaders, without his making a big deal about their gender, made a bigger impression on my views of women than any feminist views my mother ever expressed.

After about five months, my security clearance finally came through, and I started learning the professional discipline of signals intelligence. I distinctly remember the afternoon of November 22, 1963. After classes all morning, I'd eaten lunch in the base mess hall and climbed into my

Corvair convertible for the short drive back to my room in the bachelor officers' quarters. I turned the radio on and heard the first reports out of Dallas that President Kennedy had been shot. As I drove, the realization of what had happened hit me—the shock, disbelief, and uncertainty. He and the First Lady were so attractive as a couple and had captured the hearts of the American people. And I'd met him just fifteen months earlier. He'd shaken my hand and said we needed more people like me.

On base, everything stopped. There were no afternoon classes, and we were all glued to our televisions. I felt dissociated from the reality of the moment; not a participant, but just an observer of the world, a feeling I'd have again in September 2001. And also, just as after 9/11, what followed was a combination of uncertainty—that the world had changed forever and we'd have to find a new normal—and of resolution, that the nation would move forward together.

As my seminar of thirteen lieutenants wrapped up our five-month training course in early 1964, we eagerly looked forward to our assignments. The training had prepared us to be flight commanders for SIGINT units overseas, where we would supervise shifts of airmen conducting collection around the clock. I was ready to pick up the family torch of collecting Soviet communications and doing to them what I'd done to the Philadelphia PD at the age of twelve. But the Air Force, in its infinite wisdom, decided to assign me to what was euphemistically called "the Air Force Special Communications Center" at Kelly Air Force Base in San Antonio, a highly classified "Third Echelon"–type in-depth processing and analytic organization, much like NSA. It conducted longer-term analysis on the Soviet air forces.

I was appointed the deputy chief of the Soviet Air Defense Branch, a job title much more impressive than the responsibilities with which I was actually entrusted, but I set out to learn as much as I could about the technical tasks performed by the airmen I was ostensibly supervising. They seemed to appreciate my willingness to have them show me the ropes. After about six months, I was plucked out of that job and moved to what was known in the military as the "orderly room," which is the hub of military management: inspecting barracks, the mess hall, and the motor pool; administering personnel actions, discipline, and reenlistment ceremonies; and on and on. I served, for example, as a summary court officer in the case of an airman killed in a bar fight, and dealt with his personal effects and settled affairs with his family. The most indelible experience I had was processing the dishonorable discharges of two airmen who were roommates in the barracks, and who had been "outed" (which was not a term used back then) as homosexual. In the day, there was—by regulation—no other recourse. They automatically lost their security clearances and were expelled from the service. At best, homosexuals were given general discharges; some received dishonorable. These two individuals were model airmen: superb Russian linguists, meticulous about their military responsibilities, and devoted to serving their country. I remember thinking what a waste of talent it was, in addition to being a profound injustice, and it viscerally bothered me that I was forced to play a part in their unceremonious dismissals.

I was very happy to escape back to Fort Meade to visit my parents for the Christmas holidays, with the bonus of meeting up with Sue, whom I hadn't seen much of that year. We shared so many things: our values, our experiences as military brats, our love of country and appreciation for the intelligence mission. And truthfully, there was a spark between us that transcended any difficulties we'd had in the past. I went to the Hecht Company department store and bought an engagement ring for a hundred and sixty-five dollars. Sue still wears that ring (and still remembers how much it cost). I went back to Texas for a few months as Sue and our mothers made plans for the wedding, and in April 1965 we were married in the post chapel at Fort Meade, and our wedding was big, happy, and attended by many "in the business," as our families were both well-known in the NSA community. We counted driving back to Texas as our honeymoon, and we moved into a small apartment in San Antonio and began our journey through life together. Sue got a secretarial job with a small NSA detachment that had just formed at Kelly Air Force Base, the distant predecessor of what's now the huge, and hugely important, NSA-Texas facility at Joint Base San Antonio–Lackland. Once again, she was doing important work in support of intelligence operations while I wasn't doing much with my recent training and years of preparation. I started taking night classes at St. Mary's University, working toward a master's degree, which was a crucial professional accomplishment in the 1960s Air Force.

Meanwhile, the US presence in Southeast Asia was ramping up. After the Gulf of Tonkin incident in 1964—an exchange of fire between North Vietnamese patrol boats and a US Navy destroyer conducting signals intelligence operations in which both sides took damage and several North Vietnamese sailors died—Congress authorized military action. In 1965 more than two hundred thousand combat troops were shipped to the theater, and I volunteered for a one-year tour. I arrived at Tan Son Nhut Air Base, outside Saigon, in December 1965 as one of the first hundred Air Force intelligence officers to go to Vietnam on "permanent" one-year orders, under which Tan Son Nhut became my duty station, rather than on ninety-day "temporary" orders, which had loaned officers to the base while administratively they were still attached to a home in the States.

The Air Force designated me a combat intelligence officer and immediately assigned me to a midshift watch—10:00 P.M. to 8:00 A.M.—in the Indications and Warning Center. For the next four months a sergeant and I spent those ten hours, six days a week (with Sunday off), reading reports coming in from the field and culling them into a "black book" of intelligence that was carried around to each of the Air Force generals in the headquarters facility—a very distant forerunner to the President's Daily Brief, which I would oversee forty-four years later.

In those days intelligence was largely historical, telling people what *had* happened, not what *was* happening and certainly not forecasting what was *going* to happen. It wasn't part of the "find, fix, finish" operations cycle, which didn't then exist, and "intelligence automation" was pretty much acetate, grease pencil, and two corporals. My work was a tedious manual process, particularly since I only had academic knowledge about signals intelligence operations and knew almost nothing about air combat. I lamented aloud that I barely knew the difference between "flak"—antiaircraft fire—and a "frag"—a fragmentary operations order—or between an F-4 and an F-105. I imagined supergenius men with rows of ribbons and gleaming stars poring over my reports to decide where to attack and where to hold ground, making decisions with potential life-or-death consequences. Without any feedback I pressed ahead, tired and stressed, marking off the days on my calendar until I could rotate home.

The coup de grâce for my morale was a letter I received from Sue just a few weeks into my tour telling me that she was pregnant. I was despondent at the prospect of missing the birth of our first child. Then Sue's due date in June came and went, with no word from her. She had sent a telegram, but I never received it, and I hadn't been able to reach her. Jennifer was two weeks old when an Air Force general commented to Sue that I must be excited and happy to know about the expansion of my family. "Well, if he is," she replied, "I sure haven't heard it from him." The general promptly sent an official message to let me know that I was a father and that everyone was okay.

The only relief for me that year was that, coincidentally, my dad was at Tan Son Nhut as the deputy chief of NSA-Vietnam when I arrived, and our tours coincided for seven months. He was working for Colonel Hank Aplington—the same Marine who'd helped me into the Platoon Leaders Course in 1961. Dad was staying in colonel's quarters, which were way better than what I would have been able to afford in downtown Saigon, and were much quieter during the daytime, when I finally got to sleep; so I moved in with him. We made it a Sunday tradition, on our mutual day off, to treat ourselves to dinner on the top-floor restaurant of the French-colonial-era Caravelle Hotel. We ate lobster tails with butter and drank martinis while watching as A-1s bombed and strafed the Vietcong across the Saigon River. Combined with the haze I felt from working nights, sleeping days, and being completely disconnected from home, the whole experience felt surreal.

In 1966, after four months on the mid watch, I was moved to dayshift work as an air defense analyst and assigned a daunting collateral duty. Every Saturday, another lieutenant and I would drive to downtown Saigon to personally brief General William Westmoreland, the senior theater commander for all US forces in Vietnam. I had never met a four-star general before, much less talked to one, but I very quickly found myself with Westmoreland's undivided attention. After the other lieutenant briefed the entire staff on the numbers—bombs dropped, explosions, secondary explosions, bridges destroyed, roads cut, and the number of enemy killed—the general and I would step into his personal office so that I could give him the highly classified "SIGINT reflections of air strikes" report. If we dropped a bomb and then intercepted a radio transmission of the North Vietnamese talking about being hit, the general wanted to know what they said. Before I left for Saigon each Saturday, we overlaid an acetate-covered map with little "thought bubbles" containing a succinct headline for each intercepted message. During the briefing I would expand upon them from the longer signals intelligence reports.

At our first few sessions I was too nervous to notice the general's response to my report, but I was determined to read his reactions, to figure out how to brief him more effectively. Paying closer attention during our third or fourth meeting, I slowly realized that he was just nodding along without really following what I was saying, and that the general in charge of all US operations in Vietnam wasn't, in fact, a supergenius with a grand, strategic war plan well in hand. And my efforts didn't seem to make much difference to the fate of the soldiers and Marines fighting and dying in the jungle. That realization was probably the darkest moment of my career and the first time I truly struggled with the question Why do we even do intelligence work?

After a year at Tan Son Nhut, the Air Force assigned me back to Kelly Air Force Base, to another processing branch, again as deputy branch chief—the same kind of job I'd had before going to Vietnam. Sue and I began to think the Air Force just wasn't going to work out and planned for me to finish my master's degree and then join NSA as a civilian. Then one day I got a call from a friend and classmate from Goodfellow, Jack Kochanski. Jack was one of the few officers who'd wanted a stateside job after Goodfellow, and when he'd been told he was going to a SIGINT station in Pakistan, we'd tried to swap assignments. The Air Force didn't approve of our questioning its wisdom, and so Jack had gone overseas. Two years later, in the spring of 1967, Jack was working at Kelly as the aide to the Air Force Security Service commander, Major General Louis Coira. He had phoned to tell me that he had been accepted for pilot training and to ask if I wanted to interview for his aide job. I agreed, and then asked, "What does an aide do?"

That call changed my life. General Coira had been a bomber pilot during World War II and brought a self-effacing humility to command. He grasped both the details of our work and the big picture of its significance—precisely what I'd found wanting in General Westmoreland. For the next three years General Coira and I traveled the world, spending about four months of each year overseas, visiting all the Air Force signals intelligence units and observing how they ran as an enterprise. In addition to the typical military-aide duties—keeping the general on schedule, ensuring he had the materials he needed for meetings, coordinating visitors, etc.—General Coira tasked me with writing and editing much of his correspondence, which was a big responsibility for a very junior officer and gave me a new insight into the big issues with which the Air Force Security Service and its leaders dealt. Then, after a few trips together, he asked me to prepare and deliver an update on headquarters issues to each unit we visited.

The assignment was a catalyst for my career. I felt that I was doing something challenging, interesting, and worthwhile, and I also got to see the scope of the massive signals intelligence effort the United States was conducting. Because of the size of the Soviet Union and China, high-frequency Morse code was the primary way to effectively communicate across such vast distances, so the entire Eurasian landmass was ringed with SIGINT sites, stretching from Japan to Turkey to Britain. Each signals intelligence station employed hundreds of GIs—soldiers, sailors, airmen, and Marines—copying "dits and dahs" around the clock, day in and day out. Nine stations employed FLR-9 circular-disposed antenna arrays, massive things we called elephant cages, to intercept transmissions and to "direction find" where each signal came from. If two stations picked up the same transmission, we could estimate where it came from by drawing lines on a map from each station and marking where in China or the Soviet Union the lines crossed. Putting the translated content of the communication together with the transmission location gave us very useful intelligence about our adversaries' capabilities and what was going on inside their borders. Before I traveled the world with General Coira, I never could have imagined just how massive, manpower-intensive, and costly the US effort to collect and understand Soviet secrets really was.

As the intelligence and combat missions in Southeast Asia increased, the Air Force brought new capabilities to bear. In March 1968, it first deployed the SR-71 Blackbird to Kadena Air Force Base in Okinawa, Japan. It was magnificent: a mind-boggling machine that could fly at the edge of space at unbelievable speeds and collect intelligence over huge areas, virtually impervious to all contemporary antiaircraft systems. In the space of twenty minutes it could fly over all of North Vietnam and image everything that was worth imaging and intercept all the signals worth collecting. About five days later we'd get a readout of what it had collected. Of course, by then much of the data it had gathered was already obsolete. In other words, great intelligence—just too late to be useful to the combat forces.

Intelligence on the Soviets moved even more slowly. After Gary

Powers's U-2 was shot down in May 1960, the United States stopped flights over Soviet airspace and thus lost coverage of Soviet capabilities— particularly on their strategic nuclear weapons. Fortunately, the launch of Sputnik on October 4, 1957, had opened another avenue for collection. Before Sputnik, there had been a huge debate about the legal repercussions of satellites crossing national borders. Just how far up did sovereign airspace extend? If we put something in orbit above adversarial nations, what precedent would that set? Sputnik overflew national borders all over the world, sending radio signals intended—literally—to let everyone know the Soviets didn't care about national borders when it came to space flight.

In February 1959, the Air Force attempted the launch of its first "overhead" collection capability—Corona. The first launch vehicle never left the pad. In assessing America's early successes in space photoreconnaissance and just how much they changed the game against the Soviets, people tend to forget that in 1959 and 1960 our first thirteen attempts at Corona failed. Those early space collection pioneers had to answer to Congress and the president, admit to setbacks, and convince them to be patient. I can attest, those sorts of meetings aren't easy. Having given such briefings many times, as undersecretary of defense and as director of national intelligence, I doubt today's Congress would have the patience to accept multiple failures in the interest of a breakthrough in technology. I suspect that its impatience today is manifested in the constant drumbeat for "acquisition reform," as though improved bureaucratic processes for developing, building, and fielding new weapon systems, satellites, etc., would make technological progress easy and efficient.

In 1961, the CIA and Air Force agreed to establish the National Reconnaissance Office—NRO, which joined CIA, NSA, and DIA as a fourth major national intelligence agency. NRO acquired and operated satellites to collect intelligence from orbit, starting with the Corona program. I first saw Corona imagery while working for General Coira in the late 1960s and was amazed at the volume and precision of intelligence it gathered on Soviet strategic facilities. To transport these images, Corona had to launch film canisters back to earth about every six weeks. The skilled crew of a specially configured C-130 transport plane would snag a parachute conveying a canister as it descended. The film would then be processed by the "recce techs," the imagery analysts in the Air Force reconnaissance technical groups, as well as by the CIA's National Photographic Interpretation Center—NPIC. The result was an astoundingly complete picture of the way the world had been . . . a few weeks before. As I traveled the world, I found that the speed of intelligence was one of the great frustrations for our professionals deployed in the field.

In August 1969, General Coira was assigned to Japan as the vice commander of the Fifth Air Force. His deputy, Brigadier General Carl Stapleton, "fleeted up" to commander of the Air Force Security Service on August 1, which was great for me, as General Stapleton also took a personal interest in my career. I mentioned to him that I had finished all the coursework for my master's degree and only had to complete my thesis. I'd decided to write about how an equal-opportunity policy in off-base housing at Goodfellow Air Force Base—just four hours' drive from Kelly—had impacted both service members and the local community. The Defense Department had published a regulation requiring property owners who rented to *any* service members to agree to rent to all service members, regardless of race. If they refused to rent to minorities, they'd be placed on a list of owners from whom all service members were not allowed to rent. I'd dug into the literature on race relations in the United States in the late 1960s and found that while the military services were not exactly shining beacons of hope for racial harmony, Truman's order to desegregate the military in 1948 had at least forced people to work together, which led to a grudging respect for individual professional contributions, regardless of race. In theory, a regulation like the one regarding housing could extend some of that social change into the local community.

General Stapleton, who had served as commander of Goodfellow, was intrigued. He set up interviews for me both with base leaders and with city officials, and I discovered that not only was the new DOD policy good for minority service members, particularly black service members who could now find decent places to live, but economically it benefited the city and the property owners who participated. I concluded that the DOD regulation worked and had the intended impact of broadening housing opportunities for minorities. General Stapleton had copies of my thesis placed in the Security Service library and the Air University library at Maxwell Air Force Base in Alabama.

Stapleton also recognized that, while my tour as his and General

Coira's aide was a positive catalyst for my career, I needed to move on. I had mentioned on our travels together that I found the airborne signals-collection mission intriguing. We'd visited detachments of EC-47 signals-intelligence planes flying in South Vietnam and Thailand, doing essentially the same missions as the FLR-9 elephant cages while airborne. The airmen in the back of the plane would intercept a transmission, note the direction it had come from, and then intercept another line of bearing a few minutes later. They'd map out where the lines of bearing intercepted and then transmit targeting data on where the enemy transmitter was for attack aircraft or troops on the ground. It wasn't as high-tech as the SR-71, but it was timely. I'd also seen that, unlike the units in Vietnam, the detachment in Thailand had been manned by airmen solely on ninety-day temporary-duty orders. As a result, they weren't a cohesive unit, and they needed help. I volunteered to go back to Southeast Asia for a second year-long tour, as the first "permanent" commander of this detachment.

Since this assignment would include flight time over hostile territory, I needed extensive training. I attended survival training at Fairchild Air Force Base near Spokane, Washington, in March 1970, which included a lot of being cold, wet, and hungry while hiking and camping in the woods. This culminated in being "captured" and detained in a simulated prisoner-of-war camp, where I was slapped around and thrown against walls, deprived of sleep, blasted with noise, and locked inside a small box that amplified my claustrophobia in a terrible way. (Thankfully this was in the days before Survival, Evasion, Resistance, and Escape training included waterboarding.) We were told that, while the United States followed the Geneva Conventions on the treatment of prisoners of war, the North Vietnamese and Vietcong would use much worse torture techniques on captives than anything we had experienced in training. Decades later, after 9/11, I would remember the moral certitude with which our instructors in 1970 stressed that the United States would never use those techniques except to train our own troops.

I next attended water survival training at Perrin Air Force Base in Texas, where we were taught how to free ourselves from parachute rigging to avoid drowning and how to conserve energy and survive until we could be rescued. The training included five parasailing jumps, during which we were harnessed into a chute and towed behind a speedboat; upon reaching the requisite height, we disconnected and executed a water landing. Those five jumps were fun. The final exercise, however, was not: We were tossed over the stern of the speedboat in a full harness in complete darkness. I remember tumbling through the water, disoriented about which way was up, struggling with the harness, swallowing water, struggling more, and being certain I was going to drown. But I survived, graduated, and went off to attend a weeklong jungle survival course at Clark Air Base in the Philippines. I felt extremely well prepared for my assignment after enduring these courses, which I *never* wanted to take again.

The final training I took before leaving the States was voluntary, and entirely intellectual. EC-47s were weight restricted and had no room for sightseeing visitors, so the only way I could fly on operational missions from Thailand was to perform an aircrew function. I wasn't a pilot, and since the only function I could qualify for was as an enlisted airborne analyst, I attended an analysis course for warrant and noncommissioned officers at the Army's Two Rock Ranch Station near Petaluma, California, which also qualified me as a fledgling subject-matter expert on North Vietnamese Army communications practices.

I arrived at Nakhon Phanom Royal Thai Air Force Base in June 1970. The state of my unit wasn't pretty. Our "offices" were a series of semitrailers linked together with a plywood hallway that leaked whenever it rained, which was frequently. We had no latrines or running water, and we were the only flying unit with no air-conditioning in our barracks, which was against Air Force regulations for flight-crew rest. Our discipline was terrible. Our first sergeant informed me that we had the distinction of the highest venereal disease rate of any unit on base. I thought that was impressive, considering our guys were only there on ninety-day temporary-duty orders. They weren't wasting any time before getting infected on "community outreach operations." I took command, but raising our living conditions, morale, and discipline felt like swimming upstream against stiff currents.

About six weeks later, an old, seasoned inspector-general colonel from the Security Service regional headquarters in Hawaii arrived. Normally, no one is happy at the prospect of an IG inspection, but I realized that my unit needed help, so I showed him and his team every problem I'd identified and let them see anything else they wanted. Unsurprisingly he judged our unit to be barely mission capable. About a week later, I got a call

informing me that the base wing commander required my presence—
immediately. I raced to headquarters, already feeling awkward in my
combat fatigues, only to find that standing with the base commander was
four-star general Joseph Nazzaro, who was in charge of all US Air Force
units across the entire Indo-Asia-Pacific region.

The general sat and gestured for me to sit next to him. "You're running
an important mission here," he told me. "What support do you need?"
Glancing at the wing commander, I told the four-star that we lacked vehicles, air-conditioning, and running water, but that my temporary duty
crew members were making the best of the situation and were executing
five flying missions daily. My attempt to put a positive face on the situation felt very hollow. He thanked and dismissed me, and the next day we
were issued a couple of jeeps and trucks and were moved into a permanent barracks with air-conditioning. Soon after, I started getting enlisted
crew members on permanent change-of-station tours. Over the years,
I've kept tabs on the members of that unit, and I am very proud that thirteen of its enlisted airmen were eventually promoted to the highest Air
Force enlisted grade of chief master sergeant. One became the command
noncommissioned officer for all of the Air Force Security Service, a command of about twenty thousand people.

Unlike the EC-47 units in South Vietnam that were collecting intelligence for tactical strikes or raids in Vietnam, my unit was flying over
Laos, and in 1970, the secret war there did not involve conventional US
military forces. As an active participant in our missions, I'd taken my
turns in the rotation of flight analysts, looking up call signs in a technical
aid book, helping manually plot fixes in Laos, and then transmitting
them to the ground. That, combined with the interest the four-star general took in our work, confirmed what I'd suspected from early on—we
were actually working for the CIA station chief in Vientiane, Laos, who
was providing our fixes for Laotian forces that the United States was "secretly" supporting.

I flew my final mission on June 2, 1971, and just a few weeks before I
left, the same old, crusty inspector-general colonel reinspected my unit,
and this time we passed with flying colors. (I'm keeping this pun in defiance of all my editors.) I left Thailand on June 3 with a sense of professional satisfaction and personal accomplishment that I seldom
experienced during the rest of my military career. I felt I had really done

something significant, that I had molded that unit into a true capability for the Air Force and US intelligence. I was extremely proud of my troops and the unit I left behind when I flew home to my family.

After Thailand, General Stapleton decided I should see the bigger picture of the world of signals intelligence beyond what the Air Force was doing, and so he planted me at NSA as the military assistant to the director, replacing a senior Air Force lieutenant colonel as a rather junior captain. In my final performance review, Stapleton wrote, "I'm more confident in Captain Clapper's ability to be a general than I am in any of my colonels." That felt a bit over the top—even at the time—and I doubt that he mentioned that assessment to any of those colonels.

When Sue and I arrived at our old stomping grounds of Fort Meade, the NSA director was Vice Admiral Noel Gayler. He was a handsome, swashbuckling Navy fighter pilot, a certified ace for having downed five enemy planes during World War II. He was the first naval aviator to be awarded three Navy Crosses, the combat valor award second only to the Medal of Honor. Gayler was smart, capable, arrogant, and overbearing. He ruled by fear and intimidation, suffered no fools, and fired people on the spot if they didn't measure up. That said, his leadership approach was effective. People worked feverishly for long hours to get the job done on schedule, and NSA headquarters led the global signals intelligence effort for the nation. I practically lived at my desk, just outside Gayler's office, returning home only to sleep. When our son, Andy, was born, Sue remarked that the only real difference in the circumstances of his birth from Jennifer's was that I'd found out about it more quickly.

In August 1972, Gayler was promoted to full admiral and left for Hawaii to serve as the four-star commander in chief, US Pacific Command, and was replaced by Lieutenant General Sam Phillips. While Gayler was famous for his combat prowess and leadership, Phillips was known for managing large, complex, technical projects. He'd been the Apollo program director from 1963 to 1969, the driving force behind putting a man on the moon. Shortly after Neil Armstrong and Buzz Aldrin took humankind's first stroll on a celestial body, Phillips announced he was returning to his Air Force career. After command of the Space and Missile Systems Organization in Los Angeles, he came to NSA. General Phillips was quiet, courteous, serious, and brilliant. An introvert and a gentleman, he seemed the antithesis of Admiral Gayler. From observing him, I learned that, while fear and intimidation can drive people to do their jobs well, they'll only do what they are told. Under Phillips's leadership, people gave their best, as it pained them to let him down, knowing he had their backs. His staff brought him bad news without fear and let him know when things were going wrong soon enough for him to act.

There was plenty of bad news in those first few years of the 1970s. Anti-war fever had taken hold, and demonstrations were taking place all around the country. Race relations in America were at a low point, marked by riots and burning cities. The military, reflecting society at large, had its own race-relations issues, as well as problems with discipline, particularly among the draftees.

In January 1973, the United States signed the Paris Peace Accords, in which we agreed to recognize the "independence, sovereignty, unity, and territorial integrity of Vietnam." By March we'd pulled all our forces out of the country. Despite the endgame of the war, and despite the reported thaw in US-Soviet relations in the 1970s—détente, as it was called—our all-consuming target at NSA continued to be the Soviets. NSA was deeply involved with enhancing collection, particularly on their nuclear weapons programs, and we made a strong push to develop the technologies necessary to put signals intelligence systems into space.

While military aide to General Phillips in 1973, I was promoted to major, a year "below the zone"—before the time when I was supposed to be considered for promotion. I would go on to be promoted three years below the zone to lieutenant colonel, after just fourteen months as a major, and an additional year early to colonel—five years before I should have made colonel in the normal progression.

That's not to say I didn't make mistakes; I made a big career error in 1973 by following General Phillips as he picked up his fourth star and took command of the Air Force Systems Command, the organization tasked with research, development, and acquisition of new weapons systems. I admired his leadership to the point that I wanted to go with him, regardless of what work I'd be doing. At Systems Command I faced a frustrating situation, since a full colonel was already installed to do what I'd done for General Phillips at NSA. The position I now occupied had been held by the pilot tasked with flying the general around. I wasn't a pilot, and effectively having nothing to do was not "career enhancing." I realized my mistake and asked General Phillips to help. He set up several interviews, and I ended up in the intelligence office of Systems Command, in the foreign material acquisition program. This was a positive turn of events that got me involved in acquiring adversary military equipment—purchasing whole systems or collecting pieces left on battlefields to assemble into complete systems. This was a major Cold War enterprise and profoundly interesting, but it was far removed from the operational duties I most enjoyed.

After five months at the Armed Forces Staff College in Norfolk, Virginia, I was assigned to US Pacific Command—back on Admiral Gayler's staff, but sufficiently down the food chain that I wasn't in his direct line of sight again. When I arrived at Camp Smith, Hawaii, I was appointed to work shifts as a watch officer, giving me flashbacks to my time at Tan Son Nhut Air Base a decade earlier. I appealed to Brigadier General Doyle Larson, who was the senior intelligence officer—the "J-2" in military parlance—and whom I knew from the Air Force Security Service, and told him I'd already served as a watch officer in a war zone. He agreed that the assignment wasn't career progressive and moved me into the intelligence collection branch as an "action officer." Then, when I was promoted early to lieutenant colonel, Larson made me the signals intelligence branch chief. As a mentor, he influenced my next three assignments.

At Pacific Command we focused on the Soviet Far East and China, and, of course, North Korea. Open combat between the United States and North Korea had stopped with the 1953 armistice, but the war technically never ended, and soldiers from North Korea still stare across a four-kilometer-wide Demilitarized Zone—a no-man's-land between North and South Korea—at South Korean and US soldiers, who to this day warily stare back. On August 18, 1976, a South Korean working party went out to trim a massive poplar tree that blocked the view across the DMZ. North Korean troops soon appeared and ordered them to stop. In the ensuing confrontation the two US Army officers in charge of the working party were beaten to death with axes. The Pacific Command turned its attention to the tense situation and any intercepts of North Korean communications on the incident. Three days later a muscular contingent of US Army and South Korean Special Forces returned to the scene, backed up by attack helicopters, fighter aircraft, and even B-52 bombers—which the North Koreans knew could carry nuclear weapons. A North Korean convoy arrived and set up machine-gun positions, but didn't open fire. During an hour-long standoff, US Army engineers cut the tree down. The mission was aptly named: Operation Paul Bunyan.

Tensions between North and South escalated, and US Air Force B-52s continued to fly patrols parallel to the DMZ. The North Koreans, in turn, put their air-defense systems on high alert, flew MiG fighters on frequent patrols, and dispatched their submarines out to sea. We intercepted communications indicating that Kim Il-sung might order an invasion into South Korea. I stayed in the office for about three days without going home, communicating via Teletype with an Army major who was my counterpart in South Korea. The sense of an imminent war was palpable through the crisis, and it took several weeks for the situation to stabilize enough for us to fall back into a regular rhythm.

That was precisely the kind of intelligence work I'd joined the military to do, but in the summer of 1978, the Air Force decided it was once again time to invest in my education. Sue, Jenny, Andy, and I returned to the mainland so I could attend the prestigious National War College in Washington. The Air Force personnel office told me to plan on a follow-on assignment to the Pentagon, so we bought a town house in the Lake Braddock community of Burke, not far from where I'd lived with my parents when my dad was assigned to Arlington Hall. Unfortunately, I hadn't learned from my dad's experience, because after I completed my studies, the Air Force (thanks to the intervention of Doyle Larson) instead assigned me to NSA. I began making the long commute around DC to Fort Meade, in Maryland, just like Dad had. The only real difference was—for good or ill—I got to use the Capital Beltway (the proposed "circumferential highway" of the 1950s) for my commute.

In 1979 the Army, Navy, and Air Force all had cryptologic commands to conduct both signals intelligence and communications security missions—breaking and making code. The Army and Navy maintained their headquarters in Washington, whereas the Air Force Security Service was deliberately located elsewhere, at Kelly Air Force Base in San Antonio, where I'd spent so much of my early career. The Air Force needed a senior resident officer at NSA to represent its positions, and in June 1979 I took on that role. Then, in February 1980, when NSA director Vice Admiral Bobby Inman officiated at my promotion to colonel, I took charge of all the Air Force personnel stationed at NSA—several thousand people—as the first Air Force wing commander at Fort Meade.

My most demanding work mostly consisted of being the intermediary between Admiral Inman and Major General Larson, who, subsequent to being PACOM's senior intelligence officer, had become commander of the Air Force Security Service and received his second star. Larson incorporated other parts of Air Force intelligence into the agency and transformed it into the Electronic Security Command to make it more operationally relevant. It was no secret that Larson saw his natural career progression as becoming the next NSA director—a point of sensitivity with Admiral Inman, who was in Larson's way. I had to spend a good bit of my time and energy during the next year and a half as a diplomat, smoothing flag and general officer feathers whenever either was ruffled.

I consider Bobby Inman an icon and a legend—with the Navy, at NSA, and at CIA, where he became deputy director in 1981. As of this writing, he still has a full-time teaching position at the University of Texas. People everywhere have stories about his uncanny mastering of the details of signals intelligence operations or astutely handling demanding members of Congress. Many accounts involve the joint-operations policies he promoted in 1981 when, for just a few months, he was simultaneously NSA director and CIA deputy director. To me, none of the bold actions Inman is famous for hold a candle to something I saw him very quietly do to protect one NSA employee.

In 1979, shortly after I started making the daily commute to Fort Meade, Inman learned that a gifted senior civilian crypto-mathematician was gay. He wasn't living openly, but enough people knew so that Inman would have to confront the situation. For uniformed service members, like the two airmen I'd had to deal with in 1964, being outed meant immediate general or dishonorable discharge, but because civilians weren't bound by the Uniform Code of Military Justice, an extra step was required to dismiss them. Guidance for processing security clearances said that anyone who was homosexual was vulnerable to blackmail by foreign intelligence services and therefore was not suitable for holding a clearance. If anyone at a command was discovered to be gay, commanders were required to revoke their clearance, effectively ending their employment and their career.

By the time this case reached Inman, the NSA security office had already administratively removed the employee's clearance and was in the throes of firing him. Inman halted the process and asked the employee to come to his office. Inman told the man that he could not retain his clearance as long as he was vulnerable to blackmail. However, Inman reasoned that if he acknowledged his sexual orientation to his coworkers, family, and friends, he could no longer be blackmailed, and Inman could restore his clearance. The employee agreed and returned to his job. That decision was still tragic on a personal level, since it compelled someone to come out publicly on the government's terms and timetable. Still, it was a compassionate and courageous gesture, and an absolute revelation to me.

Ten years later, when I was a major general serving as the chief of Air Force intelligence in the Pentagon in 1989, I was confronted with a similar situation regarding a civilian employee who'd been outed. As the senior intelligence officer for the entire United States Air Force, I had significant authority that I certainly didn't possess in 1964, and so I followed Admiral Inman's example and restored the clearance of my employee, Mark Roth. Mark went on to serve our nation with great distinction, achieving the grade of senior executive. He is retired now, but still serving his country. My decision set a precedent in the Air Force, and I took some flak from a few of my general officer colleagues, but it was the right thing to do—for Mark, for the Air Force, and for our country. And, although I didn't admit it to myself at the time, perhaps I was also trying to atone for my part in what had happened to those two Russian linguist airmen twenty-five years earlier.

CHAPTER TWO

Command and Controversy

While mentoring from senior officers meant so much to my early career, when I arrived at the Pentagon in 1981, I met a peer who would have a major impact on me—and become a lifelong friend in the process. Rich O'Lear had been commissioned from the Air Force Academy the same year I was commissioned from ROTC, and he was also a "fast burner," having been promoted to colonel four years ahead of the typical schedule. When we were both assigned to work for the Air Force assistant chief of staff for intelligence—the senior intelligence officer at Air Force headquarters, Major General Jim Pfautz—Rich was initially slotted as my deputy. We were both type A competitive people, and I suspect those who knew us thought the competitive chemistry would put us in conflict. That didn't happen.

Rich had a very different background from mine; while I'd been focused on signals intelligence, he'd spent more time in the realm of Strategic Air Command in all-source analysis—fitting signal intercepts, imagery, and human intelligence together to discover and present the big picture of our adversaries' capabilities and intentions. But we shared a passion for getting the mission done, and we gelled from the start. General Pfautz was an exacting and demanding boss with high expectations and a sharp temper when those expectations weren't met. Rich taught me a lot about the tricks of the staff-work trade he'd learned at SAC, how to prepare and deliver briefings, and particularly, how to treat people. In many ways, his professionalism reminded me of my dad's.

I was, additionally, thankful that work was closer to home. Not having to move for another three years allowed Jennifer to spend her entire high school career at the same school, and Sue and I both appreciated giving her an opportunity neither of us had had. Establishing roots in our neighborhood somehow led to my becoming elected president of our homeowners' association, something I would never want to do again. It was akin to being unpaid mayor for thirteen hundred families, managing a seventeen-acre lake, tennis courts, a pool, and full-time office and maintenance staffs. I discovered that the only people who attended association meetings were those with fervent complaints, and I found it striking just how emotionally attached town house owners could become to specific parking places and how much hate and discontent renters could cause owners.

While I was president, our community became one of the first in Fairfax County to establish a neighborhood watch program. To get better acquainted with how the county police force worked, I asked to go on ride-alongs. By accompanying officers on patrol, I saw how they operated and how they had absolutely no idea what they would confront when they made a traffic stop or responded to a domestic dispute. My experience with the Fairfax County Police Department would prove helpful years later when I was DNI. After 9/11, the Intelligence Community worked to share information from classified sources with state and local law-enforcement officers who did not hold security clearances—the people who might actually encounter terrorists or deal with the immediate aftermath of an attack. When as DNI I met with the International Association of Chiefs of Police, those ride-alongs served as a shared frame of reference from which we could talk about much bigger issues involving the entire country.

Since Rich and I didn't live far apart, we carpooled to the Pentagon, planning our strategy for the day, and after parking, worked as a fire team to watch for the huge rats that then lurked in the Pentagon south parking lot. There were two major subordinate staff offices under General Pfautz, one focused on programs and budgets, and the other on substantive intelligence matters—actual analysis of adversary capabilities and activities. We were assigned to the first, which made me glad for the "mistake" I'd made in following General Phillips to Air Force Systems Command. That experience constituted my only familiarity with how the Air Force builds and acquires intelligence systems, providing me with just enough understanding to be absolutely blown away when I first learned about the F-117 Nighthawk and its unconventional design and stealth technology.

Within a few months, Rich became the head of the analytical "substance" directorate, at which point we reported to General Pfautz as peers. One of our chief tasks each day was to prepare him to brief the Air Force chief of staff at senior staff meetings, including preparing his slides with updates on intelligence systems and the current intelligence picture. Pentagon staff officers today often lament the rise of PowerPoint. They only complain because they're too young to remember making Vu-Graph slides and printing them on cellulose acetate transparency sheets to display with an overhead projector. Rich and I had no idea how quickly one of our presentations would gain national prominence.

On September 1, 1983, a Soviet Su-15 Interceptor fighter jet shot down Korean Air Lines Flight 007 over the Sea of Japan. The Boeing 747 had taken off from Anchorage, Alaska, with 269 people aboard, including Representative Larry McDonald, en route to Seoul. Its autopilot had been set in the wrong mode, and the plane drifted northwest of its intended course. As it approached Soviet prohibited airspace over the Kamchatka Peninsula in the dark of night, Soviet air defenses scrambled three MiG-23 fighters, which failed to intercept the airliner. KAL 007 crossed the peninsula back into international airspace over the Sea of Japan as a flight of Su-15s were launched. As the fighters approached, the KAL 007 pilot asked Tokyo Air Traffic Control Center for permission to climb to conserve fuel. Tokyo Center, which didn't have radar contact with KAL 007 and was unaware of the Soviet jets, approved the request. As the 747 climbed, it lost airspeed, and the interceptor jets flew past it. They interpreted the climb as an evasive maneuver, turned, regained visual contact, and fired two air-to-air missiles, destroying the civilian airliner and killing everyone aboard.

Immediately, and in typical character, the Soviets denied any involvement, asserting the airliner had crashed on its own, and began fabricating evidence to support their claim. In the Pentagon, General Pfautz asked Rich and me if the Air Force had any reconnaissance aircraft in the area, and whether any intelligence systems had collected data that would cast light on the matter. We pulsed all the Air Force collection stations and initially had nothing to report. We then learned that the intercept site at the northernmost tip of Hokkaido, Japan, had been conducting a test during the day and had left its receivers and recorders tuned to the Soviet air-to-ground frequency that night. The system happened to intercept the entire exchange of Soviet air-to-ground communications, although the linguists there hadn't realized immediately the significance of what they had on tape.

Rich and I reconstructed the path of the airliner and plotted it on a map. We correlated the times of the Soviet radio transmissions on the transcript with the location of the airliner. Using Vu-Graphs, we put together a slide deck that showed the failed intercept by the MiG-23s when the airliner entered Soviet airspace, and how KAL 007 had already entered international airspace, not just when it was shot down, but as the Soviet general on the ground transmitted, "How long does it take him to get into attack position? He is already getting out into neutral waters. Engage afterburner immediately. Bring in the MiG-23 as well. While you are wasting time, it will fly right out." Most damning, the Soviet general subsequently ordered the Su-15 pilots to shoot the "target" down immediately, without visually confirming its identity.

General Pfautz presented the Air Force Chief of Staff our findings, which were then sent that day to the secretary of defense and to the National Security Council in the White House. The Soviets continued their denials until the US ambassador to the United Nations played the recorded voice transmissions for the Security Council on September 5. On September 7, President Reagan declassified and published the transcript—a textbook example of a president's appropriately asserting his prerogative to declassify intelligence information.

The Soviets finally admitted their involvement, but claimed they'd confused the airliner with a US military reconnaissance plane flying at the same time. The Air Force chief of staff asked Pfautz if we'd run any missions that day. Pfautz asked me to check, and I was told we hadn't—information, it turned out, that wasn't exactly correct. We had, in fact, flown an RC-135, the specific reconnaissance aircraft the Soviets said they thought KAL 007 was, that same day, but during daylight hours, long before KAL 007 was shot down. The reconnaissance flight was unscheduled and a reaction to indications that the Soviets were going to conduct an intercontinental ballistic missile (ICBM) test launch. The launch didn't take place, but the RC-135 had been in position near Soviet airspace, ready to collect information if it had. Pfautz learned about the RC-135 flight very early Sunday morning and called me at home, yelling before I could even say "hello." For the next ten minutes, I lay in bed at the position of attention as he informed me in very specific terms about the error of my ways. That was one of the many—many—times I thought my career was dead, but I never heard another word about the incident.

Almost two months later, on October 25, US Army Rangers, Airborne, Marines, and Special Forces invaded the Caribbean island of Grenada, to "liberate it" from the leftist organization that had taken control in a 1979 coup. The invasion itself was widely criticized around the world as unnecessary overkill, and even in the United States, opinion was mixed. The operation itself was an absolutely overwhelming—if chaotic—show of force, but troops on the ground didn't have current charts from the Defense Mapping Agency and were forced to navigate the island with old maps from the Esso oil conglomerate. Communications weren't established early—famously, troops had to use pay phones to coordinate movements. Military intelligence was blamed, but the actual problem was that the invasion planners didn't bother to inform us of their plans. We were completely out of the loop and didn't catch up until the action was almost over, only a few days later. This episode brought to mind the old Air Force saw "If you want me around when the plane crashes, have me around when the plane takes off."

The coordination problem in Grenada wasn't limited to intelligence. Each military service had made its own operational plans without fully coordinating with the others, and the result was less than optimal. We were very fortunate to confront this issue during the invasion of Grenada, which put up virtually no resistance, as it influenced the reorganization of the Department of Defense with the 1986 Goldwater-Nichols Act. Under this landmark law, the Army, Navy, Air Force, and Marines—every branch of the military—were to "organize, train, and equip" the troops who would do the fighting. The combatant commanders—each with control of all the troops and equipment within their geographic area of responsibility—were tasked with planning and executing operations. In 1983, I had no idea that the nuances of Goldwater-Nichols would become important to me just a few years later.

That December, General Pfautz called me into his office and said he'd negotiated my next assignment—commander of the Air Force Technical Applications Center at Patrick Air Force Base, not far from Cocoa Beach,

Florida. Since the 1950s, AFTAC had always been commanded by an Air Force pilot, never by an intelligence officer, so I honestly wasn't sure whether he was rewarding or banishing me. Sue and I agreed that the AFTAC posting would be a pretty good "twilight tour" for us, after which we could retire and settle down. We'd also be able to keep Andy in the same high school for four years in Florida, so we bought a nice house on a corner lot in Satellite Beach, not far from the ocean.

AFTAC had the unique and important task of monitoring compliance with the 1963 Partial Nuclear Test Ban Treaty, which banned all nuclear tests except those conducted underground, and it lived by the wonderfully apt informal motto "In God We Trust, All Others We Monitor." At the time, it had about three thousand people deployed all over the world, monitoring seismic signatures, ocean acoustic signatures, and overhead satellites for anything resembling a nuclear detonation. It would then try to collect samples from the air to see if the underground test had vented particles. The AFTAC laboratory at McClellan Air Force Base in California would then "torture the molecules" for intelligence about the actual detonation. One of its major challenges was to distinguish nuclear tests from earthquakes and to try to compute the location, size, and type of detonation from this arcane data. It operated a series of small detachments intentionally located in remote, "seismically quiet" places all over the world. AFTAC had the global reach of a major command, but was small enough to be commanded by a colonel. It had a staff of wonderfully talented, dedicated people—Air Force active-duty officers and enlisted technicians and a small cadre of civilian experts, some of whom had been involved in the Manhattan Project to build the first atomic bomb. For the most part, it existed and did its work without any meddling from Washington. I arrived and took command in June 1984. During my brief tenure as commander, the Soviet Union, the United Kingdom, France, China, and, of course, the United States were all actively conducting underground tests, but we didn't observe any treaty violations. AFTAC would be the last of three Air Force organizations I would have the privilege and honor of commanding. Unique to the military, command is a special responsibility—not only for the conduct of the unit's mission, but also for the well-being of its people and their families; a heavy responsibility, but so rewarding.

That December the Air Force published the names of those nominated for promotion to brigadier general, and I was on the list. I was shocked. My parents and family were very proud, and Sue and Andy got ready to move again. (Fortuitously, Rich O'Lear succeeded me as commander of AFTAC, and he and his family rented our house.) I anticipated returning to the Pentagon as the deputy to the Air Force assistant chief of staff for intelligence, since that position was vacant, but then we got a second surprise: The Air Force was assigning me to be chief of intelligence for US forces in South Korea. My first thought was an old saying I'd heard from my dad: "There are four things in life you want to avoid: pyorrhea, diarrhea, gonorrhea, and Korea," but I learned just how little influence brigadier general selects have over their destinies.

I reported to Seoul in June 1985 and quickly discovered the obvious—although the position in South Korea was designated for an Air Force officer, it was a job much better suited to an Army officer. It was a humbling experience as a new brigadier general to ask my team of Army colonels to mentor me on things like how to properly roll up the sleeves on my camouflage battle dress uniform. They also helped with Army slang and terminology used around the post, where initially I was almost as lost as I had been when I first reported to Tan Son Nhut Air Base as a lieutenant. I found that I was not just the senior intelligence officer for US forces, but also the deputy to a Korean Air Force two-star in the US–South Korea Combined Forces Command, someone who knew very little about intelligence and was looking to me for guidance. Fortunately, both of the Republic of Korea (ROK) generals whom I served as deputy were capable, smart, and easy to work with, and we eventually found our way.

My "big boss," Commander of US Forces Korea, Army four-star general Bill Livsey, had been a lieutenant platoon leader with the 3rd Infantry Division during the Korean War and dug in on the front line when the armistice took effect on July 27, 1953. He knew his business and suffered no fools. He was salty, and in the tradition of General George Patton, excelled at colorful profanity when the occasion called for it. On day one, he made it very clear that the Korean War had never formally ended, the 1953 armistice was just a cease-fire agreement, and North Korea could, and would, invade the South if given the opportunity. From that premise, he gave me his very clear expectations for intelligence. He demanded forty-eight hours of warning ahead of a North Korean attack to give him time to activate the operations plan for the defense of the peninsula and to evacuate all US dependents in South Korea. And because taking those irrevocable actions would have huge diplomatic consequences for the United States and major political implications for the ROK, Livsey required a forty-eight-hour "unambiguous" warning—we had to know for certain that an attack was imminent, and not a bluff or a feint. General Livsey was not one for subtle nuance.

Andy enrolled at the Seoul American High School, whose wonderful principal, Sue Jackson, delivered a classic line at our first parents' town hall: "I'll make a deal with all of you. We'll take with a grain of salt any stories we hear about what happens at home, if you take with a grain of salt any stories you hear about what happens at school." We found the South Koreans generously warm and hospitable, somehow discovering our preferences and catering to them without our asking, and on our birthdays, sending enough flowers to make our house look and smell like a funeral home. As an eighth-grader, Andy took the subway in Seoul alone without our ever worrying, and we've always joked that Sue earned her black belt in shopping in Seoul's famous Itaewon shopping area, not far from the Yongsan Army garrison where we were stationed in Seoul.

As Sue and Andy got settled, and as Jennifer was starting college in Virginia, I began to try to understand the operational situation. I read all the intelligence reports I could get my hands on and memorized the North Korean order of battle. While I had mastered the details, I was having trouble seeing the larger picture. One day, I was talking with one of my senior civilian intelligence analysts and asked for his advice on how to gain a broader, more strategic perspective. He suggested I visit the post library at Yongsan to read the official US Army history of the Korean War. I ended up spending several Saturdays there, immersing myself in the archives.

At the Pentagon I'd often heard the military truism that every nation is preparing to refight its last war. Militaries are led by bureaucracies that want to prove they've learned from their past mistakes, and they'll apply those lessons to whatever situation they encounter next. The North Korea of 1985, much like the North Korea of 2018, was stuck in the paradigm of warfare in 1953. From reading the official history, I gathered that's why leaders of the Democratic People's Republic of Korea amassed their forces and supplies along the north edge of the DMZ—so they wouldn't be reliant on a lengthy mobilization and extended lines of communication.

Also, because they remembered the impact of US carrier aviation during the war, they maintained two separate attack submarine fleets, one on each coast. Importantly, I read about the North Koreans activating two corps-level command-and-control entities not long before they crossed the 38th parallel on June 25, 1950, to manage their invading divisions, and so I considered that an important indication of a potential invasion.

Correlating the history I'd learned in the library with the daily intelligence reports, with help from a couple of my senior Army colonel mentors, I developed a briefing to explain the local situation to distinguished visitors, and I tested it on General Livsey. He liked the presentation, and even more, my starched battle dress uniform with glistening paratrooper boots and properly rolled sleeves. I think he had decided to consider his Air Force one-star as a reclamation project, so he took a personal interest in me. He enjoyed trotting me out and proudly pointing out to his Army general contemporaries "his" Air Force intelligence officer, who looked and talked so very Army.

Still, on at least one occasion, I proved to be pretty clueless. Among my responsibilities as the senior intelligence officer was oversight of what was called the Eighth Army Tunnel Neutralization Team (or TNT), a small contingent of US Army soldiers attached to an ROK Army engineer battalion. This joint unit was tasked with searching for DPRK tunnels under the Demilitarized Zone, which we assessed they planned to use to sneak Special Operations Forces into the South in the first stages of an invasion. Over a period of years, three such tunnels had been found, one of which had become both a major tourist attraction and a required visit for all military-age males in the ROK. Finding a fourth tunnel would have had huge domestic political impact and so was a high priority for the ROK government.

The major role of the Tunnel Neutralization Team was to provide intelligence to the ROK Army engineer battalion, which used several water-well rigs to drill wherever we assessed a tunnel might be. The battalion searched whenever we got reports of underground compressor or drilling sounds, or when shreds of burlap, which were used to line the tunnels, turned up in nearby rice paddies. We tried to apply seismic detectors as well, but the geology near the DMZ was very "noisy." I once inquired how many holes had been dug and was told 3,400—more than 13 holes per kilometer along the 254-kilometer length of the DMZ. I suggested that if we tore off the peninsula along the resulting perforated line, it would eliminate the tunnel threat. My ROK friends didn't find the remark amusing.

One day in early December 1985, the commander of the US TNT detachment, Lieutenant Colonel Gary Kratovil, a career military intelligence officer with a master's degree in geology, came to my office to tell me, rather animatedly, that his team had located a hot prospect for the fourth tunnel. He asked me to visit the drill site both to see what his team and the ROK Army engineers had discovered and to flash my new brigadier general star to motivate the US and ROK troops. On December 17, 1985, a date I'll never forget, we boarded a UH-1 "Huey" helicopter for the short ride from the Yongsan military garrison in Seoul up to the DMZ and the drill site.

The Huey was fully loaded, with two Army pilots, Command Sergeant Major Ray Oeth, Colonel Del Morris, deputy US Forces Korea command engineer Lieutenant Colonel Mike Rodrigues, Gary, and me. I had earphones and could listen to the pilots conversing, but did not have a map. Gary had a map, but couldn't hear the cockpit. As we learned, this was a less than optimal arrangement.

It was a thirty-minute ride to the drill site in the Chorwon Valley—the nominal center of the peninsula and one of the two major invasion corridors when the North Koreans streamed south in June 1950. As we approached the site, the pilots were unable to establish radio contact with the soldiers on the ground. It was a clear day, and we were flying under visual flight rules rather than using instruments and navigation aids. Even so, pilots were required to have both radio and visual contact when flying or landing near the narrow DMZ. The copilot, Chief Warrant Officer 2 Concetta Hassan, who had led a Horatio Alger–type life and had already been the subject of a made-for-TV movie a few months earlier, was on just her second flight mission since arriving in the ROK. Through my headset, I heard her suggest that we fly higher to gain radio comms. The other pilot agreed and ascended three hundred feet. Sure enough, we heard our contacts at the landing site. Unfortunately, during the maneuver, the pilot lost sight of the pond that served as the major landmark in the area, and inadvertently lined up on another pond—just *north* of the DMZ. I began to hear a sound like popcorn in a microwave, and looked out the side of the aircraft to see white puffs below us. At about the same time, I heard a very loud, persistent, and annoying automated broadcast coming through my earphones: "Red Dog Fox! Red Dog Fox!" repeated over and over, which meant someone had crossed the DMZ. That someone was us.

Up front, CW2 Hassan took the controls, dove, turned, and after some evasive maneuvering—an unnatural act for a Huey with a full load—wheeled us around and got us back to South Korean airspace. Her maneuvers used a lot of fuel, and because we'd already traveled a long distance, we landed at a field-deployed rubber fuel bladder, gassed up with the rotor blades still turning, and then returned home to Yongsan. We didn't find out until the helicopter was back in its hangar that a round had penetrated its main rotor. Miraculously, the rotor stayed intact on the leg back to Yongsan, even with the weight of the additional fuel and a full passenger load. From the helicopter pad, my driver was waiting to take me back to my office, and I matter-of-factly told Gary that we'd need to reschedule the trip, since we never made it to the drill site. Still shaken, he gave me a quizzical look.

When I walked into my office, the red phone, a direct emergency line to the around-the-clock command post, was ringing. I had been in Korea about six months, and that was the first time it had ever rung. On the other end was a duty officer, who told me, "My God, sir, we thought you were a goner." After I assured him we were fine, another phone rang, a direct hotline from General Livsey. I braced myself and answered, and what followed made General Pfautz's Sunday morning phone call in Virginia seem like a pep talk. At high volume, General Livsey instructed me on an important distinction between practices of the Air Force and the Army. In the Air Force, the senior pilot is designated as aircraft commander, the official in charge of the safety of the aircraft, regardless of the rank of any passengers. That was not the case in the Army, so thereafter, whenever I flew as the senior-ranking officer in an Army helicopter, I made sure I always had a map and headphones and knew where I was.

To General Livsey's relief, the incident didn't get much media play outside of Korea. The United Nations Command conducted a standard investigation and conveniently determined that we'd only made a shallow penetration of the DMZ. A few days later a nervous ROK Army regimental commander showed up at my office to apologize. The incident investigation determined that the round that hit the rotor was from an

M60 machine gun, a weapon the DPRK didn't have. The commander explained that the rules of engagement called for ROK Army elements along the DMZ to assume that any aircraft flying north was defecting and to shoot them out of the sky. We'd been taking fire from both the north and south, and it turned out the ROK soldiers were better shots. I went home that night and hugged Sue and Andy.

I continued to study and to work at absorbing Army culture. I became more adept at reading General Livsey and grew to admire the way in which, with his Georgia accent, he conveniently played the "dumb Southern boy," though I knew he'd graduated first in his class from the Army's Command and General Staff College. When Secretary of the Army John O. Marsh visited and I gave him my well-honed briefing on North Korea, Marsh asked how I felt about serving as an Air Force officer in what was essentially an Army position. I told him I appreciated the institutional commitment the Army had made to intelligence and that I'd learned a lot about the intelligence profession by seeing it from the viewpoint of another service. I didn't know it yet, but assigning midgrade and senior officers to "joint duty" tours across services would be one of the major features of the Goldwater-Nichols Act in October 1986, an effort in which Marsh was heavily involved.

As the senior intelligence officer in Korea, I eventually grew confident enough in my understanding of the situation that I could honestly admit to General Livsey that we could not meet the expectation he'd demanded of me on day one. I'd become convinced there was simply no way to provide him with an "unambiguous" warning that North Korea was going to attack. I told him the only unambiguous sign he would have is when North Korean artillery shells started falling on Seoul. He didn't like my answer, but he accepted it. I also came to believe the whole idea of having warning before North Korea executed a planned invasion was moot, as the much more likely circumstance leading to a conflict would be some small incident spiraling out of control, something like the events that had preceded Operation Paul Bunyan in 1976.

Thirty years passed between when I reached that conclusion and my diplomatic visit to North Korea as DNI in November 2014. As control of the regime passed from Kim Il-sung to Kim Jong-il to Kim Jong-un, my personal assessment of the threat posed by the Hermit Kingdom never changed. If anything, the actions and the public pronouncements of the "Dear Leaders" over the decades reinforced my conclusion that none of them *wanted* to go back to fighting, but that they've kept the mechanics of war set on a hair trigger, and that any sane US policy on North Korea needed to be based on an understanding of that dynamic.

There is an unwritten, almost sacred writ of the intelligence profession that we in intelligence should avoid engaging in policy formation or execution. We support policy makers by providing them timely, accurate, relevant, even anticipatory intelligence, but we don't participate in making the policy sausage. Our objective typically is to reduce uncertainty for decision makers as much as possible, whether they're in the Oval Office, at the negotiating table, or on the battlefield. As DNI, I was careful not to advocate for specific policies in National Security Council meetings. However, Korea was one issue on which I let President Obama know—privately—that I thought his policy rationale of not discussing anything else until North Korea agreed to end its nuclear capability and ambitions was flawed, and after my 2014 mission to North Korea, I discussed my observations and views with analysts and policy makers in the national security field.

I had not fully appreciated the consuming siege mentality that pervades North Korea until I visited and engaged directly with senior officials there. The leadership elites in the North work hard to maximize paranoia among the population. Portraying the United States as an enemy that's constantly on the brink of invading it is one of the chief propaganda themes that's held North Korea together for the past sixty years. They are also deadly serious about any perceived affronts to the Supreme Leader, whom they literally consider a deity. The DPRK is a family-owned country and has been that way ever since it was founded in the 1940s. Because of its history, the DPRK sees developing nuclear weapons as its insurance policy and ticket to survival. North Korea wants to be recognized as a world power, and its entire society, including their conventional military forces, suffers for the relentless, single-minded commitment to develop and field these weapons and delivery systems to threaten the United States. Neither they nor we really know if their weapons work, but in many ways, it doesn't matter. They achieved nuclear deterrence long ago, because we have to assume that if they do launch an ICBM at the United States, it will reach our shores and detonate. They have effectively played their nuclear hand to the hilt, for without even proving they have the relevant capability, they've capitalized on nuclear deterrence.

I believe, and have advocated, that to counter North Korea, the United States needs to consider capitalizing on our greatest strengths: openness and information. The DPRK survives because it fosters isolation. Outside the ruling clique, there is great interest in the outside world. Currently, we have limited means to satisfy their citizens' hunger for information, something very difficult to do in the absence of a physical presence in the country. If we set aside for a minute our demand that they disarm before we'll talk, we could establish a presence in Pyongyang in the form of a US "interests section," modeled on the one we maintained in Havana for decades to deal with the Cuban government we didn't recognize. We would not need to present this as a reward for bad behavior, but rather as an opportunity for direct physical access, which would enhance our insight and understanding and, perhaps even more importantly, foster interaction with the people of the DPRK and enable the flow of information from the rest of the world. We would, of course, reciprocate by allowing them to establish a similar mission in Washington. I don't think this would represent a huge leap over their existing presence in the United States at the United Nations in New York.

I'm not naïve about the existence of formidable antibodies in the US government to what I'm suggesting, but I don't see any other way to resolve the impasse. The DPRK won't budge because they see us as an existential threat. If we are going to get out of the static, adversarial holding pattern we're in now, we have to be the bigger partner and make the "breakthrough," to use the preferred term the North Koreans used with me.

At this writing, the situation in North Korea seems poised for change—whether for better or for worse remains to be seen. Events and pronouncements in the first year of President Trump's administration, including increasingly successful DPRK ballistic missile tests and an apparently successful thermonuclear test, heightened tensions between our two countries. Taunts between Trump and Kim Jong-un only serve to shorten the fuses of the military forces on both sides, as the DPRK Army stands ready to rain fire down on the 10 million residents of Seoul at a moment's notice. Then, in March 2018, a South Korean envoy in Washington informed President Trump that Supreme Leader Kim was willing to discuss giving up North Korea's nuclear program. Surprising everyone, Trump accepted the invitation to talk.

What I would hope (but doubt will happen) is that the United States will enter talks with a long-game strategy in mind. America has had a substantial military presence on the peninsula for almost sixty-eight years. If we can figure out a way, over time, with sequenced, mutually verified steps, to lead the DPRK government to where they don't feel so threatened, we could move away from the rhetorical cusp of a cataclysmic war. If we can offer a road map to the US military's withdrawing much of its forces from the peninsula, while the North Koreans reduce the large conventional forces they have along the DMZ, including the huge artillery and rocketry forces that are dug in ready to fire on Seoul, that would de-escalate the situation and lessen the danger of a minor incident's quickly escalating to nuclear war. In the late 1990s, when I was out of the government, I participated in the so-called Track II dialogue with members of the North Korean UN mission in New York. Over a dinner, one of the North Koreans spoke about transforming the United Nations Command into a peacekeeping force, to serve as buffer between the North and the South. So even they have considered a different arrangement on the peninsula. A reasonable first step might be to meet their demands for a peace treaty, as all we have now is a cease-fire, which began when the warring sides simply stopped shooting. In their minds, the war could resume immediately. We remain stuck on our narrative, and they are (or perhaps merely have been until recently) stuck on theirs. Only the bigger partner can change those narratives. I hope we can think ambitiously and be willing to go long, and perhaps this is our opportunity to do so. Unfortunately, I don't think we're postured—either philosophically or bureaucratically—to achieve that.

In July 1986, I was finally sure I'd earned General Livsey's trust when he asked me to accompany him on a field trip with only his wife, Bena, and his aide-de-camp. We rode a Huey to the eastern side of the peninsula and then a truck from the landing zone into the mountains. When the truck could go no farther, we walked. Finally, wearing "battle rattle" armor—helmets, heavy Kevlar vests, canteens, and other items that all clanked as we moved—we climbed three wooden ladders to reach a mountaintop.

There we found the battle position Livsey's platoon had held when the cease-fire went into effect thirty-three years earlier. He walked around and began to describe that final day of combat in a way that reminded me of the scene in the movie *Patton* where George C. Scott, playing George Patton, recounted the battle of Carthage. Livsey looked down at the terrain and pointed to where the waves of Chinese troops had come at his platoon. He described how they'd concentrated fire to repel the attacks. He recalled the sounds and smells as they held their ground and called in air strikes. Just before the cease-fire took effect at 10:00 P.M. on July 27, both sides had opened up a massive artillery barrage, lighting up the night and making the mountainside shake. As he relived the experience and shared it with us, I felt as though I was in the presence of a demigod, returned from Hades to recount an experience that could never really be understood by mortal man.

Sometime later, Livsey summoned me to his office to ask for my thoughts on whom he should pick to become the next commanding general of the 2nd Infantry Division. He gave me three names and explained that he wanted my judgment, which he felt would be neutral and unpolluted by Army politics. I offered my thoughts, which he ultimately agreed with. A few months later, when Livsey was asked to stay for a third year as commander of US Forces Korea until he retired, I asked him if I could also remain. The tour in Korea, which I'd been so skeptical of, had turned out to be one of the most rewarding assignments for both me and my family. Livsey said he appreciated the offer, but for the sake of my career, it was time for me to move on.

In July 1987, Sue, Andy, and I moved back to Hawaii, where I was assigned to US Pacific Command as what amounted to the senior intelligence officer for all US forces across the surface of more than half the globe. In Hawaii, I quickly realized just how much the world had changed in the two years I'd been so heavily focused on the Korean Peninsula. In 1985 Mikhail Gorbachev had come to power as the general secretary of the Communist Party of the Soviet Union, giving a speech that May in which he talked about major reforms that sounded shockingly democratic and capitalist. In 1986 he introduced the Russian words *glasnost* (openness) and *perestroika* (restructuring) to the Western vocabulary. The Soviet Union had been our primary adversary, our archenemy, through most of my life, and now there was open talk of our relationship changing.

I also found that the Goldwater-Nichols Act had profoundly changed the relationship between combatant commanders and the military services. USPACOM commander Admiral Ron Hays, and then, in 1988, Admiral Hunt Hardisty reported directly to the secretary of defense, enjoying more official access and autonomy than Admiral Gayler had. As their senior intelligence officer, I liked and respected both men, but never had as close a relationship with either as I felt I had had with General Livsey.

Sue and I also found that Oahu had changed a lot since we'd left in 1978. High-rise hotels had sprung up all over Waikiki, and the island was choked with traffic and tourists. Because Hawaii was more of a magnet for visitors than Korea, I found that a great deal of my time was taken up with "distinguished visitors," either foreign dignitaries who'd come to the island on their way to the mainland, or US officials whose planes were stopping at Hickam Air Force Base, adjacent to the Pearl Harbor Naval Base, to refuel. I spent countless hours in the small auditorium that we fondly called the "blue bedroom," where polished young briefers presented the "Pacific Area Update," a scripted briefing that they had memorized. One of the many command performances was delivered to the King of Tonga, a remarkably massive man of at least three hundred pounds. Mid-briefing, the king fell asleep and began snoring loudly. Admiral Hays gestured to the briefers to keep going. The rest of us remained quiet so as not to disturb the king's slumber.

Perhaps the most bizarre VIP visit was from Vice President Dan Quayle at the very end of my assignment. His plane was stopping at Hickam in the middle of the night, and en route the VP said he wanted to play a pickup basketball game while it refueled—he and his security detail against a PACOM team . . . at 3:00 A.M. We scrambled to find five players, and the only reason it was competitive was that our side had Colonel Jack Graham, who'd played varsity basketball for the Air Force Academy a few decades earlier. We ensured the vice president's team won, but only by a little.

In 1988, I was promoted to major general. My heart's desire was to take command of the Air Force Electronic Security Command. Not only would that make for a poetic bookend for my career, taking me back to the command where I started as a young lieutenant in 1963, but it would be an especially meaningful assignment, putting me in charge of a large portion of Air Force intelligence assets and focusing them on tracking the great changes taking place in the Soviet Union, just as cracks were appearing in the Iron Curtain. But that was not to be. Instead, I received orders to report to Offutt Air Force Base in Nebraska to be the deputy chief of staff for intelligence for Strategic Air Command. Sue and I were preparing for the move when the already tense situation in China flared up.

On April 15, 1989, we monitored from US Pacific Command as students from several Beijing universities spontaneously gathered in Tiananmen Square—the massive, hundred-acre public space just outside the Forbidden City. Demonstrations against the government grew, and several thousand students demanded the party recognize them. As the somewhat sympathetic General Secretary Zhao Ziyang left on a scheduled trip to North Korea, the militaristic Premier Li Peng denounced their actions as an antigovernment revolt, promising to crack down. On the following day, close to a hundred thousand students responded with a massive protest in the square.

In crisis mode, we reported any updates from our military attachés in Beijing to PACOM leaders and to Washington. The situation worsened as the students keyed protests to a scheduled visit from Mikhail Gorbachev. Three days before his visit, three hundred thousand people staged a hunger strike and refused to leave the square, forcing the Chinese Communist Party to formally welcome Gorbachev at the airport. It was a huge embarrassment, and worse, coverage by Chinese media led to sympathy for the students across the nation. The government declared martial law and mobilized the People's Liberation Army.

All of our military attachés were put on lockdown, which profoundly cut into the quality of our intelligence picture. We still had satellite imagery—snapshots of vehicle movements—but didn't really know what units had mobilized, what they were doing, and what was happening in the streets. Outside some creative tradecraft on the ground that provided some insight into PLA activities, we were nearly blind, and unfortunately there wasn't much we could do for the student protesters.

We watched, helpless, as the PLA rolled tanks and soldiers toward the square on the night of June 3. The protesters tried to block their entrance, but troops opened fire, killing protesters in rolling skirmishes. In the dark early morning hours, the students and PLA troops had a final, violent clash. We still don't know for certain how many students and protesters died, but a very recently declassified British intelligence cable puts the number killed at more than ten thousand and details both the brutality of the slaughter and the desecration of human remains that followed. In US Pacific Command, we were shocked, outraged, and heartbroken, and for many of us, it was also a stark lesson on the limits of intelligence.

Within weeks, I had to put those somber events in China behind me and once again focus on another challenge. Just as Pacific Command forced me to open my aperture beyond the Korean Peninsula, moving to Strategic Air Command compelled a look beyond the Pacific region, as large as it was, to take in the entire globe. In 1989, SAC had responsibility for all US strategic reconnaissance aircraft (the U-2 and SR-71 spy planes), and the more prominent US arsenal of ICBMs and all the US strategic bombers (the B-1 Lancer and the B-52 Stratofortress bombers, which the North Koreans so feared). As Sue and I were unpacking in July 1989, the B-2 Spirit stealth bomber was making its first test flight.

Trying to hold on to my favorite part of living in Hawaii, I'd paid to ship my beloved yellow MG convertible to the mainland, but July in Nebraska was entirely too hot and humid to drive the car, which lacked air-conditioning. I stowed it for the summer and had a couple of months of joy in the fall until, in the first of the hard freezes Nebraska was famous for, it went into a deep coma and never recovered. As I worked to understand and master my new responsibilities, Sue and Andy settled into their own routines. Andy enrolled for his senior year in his third high school, in nearby Bellevue. Only later would we realize that he emerged from all the moves a better person. Jenny and Andy are both wonderful, and I'm incredibly proud of how well Sue raised them.

I only served at SAC for eight months, but it was a time of turmoil. In part inspired by the protests in Tiananmen Square, the Warsaw Pact countries began to shed Soviet control and free themselves of their Communist governments. During the short time I was at Offutt, we saw revolutionary elections in Poland, Hungary, East Germany, Bulgaria, Czechoslovakia, and Romania. On November 9, a confused member of the Socialist Unity Party in East Germany mistakenly announced at a press conference that guards along the Berlin Wall would begin allowing people to pass from East Berlin into West Berlin, effective immediately.

That wasn't true, but as crowds rushed the gates, the overwhelmed guards let them through. That night I watched the television coverage as people chiseled away at the Wall and celebrated in the streets. The Cold Warrior in me was amazed and delighted. The intelligence officer in me was concerned. So much instability surrounding the Soviets' massive military forces, particularly their nuclear arsenal, was inherently dangerous. At Strategic Air Command, we focused on understanding what was happening to the vestiges of Soviet military power. By the time I left in March, things in the former Soviet bloc were tumultuous.

While at SAC, I flew thirty-seven missions in the "Looking Glass" airborne command post that's featured in the film *Dr. Strangelove*. From any of the dozen or so Boeing 707 aircraft at Offutt, each specially reconfigured and redesignated as an Air Force EC-135, the command staff could maintain communications with vital elements of US strategic forces and could convey orders to the ICBM silos, strategic bombers, and ballistic missile submarines. The Air Force had a requirement that an EC-135 be airborne with a general officer aboard at all times, with no lapses ever, which translated to three missions of eight-plus hours a day. Remarkably, Looking Glass aircraft were airborne and mission-ready continuously for thirty-one years. As a two-star general, I found myself doing shift work again, taking my turns in the rotation of all the one- and two-star generals assigned throughout SAC. While airborne, we ran exercises to assess our readiness to respond if threatened. We could *always* respond with catastrophic force. We could *never* prevent the annihilation of our homeland. No one who'd held the responsibility for deploying nuclear weapons during an exercise could deny that reality. It was this experience that convinced me that neither side would ever intentionally inflict a nuclear attack on the other. Thankfully, the most exciting thing that ever happened on those flights was when an occasional Boy Scout troop or Chamber of Commerce group visited the underground SAC command post for a tour. They would call up Looking Glass, and I would answer as the disembodied voice in the sky, giving them a short, scripted briefing and reassurances they were well protected.

The orientation flight I took in January 1990 in a two-seat U-2 spy plane was a much more exciting experience. Over 68,000 feet up, at the edge of space, I could see all of Northern California. The sky was purple, fading to black above me. All the world's problems—North Korea's aggression, China's oppression of its own citizens, the uncertainty of what was happening to all those Soviet weapons—seemed small and far away. For four short hours, the pilot and I were above all other concerns. "Fun" doesn't fully capture the experience. It was transcendent, although I did wonder what I would do if the pilot had a heart attack. That March, the highly esteemed Air Force chief of staff, General Larry Welch, summoned me back to the Pentagon, where fun goes to die.

I left almost immediately, while the commander of SAC, General Jack Chain, graciously allowed Sue and Andy to stay in our quarters at Offutt so that Andy could graduate. Back in Washington, I joined the Air Force staff as its senior intelligence officer. I briefly lived with Jen and her husband, Jay, in their town house until Sue joined me in government quarters at Bolling Air Force Base in July.

While my two most recent career moves had opened my view of the world, my focus from the Pentagon narrowed to a tiny nation in the Middle East—Kuwait—and to the airspace above its neighbor—Iraq. Throughout the 1980s, the United States had grudgingly backed Iraq in its war with Iran, preferring almost anyone to Iran after the 1979 revolution. Invading Iran in 1980 had been a terrible miscalculation by the new Iraqi president, Saddam Hussein, and support from the United States and Saudi Arabia was really the only reason Iran had not reversed the invasion and conquered Iraq. In the two years since the Iran-Iraq War had ended in 1988, Hussein had ruled as a brutal dictator, using executions as a management tool and even inflicting mustard gas and nerve agents on his own people in the ethnically Kurdish north. He had aggressively rebuilt his army after the war and boasted that he had a million soldiers, although US intelligence estimated the number as closer to six hundred thousand.

When I returned to the Pentagon in March 1990, the only person in the US government who really thought Iraq would invade Kuwait was Defense Secretary Dick Cheney. Of course, he also thought Gorbachev was about to be overthrown and the Soviet Union was going to come roaring back. General Welch retired and was succeeded by General Mike Dugan, who only lasted six weeks before Secretary Cheney fired him, a move I believe was more about Cheney's asserting civilian control over the military than about Dugan's allegedly overstepping his bounds with the media.

Meanwhile, Saddam had massed his troops at the Kuwait border, including his elite Republican Guard. A nervous consensus evolved that Saddam was bluffing. At that point, we were still sharing intelligence with Iraq and selling them arms. On July 31, General Norman Schwarzkopf, the commander of US Central Command and, under Goldwater-Nichols, the general responsible for running any military operations in and around Iraq, briefed the Joint Chiefs of Staff, including General Colin Powell, in "the tank," the JCS's secure briefing room in the Pentagon. He said that there were a lot of reasons for Saddam Hussein to bluff, most of them having to do with money Hussein owed Kuwait or his desire to manipulate oil prices. He concluded that the chances of Iraq invading Kuwait were "slim."

Obviously, US intelligence hadn't served General Schwarzkopf well in the weeks leading up to that meeting. We had an exquisite overhead capability to take digital pictures from space and beam them directly to the agencies in and around the Washington area. We had analysts who could count the precise number of tanks and artillery pieces in each formation, and we knew the Iraqi order of battle and its capabilities cold. We just were not as good at determining what Hussein intended to do with them. Schwarzkopf later said he hated the intelligence "words of estimative uncertainty" and that we almost never told him something was "certain" or "almost certain." He heard a lot of "probably," "probably not," and "chances about even," which he found particularly unhelpful. He also found it dysfunctional and less than helpful that the major intelligence agencies and the service intelligence components were all telling him different things, and no one was figuring out why they all seemed to disagree.

In 2014, when I was DNI and Russia had troops massed on the border of Eastern Ukraine, I remembered General Schwarzkopf's complaints. We didn't have any better insight into what was going on in Putin's head in 2014 than we did in Hussein's in 1990, but with the advent of social media and our expanded use of satellite imagery provided by commercial companies, we had progressed in seeing indications and providing warning of impending action. In the end, though, having such insight didn't stop Putin from annexing Crimea in March 2014.

On August 2, 1990, two days after Schwarzkopf's Pentagon briefing, Iraq invaded and then overran Kuwait. In less than two days, Saddam gained control and declared Kuwait the "nineteenth province" of Iraq. He parked his tank formations and his massive army along the Kuwaiti border with Saudi Arabia, pointed at the Saudi capital of Riyadh, less than three hundred miles away, about the driving distance from New Haven, Connecticut, to Washington, DC, with nothing but open desert in the way.

On August 3, General Schwarzkopf asked Lieutenant General Chuck Horner, the commander of the 9th Air Force and the Combined Forces Air Component commander for US Central Command, to design the coming air campaign and to work as the forward deployed commander of CENTCOM forces. He then dispatched Horner to Riyadh to receive US troops and equipment as they arrived in Saudi Arabia. My primary job in all this was to support the Air Force chief of staff as he managed the provision of Air Force resources to Schwarzkopf and Horner, so that they could defeat the Iraqis when President Bush gave the order in January 1991. Unfortunately, not everyone in the Pentagon saw it that way.

Four years later, in 1995, the Air University published a breathless account of Colonel John A. Warden III, the Air Force deputy director for warfighting concepts, and his "Checkmate" think tank in the basement of the Pentagon at the time. It described how Colonel Warden flew to Riyadh to present General Horner with the Air Force's plan to win the war solely by using "Air Power"—a phrase always capitalized—without the need of any other military services. Horner unceremoniously dispatched Warden back to Washington but kept some of his staff who'd made the trip, including Lieutenant Colonel Dave Deptula, who ended up doing a lot of the real planning for Desert Storm when US and coalition forces routed the Iraqis the following January. I got to know and respect Dave as he advanced through the ranks ultimately to lieutenant general, and I often sought his opinion when intelligence and Air Force operations crossed paths.

On August 9, before Colonel Warden's ill-fated attempt to lecture General Horner in Riyadh, Warden's boss, Major General Minter Alexander, called and asked me to break off some of my intelligence staff, who were quite busy trying to keep the Air Force leadership current on the daily situation, and send them down to Warden in "Checkmate" to help him pick targets in Iraq. I'd been in contact with General Horner's intelligence chief, and I knew Horner had no idea that the Pentagon staff were designing an air campaign. I don't remember the specific words I used on the phone with Minter, but having had the experience of serving in

Korea, at Pacific Command, and at Strategic Air Command, as well as having the ability to imagine how General Livsey would have reacted if a staff officer from the Pentagon basement showed up in Seoul to give him a battle plan for defeating North Korea without having to worry about ground forces, I told Minter in my politest two-star general peer-to-peer phrasing that I believed General Horner was in charge of the air war and that, regardless, my staff wasn't configured to comply with his request.

Minter then appealed to the Air Force vice chief of staff, four-star general Mike Loh, who tried to force my hand. I believed they were way out of their lane and were not helping the efforts of Schwarzkopf and Horner, who actually had to fight the war. So I didn't budge. General Loh, along with all the Air Power advocates, labeled me as recalcitrant, someone who just didn't "get it." The Air University account goes much further in excoriating me as an Air Power nonbeliever. My telephone conversation with Minter Alexander is scripted over three pages of direct quotes, which I informed the Air University commander were all fabricated, but he printed them anyway. Shortly after the book came out, I received a classy note of apology from Minter Alexander.

Obviously, this matter still sticks in my craw, but I'm writing about all of this because so much of the doctrinal infighting impacted me years down the road. The book correctly points out that Colonel Warden in the Pentagon had much better imagery intelligence than General Horner did in Riyadh. We had these great digital pictures in Washington, but to get them to the American forces in and around Kuwait, we had to print them out and fly them to the war zone on a courier plane, literally halfway around the world. We still had the same problem we'd faced in Vietnam— intelligence arriving too late to be useful. It was a great frustration at the time.

Also, in many ways the Air Force's resistance to the reforms dictated by the Goldwater-Nichols Act of 1986 foreshadowed the opposition some intelligence agencies—particularly the CIA—would have for the measures dictated by the Intelligence Reform and Terrorism Prevention Act of 2004, which created the director of national intelligence. There are obvious differences between those two landmark laws, but both ask the individual elements (military branches or intelligence agencies) to subordinate their primacy to the larger enterprise. Four years after Goldwater-Nichols, powerful figures within the Air Force still resisted its role as force

provider to the combatant commanders and were fighting a rearguard bureaucratic insurgency. Similarly, when I became DNI five and a half years
after legislation to reform the IC was enacted, some influential voices
within the intelligence agencies were still exhibiting passive-aggressive
opposition to the notion that their component missions were part of the
larger intelligence enterprise.

On October 30, 1990, General Tony McPeak became Air Force chief of
staff. McPeak supported Goldwater-Nichols and General Schwarzkopf's
authority, through General Horner, to execute operations in the Central
Command area of authority—which effectively ended the fight over the
Air Power plan. But he also was a dyed-in-the-wool fighter pilot who had
a reputation for disdain for the intelligence profession and those who
engaged in it, a conviction shaped by his combat experience in Vietnam,
when he believed intelligence professionals had held back information
that pilots needed to safely and effectively conduct their missions. As the
senior intelligence officer of the Air Force staff, I was in McPeak's direct
line of sight and, potentially, line of fire. I told Sue that we'd had a pretty
good run, and that achieving the rank of major general was a respectable
accomplishment.

On January 17, 1991, with doctrinal disputes behind us, General
Schwarzkopf's forces switched from Desert Shield to Desert Storm and
went on the offensive. For the next five weeks, Air Force and Navy jets
bombarded the Iraqi forces, quickly destroying their air and antiair capabilities and then command and control. Under General Horner's direction, coalition forces flew unopposed bomb runs on Iraqi Army positions.
The only seemingly difficult task in the air war was trying to find the
camouflaged, mobile Scud-missile launchers in the desert before they
could fire toward Israel or Saudi Arabia. Still, everyone braced for a brutal ground confrontation with the massive numbers of supposedly elite
Iraqi troops in Kuwait and along the border of Saudi Arabia. We particularly were concerned that the Iraqis would use their stockpiles of chemical weapons on the invading coalition troops.

On February 24, after feinting a Marine Corps amphibious assault
into Kuwait City from the Persian Gulf, coalition forces swept into Kuwait and Iraq from Saudi Arabia. US Army M1A1 tanks and Air Force
A-10 Thunderbolt close-air-support jets dominated Iraqi armor. Iraqi
forces put up almost no resistance, either laying down their arms and

surrendering or running before the fight reached them. Schwarzkopf said he could have driven straight to Baghdad if he had been ordered to, but we stopped after liberating Kuwait, ending the ground assault just a hundred hours after it started.

In the months following the war, General Schwarzkopf gave high praise to almost everyone involved in almost every aspect of the operation. The one exception was intelligence. We had counted the Iraqi order of battle down to a level of detail that was probably unnecessary. What we failed to do was to give any insight into the Iraqi soldier's will to fight. In that respect, we'd vastly overrated the Iraqi Army, something we'd do again in 2014, when cities in Iraq were depending on it to defend them from the Islamic State.

Schwarzkopf had two chief complaints. First, as combatant commander, he had control of all the mainline, traditional military forces in the theater from each of the services, but he had no idea what Special Operations Forces or the CIA elements were doing. Bob Gates, who became director of central intelligence and of the CIA in November 1991, took that complaint seriously and set out to address the matter. Schwarzkopf's second complaint centered on his disappointment with the imagery intelligence he'd received. He argued widely, loudly, and correctly that he'd had no wide-area imagery to see the total expanse of his battlespace. We'd provided him "postage-stamp" photos, tiny pictures without any context of how they fit into the overall theater of war, which was like looking at a patch of land through a soda straw. Worse, we'd provided these images far too slowly to be useful. And, to his frustration, there was no single agency he could contact to coordinate imagery collection and analysis and get results to him quickly.

Given General McPeak's antipathy toward intelligence officers and my conflict with senior generals in the Pentagon over who should design and control the air war over Iraq, I figured my time in uniform would soon be over. So, once again, Sue and I started making retirement plans, but my military career had one more assignment in store.

CHAPTER THREE

The Peace Dividend

In 1991, the US Intelligence Community included four large, full-time intelligence agencies and the four intelligence components of the military services. The Department of Defense harbored three of the major intelligence agencies: the National Security Agency, NSA—the lead for intercepting signals and communications (established when I was in grade school in 1952 and that my dad, Sue's dad, Sue, and I had served in); the Defense Intelligence Agency, DIA—the central hub for intelligence on foreign military capabilities and intentions; and the National Reconnaissance Office, NRO—the organization that designed, launched, and flew intelligence satellites, including all the overhead missions to keep tabs on the Soviets. In 1991, NSA and DIA were led by three-star military officers and NRO by a senior civilian, all three of whom reported to the secretary of defense. The CIA operated independently as the fourth major agency with a civilian director who was "dual hatted" to lead the entire Intelligence Community as the director of central intelligence, as well as serving as the director of the Central Intelligence Agency. He reported to the president. Each intelligence component of the military services—Army, Navy, Air Force, and Marine Corps—was run by a general or admiral, and each service had intelligence analysis centers tailored to the needs and interests of its service missions. In October 1991, the Air Force would consolidate all of its major strategic intelligence activities under the Air Force Electronic Security Command and rename it the Air Force Intelligence Command, a consolidation I'd helped to foster from the Pentagon.

In addition to the eight organizations nominally thought of as the Intelligence Community, the Coast Guard conducted intelligence missions, but did not really have a dedicated intelligence cadre, and the Departments of State, Treasury, and Energy also contained small intelligence offices, tightly focused, respectively, on intelligence to support diplomacy, financial intelligence, and on the security of DOE's laboratories as well as tracking the proliferation of nuclear weapons around the world. I had some familiarity with DOE's intelligence capabilities because of my tenure at AFTAC. But no one thought of the offices outside CIA and DOD as being part of an Intelligence Community and no one had any illusions about any of these organizations operating as an integrated enterprise.

By 1991, I'd spent most of my career as a staff intelligence officer—either on an operational staff or as a cog within the Air Force Intelligence Command or NSA. I'd had a lot of contact with the major agencies, but NSA was the only one in which I'd spent any significant time. So I was shocked when General McPeak called me to say, in a routine business tone, that Army Lieutenant General Ed Soyster was retiring as DIA director, and McPeak intended to nominate me for a third star to succeed him. It took me a moment to process what I had just heard, but once I grasped it, I was thrilled. In my brief interactions with the agency, I had been impressed with DIA's mission and staff, and the more I thought about it, the more it seemed to be another serendipitous turn for my career, leading in a direction I found appealing.

McPeak proposed my nomination to the Joint Chiefs of Staff in March, and I was considered alongside generals and admirals from the other services. In June, the JCS reached consensus with the assistant secretary of defense for command, control, communications, and intelligence, Duane Andrews, and forwarded my name to the White House to officially nominate me to the Senate Armed Services Committee, which would ultimately send my name to the floor to be confirmed by the entire Senate for my third star.

Filling the position of DIA director didn't, in and of itself, require Senate confirmation, and typically, after consideration by the SASC, the nomination to promote someone to three-star general would quickly advance to the floor of the Senate for a pro forma vote. Not so for me. The Senate committee was at the time attempting to extort information from DOD on a completely unrelated program, information the Pentagon didn't want to surrender. My nomination provided it with convenient leverage, and so the committee simply refused to consider it, leaving me to spend five months as an unemployed two-star general residing in bureaucratic limbo. Suffice it to say, I don't do well when unoccupied and bored. I passed the days receiving briefings from the DIA staff on their work, reading intelligence reports as the Soviet Union imploded, going to the Pentagon gym a lot, and driving staff officers crazy with requests for information to read to fill my time. The one pleasant surprise was acquiring General Tony McPeak as a mentor and discovering that the super fighter-pilot was much more reasonable in person than his reputation suggested.

During those five idle months, one of General McPeak's decisions put me into an awkward situation in public. Under his leadership, as part of a historic reorganization of the Air Force, the forty-year-old institutions of the Strategic Air Command, Tactical Air Command, and Military Airlift Command—SAC, TAC, and MAC—were all disbanded, almost overnight, and yet almost no one in the Air Force complained. The entire service was then too distracted by his decision to also change the Air Force uniforms for a redesign that was universally panned. Officers' attire was particularly abhorrent, as it omitted the traditional brass rank and "US" insignia and put stripes on the coat sleeves, much like the Navy did. When McPeak unveiled the new uniforms at a press conference, a reporter instantly summed up everyone's thoughts: "These look like airline pilot uniforms." General McPeak's succinct response was "Guilty." I always wondered if he'd intentionally created this issue as a distraction from shutting down the three iconic commands.

I was "randomly" picked to be one of a few hundred service members to test-wear the two versions of the proposed new uniforms, both to model them for others and to assess their utility. One version failed me at the worst time. On Memorial Day 1991, Sue and I were to attend a concert on the National Mall and had been invited to a military reception before the event in the Capitol. Just as we stepped out of a car to walk the hundred yards or so to the Capitol building, a sudden, torrential rainstorm hit. As a traditionalist, I didn't carry an umbrella, even in the face of a darkening sky, and by the time we reached the reception, we were drenched. As it dried, my uniform began shrinking around my arms and legs. I sensed an uncomfortable tension from the tightening fabric, and when a button on my chest actually popped, I felt absurdly like the Incredible Hulk in the early 1980s TV show. I tried to melt into the crowd, but too late. General Colin Powell, of all people, resplendent in his dry dress Army service uniform, spotted me, smiled, and with obvious joy and great zeal, launched into a public razzing about Air Force uniforms and dress standards. It took my bruised ego several months to recover.

The five-month respite from the pressure of day-to-day duties did give me abundant time to ponder what I wanted to accomplish as DIA director. I'd spent a great deal of my career at operational commands in which my bosses had been intelligence customers, rather than practitioners, and I thought defense intelligence could serve its operational customers better than it had. I was frustrated that we could beam imagery into the Pentagon but still could not put timely intelligence into the hands of the combat forces at scale.

I was also struck that, while the director of central intelligence consolidated and presented the combined "national" intelligence picture to the National Security Council and the president, the "defense" intelligence picture was often conveyed to the Joint Chiefs of Staff and the secretary of defense erratically and in separate, often competitive streams from DIA and the intelligence components of each military service.

From my three combatant command senior intelligence officer jobs and as Air Force chief of intelligence, I appreciated alternative views. Constructive dissents can be helpful because they illustrate how the same source material can be viewed differently by different analysts or agencies. But the secretary of defense, or for that matter a warfighting commander like General Schwarzkopf, could receive five intelligence reports, one from DIA and one from each service, that all expressed opposing assessments, with little explanation as to why; or conversely, such reporting could effectively consist of five redundant echoes, none of which added any new information or insight. I was determined to try to fix those two problems as DIA director, and believed that the sudden demise of the Soviets would give me the space and time to do so.

The tedium ended when I became (I believe) the first DIA director nominee ever to appear for a formal confirmation hearing, which made me a bit apprehensive but passed without incident. After the hearing, I was quickly confirmed, appointed, and took my oath of office—all in November 1991. General McPeak presided at my pinning. I will never forget the grace he brought to that ceremony, in the presence of my mother and father, who were both beaming. I arrived at DIA just in time to see the Soviet Union finally collapse and officially dissolve on December 26.

One of the first decisions I had to make was what to do with the tenth issue of DIA's annual *Soviet Military Power*. In the late 1970s the defense establishment believed that, while Americans felt a visceral animosity toward the Soviet Union, the public and the world at large didn't truly understand the menace the Soviets posed to global peace and security— just as very few understand the threat Russia poses today. In 1981 DIA sought to show the magnitude and capability of Soviet forces and strategy by drawing on experts from across the Intelligence Community and amassing their consolidated knowledge in a profusely illustrated volume. They then performed the difficult work of declassifying the information, which meant going back to the systems and the people the intelligence originated with and working line by line to determine what facts and assessments could be published without revealing the sources and methods used to collect them. The initial one hundred-page publication was a compelling graphic example of what DIA could achieve when it worked to integrate the intelligence efforts of the military services.

Soviet Military Power was so successful that the agency decided to publish annual updates, starting in 1983. By the time I arrived at DIA, it was printing more than four hundred thousand copies each year in nine languages, including Russian. The 1991 issue was in its final edits when I took my oath of office, and with the Soviet collapse imminent, DIA was discussing just shelving the project. With no Soviets to make a public diplomacy case against, why bother? As the new director, I pointed out that none of the Soviet bombers, submarines, and ICBMs was about to magically disappear, and that our publication could explain what was happening during a crucial transformation. We published the 1991 issue as *Military Forces in Transition,* a title that set the tone for one of our biggest challenges over the next four years—keeping track of strategic Soviet military equipment.

I began to look for other ways to extend and institutionalize that cooperation among the services. Within DIA, a small but very capable group was tasked with aggregating the General Defense Intelligence Program. The GDIP (Gee-Dip we called it) encapsulated everything intelligence organizations did with the manpower and money Congress allocated for defense intelligence. The GDIP staff collects and summarizes that activity in a single report to help Congress decide what activities to continue appropriating. Other agencies prepared similar documents for cryptologic, human intelligence, counterintelligence, and other intelligence programs. Today, all of them are rolled up into just two consolidated program reports—one from the director of national intelligence and one from the undersecretary of defense for intelligence, positions that did not exist at that time.

In 1991, the GDIP staff had just welcomed its new deputy director—and later director—who was known and respected across the eight organizations of the Intelligence Community. Joan Dempsey was one of the most savvy intelligence officers with whom I've ever served—astute and pragmatic about both intelligence work itself and the ways of Washington. She compensated for my blind spots when it came to the art of dealing with Congress and the nuances of working with a civilian workforce, which constituted 75 percent of DIA. When I'd given direction as a commander, people in uniform typically responded, "Yes, sir." Civilians at DIA sometimes reacted to me as their director with an attitude closer to "We'll think about it." Joan saved me from responding poorly—often and early.

Right out of the gate, Congress handed me a challenge disguised as a gift. They'd been pushing to consolidate GDIP resources under a single command and proposed taking five major intelligence centers from the military services and moving them all under DIA. In the end, it was decided that DIA would gain only the Missile and Space Intelligence Center (MSIC) and the Armed Forces Medical Intelligence Center (AFMIC), under the rationale that they were both predominantly staffed by civilians, who could be more easily absorbed into DIA. I quickly learned that "empire building" is not all it's cracked up to be, and that feathers get ruffled when Congress takes something from one organization and gives it to another. While AFMIC had been a joint command with each of the services represented, MSIC had belonged to the Army, and so it was the Army that felt most aggrieved and complained the loudest. Fortunately for me, the two moves went "final" on January 1, 1992, when I'd been on the job just a month and a half, and so the Army didn't hold me personally responsible. Still, MSIC was the source of one of my first real headaches as DIA director.

The Missile and Space Intelligence Center essentially studied the capabilities of any foreign missile launched from the ground that wasn't an ICBM. During the 1990–91 Gulf War, because DIA needed its expertise to understand the surface-to-air systems in Iraq, as well as the mobile Scud missiles that Iraq kept trying to launch into Israel and Saudi Arabia, MSIC sent analysts from its headquarters in Huntsville, Alabama, to Washington on temporary duty orders. One of those civilian analysts had a girlfriend in Washington, and the temporary duty was a convenient arrangement he wanted to maintain. With the war over, I canceled the temporary duty arrangement and sent the MSIC people home. This analyst reached out to Alabama senator Richard Shelby's office and found a sympathetic ear in his staff. Shortly after, I received a letter with Senator Shelby's signature, informing me in no uncertain terms that I was an incompetent, unprofessional hack for having closed down the MSIC cell in the Pentagon. I hit the ceiling. I couldn't believe that a senator could be so disrespectful to a lieutenant general (oh, how naïve I was), and I directed my staff to prepare a barn-burner response.

Fortunately, Joan had a better idea. She pointed out that the letter had been signed by autopen, probably without Senator Shelby's knowledge, and suggested that I view the letter as an opportunity. She knew that MSIC's fifty-year-old facility in Huntsville was in disrepair: the roof leaked, the plumbing was unreliable, the electrical system was overstressed, and the air-conditioning and heating systems were obsolete. Using the letter as an excuse to engage with his staff, she set up a meeting with Senator Shelby to discuss building a new facility. On the way to Capitol Hill, she prevailed upon me not to bring up the letter, and I didn't. Instead, we discussed how both DIA and the state of Alabama would be greatly served if we could find military construction funding to give the superb workforce of MSIC (all constituents of Senator Shelby) a state-of-the-art facility. We quickly struck a deal. After that, I sought Joan's opinion before any major decision, in many ways viewing her as an unofficial second deputy director. Not for the first time, I came to regard someone who ostensibly worked for me as a mentor.

Joan was a trailblazing role model for an entire generation of women in the IC. She supervised a number of intelligence officers on the GDIP staff who would leave a substantial mark on the community, including Deborah Barger, Jennifer Carrano, and Linda Petrone. Joan's protégée

and successor as GDIP staff director, Tish Long, later became the first
woman to direct a major intelligence agency. It's a great injustice that
Joan never had that opportunity. Over the years, Joan and Tish, and later
Betty Sapp and Stephanie O'Sullivan, helped me be successful, not the
other way around. From what I saw, these women proved themselves to
be not merely *as* competent as their male contemporaries, but better. Borrowing an old expression, Joan used to say that women in the Intelligence
Community had to follow the example of Ginger Rogers—Ginger performed the same dance steps as Fred Astaire, but backward, and in heels.
Joan and many other powerful women in my life managed this with un-
complaining grace and good humor. I've just asked them to remember
me kindly when they eventually take over the world.

While the struggle those women endured for recognition of their efforts and accomplishments was very visible to me as director, the fact that
we had racial tensions and discriminatory practices was sprung on me
one afternoon. Sandy Wilson, an African American Air Force captain
who had come with me from the Air Force, invited me to a brown-bag
lunch meeting. Instead of the half dozen employees I'd expected, well
over fifty had shown up, and I noticed that I was the only white guy in the
room. I sat down and went into "receive only" mode for the next hour-
plus. Many of those employees shared personal stories about the culture
and atmosphere at DIA, starting with the fact that the mailroom was
commonly referred to as "the plantation." It challenged my entire belief
system to hear that some people would treat others with that kind of
disrespect. I realized with a growing sense of horror that this wasn't an
isolated problem but one that infected many parts of the agency.

After that meeting, I established an equal opportunity and diversity
officer at the senior executive level, whose full-time job was to root out
and deal with issues of inclusion. I told him that the point wasn't just to
increase the percentages of underrepresented minorities employed at
DIA, but more importantly, to make all employees feel valued as part of
the agency community. I told the employees at the brown-bag lunch that
my office was open to them whenever they felt they were being treated
with anything less than the respect they deserved. Many of them took me
up on that offer, and we painstakingly resolved each case. Beyond doing
what's "right," if racial issues are allowed to fester, they will negatively
affect the mission—a lesson that stuck with me for the rest of my career.

I'm proud of the positive impact we had on the culture at DIA over just a few years. I'm not one to cite awards I've received, and I certainly didn't undertake this work for recognition, but I'm still very proud that the NAACP presented me with a meritorious service award in July 1994 for my "contributions in promoting equal opportunity policies and programs."

I tried to fix such institutional problems as publicly—within the agency—as possible, whereas I felt it best to help out individual officers as quietly as possible. One morning JCS chairman General Colin Powell called me to his office. He never summoned me to tell me how happy he was with the job I was doing, so I fully expected I was walking into an "enhanced counseling session." Instead, Powell asked me, "Do you know this Mike Hayden guy?" I said I'd heard of him as a fast-rising colonel assigned to the National Security Council staff who was on the brigadier-general promotion list, but I didn't know him personally. Powell said he'd been told that someone on the NSC had slated Mike to become the next US defense attaché to Moscow, apparently based on his earlier assignment as the Air Force assistant attaché to Bulgaria from 1984 to 1986. Powell informed me that wasn't going to happen. As JCS chairman, he was deeply involved in trying to forge a new relationship with a post-Soviet Russia and wanted his own trusted agent to represent him in Moscow. Since DIA managed all the military attachés worldwide, Powell told me, "You'd better find him another job." I eventually helped swing a deal to get Mike appointed as director of intelligence at European Command, a high-profile job at which he excelled. I don't think Mike ever realized I was involved, but I've enjoyed the thought that I helped set him on the path to ultimately serving as director of both NSA and CIA and achieving the very rare distinction of four-star general.

Just a few weeks before I took my oath of office as DIA director, Bob Gates took his as director of central intelligence and of the CIA. Bob was, at that point, the only DCI to have risen through the CIA analytic ranks to be appointed director, and because of his extensive agency background was better able to balance his time and see past agency concerns. For me, that was great, as he encouraged me to lead the intelligence components of the military services as the unofficial "director of military intelligence."

With his support, the military intelligence leaders agreed to have me represent them when National Intelligence Estimates came up for approval. NIEs represent the apex of the Intelligence Community's long-term, strategic analysis product line, in direct support of senior policy makers across the government, to include the president. When I was DIA director, NIEs particularly focused on the dissolution of the Soviet Union, the trajectories of its former satellite nations, and the disposition of its military capabilities. As ex officio director of military intelligence, I spoke from a stronger position at meetings to discuss community approval of draft NIEs, since the views I expressed carried the weight of all the military components. They also agreed to my ideas about how to organize analysts deployed to the combatant commanders and the Pentagon. I quickly found that the military services supported almost any proposal I put forward, as long as I was transparent with them and they didn't lose resources.

That lasted about a year. Then, with the legislation that appropriated funds and authorized activities for Fiscal Year 1993, Congress directed us to start "reaping the peace dividend"—meaning the US government, and presumably taxpayers, would collect the reward of the end of the Cold War by no longer investing so heavily in the forces we'd built to confront the Soviets, and channel the funds elsewhere or use them to pay down the national debt. Every military service and every intelligence agency had its budget slashed, and I was informed that DIA's resources would need to be cut 20 percent over the following five years. Because such a large percentage of the agency's budget went into salaries, that meant I had to get rid of one fifth of our workforce.

We addressed that mainly by offering early retirements and freezing hiring, which we recognized would also affect our talent pool, but we didn't have much choice. From planning sessions, I soon realized that because of the staff cuts we would have to reorganize the agency to match our manpower levels. We took the decisive step of combining our two major analytic organizations. Before, one directorate had focused on strategic estimates, and the other generated the daily production of analysis on a tactical deadline. After the reorganization, the consolidated analytic organization would not distinguish strategic analysts from tactical, nor analysts who studied the technical capabilities of foreign military weapons systems from those who studied the overall military capabilities of adversary nations. We knew this was going to hurt, but the advice of General George Patton came to mind: "The time to take counsel of your fears is before you make an important battle decision. That's the time to listen to every fear you can imagine. When you have collected all the facts and fears and made your decision, turn off all your fears and go ahead."

When I set aside my fears and announced the decision, however, the workforce revolted. My mistake was in not considering its civilian nature. While military service members frequently move between duty stations, many DIA civilian employees had sat at the same desk for eight straight years since the building opened, and now many employees were forced to play musical cubicles. We literally experienced scuffles between employees over whom a particular desk belonged to and who was going to occupy it. I realized very quickly that, whatever merits our reorganization plan had, we hadn't sufficiently talked with the employees and worked out the details. We ultimately ended up executing a second reorganization to undo the ill effects of the first. I learned that gaining employees' buy-in before making big changes is essential, and that there are cultural differences between military and civilian employees.

Of course, this same downsizing was going on everywhere, including with each of the service intelligence components, as well as with combat and combat-support structures throughout DOD. Then, in the midst of everyone's reorganizing to "reap the peace dividend," the US military was ordered into combat.

By late 1992, Somalia had no central government and had achieved "failed state" status. Warlords ruled the lawless streets, and human suffering was widespread. In December, the UN Security Council passed a resolution authorizing force to restore order, and President George H. W. Bush—who had just lost his reelection bid to Bill Clinton—ordered the US military to prepare. At DIA, we realized we had very little foundational intelligence on Somalia. We needed maps of the infrastructure, roads, ports, and terrain. We needed information on the warring clans. We needed profiles on the warlord leaders. The Intelligence Community had essentially closed shop in much of the Horn of Africa, and there were no reliable assets on the ground.

We did what we could to collect overhead imagery from satellites and overflights. We deployed DIA officers with the combat forces and painstakingly built the intelligence picture from the ground up. I wish I could say our work led to stabilizing the situation and allowing aid to reach the Somali people in need, but that didn't happen. On October 3, 1993, US special operators conducted a disastrous raid that left eighteen Americans dead and seventy-three wounded. Rescue operations continued the following day, and one American was held hostage for eleven days. We don't really know how many Somalis died in the battle of Mogadishu, but estimates range from the hundreds to the thousands.

After the clash, televised images of American casualties being dragged through the streets of Mogadishu reached the States, and two days later, President Clinton announced that he was recalling all US forces from Somalia. The Joint Special Operations Command commander took responsibility for the disaster, saying in part that he blamed himself for sending the special operators in Task Force Ranger on the mission without adequate intelligence. This series of events was heartbreaking for DIA, as the special operators were close partners of ours, and many of us took their loss very personally.

In the spring of 1993, as President Clinton's defense team came into shape, new Deputy Secretary of Defense Bill Perry saw another opportunity for consolidation of resources under the nominal auspices of my new, self-proclaimed role as director of military intelligence. Dr. Perry asked me to research the human-intelligence programs in each of the military services and return to brief him on the potential for creating a single, unified, strategic, military HUMINT service. The idea was to generate efficiencies by consolidating the costly management and support structures of each military service within DIA—theoretically to gain more operational "tooth" by reducing management "tail." It would also mean moving three thousand people and their attendant funding out of the service intelligence components. They howled, and I didn't blame them. Unfortunately, it was the Army that again had the most resources to lose, and the service turned from complaining to me, to waging a political-guerrilla campaign against DIA with Congress.

This effectively left me in the position of adding thousands of people to a workforce I was simultaneously cutting by 20 percent. In planning for the consolidation, we severely underestimated the support structure that such a large HUMINT service would need (comptroller, personnel, logistics, contracting, etc.), and I failed to secure the necessary resources and billets for administrative and support people.

I was successful in divesting just one of my own responsibilities as DIA director, and it was by far the most politically charged, controversial, and depressing issue of my tenure. In 1973, as the Paris Peace Accords were signed—temporarily stopping the North and South Vietnamese armies from fighting and permanently ending US participation in the conflict—3,237 US service members were listed as either "missing in action" or "killed in action/body not recovered," but only 591 POWs returned in Operation Homecoming. The Department of Defense, working with intelligence agencies and the South Vietnamese government, searched South Vietnam for two years, recovering and identifying the remains of just 63 servicemen. In 1975, Saigon fell to the Communists, and searches stopped. That's when things got complicated.

The National League of Families of American Prisoners and Missing in Southeast Asia had formed during the war to bring the abuse of POWs to the forefront of the national discussion, and after hostilities ended, the league switched its mission to advocating for the prisoners' return. Many people affiliated with the league believed they were alive and that the US government wasn't doing enough to bring them home. DIA had established a dedicated office to gather, analyze, and investigate any intelligence leads, particularly reported or alleged sightings of people believed to be American POWs. Although none was ever found alive, by the 1980s, conspiracy theories abounded, fueled in part by the success of *Rambo: First Blood Part II,* a fictional account in which Sylvester Stallone's character finds and dramatically rescues POWs being held in bamboo cages, to the astonishment of government officials in positions similar to mine who'd insisted there were no more prisoners of war.

I got involved with the League of Families, supported their efforts, and attended and spoke at their annual conventions. Those gatherings were heartbreaking, and all I could say to grieving families was some variation of "I understand how you feel. The odds are against your loved one being alive, but DIA will persevere and will keep looking. We take every lead seriously and will do all we can to resolve all of them." Because of the nature of DIA work, I couldn't go into nearly as much detail about what we were doing as I wanted, much less to their satisfaction. It eventually became clear to me that it was simply inappropriate for an intelligence agency to be in charge of resolving casualty issues, which should have been handled more openly and transparently than we had the ability to do. The media excoriated what they perceived as our "mind-set to debunk" the false live-sighting reports and portrayed us as cruel and heartless. Because we were a "spy" agency, the conspiracy theorists also alleged that we were covering up crimes in which the US government was complicit. I received several anonymous death threats, which we then wasted more resources tracking down.

Vietnam veteran and Republican senator Bob Smith of New Hampshire constantly criticized DIA and told families that he was holding our feet to the fire. In August 1991, Smith had persuaded the Senate leadership to establish a Senate Select Committee on POW/MIA Affairs. The committee investigated for a year and a half, calling witnesses ranging from former secretary of state Henry Kissinger and former Vietnam Army colonel Bui Tin to Defense Secretary Dick Cheney and even me. In January 1993, just weeks before the end of President Bush's administration, the committee released its report, which was highly critical of Intelligence Community practices but also found no compelling evidence that any American POWs were still alive in Southeast Asia. After President Clinton's administration took office, I gave DIA's POW/MIA resolution office to DOD, lock, stock, and barrel. As of this writing, more than sixteen hundred service members are still unaccounted for. No nation expends more effort to recover prisoners of war and those missing in action than we do, but it's unlikely more than a few more from the Southeast Asia war will ever be identified.

I gave up the POW/MIA mission quite voluntarily, but I also discovered what it felt like to have a valued mission taken away from my agency. It took four years of study and debate after the Gulf War before national leaders were willing to do something about General Schwarzkopf's imagery intelligence complaint. They eventually reached the conclusion that the problem would never be solved until there was a single agency responsible for imagery in all its forms at the same depth that NSA was responsible for cryptology in all its forms. The direction from above was therefore to move all the imagery analysts from CIA's National Photographic Interpretation Center, with all its attendant resources, along with people and resources from other elements, including those at DIA, and combine them with the mapping, charting, and geodesy mission performed by the Defense Mapping Agency. We were told the resulting National Imagery and Mapping Agency—NIMA—would join CIA, NSA, DIA, and the NRO as the fifth major intelligence agency.

As DIA director, I stood to lose some five hundred imagery analysts and an entire mission area to NIMA. Within DIA, the imagery analysts were sometimes treated as second-class citizens by all-source analysts, but their work was integral and crucial to our analysis process. To protect DIA, I fought NIMA's establishment right up to the day of my retirement, a battle that in retrospect was both misguided and hopeless. In the end, when NIMA was officially established on October 1, 1996, I was glad to see such a concrete step taken toward accountability for making useful imagery available on a timely and high-volume basis.

In our shrinking fiscal environment, we didn't have the resources to invest in any large, new-technology project, but one small team at DIA was in charge of creating a Joint Worldwide Intelligence Communications System, and I tried to give them as much support as I could. Their charter was signed in 1990, the same year Tim Berners-Lee invented the World Wide Web. Because the idea of going online to search for information was completely new and largely untested outside the research offices of DARPA (DOD's technology research arm, which created ARPANet, the forerunner of the internet) and CERN (the European nuclear research organization where Berners-Lee created the World Wide Web), and email didn't become prevalent until later, this team was tasked with something much more modest—creating a secure video teleconference capability with which we could conduct virtual meetings to discuss classified information, led by Air Force Captain Mike Waschull. In those early days the system was fraught with problems: The bandwidth was limited, images constantly froze on the screen, and the audio was bad. But we all saw the tremendous possibilities for what JWICS could do to make intelligence sharing faster and more operationally relevant.

President Clinton visited the Pentagon for briefings on Operation Uphold Democracy, the US-led, UN-authorized mission to remove the military regime installed by the 1991 Haitian coup d'état. We used JWICS for those sessions, and the president liked it so much that he arranged to import the capability to the White House Situation Room. Over the next two decades, every time I suffered a relapse and returned to government, I found JWICS continuing to grow, expanding to include secure internet and secure email. Later, when I was DNI and the time came to integrate the archipelago of agency IT systems and networks into a single Intelligence Community IT enterprise, JWICS served as its infrastructure backbone. It's been a fortunate pattern in my career to have been appointed to places where people were already doing exceptional work. If you can spot such pockets of innovation and excellence and then champion and provide "top cover" for them, it will do wonders for your own career progression.

I also spent a great deal of time on the road while DIA director. Many of my trips were to bond with our close partners, particularly among the five English-speaking "Five Eyes" nations, but I dealt with many other countries as well. In 1994 our intelligence collection revealed that Saddam Hussein was again moving a massive number of troops and equipment to the south, toward Kuwait and Saudi Arabia, so I took John Moore, the defense intelligence officer for the Middle East and the senior subject-matter expert, to Kuwait City to brief the six ministers of foreign affairs of the Gulf Cooperation Council states. They took the news gravely and contemplated another invasion that, thankfully, didn't come. From Kuwait, we flew to Saudi Arabia to brief the minister of defense and discuss preparations in the event we needed to rapidly deploy US forces again. The minister patiently listened to us and responded that he would have to reserve judgment, observing, "We can't have your women in T-shirts driving trucks around here again."

In the air, on our way home, we were told to divert to Egypt to brief President Hosni Mubarak, an imposing figure with a reputation for ruling with an iron fist. After we exchanged uncomfortable pleasantries, he inquired if I'd been to Egypt before. John piped up and said, "Hey, general, why don't you tell the president about that time your dad took a swing at King Farouk?" Mubarak, who speaks fluent English, turned his gaze on me, and I nearly choked. I stuttered for a moment, sure an international incident was under way, but after I told the story, he roared with laughter and kept us way past schedule. In one of the more surreal moments of my life, as we were leaving, I caught sight outside Mubarak's chamber of Yasser Arafat, looking extremely cranky, accompanied by two dour, heavily armed bodyguards who glared at me.

Many of my foreign visits were to coordinate and reaffirm existing alliances. Others were intended to forge new relationships behind the former Iron Curtain. It was such a strange reversal, given that the US Intelligence Community had battled the Soviets in the shadows for decades, and many times I'd felt like we were losing. The media had dubbed 1985 "the Year of the Spy," for the eight high-profile arrests of Soviet agents in the United States, and that year wasn't really an outlier for Soviet penetration of the US national security structure. Much controversy has swirled around the "failure" of the Intelligence Community—CIA and DIA specifically—to have predicted the precipitate collapse of the Soviet Union and the unraveling of the Warsaw Pact. We were well aware of the fundamental rot of the entire Communist system and confident in its ultimate demise, but it's nearly impossible to predict spontaneous events that lead to momentous change—not with the Soviets, and not decades later with the Arab Spring.

When I first went to Russia in 1992, I was taken aback, even disappointed, at seeing the run-down infrastructure and the plight of Russian citizens. It was graphic evidence that behind the formidable Soviet military power was a third- or fourth-rate economy. On a subsequent trip, I visited GRU headquarters—the Russian military intelligence agency that was DIA's nominal counterpart, much as the KGB was CIA's. (I don't know if I was the first DIA director to visit GRU, but I do know that Lieutenant General Mike Flynn was not the first DIA director to visit there in 2013, as he claimed.) There we found Soviet military equipment being sold at bargain-basement prices to raise funds to keep the agency functioning, so DIA bought jets, tanks, guns, antiaircraft systems, and whatever else we thought would be useful to study and exploit, as well as anything we wanted to keep off the black market.

In 1993 I visited Ukraine to establish a relationship with the former Soviet intelligence apparatus there. Ukraine was (and still is) a very poor country, but they rolled out the red carpet, taking me to some of their most sensitive intelligence sites and greeting me at each one with the traditional bread, salt, and vodka. We ate a lot of fish, and in the shadow of Chernobyl, wondered if it was safe. We stopped at a Ukrainian air defense training school, and I saw pictures of US aircraft on the classroom walls as training aids for learning how best to shoot them down. When touring a signals intelligence site, I walked up behind a Ukrainian intercept operator and saw from the notes he was transcribing in English that he was listening "live" to the communications of an airborne NATO AWACS aircraft—the Boeing 707 with the giant rotating radar dome used for all-weather surveillance, command, control, and communications. It was a surreal experience for a longtime Cold Warrior to watch our former adversary's SIGINT operation actively surveilling us. We were given such unprecedented access because Chief of Ukrainian Military Intelligence Major General Skipalski was interested in having the US subsidize their SIGINT stations to respond to NATO tasking. We had to decline, mainly because their massive equipment was old and analog, and their intercept antenna complexes were all oriented west to collect on the US and NATO and wouldn't have any real use for us without a substantial investment.

We drove to the Ukrainian base housing the Mach 2 Tu-160 Blackjack nuclear-payload jets we'd tried to collect intelligence on for years. The base commander initially seemed terrified that a three-star American military-intelligence "spy" had come to tour his base, but after several toasts of vodka, he relaxed—a lot—even inviting us to tour the flight line, where my senior expert on Russia pointed out birds' nests inside the wheel well of a Tu-160. As we were getting ready to leave, I asked, as a point of professional curiosity, just how many Tu-160s were on the base. The commander immediately sobered, blanched, and said that was a state secret. General Skipalski motioned for me to join him, and as we drove up and down the flight line, I counted the planes. Back at the starting point, he asked how many I'd counted. I said nineteen. He asked if that was the number we'd counted with US intelligence systems. I told him it was. He smiled and nodded.

Of all the trips I made behind the Iron Curtain in the early 1990s, by far the most sobering was to East Berlin, which actually took place before the Soviet Union dissolved and before I moved to DIA. The idea of revisiting the city after so many years was appealing; the reality was not. We toured two former Soviet *kasernes*—military encampments—and found that the Russians had stripped every building of anything of value (including window fixtures, doors, and plumbing) when they withdrew from the country, and left behind an environmental disaster. At the motor pool facilities, they had changed tank oil by just dumping the old oil onto the ground, which now covered and penetrated everything with its stench. And all the buildings were black from the residue of the coal they'd burned.

The most indelible impression left on me occurred when the German defense intelligence chief led us through the headquarters of the Stasi—the East German secret police—an eerily timed tour, given that it occurred simultaneously with the trials of former Stasi officers for their crimes against humanity. The Stasi was known for its massive spy networks throughout East Germany, for recruiting kids to inform on their parents, and for rooting out dissidents and destroying them, either physically or psychologically. We saw displays of medals, plaques, and monuments—rewards for those who'd spied and reported on their families. Even their files were preserved, row after row of floor-to-ceiling shelves filled with personal information on the citizens of the German Democratic Republic. I touched some of the files, aware that each contained the private secrets of real people whose lives may have been ruined by this invasion of their privacy, or simply by knowing it was a parent or child or sibling who'd betrayed them. It was chilling to imagine living in such a state.

Seeing the stark reality of what the Stasi did stayed with me. This was what happened when a state surveillance apparatus ran amok with no limits and no checks. The people of East Germany never asked for such intrusiveness, and there was no oversight—no legislative review or judicial restraint over their pervasive, Orwellian surveillance. The experience also tempered my attitude about collecting intelligence on innocent citizens—in our country or anywhere else. That was a concept I didn't need to confront before the collapse of the Soviet Union; anyone communicating on Soviet networks was aligned with the Soviets. Within just a few years, the internet and global telecommunications companies would erase the lines between East and West and between innocent civilian and government agent. Because of that visit to East Berlin, I was conscious of the Stasi legacy when those global shifts happened, particularly years later when, as DNI, I had an oversight responsibility for all US intelligence activities.

In 2013, after Edward Snowden released a massive collection of IC secrets into the wild, the word "Stasi" appeared more than once in the media to caricature our work. That reference may or may not have been hyperbole to those who uttered it, but the comparison—and the accusation inherent in it—hit home. The memory of Stasi headquarters in East Berlin was in my mind when I pushed for greater intelligence transparency, for declassifying documents that explained the legal basis for what we were doing, how the process of establishing collection targets worked, and how all three branches of government conducted oversight to ensure the protection of civil liberties and privacy. I wanted the American people to have a better understanding of what their Intelligence Community did and the limits of just how intrusive we should be in their lives—a dialogue East German citizens never had with the Stasi.

Despite all this transparency and communication, I don't think Americans had resolved this issue in their own minds before I retired as DNI in 2017. The public continued to send mixed messages about its desires regarding the balance between safety and security on one hand, and civil liberties and privacy on the other. Most of the time, people leaned toward a less-intrusive intelligence enterprise that respects their civil liberties to the greatest extent possible, a position I appreciate and agree with. Yet every time an American citizen committed a mass shooting or set off an improvised bomb, particularly if that person invoked Allah before committing such an atrocity, people demanded to know why we weren't reading that person's email and social media posts, why we weren't listening to his phone conversations, and why we weren't infiltrating the personal space of others who might perpetrate such tragedies.

Every time this subject was raised, I'd think, *Well, we could do that.* It would take time and a significant investment to build the infrastructure necessary to get intimate with the private lives of American citizens, and it's a measure I would oppose vigorously, but we could be much more intrusive than we have been. The question for me is, to what extent are we as a society willing to sacrifice personal liberties in the interests of common safety? We stop at red traffic lights. We submit to security screenings before boarding airline flights, which represent infringements on our civil liberties and privacy. Would we agree to having an inward-facing domestic intelligence apparatus? Should we? It's a question that would assert itself with increasing frequency in the years after I took off the uniform, and I believe the US public has yet to reach a clear and consistent consensus.

I retired from active-duty service in September 1995. The Air Force had extended me for a fourth year as DIA director, to keep me in the running to potentially fill the position of deputy DCI, but when John Deutch was nominated to succeed Jim Woolsey as DCI, he preferred to have a deputy with White House experience—who turned out to be George Tenet—rather than someone with a military background. Deutch later informally offered me the job of NSA director, to replace Vice Admiral Mike McConnell. When I discussed this offer with Sue, she pointed out that we'd moved twenty-three times in thirty-two years. If I wanted to go to Fort Meade, she said, I should do so, but she wanted to put down roots in Virginia with her own house and her own garden. I decided it was her turn to decide where we'd live and submitted my retirement request. Secretary Perry said some generous things about me and my career at my retirement ceremony. After the reception, Sue and I stopped by the base's Pass and ID office to pick up our retired-military identification cards, and I drove off a military installation for the last time in uniform. Just like that, it was over.

Retirement after thirty-four years of military service was, not surprisingly, something of a jolt. For some reason, I thought multiple employment possibilities would come rolling in. That didn't happen. However, a friend from my University of Maryland ROTC days made a great offer for me to become a vice president of his small company, which provided systems acquisitions support to the Navy. It didn't take me long to realize that my main value was to be a corporate hood ornament, and that it was not a good fit for me. I started looking for a graceful departure that wouldn't embarrass me or the firm, which had been very generous. That elegant exit soon presented itself—unfortunately, by way of a national tragedy.

With Saddam Hussein still in power after the Gulf War concluded in 1991, the United Nations wanted to prevent his Sunni-led government from inflicting its wrath on the non-Sunni communities in Iraq. The most straightforward way to accomplish this was to establish no-fly zones above the Shia population in the south and the Kurdish population in the north. That left Baghdad open to airline traffic approaching from the east or west, and it kept Hussein's military from bombing the disenfranchised people of his country. The US Air Force led the coalition forces enforcing the no-fly zone south of the 32nd parallel—about half the land area of Iraq—flying missions out of the air base in the Saudi city of Dhahran, on the gulf coast near the island of Bahrain. Most of the contingent lived in an on-base apartment complex called Khobar Towers. On June 25, 1996, Iran and Hezbollah orchestrated the detonation of a massive truck bomb at the back of an eight-story apartment building, where each of the units had a sliding glass door. The blast caused the nonshatterproof glass to break into supersonic shards that killed nineteen airmen and wounded hundreds of people, both Americans and Saudis.

In early July I got a phone call from Wayne Downing, a four-star

Army general who'd retired from his position as commander of US Special Operations Command just five months earlier. Defense Secretary Perry had appointed Wayne to lead a joint task force to investigate the incident, to identify who if anyone should be held accountable, and to determine how to prevent something like that from happening again. I knew Wayne from our time together on active duty and held him in high regard. He told me he didn't want me to be a formal member of the task force, but asked if I would serve as a senior adviser on intelligence and counterintelligence matters. I accepted, leaving the job at my friend's company and rejoining the government as a temporary senior executive employee. We flew almost immediately to Saudi Arabia. As we stood on the tarmac at Dhahran, I was hit by the memory of standing in Dhahran in 1948 as a seven-year-old boy in short pants on the way from Eritrea to the United States, the wind blowing sand so hard that it stung my legs. Forty-eight years later, I was back in Dhahran, again uncertain about what I was about to encounter.

We spent about two weeks in Saudi Arabia, half at Khobar and the remainder in Riyadh. Most of our investigation centered on the question of how, precisely, the conspirators could simply back a large truck up to the fence near the two apartment towers, detonate a powerful bomb, and escape. We interviewed many who were stationed at the base, and I spoke with a young Air Force major who was, like most people, assigned there on ninety-day temporary orders, in his case as the wing intelligence officer. His entire focus was on threats to the aircraft patrolling the airspace over Iraq, not local threats in Saudi Arabia. In fact, he said he had no resources to monitor the local garrison, even if it had occurred to him to worry about it.

I also spent a good deal of time with the commander of the local Office of Special Investigations (OSI) detachment. The OSI is the rough analog of the FBI for the Air Force, charged with law enforcement investigations and counterintelligence. It was "stovepiped," meaning that while its small units were deployed to virtually every major Air Force installation across the globe, they were centrally commanded from its headquarters in Washington. The young OSI captain, who had been at Khobar for about thirty days, was very open and cooperative and let me look through his office files. I found a copy of an assessment done by his temporary-duty predecessor the previous April, which had forecast the attack scenario as it occurred on June 25 in a chilling level of detail. Because of the stovepipe nature of OSI, the wing commander, Brigadier General Terry Schwalier—who had been scheduled to pass the baton of command the day after the attack—never saw this report.

As Wayne and his team were writing the assessment, I worried that the Air Force would come down unduly hard on Terry to avoid institutional accountability. I wanted to share my concern with Wayne, but given my advisory status, I was excluded from the "small group" meeting to finalize the task force's recommendation on accountability. I wrote a memo to Wayne, stating my belief that the fault didn't lie with the local commander but rather with Air Force institutional shortfalls relating to base-level security practices, many of which were corrected after the bombing. As it happened, the Air Force didn't hammer Terry. It was Secretary of Defense William Cohen (Dr. Perry's successor) who did the hammering. Over objections from the Air Force chief of staff, Cohen pulled Terry's name off the promotion list to major general, prematurely ending the career of a good officer. Some in the Air Force were angry that I hadn't resigned from the task force in protest, overlooking the fact that I was an adviser and not actually a member, and that I was specifically excluded from accountability deliberations by the task force senior leaders and unaware that there was anything to resign over until it was too late.

For me, the investigation of the Khobar bombing was an epiphany. I will never forget climbing the stairwell of the apartment building adjacent to the one that had absorbed the brunt of the bomb blast. Its stairs, handrails, and walls were smeared in blood. I instantly "got religion" about terrorism. And I learned that it is simply impossible, after the fact, to re-create events as they actually happened. That is, it is not possible to reconstruct the contemporaneous conditions and environments in which people make judgments and decisions. It was not the last time I'd reach this conclusion.

Another key lesson I took from the experience is that differences in service cultures have an impact on how we view the actions of others. As a ground-combat-arms Army officer, Wayne Downing viewed garrison security much differently than I did or Terry Schwalier had as Air Force officers. Taking into account factors like perimeter defense, surveillance and countersurveillance, and potential field of fire is instinctive with experienced Army and Marine Corps officers, but not necessarily for Air Force or Navy. The accountability determination was therefore conducted on an Air Force officer from an Army perspective. This small but important fact influenced future accountability investigations, which would be led by officers of the same service as the officer being investigated.

I returned to life in Northern Virginia and was hired by Booz Allen Hamilton, where Mike McConnell was a partner. I stayed with BAH for about a year and a half and found that I wasn't particularly good at helping to win contracts and expand the firm's footprint. I also discovered just how frustrating it could be to engage with the government and just how much companies were willing to invest in preparing proposals to compete for work—proposals that in themselves didn't provide any intrinsic value to the government. I also realized I didn't want to be responsible for company profit or loss or for employee payroll, and the firm really didn't want a partner who didn't have a driving interest in generating profit.

So I continued to float around, consulting for the government and for the nonprofit Potomac Institute for Policy Studies. I was asked to join the NSA Advisory Board and spent a lot of time driving to and from Fort Meade, doing what I could to help NSA transition into the internet age. I was elected president of the Security Affairs Support Association, which would later become the Intelligence and National Security Alliance, one of the three major organizations that interface between the Intelligence Community and industry partners. In 1998, I moved to SRA International as a vice president for intelligence. SRA was a better fit than BAH, mostly because its leaders tolerated my pro bono work for the IC, but in truth, helping make the owners of the companies I worked for richer just never moved me.

In 1998 I was invited to become a member of the congressionally mandated Advisory Panel to Assess Domestic Response Capabilities for Terrorism Involving Weapons of Mass Destruction, chaired by Virginia governor Jim Gilmore. Initially, Don Rumsfeld was on the commission, but it quickly became clear that Rumsfeld's and Gilmore's personalities could not coexist in the same room. In 1999, 2000, and 2001, I helped write three iterations of the annual Gilmore Commission Report, and each year, I testified to Congress on behalf of Governor Gilmore, presenting our findings, which were not very reassuring. Gilmore publicly expressed—in no uncertain terms—that it was not a question of if, but when the homeland would be attacked by terrorists possessing a nuclear, chemical, or biological weapon. In 2001, after the Bush administration came to power, we briefed Vice President Dick Cheney, and Gilmore's concerns resonated with him.

I didn't share the certitude that Gilmore and Cheney felt about an impending nuclear, chemical, or biological attack, but from my other pro bono work, I knew that neither resources nor morale was healthy in the Intelligence Community. The "peace dividend" cuts had continued, and every year, each agency cut a "salami slice" across programs and capabilities, whittling everything down until its capabilities suffered, and many no longer functioned as intended. Across the community, global presence and analytic coverage were reduced, CIA stations overseas were closed, and capabilities for processing, exploiting, and dissemination were shrunk. The community lost one third of its all-source analysts and a quarter of its HUMINT collectors. Of twenty-three SIGINT satellites in orbit, twenty-two were beyond the end of their design life, as were two of our three imagery satellites. The community was forced to neglect the basics of power, space, and cooling within its far-flung facilities, and the agencies retreated defensively into their respective discipline cocoons, a condition not conducive to collaboration and coordination. So, while I wasn't certain an attack was imminent, I also wasn't confident that our Intelligence Community was prepared to detect one coming, and if one occurred, to respond resiliently.

For me personally, life was pretty good. Since I had retired from active military service, my responsibilities had decreased while my income had increased. I was home at night. I was getting to know the terrific young adults that Sue had raised. Two or three times a year, Sue and I went on luxury cruises. However pleasant it was, I just wasn't getting the "psychic income" that public service offered. Then, in late summer 2001, I got a call from retired Vice Admiral Staser Holcomb, who had been Secretary Rumsfeld's military assistant the first time he'd served as secretary of defense and who was now serving informally as Rumsfeld's "executive headhunter," recruiting people for senior positions in DOD. Staser simply asked, "Would you consider coming back to government service?"

CHAPTER FOUR

9/11 and Return to Service

S taser explained that the Pentagon was looking for a new director of the National Imagery and Mapping Agency and wanted to consider candidates other than military officers. To this day, I really don't know why I was approached to interview for a job directing an agency whose creation I'd opposed as one of my last acts leaving the military. But with the benefit of six years of hindsight, I could see how the challenge of directing NIMA would be worthwhile. In theory, it made sense to fuse the nation's mapping and geographic analysis capabilities to create a new intelligence discipline. The raw collection for both endeavors emanated from the same sources—our overhead-reconnaissance satellite systems. In practice—and as the result of a shotgun marriage arranged by Congress and a very small group of executive branch leaders—the mappers and imagery analysts worked as two wary partners forced to live under one roof. NIMA needed someone to forge these two communities together and focus them on a united mission.

I called Sue right away to tell her about this "bolt-from-the-blue" phone call and that I was interested in the job. "You're kidding me," she replied, and the conversation later that evening lasted through more than one glass of wine. I think she understood from the outset that I really missed public service, but she did *not* miss playing the role of military wife. With Andy and Jennifer leading their own lives as independent adults, she enjoyed the quiet work she'd found and the satisfaction it brought to her. I'd known that social duties had never been her favorite part of military life, but I was surprised by the vehemence of her opposition. She'd also become used to having me around, taking cruises, and traveling together. I reassured her that NIMA wasn't a military command and she wouldn't have to be a military wife again. There would be foreign visitors and social receptions, but she would only have to be involved to the extent she wanted to be. I told her I wouldn't take the job without her support, but I really wanted to do it. Though skeptical, she ultimately relented.

NIMA's challenges were an open secret. In the five years since the agency had been formed, ten separate studies had been commissioned to prescribe a cure for its alleged maladies. Studies, of course, are one of Washington's time-honored pastimes for simultaneously responding to criticism and conveying the image of taking action while kicking any big decisions down the road, and NIMA had become the study piñata of the Intelligence Community. The most recent, a joint secretary of defense and DCI study directed by Congress, had begun in late 1999 and had just published its report in December 2000. The commissioners wrote that the proximal event leading to their appointment was the failure of the Future Imagery Architecture systems, which the *New York Times* called "perhaps the most spectacular and expensive failure in the 50-year history of American spy satellite projects." FIA was largely an NRO disaster, but NIMA owned a lot of the problems with integrating ground systems to task and deliver imagery analysis. The commissioners' list of grievances echoed General Schwarzkopf's complaints after the Gulf War, which were precisely what the agency had been founded to address five years earlier.

I didn't read this critique as an indictment of the first two directors, but rather as recognition of how hard it is to change institutional and cultural mind-sets. Culture, custom, and resistance to change are formidable obstacles that take time to overcome. As the commissioners wrote, "Although some progress has been made, the promise of converging mapping with imagery exploitation into a unified geospatial information service is yet to be realized, and NIMA continues to experience 'legacy' problems, both in systems and in staff."

The report praised NIMA's forays into using satellite imagery produced by the commercial companies for the energy exploration, natural resource management, urban development, disaster relief, and environmental research industries, among others; but then the report rebuked the agency's failure to think beyond what the current technology was capable of doing. It laid out specific actions that needed to be taken by the director, such as appointing a chief technology officer, but also steps that might require congressional action—for instance, allowing US commercial satellite companies to collect and produce images at much higher resolution so that NIMA could stop expending so much time and resources on getting its legacy systems to do that job.

The commissioners observed that NIMA had failed to integrate the work of the technical experts filling not just two, but "two and a half roles"—imagery analysis, cartography, *and* acquisition. The joint report laid out a road map for integrating the work of those specialists, eventually employing analysts who were trained in each field from the beginning of their careers. The commissioners described a future vision of integrating signals intelligence with geospatial intelligence to intercept the content of an adversary's communications and then identify where on the globe the transmission emanated from—what I'd done manually on my EC-47 missions over Laos and Cambodia thirty years earlier, at scale and with the value of imagery analysts. If we could make that happen, we'd be onto something revolutionary for national security.

The commissioners made one other recommendation that was more personal for me, writing that this kind of change would never happen during a two- to three-year tour of a military director, and urged "that the Director of the National Imagery and Mapping Agency serve a term of not less than five years." I decided I wouldn't take the job unless I had support from the secretary of defense to serve that term. I noted that a full five-year tour would also qualify me for a (very modest) civil service pension (which was not, by the way, a persuasive argument for Sue).

Because the NIMA director was appointed directly by the secretary of defense, I assumed I would just have to pass muster in an interview with Secretary Rumsfeld. I'd studied the diagnosis in the commission report, I'd talked to people in the agency and to many of its stakeholders, and I'd decided how I'd administer the prescription. I was ready, or so I thought.

My formal interview for the job was unusual, to say the least. Staser accompanied me into the secretary's cavernous office, and we sat around a small table once used by Jefferson Davis when he was the secretary of war, five years before he became president of the Confederate States. Almost as soon as I sat down, Rumsfeld was off on a rant about Congress, complaining about partisan politics and how too many members catered to their constituents over the best interests of the nation. He seemed genuinely frustrated with congressional demands for reports, which had increased exponentially from the first time he had served as secretary. I mentally, if not verbally, agreed with him. He paused to ask what I thought about a few of our mutual acquaintances. I diplomatically hedged my answers regarding people with whom I might soon be working, but my impression was that he wasn't paying attention, and my responses didn't matter. He went back to his congressional rant, saying that Congress hadn't tried to micromanage him the first time he'd been secretary of defense. I nodded along, interjecting an occasional "Yes, Mr. Secretary," or "I certainly understand," and listening for any openings to bring up the points I wanted to make about NIMA. As my thirty-minute appointment extended to forty-five minutes, I thought that if I was a wagering man, I'd bet he'd be out of the job before Christmas. The interview came to a merciful end. He stood, shook my hand, and wished me luck. Outside, Staser saw my quizzical look and told me I had the job.

I had only a few weeks to finish preparing. I met with NIMA's outgoing director, Army Lieutenant General Jim King, who was to retire on Thursday, September 13, 2001, and then I started on-site visits to each of NIMA's seventeen legacy facilities spread around the Washington metro area. On September 10, I flew out to visit the NIMA facilities in St. Louis, a legacy of the Air Force Aeronautical Chart and Information Center that had been absorbed into the Defense Mapping Agency in 1972. About a third of NIMA's workforce was posted there.

On the morning of September 11, I was sitting in a conference room at yet another NIMA facility in Arnold, Missouri, near St. Louis, receiving a series of briefings on their mission and capabilities. A secretary soon interrupted the meeting, saying she thought we'd want to know that a plane had crashed into the World Trade Center in New York. It sounded like a tragic accident, and we wondered aloud for a few minutes about civil aviation in and around New York City and how someone could have gotten that lost, particularly since it was a beautiful, clear day across the country. The briefer had barely hit his rhythm again when just after 8:00 the secretary returned, going straight to the TV and turning it on. The South Tower was ablaze, and the North Tower spewed smoke behind it. In just a few seconds of viewing these terrible images, I realized that directing NIMA was going to be a lot more challenging and a lot more critical than I'd realized.

At about 8:40, a reporter announced that the Pentagon had been hit, and a few minutes later, the station went to a live stream of the building in flames. I'd spent almost ten years working there, and I oriented immediately. The camera was streaming from somewhere near the gas station to the southwest of the building. Just out of the picture to the right was the parking lot where Rich O'Lear and I had fought off the huge rats every morning. Just out of the picture to the left was Arlington Cemetery, the lines of white headstones on the hills of green grass. Black smoke poured out of the massive, crumbling structure. I wondered how many casualties there were, and if anyone I knew was among them. The camera cut back to New York, where people were jumping from the World Trade Center's top floors. It was painful to watch but impossible to turn away from. Just before 9:00 central time, the South Tower fell, followed thirty minutes later by the North Tower. Twenty minutes after that, the west face of the Pentagon collapsed. That image is still seared into my memory—the Pentagon, where I'd spent so much of my life and so much of my energy, in smoldering ruins.

I called Sue to check in, and then tried to reach Jim King so that I could offer my support and to ask if his instinct to postpone a leadership change was the same as mine, to provide some sense of continuity to the workforce, which would be pressed hard by events to come, particularly if we were in for more attacks. The aeronautical navigation specialists in St. Louis were concerned about where all the planes in US airspace were being diverted, where our military assets were grounded, and where we might be vulnerable for a potential next round of attacks. Soon they would turn to helping track down the perpetrators. When we finally reached Jim that afternoon, he said he'd already canceled his retirement ceremony.

After we spoke, I felt an overwhelming urge to get back to Washington, to Sue, and to NIMA headquarters—to do *something*. Of course, all flights were grounded, every rental car not already occupied had been snatched up by grounded air passengers, and there were no train tickets to be had. Finally, two other senior executives who were visiting from NIMA headquarters and I commandeered a car from the Arnold facility motor pool and hit the road. The drive was more than eight hundred miles, almost entirely on monotonous Interstate 70. I struggled to stay awake when driving, and then I struggled to stay awake while trying to help my two companions stay awake. It was stupid and dangerous, and we were lucky to arrive in the Washington area alive twelve hours later, on the morning of Wednesday, September 12.

I let Jim King know I was back, realized there wasn't much I could do, and headed home to sleep. On Thursday and Friday I drove to the Bethesda facility, continuing to get up to speed and trying to help where I could. On late Friday afternoon Jim and I were formally notified that the Pentagon—likely Secretary Rumsfeld—had overruled our informal agreement to postpone our turnover. So I'd officially been director for two days without knowing it. A personnel officer administered the oath of office to me in his modest office, and that was it—no passing of the NIMA flag and no ceremonial rituals normally observed in such a transition.

That day the State Department demanded in writing that the Taliban government provide all information it had about Osama bin Laden and his whereabouts, and that it expel anyone affiliated with al-Qaida. Similarly, Congress passed a joint resolution authorizing "the use of United States Armed Forces against those responsible for the recent attacks launched against the United States." That same afternoon, President Bush stood on a pile of rubble at Ground Zero, holding a bullhorn and trying to address the emergency responders who had crowded around. When one of them yelled, "I can't hear you," Bush responded, "I can hear you. I can hear you. The rest of the world hears you. And the people—and the people who knocked these buildings down will hear all of us soon." I thought that was an inspired, and inspiring, statement to those responders and to the nation, and I wanted to get to work. On Saturday the fifteenth, when I drove my mighty Mustang onto the NIMA compound and parked in the space marked "Reserved for Director," a very polite security guard informed me I wasn't authorized to park in the director's parking spot. I extended my hand and said, "Hi."

On Monday I addressed the senior staff at NIMA for the first time as their director. I told them that I was gratified to return to government, but circumstances were not what any of us had expected or wanted. I said we would all remember what we were doing when we were attacked, much like what many of us had experienced on November 22, 1963, except that in many ways September 11, 2001, would be more profound, because people we personally were acquainted with had been affected. I knew seven DIA employees who had been lost, and a husband-and-wife tandem of flight attendants who were on the airliner that crashed into the Pentagon were related to my son-in-law, Jay. I told the NIMA staff that the real shock would set in as our nation endured three thousand funerals and many more memorial services in the coming weeks.

Finally, I said that we were in the privileged position of being able to do something about the tragedy, to make a direct contribution to whatever was coming next. My impression was that people in NIMA were thinking of their responsibilities as a sacred public trust, and they were reacting accordingly. I acknowledged that in 1995, as DIA director, I'd been against the formation of NIMA, and that I'd been wrong: NIMA could play a leading role in integrating and unifying the Intelligence Community. I stressed that NIMA drew its institutional strength and relevance from the fact that, fundamentally, "Everything and everyone must be someplace," including the people who had attacked us on September 11. If NIMA met its potential, managing the functional synthesis of imagery and mapping into a new intelligence field, every other agency and every other discipline would build upon the geospatial foundation we would provide. We would need to make major changes, working simultaneously on three time frames: now, next, and after next.

Soon after that first meeting, we established a task force for integrating our imagery analysts with the mapping and charting experts, and we set it loose. I authorized my newly arrived deputy director, Joanne Isham, an experienced senior CIA officer, to take whatever steps were necessary to facilitate the transformation. She would work on changes inside the agency, and I would work on support we needed from outside. And then, we went to work, and NIMA went to war.

One of our big goals was to get people with different skill sets to physically and functionally work together. Under Jim King, NIMA had experimented with assigning mappers and imagery analysts to a single workspace to see what they could accomplish, but NIMA needed to scale Jim's experiment up so that the entire agency worked that way. In the meantime, we were fixated on filling the blank space that was Afghanistan, where al-Qaida was hiding and training. We started almost from square zero, since the little data we had was not current, and without basic information on the country's geography, demographics, and infrastructure it would be virtually impossible to conduct military operations there. We began obtaining raw data and buying all the commercial imagery of Afghanistan as it became available. I was accused in some trade media of exercising a "checkbook monopoly," trying to corner the market on commercial imagery, but I was fine with that criticism, as we needed all the data we could gather, from whatever source—to locate the terrorists, and then produce maps and charts to target them.

On September 21, in an address to a joint session of Congress, President Bush spoke to the world, saying, "Every nation, in every region, now has a decision to make. Either you are with us, or you are with the terrorists." Even more directly, he addressed the government in Afghanistan: "The Taliban must act and act immediately. They will hand over the terrorists, or they will share in their fate." Before the month was out, CIA operatives were in the country, laying the groundwork to support an invasion. On October 7, less than a month after the 9/11 attacks, the United States began air strikes in Kandahar, Kabul, and Jalalabad. On October 19, Special Operations Forces initiated the ground war. Very quickly, Taliban and al-Qaida fighters were on the run. As someone who had witnessed the gradual buildup to the Gulf War and Operation Desert Storm from the Pentagon, the rapidity of Operation Enduring Freedom was impressive. Everyone at NIMA was working hard to support the war effort. With advances in digital technology, we were pushing imagery not only to the Pentagon, but also to General Tommy Franks and Central Command, and to commanders on the ground in Afghanistan. However, we were still effectively functioning as practitioners of two separate disciplines.

I've never been a big fan of off-site meetings with team-building exercises and other touchy-feely whatnot, but I thought it would be beneficial if the agency leadership and I collectively paused, caught our breath, and took stock of the course we'd charted for the agency. After the Christmas holidays, I asked the top forty leaders to join me at a secluded spot away from Washington to assess the agency's collective performance. Once I had them captive, I asked, somewhat rhetorically, whether we'd all been "singing 'Amazing Grace' at the wake of DMA and NPIC long enough," and if the time had come to fully unite, integrate our work, embrace "geospatial intelligence" as a new discipline, and ultimately change the name of the agency. They unanimously agreed. It took almost two years for legislation to officially rename NIMA to the National Geospatial-Intelligence

Agency in November 2003, but I believe geospatial intelligence was officially born at that off-site meeting in January 2002.

The prospect of changing the agency's name turned out to be an emotional, controversial issue with the workforce. I received many cards
and letters expressing support, angst, or outright resistance to rebranding
after only five years. People also succumbed to the temptation to try to
pronounce "NGIA" as a word, and I heard from several black employees that they were uncomfortable with the result. I didn't disagree, so
we added the infamous hyphen to make it the National Geospatial-
Intelligence Agency. When people said "NGA," they sounded out each
letter: N-G-A; and NGA has three letters, like the other big agencies. I
still get my chain pulled about the decision to hyphenate the name, even
by friends like Mike Hayden and Bob Gates, who consider it "awkward"
and "unfortunate." I don't regret it. NGA is the only agency I ever got to
(re)name, and I still think the name fits.

On January 29, President Bush delivered his first State of the Union
address since the attacks, explaining that the administration's goals went
well beyond taking out the group of al-Qaida terrorists who'd planned
and perpetrated the attacks on New York and Washington: "What we
have found in Afghanistan confirms that, far from ending there, our war
against terror is only beginning." We would root out terrorism wherever
it could be found, and any nation that supported terrorism or allowed
terrorists to exist within its borders was complicit. His message for those
nations was clear: "Some governments will be timid in the face of terror.
And make no mistake about it: If they do not act, America will."

What followed became the standard answer among intelligence and
national security leaders to the question, What keeps you up at night?
"Our second goal," Bush announced, "is to prevent regimes that sponsor
terror from threatening America or our friends and allies with weapons
of mass destruction." He cited North Korea, Iran, and Iraq, saying that
they "and their terrorist allies constitute an axis of evil." He saved his
most damning rhetoric for Iraq: "This is a regime that has already used
poison gas to murder thousands of its own citizens—leaving the bodies of
mothers huddled over their dead children. This is a regime that agreed to
international inspections—then kicked out the inspectors. This is a regime that has something to hide from the civilized world." He concluded
with the warning, "The price of indifference would be catastrophic."

Shortly after that speech, we heard that Vice President Cheney was pushing the Pentagon for intelligence on Iraqi weapons of mass destruction, and then the order came down to NIMA to *find* the WMD sites. We set to work, analyzing imagery to eventually identify, with varying degrees of confidence, more than 950 sites where we assessed there might be WMDs or a WMD connection. We drew on all of NIMA's skill sets to determine whether and how the suspect WMD sites might be interconnected and mutually supportive. This served as a compelling, persuasive example of what the integration of our two major legacy professions could achieve . . . and it was all wrong.

With the same "slam-dunk" certitude expressed by CIA director George Tenet, we fed our findings into the classified work being prepared at that agency, and in September, I represented NIMA as a member of the National Foreign Intelligence Board, participating in the review process that would certify the National Intelligence Estimate on Iraq's Continuing Programs for Weapons of Mass Destruction as a consensus view of the IC. The White House aimed to justify why an invasion of and regime change in Iraq were necessary, with a public narrative that condemned its continued development of weapons of mass destruction, its support to al-Qaida (for which the Intelligence Community had no evidence), and the atrocities Hussein had inflicted on the Kurdish people within his borders (which were terrible, but atrocities were not unique to Hussein's Iraq). After the Intelligence Community presented its consensus, the White House homed in on Iraq's WMD programs and on Hussein's flouting of weapons inspections.

On February 5, 2003, Secretary of State Colin Powell gave an impassioned, persuasive, and seemingly well-documented briefing to the United Nations in which he presented evidence of Iraq's reconstituted chemical, biological, and nuclear programs. To support his speech, NIMA had gone through the difficult process of declassifying satellite images of trucks arriving at WMD sites just ahead of weapons inspectors to move materials before they could be found, and my team also produced computer-generated images of trucks fitted out as "mobile production facilities used to make biological agents." Those images, possibly more than any other substantiation he presented, carried the day with the international community and Americans alike.

Having made its case, the United States led a multinational force, joined by contingents from the UK, Australia, Spain, and Poland, in an invasion of Iraq on March 20, six weeks after Powell's speech. NIMA provided unprecedented support to the effort, both for the military planning against Iraq's defenses and for the teams that would seize any weapons of mass destruction they found and secure the sites we'd helped identify. We prepared a prioritized list of our suspect sites with specific locations, the best approach routes, and any noted defenses, transmitting this data directly to the theater, using capabilities that weren't available during the 1991 war. We maintained secure communications with deployed forces, including the fourteen-hundred-member international Iraq Survey Group. Using this information, they went from site to site but found almost nothing. We were shocked. In September the survey group admitted in its public report that they'd found only trace amounts of chemical weapons, not enough to use in combat. The trucks we had identified as "mobile production facilities for biological agents" were in fact used to pasteurize and transport milk.

In late October, I spoke at an off-the-record breakfast event with Washington media to discuss the state of the wars in both Iraq and Afghanistan. I talked about the imagery situation in Iraq and explained that we'd made some assumptions we shouldn't have, though the circumstantial prewar evidence seemed compelling, and admitted that I was still baffled that no WMD sites had been discovered. I mentioned that in the days before the invasion started, we saw a lot of cars and trucks fleeing the country into Syria, and Bill Gertz from the *Washington Times* asked if it was possible that the vehicles were removing WMD caches ahead of the invasion. I replied that it was impossible to determine who or what was in them. I probably should have clarified what a great stretch it would have been to assert that Syria's Alawite-led government, aligned with Shia Iran against Iraq's Sunni-led government, would conspire with Hussein to harbor Iraqi weapons. The following morning, I was amazed to read the *Washington Times* headline: SPY CHIEF SAYS IRAQ MOVED WEAPONS: SATELLITE IMAGES BEFORE WAR SHOW HEAVY VEHICLE TRAFFIC INTO SYRIA.

In the years that followed, I've heard many, including some in the Intelligence Community, theorize that Saddam Hussein had bluffed his way into a US invasion, that he feared Iran more than the United States, and that he wanted Iran and other neighbors to *think* he had chemical, biological, and nuclear weapons programs, to intimidate them and to prove to his own government and people that he was firmly in control, defiant to the world, and a force in the region. This theory holds that he *purposely* built facilities to look like WMD sites, and that he *deliberately* moved trucks on and off those sites prior to UN weapons inspections to create the *illusion* that he was hiding a covert weapons program. This was not, however, the case. The theory accords far too much credit to Hussein and doesn't attribute the failure where it belongs—squarely on the shoulders of the administration members who were pushing a narrative of a rogue WMD program in Iraq and on the intelligence officers, including me, who were so eager to help that we found what wasn't really there.

It wasn't until a few months later, at a closed hearing with the Senate Armed Services Committee, that I first heard the code name "Curveball." I was seated almost directly behind George Tenet as he and a few of his senior analysts told the committee about a man who had escaped Iraq and fled to Germany. He'd asked for asylum, claiming that he'd worked on a team that built mobile production facilities for biological agents. Listening to Tenet's account, I felt a sinking feeling. He said that before the war, the CIA had never had direct access to Curveball, only to the intelligence from him the Germans had passed to us, which CIA and DIA sources confirmed through another source in the Middle East—who, it turned out, had gotten his information secondhand from Curveball. Our original and corroborating sources were therefore the same person. Worse, Curveball turned out to have been an alcoholic who'd worked for a TV station owned by Saddam's son Uday, and he'd fled Iraq because he'd stolen money from his employer, who wasn't known for lenience with those who'd shown disloyalty. Sitting in that classified hearing and listening to George and his officers brief the committee, I felt a lot more naïve than someone with forty years of experience in the intelligence business should have felt.

George, to his credit, took all of the heat for the atrocious intelligence work. As DCI, he was ultimately accountable, but we were all responsible. I'd sat as a member of the National Foreign Intelligence Board that had approved the October 2002 National Intelligence Estimate, and I'd never thought to question CIA's "spooky source" that had given us all that amazing—too amazing—intelligence. Years later, when I attended National Intelligence Boards to review National Intelligence Estimates ("foreign" was dropped when the Department of Homeland Security and the FBI were added), the procedure had changed so that the very *first* topic discussed was the sources used to reach any conclusions about the intelligence in question—one of a number of reforms the community instituted after Iraq.

While the larger IC sorted through these big questions, NIMA pressed on. The idea of geospatial intelligence was taking root within the agency, and we needed the industrial base that we relied on for technical solutions and to supplement our government workforce to get in sync too, so in October 2003, through Joanne's aegis, we worked with a small number of corporate leaders to hold an unclassified symposium we called "GEO-INTEL 2003" at the New Orleans Marriott Hotel. Notably, Steve Jacques, who had recently left Raytheon to start his own company, and Stu Shea with Northrop Grumman led the corporate effort. We billed the event as an opportunity to hear the government "highlight the role of geospatial technologies in national security," and discuss geospatial intelligence in Iraq and Afghanistan, as well as to see the technology that we were using at nonmilitary events, such as the 2002 Salt Lake City Winter Olympics.

NIMA hoped to entice enough industry partners to be worth the effort, but even we were surprised when more than a thousand people showed up. Energized by the showing, Steve and Stu joined with other industry members to form a nonprofit alliance, the US Geospatial Intelligence Foundation, to work across corporate lines on the tradecraft and technology behind geospatial intelligence. They took responsibility for continuing the forum, rebranding it from "GEO-INTEL 2003" to "GEO-INT 2004." The following October, I appeared onstage with Lieutenant General Mike Hayden, who'd become NSA director in 1999, to talk about how signals intelligence and geospatial-intelligence professionals were working together in unprecedented ways. A decade later, more than four thousand GEOINT practitioners in government and industry attend each year, making the GEOINT Symposium the largest such gathering of government and contractor intelligence professionals in the United States.

I was grateful for the energy our workforce and USGIF put into developing tradecraft and growing the GEOINT community, particularly in the year between GEO-INTEL 2003 and GEOINT 2004, which was a dark period of reckoning for the Intelligence Community. In February

2004, President Bush established the Commission on the Intelligence Capabilities of the United States Regarding Weapons of Mass Destruction, known in shorthand as the Iraq WMD Commission. The feeling around the community was that, unlike the 9/11 Commission, which had ostensibly started with a blank slate and set out to discover what happened, the Iraq WMD Commission had already judged the ways in which we'd fallen short, and was looking to document any and all mistakes—even honest ones—and hold everyone involved accountable.

Then, in April 2004, an event completely unconnected to the IC put us under even more intense scrutiny. On April 28, *60 Minutes* aired a report on prisoner abuses at the Abu Ghraib prison in Iraq and included leaked photos of uniformed US Army guards taunting naked Iraqi prisoners on leashes. Army Reserve Sergeant Joe Darby at Abu Ghraib turned a disk with the pictures over to the Army Criminal Investigative Command, and after its investigation was under way, other people with copies of the pictures leaked them to the press. More photos seemed to leak out every day, and attention to the prisons in Iraq eventually turned to questions about the Guantanamo Bay, Cuba, prison in which the CIA was operating. Human Rights Watch and other rights groups began to talk about the "extraordinary rendition" of terror suspects to CIA "black sites" or to nations that had fewer qualms about what methods they employed during interrogations. At NGA, processing geospatial imagery, we were about as far from the scandal as an IC agency could get, but the revelations about prisoner abuse still bothered us, because we were an integral part of the Intelligence Community. I remembered back to the promise made by the instructors at Air Force survival school in 1970, before I deployed to fly missions over Laos—that the United States would never treat prisoners the way the Vietcong treated our service members they captured.

Meanwhile, in July 2004 the 9/11 Commission published its report, which included a narrative of what happened that day, an investigation of the events that led up to the attacks, and an examination of what could be done in the future to prevent anything like it from happening again. The 9/11 commissioners graphically described the intelligence picture for the summer before the attacks with the phrase "the system was blinking red." One passage in particular succinctly crystallizes the problems we had as an Intelligence Community: "The agencies cooperated, some of the time. But even such cooperation as there was is not the same thing as joint action. When agencies cooperate, one defines the problem and seeks help with it. When they act jointly, the problem and options for action are defined differently from the start. Individuals from different backgrounds come together in analyzing a case and planning how to manage it."

The joint action they described meant getting all the agencies and smaller elements to realize they were all engaged on the same mission and would mutually benefit from working on it together. NGA was in the process of developing tradecraft for geospatial intelligence, for which we were the nascent functional manager. The other agencies had developed tradecraft for their own specialties over the course of decades, particularly CIA (the functional manager for human intelligence) and NSA (the functional manager for signals intelligence). I'd been in the SIGINT world and around the rest of the community long enough to realize that each agency needed to embrace its own culture, traditions, and capabilities. After honoring that, we could inspire them to cooperate to take advantage of one another's complementary strengths. It was the same reasoning for why we needed a diverse workforce: bringing together different perspectives and experiences enabled us to formulate a range of different options for action. In the Intelligence Community, the old saying "the sum is greater than the parts" has profound meaning.

From NGA, I'd seen the major agencies take important steps to realizing this integrated approach. NGA embedded its own experts within the NSA, CIA, and DIA workforces to provide a common GEOINT foundation. I also realized it was easier for them to collaborate with us than with one another. When I'd started in the intelligence profession in 1963, CIA and NSA just didn't come in contact in the field, but as both agencies grew in capability and expanded their global reach—and as the world effectively shrank—they increasingly found themselves operating in the same space. Competition, however friendly, often begets turf battles, and leading up to 9/11, each agency sometimes viewed the others with distrust. NSA, for example, often institutionally felt more comfortable sharing SIGINT with their Commonwealth partners from the UK, Canada, Australia, and New Zealand than with CIA. NGA, in contrast, was too new an entity to represent a threat, and we were developing tradecraft that was by its very nature collaborative. So we looked at the other agencies as partners, not competitors, and they reciprocated.

The release of the 9/11 Commission Report in the summer of 2004 was an epiphany moment for our nation and a catalyst for the Intelligence Community, although at the time, reading that document felt like scraping a wound that had just begun to heal. The immediate response from Congress and the White House was to do *something*, but there were wide disagreements about what that something should be. Some in the Senate proposed choosing a strong, empowered Intelligence Community leader to serve as a Cabinet secretary. Some in the House wanted to create a position for a coordinator of intelligence sharing, but supported Secretary Rumsfeld's view that a national intelligence director shouldn't have any authority to direct agencies. Rumsfeld found an ally in House Armed Services Committee chairman Duncan Hunter, who foresaw that a "Secretary of Intelligence" would risk compromising his Armed Services Committee's influence over the National Intelligence Program budget.

The Senate effort, at least, was driven by two people who were genuinely committed to reform of the IC. Majority Leader Bill Frist logically could have assigned writing and negotiating the Senate bill to either the Armed Services Committee or the Select Committee on Intelligence, both of which had turf to protect. Instead, he gave the pen and the power to negotiate with the House to Senators Susan Collins and Joe Lieberman, the chair and ranking member of the Senate Homeland Security and Governmental Affairs Committee. It was a deft move by Frist, as neither Collins nor Lieberman was fighting for control of the agencies, so they could at least notionally focus on what was best for the nation—not just for their committee.

In March 2015, at an event where we were both speaking, Senator Collins said something about the struggle to forge that legislation in 2004 that really struck me. She said that her inspiration had been something she'd been told by Mary Fetchet, a mother who had lost her son on 9/11: "When American lives are at stake, inaction because of inertia is unacceptable." Collins said that every time she thought about throwing in the towel, she remembered Mary Fetchet's words. Collins was serious enough about introducing legislation that she asked the CIA to detail someone from the Community Management Staff to her office to help with coordination and provide a sanity check on proposals. CIA sent Deb Barger, one of the intelligence officers who had worked with Joan Dempsey when I was DIA director.

In his book *Playing to the Edge,* Mike Hayden recounts that in a closed session of the House Intelligence Committee, he as NSA director and I as NGA director warned that creating a powerless intelligence director would make things worse, as the agencies affected wouldn't know who was in charge and whether to follow the new director, or the director of CIA, or the secretary of defense. We recommended, if they were going to go, to go big. Mike describes how soon after, in August, we met with a group of Intelligence Community seniors in an off-site leadership course for an off-the-record discussion about the state of play in the community.

At that session, Mike and I were quite candid. I pointed out that in my forty years in the business, every DCI had started out with great intentions of making the community more collaborative, but sooner or later (mostly sooner), they had all become consumed with agency-centric issues, and managing the community became a second-tier priority. To me, the most prominent exception was Bob Gates, who'd served as a career CIA officer and because of his familiarity with the agency was better able to balance his time and energy between both of his "hats." I went so far as to argue that if we were going to create a director of national intelligence, we should consider moving the three agencies whose names started with "N" (for "national")—NSA, NGA, and NRO—out of DOD. Each of those agencies had a role in supporting combat troops, but the vast majority of their funding and effort was focused on strategic intelligence to support the president, the National Security Council, and the whole of government efforts to benefit national priorities—priorities that didn't necessarily align with those of the secretary of defense. The fact that Mike and I were the directors of two of those "national" agencies did not escape the senior executives present, and our assertions weren't mitigated much by the fact that we said DIA, whose "D" stood for "defense" and whose focus was more squarely on supporting troops, should probably stay with DOD when the others left.

A few days later, Mike and I found ourselves at an uncomfortable lunch in Secretary Rumsfeld's private dining room. We were seated across from Rumsfeld, Deputy Secretary Paul Wolfowitz, JCS chairman General Dick Myers, and Undersecretary of Defense for Intelligence Steve Cambone. Of that group Cambone had by far the most to lose if the "national" agencies left DOD. His position had been created in March 2003, with

Rumsfeld's support and the strong backing of Duncan Hunter in the House, ostensibly to coordinate DOD's intelligence budget and to oversee the four DOD agencies and the intelligence components of the military services, and implicitly to be a counterweight to the yet-to-be-legislated DNI. If three of the four agencies were pulled out from under Cambone, his authority would be greatly diminished.

Mike has compared this infamous lunch to sitting at the DMZ, negotiating across the table with North Koreans, which was an apt analogy. When I'd served as DIA director, I'd found many occasions to speak truth to power. I'd testified honestly about how reaping the peace dividend was undermining our workforce. I'd briefed Congress and the secretary about our lack of confidence in what would happen to the Soviet nuclear capability with the breakup of the USSR. I'd delivered a lot of bad news, a lot of assessments, and a lot of my own personal judgments that those listening probably would have preferred not to have heard. But since taking the helm at NGA, I'd found that I was even less inhibited than I'd been as a three-star general. To our credit—particularly Mike's— we didn't back down from the positions we'd expressed at the off-the-record session, but as a civilian agency director on what I knew (or thought) was my last hurrah in the government, I was not as circumspect with my words.

At that lunch, Mike and I both advocated establishing a strong DNI, rather than creating a weak figurehead that would diffuse or confuse authority, and we told the secretary that he should back legislation that would align the three "national" agencies under a DNI. The agencies could still fulfill their combat support responsibilities, but they would produce better intelligence under an authority whose full-time focus would be on integrating their work. We appealed to him to support improving how intelligence functioned, rather than protecting the existing bureaucracy. Secretary Rumsfeld cut short the lunch and left, missing a good dessert. Mike would later say that my discourse that day was the reason my NGA directorship was ultimately terminated early. Not completely, but I certainly believe it put me on Rumsfeld's and Cambone's watch list. I stuck around for almost another two years and later learned the final impetus for my dismissal was much more petty.

On September 23, 2004, Senator Collins introduced her committee's legislation to create a strong director of national intelligence with clear authorities. The Senate bill passed on October 6, and the far weaker House bill on October 16. When the two chambers couldn't reconcile differences before adjourning for the November 2 election, most observers assumed the bill was dead. Postelection lame-duck sessions rarely pass any meaningful legislation, and the House and Senate were still far apart, with the House in a much stronger position, because the Senate really wanted to pass the bill, and the House would've been happy to let it die. That enabled Duncan Hunter and his committee to extort whatever concessions Rumsfeld wanted under the rubric of "compromise." If they didn't get what they demanded, the new Congress would have to start over with new legislation in January, and for opponents of a strong DNI, that was all to the good. That seemed the likely course—until someone creatively inserted the word "abrogate." The House agreed to pass the bill if the Senate would consent to add Section 1018, which read:

> The President shall issue guidelines to ensure the effective implementation and execution within the executive branch of the authorities granted to the Director of National Intelligence by this title and the amendments made by this title, in a manner that respects and does not abrogate the statutory responsibilities of the heads of the departments of the United States Government.

This essentially neutered the entire legislation, by stipulating that anything the DNI asked an intelligence component to do could be overruled by the Cabinet secretary who controlled that component, but this was the final offer. Collins and Lieberman realized that their choice was either to accept it or start over. The Senate acquiesced, and Congress passed the bill to the president, who signed the Intelligence Reform and Terrorism Prevention Act of 2004 into law on December 17. IRTPA, like all major legislation, was flawed. Actually, with the addition of Section 1018, it overachieved at being flawed, but it did manage to codify intelligence reforms and establish in statute the Office of the Director of National Intelligence.

Unsurprisingly, considering the act's weak legislative charter, President Bush encountered difficulty in finding someone willing to serve as the first DNI. Bob Gates has written about how he turned the job down, as he believed that the position involved huge responsibility but granted little authority to make anything happen. I remember thinking it was a job I certainly wouldn't want.

In April 2005 John Negroponte, a distinguished State Department diplomat who'd been an intelligence customer his entire career but never an intelligence officer, took the oath of office as the first DNI. I like and respect John and appreciated his taking on this challenge, but I thought the position should have been filled by a career intelligence officer, someone steeped in intelligence culture, particularly as the first incumbent. In fairness, I would never advocate that a career intelligence officer lead the State Department. I was heartened by one of the first decisions John made, bringing Mike Hayden from NSA to be the principal deputy DNI. Mike pinned on his fourth star—the only four-star intelligence officer at the time—and became John's close partner in leading the IC.

John and Mike set to work, bureaucratically outgunned by Rumsfeld and the large Office of the Secretary of Defense. The DNI had a tiny staff scattered among a few offices in the New Executive Office Building near the White House and in CIA headquarters. I heard about meetings where the four deputy DNIs crowded into the chief of staff's office. Two sat in chairs that got hit whenever the door opened, a third sat on a safe, and the fourth leaned on the doorframe. That was how the senior brain trust for the US Intelligence Community was initially accommodated. John, to his credit, persevered through a very difficult launch.

My immediate concerns for NGA were more parochial and more practical. Congress and the president had authorized DOD to close military bases around the world to reduce operating costs, and the Pentagon's recommendations to the Base Realignment and Closure Commission were due May 13, 2005, to include how it would allocate funding for new facilities. In January 2004 Secretary Rumsfeld had asked all installation commanders to begin to gather information and data. We were far ahead of the curve, having already studied how to consolidate NIMA's miscellaneous facilities in my first year on the job. By the time the commission activated, the decrepit NPIC building in the Washington Navy Yard in Southeast Washington was nearly closed, and we had identified a site in Springfield, Virginia, to build NGA's future headquarters that, sometime after 2010, would bring together the two thirds of the agency workforce in

NEWARK PUBLIC LIBRARY
121 HIGH ST.
NEWARK, NY 14513

the Washington area. We just needed the commission and armed services committees to authorize us to spend $2.4 billion to build the new head-quarters, as well as a smaller new facility near St Louis. We'd calculated how, over time, the cost of this construction would be amortized, and we'd convinced DOD we'd save money from the initial investment.

On Thursday, May 12—with a day to go before deadline—the secretary of defense still had not finalized the list of bases selected for closure or realignment, and there was a scramble across DOD for each service and agency to protect its equities. That morning, Cambone told NGA he'd decided unilaterally that we couldn't put the money Congress had previously allocated for us to relocate NPIC toward construction of a new facility, so we didn't have enough to build a new headquarters. I spent most of the day on a series of tense phone calls with Cambone, Mike Hayden, and Pentagon logistics chief Mike Wynne, who was responsible for finalizing recommendations for the secretary. In the space of two hours, the funding pendulum for NGA swung from zero to $2.4 billion for both new facilities before settling on $2.1 billion for just the headquarters building in the East. At the end of the day, I felt I had another strike against me on Cambone's ledger, but I also felt it was well worth it.

Then, on August 29, 2005, NGA and the nation suddenly faced a new kind of challenge. At 6:10 A.M. local time, Hurricane Katrina leveled miles of Mississippi and Louisiana coastline and left large sections of New Orleans underwater. In the aftermath, the Coast Guard commandant and chief of hurricane relief operations, Admiral Thad Allen, reached out to NGA for help in assessing the magnitude of damage to the city—how it had affected the waterways, blocked the ports, and disrupted the infrastructure, including knocking out all communications into or out of much of Louisiana and Mississippi. Plainly stated, he asked us to help him acquire the situational awareness he needed to manage disaster response and prioritize relief efforts.

NGA felt a special connection to New Orleans, since we had a small number of employees who lived in the affected area and because we'd held GEO-INTEL 2003 and GEOINT 2004 in the city. We deployed two Humvees adapted to establish communications and seventy-five people with GEOINT workstations. They created new maps and charts from aircraft and satellite imagery and produced analysis that was critical to helping Thad determine the quickest ways to restore phone systems and other critical infrastructure and to map passage in and out of damaged neighborhoods. We even helped with tracking derelict oil rigs that had broken loose and were adrift in the Gulf of Mexico. The Coast Guard and NGA ended up working closely together, and I believe we saved lives and helped put the region on the path to recovery. We responded to an urgent request for help with the resources we had available, and that was my apparent undoing as NGA director.

In the immediate days after the storm struck, the White House convened daily interagency meetings to review the government's response. I was told later that the Coast Guard and NGA were consistently singled out as exemplars for the federal response to Katrina. Secretary Rumsfeld wasn't aware that NGA had deployed so many people and assets, and that was the final straw. In September I received a one-line memo from Rumsfeld that simply read, "You are relieved of duties as NGA director as of 13 June 2006." That was still nine months away, but it was three months short of my planned and announced departure date of September 13, and everyone would know my five-year tour had been cut short. Having essentially been fired, I'd be a lame duck for the remainder of my tenure. I called Tish Long, who was by then a senior executive in Steve Cambone's office, and asked if she knew anything about Rumsfeld's decision. She didn't, but gave me Cambone's personal cell phone number. I called him and asked for an explanation I could share with the workforce and with my family. He replied, "I can't tell you." I said, "Thanks a lot," and the conversation ended. The decision was never officially explained to me, although someone in Rumsfeld's office, whom I trust, later told me it was because we'd supported Katrina operations without first asking for permission. I didn't do so because we were complying with a long-standing written agreement with the Federal Emergency Management Agency, already approved by DOD, to respond automatically to requests for support in the event of natural disasters.

In the intervening weeks I began to realize that, aside from the public humiliation, expelling me on June 13 instead of September 13 meant that I would be three months short of being vested in a very small government retirement annuity. Again, Sue was not amused. Joanne Isham came to my rescue, arranging to enroll me in a ninety-day CIA course designed to help career employees transition to the civilian world, which would extend my time in service to precisely five years. Cambone approved the training course, under the condition that I not show my face around NGA after June 13.

One postscript on the Katrina episode: In the process of working with the Coast Guard, I got to know Thad Allen pretty well professionally. After he learned about the circumstances of my premature departure, he brought me to his headquarters and presented me with the Coast Guard Distinguished Public Service Award. The Coast Guard had adopted me as something of an unofficial mascot, and it was a status that served me well for another decade and more. Some of the most personally gratifying experiences I had as DNI were at Coast Guard facilities and ships, where I always received a family welcome. In 2015 Sue and I had dinner with Thad and his wife, Pam. As old warhorses are wont to do, we reminisced as he showed us around his house. He recalled the superb work NGA did after Hurricanes Rita and Katrina, as well as in the aftermath of the BP oil spill, and I found that he still displayed a three-dimensional topographical map of New Orleans that NGA gave him when he retired.

Katrina was a watershed moment for the Intelligence Community, and particularly for NGA. In the years that followed, NGA would put its tradecraft to work on natural disaster recovery efforts around the world, as well as in response to the Ebola outbreak in West Africa in 2014. Today, GEOINT is a tremendous force for good in the world, making positive impacts that extend beyond the dimensions of its intelligence mission. On my final day as director, the people of NGA made sure I felt their respect and affection as they wished me farewell. Lacking an auditorium, they set up a massive, air-conditioned tent to accommodate the ceremony and reception and invited foreign partners and dignitaries, and we celebrated what we'd become—not mappers and imagery analysts, but geospatial-intelligence professionals.

Leaving NGA in the summer of 2006, I had a much better idea of what the corporate world offered, and quickly found work at a company called Detica. My connection was Denny Reimer, the former Army chief of staff whom I'd served with in Korea twenty years earlier. I'd determined by this point that I both could and would find my psychic income somewhere outside the contracting world. I had absolutely no intent to ever go back to government service, but found another outlet when Georgetown University hired me as their Distinguished Professor in the Practice of Intelligence, a title that sounds far more impressive than I deserved. I

taught just one course a semester, a lecture and discussion class for graduate students, an interesting mix of recent Georgetown graduates and
older intelligence professionals who were going back to school for their
master's degree. I found that neither category of student took anything
for granted, and so I struggled to stay one class ahead of these very bright
students.

I was very fortunate to have a postgraduate assistant assigned to help
me with designing the curriculum, selecting readings, and anticipating
the academic discussions that would follow. Hannah Powell was a recent
master's program graduate who had studied in Spain and completed two
internships with the State Department at embassies overseas. She was
savvy in the ways of the academic world, Washington, and international
diplomacy, and as it turned out, I needed her for all three.

Occasionally, after class I met a few students at the Tombs—a famous
Georgetown watering hole—to discuss world events and issues with
which they were dealing. I enjoyed mentoring my students at least as
much as I enjoyed teaching, and it was a lot less stressful to consider
world events through an academic lens. On October 9, North Korea conducted its first underground nuclear test. I'm sure I described to students
how AFTAC would be scrambling to identify how large a detonation
had occurred and how successful it was. Happily, I felt far removed from
the action.

In early November, President Bush announced that he was replacing
Don Rumsfeld with Bob Gates—of all people—as secretary of defense. I
told my students that appointing Gates was a great move for the nation,
as he had been a tremendous DCI and had a great understanding of how
the national security apparatus worked. I also read between the lines of
Bob's public statements that he didn't want to leave as president of Texas
A&M, but was answering the call out of a sense of duty to the nation. In
conversations in the Tombs, I said I didn't envy Bob's having to go
through the confirmation process, with its onerous volumes of paperwork on personal finances, intrusive written questions from Congress,
and preparation for a confirmation hearing. I said I'd never want to go
through any of that again.

A few weeks later Bob called to ask if I'd consider finishing out the
Bush administration's term with him, as his undersecretary of defense for
intelligence. I could feel the schadenfreude inherent in being asked to

replace Steve Cambone as USD(I), but I also knew the job wasn't easy—and I'd have to go through confirmation. Still, it was a chance to serve again, and I'd be working for someone whom I admired and respected greatly, and whom I considered a mentor. I told Bob I was interested, but that I'd have to talk to Sue, a conversation I correctly surmised would not go well. "How can you go back to work for this administration?" she asked that night. "They just fired you!" When I replied, "But it's Bob Gates," she only repeated, "They *just* fired you."

A few nights later I met Bob for dinner at the Willard Hotel. There was no big wooing involved; he asked if I'd take the job, and I said yes. When he asked if there was anything he could do to help me, I told him, "It would really help if you called my wife." He laughed and said he would, and we then got to business. He explained that he wanted someone he knew and trusted to end the abject bureaucratic warfare between the Pentagon and the relatively new Office of the DNI. He felt with Mike Hayden as the new CIA director and me as USD(I), we would have a team that trusted each other and could work together. He also wanted me to rein in the Pentagon's human intelligence apparatus, which had grown up under Rumsfeld and Cambone, and to cede proper authority back to the CIA. We ended up closing the restaurant down after a lengthy conversation about how to heal wounds and patch the divide between DOD and the Intelligence Community.

Bob was good to his word. He called Sue to ask her leave to "borrow" me for a while. According to Sue, the conversation ran something like this:

"Hi, Sue. This is Bob Gates."

"I know who you are."

"I was told I had to get your permission for Jim to come back to government."

"That sounds right."

"I promise, I only want him through the end of the administration, less than two years once he's confirmed."

"Okay. You can have him."

Bob's version of the conversation paints Sue in a more gracious light than her own version, but either way, the result was that I was cleared to proceed. Bob was confirmed by the Senate and took office in December 2006. I set to work, researching and completing financial disclosure questionnaires and eighty-three questions on topics ranging from my understanding of how detainees should be treated under Common Article 3 of the Geneva Conventions to my opinion of the organizational structure of both defense intelligence and the Office of the DNI. All except the final four were essay questions. Each of the last four asked for my agreement to testify and to provide documents to congressional committees if asked. If I provided any answer other than yes, I wouldn't have had to worry about showing up for a confirmation hearing.

Again, because of politics beyond my control, my hearing was delayed until March 27, but things seemed to be going smoothly—until about two weeks before I was scheduled to testify, when I got a call from the White House personnel office. They wanted to know why I'd spent eighty thousand dollars on my NGA farewell reception the previous summer. I had no idea what they were talking about. I was certain there had been an error somewhere and called NGA. The error, as it happened, was mine in not asking the "perfect question." While I had noticed the large tent— with its air-conditioning, hard flooring, and wood-paneled "Don's Johns" porta-potties—going up during my last days as director, I'd failed to ask, "How much does that tent cost?" Nine months too late to do anything about it, I learned the answer was eighty thousand dollars. No one had run the cost estimate past me. The staff had just asked me whom to invite. But three weeks before my confirmation hearing, two disgruntled NGA employees had sent an anonymous letter detailing the tent rental charges to the Senate Armed Services Committee, which had, in turn, contacted the White House. We very quickly checked all the paperwork and accounting, and NGA had jumped through all the required legal hoops and received approval from the appropriate offices in the Pentagon before ordering the tent. They'd spent a lot of money to celebrate my four years and nine months at the helm of the agency, but they'd done it by the book.

After that drama, my hearing was relatively quick and painless. Senator John Warner, the ranking Republican on the committee, was my sponsor and graciously introduced me. Senator Carl Levin, as committee chair and senior Democrat, was enamored of everything Bob Gates was doing in the post-Rumsfeld era, and so, with my family in attendance, I received warm bipartisan support. After the hearing, the two senior senators invited me to a private anteroom, where they took me to the woodshed over the tent rental. I took responsibility and walked them through the approval procedures that NGA had gone through. They thought that level of spending was ridiculous and vowed to conduct an investigation into how much farewell ceremonies cost throughout DOD. I can only imagine what they would have found if they'd put that vow into action.

In any event, the committee approved my nomination and sent it to the full Senate for vote. We thought I might be confirmed on Thursday, March 29, before the Senate adjourned for their Easter recess on April 8, but by my Thursday evening class at Georgetown, I still had no word on the Senate vote. When I gave the class a break at the midway point, I had a voicemail from Jack Dempsey, USD(I)'s legislative liaison officer (and Joan's husband, by the way). He said that some unknown senator had put my nomination on hold, and there was nothing anyone could do, as the Senate had gone on recess. A few days later Gates's legislative affairs office called to say that Senator Jim Bunning of Kentucky, the former major-league baseball star, had placed the hold on me and asked what my connection to Bunning was. I had no idea, as I'd never worked with his office, never appeared before him for testimony, and never even met him. We were all mystified.

Hannah Powell ended up saving me from the pain of an extended hold. Online she discovered that Senator Bunning had put a similar hold on Art Money's nomination for assistant secretary of defense in 1999 and didn't lift it until DOD agreed to buy a large quantity of electromechanical safe locks from Mas-Hamilton Group, a company based in his home state of Kentucky. Sure enough, the lock contract was expiring, and Bunning wanted it renewed. Hannah quietly forwarded links to the news articles from 1999 to the *Washington Post,* which contacted Bunning's office. Returning from Easter break, his office quickly removed the hold on my nomination and denied ever having issued it in the first place. The Senate went back into session Tuesday and voted to approve my appointment on Wednesday, April 11. Gates, who'd had enough, told me to bring Sue and any other family I could find, which ended up being just my two oldest grandkids, to his office, where he promptly swore me in that afternoon. This is how things work in Washington.

Sue made a point of presenting me with an electronic countdown clock that would tick off the days, hours, and minutes until January 20, 2009—the end of George Bush's presidency, when I would rejoin her in the land of luxury cruises. She intended it to have a place on my desk, where I could keep an attentive eye on it. A few weeks later Andy gave me a less serious gift—Jim Bunning's baseball card, which likely had been hard to come by. He suggested I get it autographed the next time I was on Capitol Hill. I never asked Bunning to sign it, but I kept the card, and the story lives on as a family joke.

As soon as I was sworn in, Gates confirmed my marching orders: get Pentagon intelligence back in line and fix the relationship with the DNI. He then pretty much left me on my own, as he focused on winning the wars in Afghanistan and Iraq. The equation for meeting his expectations had changed a bit during my confirmation process, and all for the better. In February John Negroponte had stepped down as DNI, returning to the State Department as deputy secretary, and was succeeded by Mike Mc-Connell. Mike and I had first worked together in the late 1980s, when I'd been the senior intelligence officer for US Pacific Command and Mike for US Pacific Fleet, the Navy's service component in Pacific Command's area of operations. Later, of course, Mike had served as NSA director when I'd been DIA director and Bob Gates CIA director, and Mike had also been a partner at Booz Allen Hamilton when I'd been hired.

My first order of business as USD(I) was to address the combative relationship between the Office of the DNI and the Office of the Secretary of Defense, and we immediately found a target of opportunity. The 2004 IRTPA legislation, in addition to creating the DNI, made it a requirement that, to become eligible for promotion to senior executive, all intelligence officers get broader IC experience by serving outside their "home" intelligence element. One of the bureaucratic fights between ODNI and OSD had been over who had the authority to "certify" someone from a DOD agency or military service as having met that "joint duty" requirement. The whole matter was a little silly, putting bureaucratic infighting ahead of the welfare of employees, but it also gave me an idea. I proposed to Bob that I be assigned a "dual-hat" position on Mike McConnell's staff as the DNI's "director of defense intelligence," putting me on both Mike's and Bob's staffs. Bob supported the idea, and Mike was also on board. We signed a memo to create the new position on May 28, just forty-seven days after Bob swore me in, which has to be some sort of DOD staffing record. Shortly after, Mike and I began an exchange of hostages, wherein he sent a representative to my staff meetings, and I sent Linda Petrone to his, one of the notable intelligence officers who'd worked with Joan Dempsey at DIA.

Simultaneous to making peace with ODNI, I began examining the infrastructure of questionable human intelligence capabilities that had developed on the secretary's staff. Before he'd taken the job, Bob had said publicly that he intended to get DOD out of CIA's business. Representative Duncan Hunter, who'd worked to make sure IRTPA didn't "abrogate" any authority from the secretary of defense to the DNI, insinuated before, during, and after Gates's hearing that Bob would change his mind about giving up that power and leverage once he took office. When Bob stood firm, congressional Republicans were at first dismayed, and eventually apoplectic, raging at both Bob and me for killing off what they considered to be critical DOD assets. Frankly, I didn't think it was appropriate to be operating *any* intelligence collection or analysis capability on the bureaucratic OSD staff. My personal responsibilities meant I had to focus on policy issues and budget, not on whatever was happening that day in Syria or North Korea. Moreover, some of the new capabilities that had arisen in DOD were redundant with those handled elsewhere in the community—namely at CIA—and, following Bob's lead, I was more interested in making the IC work than accumulating power.

By the time I'd moved into my Pentagon office, the IC had settled at seventeen distinct elements. Of those, only five were intelligence "agencies," with the lion's share of their resources focused on conducting intelligence as their primary mission, except for a portion of CIA's budget allocated for covert action and NSA's responsibilities for assuring the government's ability to communicate. Those five agencies were responsible for conducting national intelligence to keep the warfighters, the national security structure, and the president informed, and each agency had its specialty: CIA—human intelligence and covert operations; NSA—signals intelligence and cyber; NGA—geospatial intelligence; DIA—military intelligence; and NRO—building, buying, launching, and flying reconnaissance systems in space.

Eleven of the other Intelligence Community members were smaller offices, responsible for supporting their parent organizations. The four DOD service intelligence elements mostly served their respective military service: Army, Navy, Air Force, and Marine Corps. Four other elements directly served Cabinet departments and secretaries: State, Treasury, Energy, and Homeland Security. And three other elements served large organizations within two other Cabinet departments: the Coast Guard within DHS, and the Drug Enforcement Administration and the FBI within the Justice Department. The intelligence component of the FBI, grown after 9/11, is a bit of an anomaly, as it is closer in scale to an actual agency, with a significant focus on counterterrorism, counterintelligence, and cybersecurity. The FBI occupies a unique position, looking outward at threats beyond our borders, like the "Big Five" agencies, and inward at domestic threats, with one foot in each of the worlds of intelligence and law enforcement.

The final IC element was the Office of the DNI. The ODNI was and is relatively small, particularly compared to the sprawling Office of the Secretary of Defense and the Joint Chiefs of Staff, but the ODNI wasn't solely dedicated to coordinating budget and resources, as the USD(I) staff was. More than half of ODNI's staff of fewer than two thousand people was and is focused on operational missions through their cross-community "centers": the National Counterterrorism Center (NCTC); the National Counterproliferation Center (NCPC), countering the spread of weapons of mass destruction; and the Office of the National Counterintelligence Executive (ONCIX, later renamed the National Counterintelligence and Security Center, NCSC), monitoring other nations' efforts to spy on us. In 2007, the ODNI added the Intelligence Advanced Research Projects Activity (IARPA) to conduct technology research for cross-community missions. In addition, the President's Daily Brief Staff and the National Intelligence Council (which generates high-level community analytic products, including National Intelligence Estimates) work for the DNI. While ODNI operates as a default headquarters for the Intelligence Community, I came to consider it an active participant in the intelligence process and properly the seventeenth IC member. Years later, when I was DNI, our social media manager, Michael Thomas, succinctly summed up how the rest of the world views the ODNI: "If the CIA is the New York Yankees, we're the Commissioner's Office. We don't have any fans, and no one buys our jerseys."

As USD(I), I was afforded access to the President's Daily Brief for the first time in my career, and the best part of that access was my conversation each day with my assigned briefer. I still value the relationships I've had with those individuals over the years. My primary job, under the 2003 legislation that created USD(I), was making sure DOD intelligence components had the resources to operate, a task made easier by the fact that we were at war. As the fighting in Iraq and Afghanistan continued and we uncovered terrorist networks and plans to attack in the United States and Europe, every year we asked for an increase in funding for the Military Intelligence Program. And every year we got it.

Much more difficult and controversial was granting authority. One of Bob Gates's stated reasons for declining the DNI position had been the director's lack of influence in hiring and firing IC component heads. Going completely against the Washington mantra of "Where you stand is where you sit," Bob still felt the DNI should have at least some say over who led the IC agencies. We couldn't give the DNI direct hiring authority without changing the IRTPA legislation, and Congress was having a hard enough time just passing a budget. So Bob, Mike, and I set out to remedy the situation as best we could, focusing on Executive Order 12333 (pronounced by everyone as "twelve triple-three"). President Reagan had signed this landmark executive order in 1981 as an underpinning for the organization, mission, authorities, and limits imposed on the IC. President Bush had last amended it in 2004, before IRTPA created the DNI. As a consequence, the executive order no longer comported with the spirit and intent of the law.

Bob and Mike got White House approval to amend the executive order again, and I worked with David Shedd, one of Mike's four deputy DNIs, to draft and coordinate new language with the White House. Our most significant proposed change was to stipulate that the secretary of defense coordinate with and receive the concurrence of the DNI to hire and fire directors of the four DOD agencies. For the military service intelligence chiefs, the respective secretaries were required to consult with the DNI. (Only in the government is the distinction between the words "consult" and "coordinate" so important.) The changes also gave the DNI authority to set IC collection and analysis priorities and to coordinate areas of responsibility.

President Bush signed the revisions on July 30, 2008, and the next day Mike McConnell and I went to Capitol Hill to brief the House Intelligence Committee. In one of the most childish displays I ever saw on Capitol Hill—and that's saying a lot—committee ranking member Pete

Hoekstra stood up and led four Republicans out of the hearing room in protest over the fact that we'd changed an executive order—an *executive* order—without their concurrence. What made the display so absurd is that Mike and I were there representing a Republican administration, briefing them on an executive order being revised by a Republican president. I doubted the same thing had happened when President Reagan signed the original order in 1981.

I found that my best work as USD(I) relied less on the authorities I had and more on the fact that I'd been around the intelligence business long enough to be acquainted with everyone involved. I'd met Lieutenant General Keith Alexander, the NSA director, when he was an up-and-coming Army major in the 1980s. Vice Admiral Bob Murrett had succeeded me at NGA, and we'd kept in contact. I'd known Lieutenant General Ron Burgess at DIA since he'd served as the senior intelligence officer for Southern Command, starting in 1999. And Scott Large and I got to know each other as we sorted through NRO's major systems acquisitions.

One of the other relationships that was invaluable was with Mike Vickers, who had a lengthy correspondence signature block as "Assistant Secretary of Defense for Special Operations/Low Intensity Conflict & Interdependent Capabilities." Basically, he conducted policy oversight for Special Operations Forces and for military activities that were more "spooky" than regular warfare—a large and growing field of work in both Afghanistan and Iraq. He also served as a networker among the special operations community, CIA, and the secretary of defense. Mike was uniquely qualified for this role, as he'd served behind the scenes in the CIA's effort in the 1980s to arm and finance the mujahidin in Afghanistan to resist and eventually overthrow the Soviet occupation. Mike was a featured character in *Charlie Wilson's War*, both the book and movie, and he was a legend among both intelligence officers and special operators.

Mike and I spent many hours bonding in adjacent witness chairs in congressional hearings, and we traveled together a lot. One of the more interesting experiences of my career was going to Afghanistan with him in June 2009, visiting his old haunts as he narrated what had occurred in each place. I got a guided tour of the most successful covert action in history from a legendary figure who played a crucial role in making it all happen, who was also a great friend. I struggled to chronicle everything we saw, heard, and discussed as we hit stops in multiple countries, and I took pages and pages of notes. When I got back to the office, I always found holes in my trip report, things I only vaguely remembered doing. Mike carried only a single three-by-five-inch card on which he took teeny-tiny notes, which he managed to turn into complete and readable novel-length reports that included every detail of our visits. I still don't know how he did that.

Years later, when I was DNI, Mike and his wife, Melana, invited Sue and me over to their house to watch *Charlie Wilson's War*. Mike kept pausing the movie, sometimes to debunk what was happening onscreen and sometimes to elaborate and embellish. In the film, Mike's character is introduced to the audience (and to Tom Hanks, playing Representative Charlie Wilson) as "the nerdy-looking kid in the white shirt," who was playing chess against four guys simultaneously. One thing I learned while watching *Charlie Wilson's War* at Mike's house is that the real Mike Vickers doesn't play chess.

On November 4, 2008, Barack Obama was elected to be our forty-fourth president. He had run on a campaign of "hope and change" and in large measure on not being George W. Bush. He was young and charismatic, and his father was black. I marveled on that day, and occasionally throughout his presidency, at just how far America had come in my lifetime. It was a tremendous milestone for our nation, and one I was very proud of us for. At the same time, I knew only a few months remained for me to cement the progress we'd made in defense intelligence before someone else took the job of USD(I).

Of course, neither Bob nor his senior intelligence adviser—me—expected President-elect Obama to stage a covert meeting in a hangar at Reagan National Airport to ask Bob to stay on as Secretary of Defense. During the first week of December I was in Wellington, New Zealand, on yet another "farewell trip." Having previously bid farewell to my Aussie and Kiwi counterparts as DIA director and as NGA director, I was getting pretty good at it. Then, on December 5, I got word via official communications channels that Bob was going to call me. I figured he wanted to thank me for my service, which would be the nice way of saying I was to be replaced. That shouldn't have been an urgent matter, but Bob phoned at 9:30 A.M. on Friday in Washington—2:30 A.M. on Saturday in New Zealand. He informed me he was staying on as secretary and wanted me to continue as USD(I), but was checking to make sure I'd agree to do so before he approached the president-elect's transition team. It took me a long few seconds to process his message, and I mumbled something about being honored that he'd ask me to stay, and that he didn't need to check with Sue again. When I called Sue at a more reasonable hour, she was supportive, although she asked if the countdown clock she'd given me could be reset.

In the following months, nearly all of the people I'd grown accustomed to working with turned their responsibilities over to successors. One choice of President Obama's that I found baffling was Leon Panetta to lead CIA. Panetta was a politician—a former representative and President Clinton's White House chief of staff—and his taking charge of the agency tasked with conducting human intelligence and covert actions made little sense to me. Politicians had a very mixed track record as CIA directors, and I recalled the short and controversial tenure of Porter Goss, who'd preceded Mike Hayden. Fortunately, I was very wrong about Leon. He has a great touch with people, and he became one of the most beloved and revered directors the agency has ever had.

President Obama's pick for DNI, retired four-star Navy Admiral Denny Blair, at least made sense to me, although I wondered if he was the right fit. The DNI job, like that of the USD(I), had very little line authority and required gentle powers of persuasion among close associates, but going in he didn't have close relationships with any of the agency directors. Denny reminded me a lot of Vice Admiral Noel Gayler, whose military assistant I'd been at NSA, as he cut the same handsome, charismatic, articulate figure, and they had both finished their naval careers in the same demanding, high-profile job—commander of US Pacific Command. Remembering the surprise I'd felt in 1991 when the civilians at DIA didn't necessarily move when I said "jump," I wondered how someone who had distinguished himself in a career of military command would function in the culture of intelligence. Despite Gates, McConnell, Shedd, and my work revising EO 12333 the previous summer, the DNI still had very little real authority.

My first interaction with Denny went a long way to alleviate my fears. He was amicable and interested in what I had to say, and as soon as he had grasped my dual-hat arrangement as Gates's USD(I) and as his director of defense intelligence, he invited me to personally attend his senior staff meetings at ODNI headquarters, an offer on which I took him up. In the first few meetings the ODNI staff was reluctant to bring up "inside-baseball" issues in my presence, asking instead to discuss such matters privately. I, meanwhile, was very open about issues in DOD, asking for help where I could get it, and the staff soon decided I wasn't there simply to spy on them and began to open up.

A new wrinkle on the national intelligence stage under President Obama was John Brennan's role as "Deputy National Security Adviser for Homeland Security and Counterterrorism and Assistant to the President," another insufferably long title. John had been a career CIA officer and the first director of the National Counterterrorism Center, getting it up and running well before it was incorporated into ODNI in April 2005. People in Washington circles knew that President Obama had wanted John to be his CIA director, but being associated with the Bush CIA made confirmation difficult, and so John assumed a special advisory role in the White House. John and I weren't intimate friends, but we'd held each other in mutual respect for some years. As USD(I), not involved with the substance of intelligence reporting, I didn't see much of John until the final year of my tenure.

Fortunately, none of the DOD agency directors were up for replacement because of the transition. Unfortunately, Blair, Gates, and I had to make a hard call with respect to the National Reconnaissance Office leadership. NRO was going through a difficult period, with a reorganization that didn't "take" and still suffering the aftereffects of high-profile satellite system failures, notably the multibillion-dollar Future Imagery Architecture program, which was canceled in 2005 and, in 2008, lost control of a satellite that had to be destroyed in orbit. When the NRO director retired in April, we moved Betty Sapp, my USD(I) deputy for portfolio, programs, and resources, to NRO as the principal deputy director. She served as acting director until June, when we hired recently retired Air Force General Bruce Carlson. I didn't like losing Betty from my staff, but having someone with her technical experience and disciplined nature at NRO was a big plus, in addition to having someone there with whom I worked well and whom I trusted. With Bruce and Betty in the front office, NRO began to dig itself out of a hole.

Then, in the summer of 2009, Lieutenant General Ron Burgess took seriously an idea of mine that other generals might have considered half-baked. As DIA director, he had the same responsibilities to fill senior defense intelligence jobs as I'd had, way back when. While I'd once had to find a position for Brigadier General-select Mike Hayden, a problem easily resolved, Ron found that he had a gap in filling a critical post—specifically, the senior intelligence job for the Joint Chiefs of Staff. None of the qualified two-star generals or admirals could leave their current positions, and moving one of them early would mean moving everyone early, to backfill one another in the resulting daisy chain. I suggested to Ron that he appoint a civilian—Robert Cardillo—DIA's director of analysis, to serve temporarily. Robert had spent most of his life as an analyst, but he'd been a great "utility infielder" for me at NGA, even running NGA's public affairs and congressional affairs shops. I assured Ron that Robert could handle coordinating intelligence for the JCS and briefing Chairman Mike Mullen. Of course, it required a leap of faith, since no civilian had ever held that position before. Happily, Robert filled the year-long gap successfully. Admiral Mullen had great regard for Robert and his work, Robert gained valuable experience that would be very useful to him (and to me) later, and Ron was able to bring Robert back to DIA as his deputy director in 2010, filling another critical vacancy.

For two and a half years, from April 2007 through November 2009, I managed to work in the trenches trying to strengthen both DOD and the IC and bringing both enterprises more closely together without drawing much public attention to my existence. But on November 5, 2009, Army major and practicing psychiatrist Dr. Nidal Hasan walked into a medical screening facility at Fort Hood, Texas, shouted, "Allahu Akbar!," and began shooting, intentionally targeting soldiers in uniform over civilians and pursuing them as they fled the building. The rampage only ceased when Hasan stopped to change clips, and civilian police sergeant Mark Todd took him down with return fire. Thirteen people had been killed and another thirty-two injured. From the White House, John Brennan tasked the DOD, FBI, and NCTC with conducting a joint investigation into how an active-duty, commissioned Army officer could become radicalized without the Army's knowing.

The FBI's superb deputy director, John Pistole, and I dug into the evidence and started conducting interviews. A number of Hasan's coworkers testified that he was very upset about his impending deployment to Afghanistan, and others said he'd been torn about what he saw as a choice between the United States and Islam. We learned that Hasan had visited radical Islamist websites and expressed admiration for Anwar al-Awlaki, the radical Islamist imam who'd counseled three of the 9/11 hijackers from his mosque in Virginia, and who—eight years later in Yemen—was radicalizing and recruiting Western Muslims to the cause of al-Qaida online. The FBI found sixteen emails ranging from December 2008 to June 2009 between the two, almost all from Hasan to Awlaki. The content of a few of those emails was concerning, particularly Hasan's desire to see Awlaki again in the afterlife. Hasan had recently paid a visit to Guns Galore in nearby Killeen, and asked for whichever handgun had the "highest magazine capacity." He'd purchased the weapon the next day, and then practiced firing it rapidly on a gun range until he was proficient.

On December 9, we held a press conference, and John told members of the media that Hasan had been in electronic communication with an FBI target. It didn't take the media long to figure out that it meant that Hasan had emailed Awlaki. In the months that followed, John and I answered a lot of questions from a lot of people, including in closed congressional hearings. As people sought to assign blame, I was continually reminded of Terry Schwalier and the Khobar Towers attack, and how hindsight is always 20/20. But as I was asked again and again why FBI or intelligence elements hadn't been reading Hasan's emails and monitoring his internet usage before his rampage, a new, unsettling thought occurred to me: I wondered just how intrusive people wanted or expected us to be. Hasan was an American citizen, a commissioned officer in the Army, and a psychiatrist. Did he give up his privacy rights or right to practice his religion when he became an active-duty service member? When he visited radical sites online? The FBI determined they didn't have enough evidence to get a warrant for a search. Did Americans want their Intelligence Community to start monitoring citizens without a warrant? How many steps away from a Stasi-type environment were we? As we concluded our investigation and briefed executive and legislative branch leaders, I didn't find any satisfactory resolution to these unsettling questions. I still haven't.

In the midst of struggling with the quandary of how to protect both public safety and individuals' right to privacy, I witnessed one of the most morally courageous acts I've ever seen. On January 27, in his 2010 State of the Union Address, President Obama announced his intent to repeal the Clinton-era "Don't Ask, Don't Tell" policy in DOD, thus allowing gay and lesbian service members to serve openly. Secretary Gates and JCS Chairman Mullen were called to testify on the proposed repeal six days later.

In their opening statements, both spoke in support of the president's position, while cautioning that DOD needed time to study how the repeal would affect troops, particularly those deployed in war zones. This was the circumspect, reasoned, well-justified position of the department. At the conclusion of his opening statement, Mike said six words that always riveted my attention: "Speaking for myself and myself only."

Generals and admirals are expected to answer congressional questions candidly, giving their personal views when asked. In my experience presenting both intelligence briefings and sworn testimony as a general officer and as a senior civilian, I had been very careful to differentiate between when I was speaking for the government and when I was breaking with the party line of the bureaucracy—the "company policy," as I called it—knowing that expressing my personal views could influence decisions in ways for which my bosses and the institutions we represent may not have been prepared. For the chairman of the Joint Chiefs of Staff to make any such remark, particularly planned and scripted in his opening statement, was of consequence. Pausing just a moment, Admiral Mullen addressed his personal views to Senator Carl Levin:

> Mr. Chairman, speaking for myself and myself only, it is my personal belief that allowing gays and lesbians to serve openly would be the right thing to do. No matter how I look at this issue, I cannot escape being troubled by the fact that we have in place a policy which forces young men and women to lie about who they are in order to defend their fellow citizens. For me personally, it comes down to integrity—theirs as individuals and ours as an institution.

For the seventeen years since the imposition of the Don't Ask, Don't Tell policy, no service chief had spoken publicly against the policy, and no service chief, much less a JCS chairman, had ever advocated for allowing gay service members to serve openly. On February 2, 2010, the JCS chairman spoke truth to power, in the process pointing out that an institution—*his* institution—that placed a premium on personal integrity was forcing its members to sacrifice theirs. To me, at least, Mike's simple, direct statement made the moral obligation to repeal Don't Ask, Don't Tell self-evident. In the span of twenty-nine seconds, Mike Mullen forever became a personal hero of mine, after which I would always consider lesbian, gay, bisexual, and transgender issues from the perspective he expressed that day.

Simultaneous with the Fort Hood shooting investigation and the initial efforts to repeal Don't Ask, Don't Tell, I watched from the sidelines as Denny Blair's tenure as DNI began to unravel. For much of 2009, he and Leon Panetta had been in a bureaucratic spat over whether the CIA director or the DNI should designate the senior intelligence officer at a given foreign location. The whole idea of having a CIA station chief was to make a senior person cognizant of all US intelligence activity taking place in the country in question, who was in turn accountable to the diplomatic chief of mission there—typically the ambassador. This arrangement had been memorialized in an agreement between Secretary Rumsfeld and DCI Porter Goss. Denny could, and did, make an argument for the DNI to be able to pick someone outside CIA to be the senior officer, for instance, in a country where NSA has a larger US intelligence footprint than CIA. Either way, it seemed to me to be a less than critical issue on which to draw a line in the sand, but that's where Denny chose to draw his line.

Leon, for his part, was right to push back, both on principle and because, in the charged atmosphere of 2009, the CIA workforce needed someone to have their back. Both public opinion and elected officials had turned against the agency over work it had carried out—work that it had been ordered by the president to do, that was deemed legal, and that was approved by those briefed in Congress. And many in the CIA believed it had been critical to preventing another tragedy in the years immediately after 9/11. Particularly frustrating was the fact that the programs in question—the use of "enhanced interrogation techniques" and "extraordinary rendition" to black sites—had ended long before many in the agency were even aware of their existence.

Leon was not going to acquiesce, but even those circumstances could have been worked out if he and Denny had held the argument in private. Instead, Denny issued a cable—an official communication—notifying everyone overseas that he was in charge of picking the senior intelligence officer in each station. CIA officers took that as yet another attempt to marginalize the agency and its traditional authorities abroad. Leon immediately issued a cable countermanding Denny's. Denny in turn appealed to the White House, essentially to determine if he was in fact in command of the Intelligence Community. In October Vice President Biden brought the two men into his office to mediate their differences. Leon wasn't giving ground, and Denny wasn't disposed to mediation with someone he felt reported to him, so it was left to Biden to make the final call. Weeks later he decided in favor of the CIA and Leon. Denny had picked his battle and lost.

The situation worsened on Christmas Day 2009, when Umar Farouk Abdulmutallab, a young Nigerian man aboard Northwest Airlines Flight 253 from Amsterdam to Detroit, tried to set off plastic explosives hidden in his underwear. The explosives fizzled, setting his underwear on fire. Other passengers noticed what was happening and overwhelmed him with physical force. In the weeks that followed the attempted attack, the White House identified shortcomings at the National Counterterrorism Center, made worse by NCTC director Mike Leiter's delay in returning from a ski vacation upon learning of the attack. NCTC postured itself as independent, but Leiter worked for Denny, and when John Brennan, the founding NCTC director, pointed out NCTC's problems, it reflected poorly on Denny.

In the years since 2010, people have theorized that Denny Blair didn't last as DNI because of his feud with Leon Panetta, or because of the "intelligence failure" regarding Abdulmutallab, or because of any of his public gaffes, gaffes that we're all prone to. I simply think he was an intelligent, capable, patriotic man who was not the best fit for that particular job. He had thirty-four years of experience in uniform as a consumer of intelligence, leading to his command of all US forces for more than half the surface of the globe. I learned later that as DNI, he'd forcefully engaged White House and National Security Council meetings with his views on how, when, and where to project force, which makes sense in the context of Denny Blair, presidential adviser. As a lifelong intelligence officer, I instinctively live by the first, fundamental, unwritten law of intelligence work: Speak straight, unbiased intelligence truth to power, and leave the business of policy making to the policy makers. I've described all this here not to criticize Denny, but because his experience had an impact on decisions I would make when I succeeded him, and it influenced how I dealt with the IC leadership, particularly the three CIA directors who served during my tenure as DNI.

CHAPTER FIVE

The Second Most Thankless Job in Washington

In early April 2010, with Denny Blair still on the job, Bob Gates called me to his office and said simply, "Jim, we need you to be the DNI." My immediate response was a flat no. I'd watched three successive DNIs in less than five years struggle with the responsibility of occupying a Cabinet-level position without congruent legislative authorities. The DNI was tasked to be the president's senior adviser and to lead, integrate, and manage the consolidated budgets of seventeen disparate intelligence organizations, transforming them into an actual Intelligence Community, but had zero line authority over any agency. I knew all too well from my time at the NIMA/NGA how hard it could be to integrate different cultures, and NIMA had involved only two groups of people, both within the agency I directed. Fifteen of the seventeen organizations for which the DNI was responsible reported to six Cabinet departments, led by six Cabinet secretaries, and the legislation that established the DNI included a clause granting deference to those secretaries. I wasn't sure it was possible to actually *do* the job of DNI. Moreover, as I told Bob then, I was pushing seventy (today, of course, I'm dragging it closer to eighty), and I had absolutely no interest in enduring another confirmation process.

Most important, I'd already taken two postretirement jobs with Sue barely acquiescing. I'd retired after DIA at her behest, and it seemed to me that it was again time for us to follow her wishes. That night I told her about the job offer and how I'd declined it, expecting she'd be pleased and impressed. Instead, much to my surprise and chagrin, she replied, "How could you turn that down?" Once again I found myself in a late-night conversation in which Sue tried to straighten out my priorities over a glass or two of wine. She argued that this job was fundamentally different from NGA director or undersecretary. The DNI's scope was wider, I would have a chance to make a difference for the entire community, and I'd be working directly with the president. The next morning I dropped off a note to Bob that read, "I talked to Sue and thought about it, and if you and the president think I'm the right person for the job, I'll do it."

I then went back to work as USD(I) and heard nothing for weeks. On Tuesday, May 4, I was on my way to Andrews Air Force Base for a flight to Ottawa to meet with my Canadian intelligence counterparts, when Robert Rangel, Bob's chief of staff, called to say I had an appointment with the president the following morning. When I told him I was on my way to Andrews to fly to Ottowa, he replied, "You don't understand. You have an appointment with the *president* tomorrow—alone." He explained that it would be an interview for the DNI position. I believe my entire response was "Oh," and I canceled my trip.

I arrived in the anteroom outside the Oval Office fifteen minutes early. Over the next seven years, I'd get to know that anteroom well. It wasn't much bigger than a few office cubicles, but it was a central hub, with one door leading to the main entrance to the Oval, another to a hallway toward the Roosevelt Room, a third to the Cabinet room, and a fourth leading to the president's outer office and a back entrance to the Oval. When I was finally led to the Oval Office entrance, I saw President Obama standing at a credenza in front of his scheduler's desk, casually looking over the front pages of a pile of newspapers. He looked up, gave me his patented smile, stepped over, and shook my hand. I have no doubt that his greeting was choreographed to put me at ease. I don't recall precisely what he said, but after some pleasantries, he gestured for me to follow him into the Oval—another room I would get to know very well.

This wasn't my first time in the Oval Office, as earlier in my career I'd been part of a group of "straphangers" attending a personnel announcement there. But this was certainly my first time alone with a president, an experience even Cabinet secretaries seldom have. It would be repeated for me twice more in the next seven years—both times for discussions about replacements for the CIA director. I observed, as I entered, that the office is designed to impress and intimidate. My eyes took in the blue presidential seal, embedded directly in the center of the oval rug. Rays of gold and bronze radiated out from it across the rug and projected onto the vertically striped walls. Between my meeting in May and my first President's Daily Brief in September, President Obama would swap out the radiant rug for a solid, cream colored one with a white presidential seal. His more muted color scheme projected a still confident but more relaxed commander in chief, one who embraced the power of the office but equally exhibited the humility inherent in his character.

At one end of the room under three tall windows stood the famous "Resolute desk," constructed from the timbers of HMS *Resolute*, a British ship trapped in Arctic ice, abandoned in 1854, and then recovered and returned by Americans two years later. When *Resolute* was retired, Queen Victoria had the massive, ornate, and magnificent desk made and presented it to President Rutherford B. Hayes in 1880 as a sign of gratitude and friendship. It both symbolizes and embodies the power and grandeur of the office of the president. I rarely saw President Obama behind that desk, except during signing ceremonies and photo ops.

At the other end of the room, a portrait of George Washington hung over the fireplace mantle. The president walked over to the chair to Washington's left, motioning for me to join him in the chair to Washington's right, which Oval Office etiquette typically reserved for the vice president or foreign dignitaries. He asked how I felt about taking the DNI job, letting me present my prepared talking points up front. I told him I hadn't campaigned for the job, that I was nearly seventy years old and "already had one foot in assisted living," but acknowledged that I was a "duty guy at heart," and if asked, I'd do my best. I felt that the DNI was an important position and a vast improvement from the DCI system, because the Intelligence Community leader is not a part-time job for an agency director. He chuckled at my "assisted living" line and said I looked as if I was in pretty good shape. He asked if I worked out, and I told him my schedule of alternating days between lifting weights and doing cardio. We talked about balancing the rigors of our jobs with taking care of ourselves and kept it light, but he was clearly taking stock of me. After about fifteen minutes, he smiled, rose, shook my hand, and walked me out.

The next day, I visited Bob in his office and discussed the interview. I enjoyed shooting the breeze with the president, but I had more thoughts on what it would take to make the DNI job actually work that I hadn't had a chance to express. Bob suggested I write a letter to President Obama, which he would personally hand deliver.

On Thursday, May 20, Denny Blair announced his resignation. The media hyperventilated, speculating about what had happened to prompt his removal. Many associated it with a May 18 Senate report on Abdul-mutallab's Christmas Day attempt to set off explosives aboard Flight 253. Since the release of that report, I'd been rumored as Denny's replacement, and after his resignation, my face was all over the cable news networks. I sat down to finish my letter to the president, writing that I hoped my thoughts would be "universally" useful to him, whether I ended up as the official nominee or not. I also cautioned, "I think the position of DNI has about one more chance to succeed before the Congress gets serious about trying something else (e.g., a 'Department of Intelligence,' which I think would pose major civil liberties challenges)." I didn't share my experience of touring the Stasi headquarters in East Berlin, and I didn't express how strongly the idea of an all-powerful American intelligence czar went against my perception of who we were as a nation.

In the two and a half weeks since Bob had suggested I write a letter, I'd wondered about just how candid I should be. Finally, with the understanding that if I couldn't write complete truth in that letter, I would never be able to do justice for the Intelligence Community and the country as DNI, I decided that President Obama deserved my full candor, so I offered seven key observations.

Regarding his expectations, I wrote:

> If the expectation is that the DNI—and the Community which he/she is the nominal leader—is to be held to the standard of perfection, batting 1.000 all the time, then you may want to look for someone who is far more clairvoyant than I. Too often people confuse mysteries and secrets, and expect the Intelligence Community (IC) to be equally adept at divining both. We're not. In the minds of many in the IC, Denny Blair's departure seems to substantiate the old simplistic saw about there being only two conditions in public life: policy success or intelligence failure.

My second point concerned defining some "lanes in the road" for the relationships between CIA director Leon Panetta, Homeland Security Adviser John Brennan, and the next DNI, "first and foremost in your mind, and then, of course, to them, and importantly, for the Intelligence Community at large. Right now, there is confusion about who is really in charge of intelligence and what you expect of each." Further:

> Both the optics and substance of your interactions with the DNI are crucial. If you consistently treat the DNI as your senior intelligence adviser, that in itself will empower the position. . . . If, on the other hand, you engage directly with the Director of CIA, without at least the knowledge—or preferably the participation—of the DNI, the stature and imputed authority of the DNI are marginalized accordingly.

Thirdly, I agreed with Bob Gates's idea that the DNI should function as something like an "avuncular, sage, strong Senate committee chairman, in the tradition of, say, John Warner or Sam Nunn," bringing other leaders together on the merits of an idea, rather than issuing line orders. Further, I endorsed the idea that only a career intelligence officer could follow the model that Bob had set as DCI, explaining that because of his vast experience, "He was a 'DNI' way before anyone thought of it," and concluding, "That, by the way, is a strength of the DNI arrangement—someone who can preside over the entire community, without the distraction of running a large, complex agency."

My fourth observation was that I would need to make some changes to the ODNI organizational structure and staff. My fifth was "I am a 'truth to power' guy." I described the trouble that that conviction had gotten me into when I spoke my mind to the previous secretary of defense, and noted that I wasn't going to change: "I would always insist on giving you privately the facts, to include what we don't know." Within that sentence, I'd deliberatively chosen the adverb "privately."

I thought those were five reasonable, defensible observations. My sixth, not so much:

> I have always sought to be "below the radar"; I do not like publicity. I've spent the last week cringing every time I saw my name in the paper, or my face on the tube. I think it is part of the unwritten code of professional intelligence officers to stay out of the media. I don't believe the DNI

should be out making speeches, appearing on talking-head shows, or giving interviews.

I certainly didn't believe the DNI should *ever* write a memoir.

Finally, I noted that, if I was chosen as DNI, and "if the first inklings of discomfiture with me arise," I would not be offended if asked to leave, and "There should be no agonizing over such a decision." I signed it, "With great respect, Jim Clapper." I never received a direct reply to the letter, although my later interactions with the president led me to believe he'd absorbed both its substance and intent.

On Saturday, June 5, I returned to the Oval Office, this time so that the president could announce my nomination. Sue and Jennifer and her family accompanied me, and President Obama laughed and kidded with them, radiating his irresistible charm and good humor, putting all of us at ease. My two oldest grandkids, Ryan and Erin, were wide-eyed, both at meeting the president and just being in the White House. As we were walking out to the Rose Garden to face the phalanx of media cameras, the president paused and commented to Erin, "I appreciate your grandfather's willingness to take on the second most thankless job in Washington." I thought he was joking. Nope.

On Monday I received a call from Kathleen Turner. I knew her from my time as DIA director as a sharp Soviet subject-matter expert who'd risen through the ranks to become at thirty-two the youngest DIA officer ever to reach senior executive. I'd appointed her as DIA's human resources director, and after I moved on, she'd continued to impress in roles of increasing responsibility until, in 2005, she left DIA to serve as the first ODNI legislative affairs director. I was very happy to hear her say she'd be my Sherpa, my experienced and knowledgeable guide through the confirmation process. I was filling out volumes of paperwork from the White House, all the typical security clearance and conflict-of-interest forms, but also much more intrusive questions, such as what I might have ever written or said that could embarrass the president, and how I was getting along with my wife. They served as a fair warning of the public profile of the job I was about to take.

I also got a call from Leon Panetta, congratulating me and inviting me to lunch with him and Senate Intelligence Committee chairman Dianne Feinstein, whom I didn't know personally and with whom I hadn't always

had the most positive and satisfying exchanges during
wanted both to help me with my confirmation and to beg
breach between the CIA and ODNI. The lunch succeeded o
I didn't say much, but Leon slipped in some good words for
ing Feinstein, who was skeptical of military retirees, that I'd
active-duty uniform fifteen years earlier and left that mind
me. I told her that as DNI I'd focus on integration of communit
the reason I felt Congress and the president had created the posi
of the few things she said directly to me over lunch confirmed
cern I'd expressed to the president: There would probably not be a
chance to make the DNI concept work if it didn't work this time.

Leon helped me with one other issue that summer, something
probably contributed to my success more than any other. I told h
needed the principal deputy DNI to be a CIA person, someone who
insight into and credibility and influence with the agency, someone w
could cover my blind spots when CIA issues came up. Leon offered hi
number three—Stephanie O'Sullivan, CIA's associate deputy director. I
knew her by reputation as a brilliant technical engineer who'd spent most
of her career building systems to which I often didn't have access. When
we spoke, I told her my principal motivation in taking the DNI job was
to make the enterprise better. I proposed that, generally, I'd work the
outside—the White House, Congress, foreign partners, agency directors—
if she'd work the inside—ODNI staff and Intelligence Community issues.
This resonated with her, and we bonded right from the start.

Of course, before I could put any of that into action, I had to be confirmed. Kathleen Turner guided me through meetings with each of the
senators on the Intelligence Committee, who would all ask questions at
my confirmation hearing and would ultimately vote on sending my name
to the Senate floor. I laid out my case to each, and they all seemed to hear
me out before turning to their own pet issues. Many expressed concerns
about installing yet another retired military officer in a senior civilian
intelligence position. I reminded them that I was one of only a few who
had served as a military service intelligence chief, twice as an agency
director—once in uniform and once in a suit—and as a political appointee at the undersecretary level, experience that gave me a fair understanding of what it took to make all of those jobs work, and that I would bring

to bear as DNI. Many expressed serious doubts and warned again that I represented the last chance to get this right, but Kathleen always put a positive spin on events and, on more than one occasion, talked me down from backing out of the nomination.

By far, the most comfortable meeting I had was with Senator Barbara Mikulski from Maryland. We already had a rapport from working through Base Realignment and Closure issues when I'd been NGA director. Senator Mikulski and I would both retire in January 2017, and in the seven years I worked with her, my impression never changed. She was the rare Capitol Hill politician who always advocated for her positions—which consistently included the IC and our workforce—but never let the culture of politics compromise her fundamental sense of right.

Meanwhile, the defense intelligence world didn't stop turning, and two important events occurred on my watch as USD(I) that summer. For several years, the Pentagon had faced the growing realization that it needed to organize for military activity in the cyber realm—both on defense and offense. In time-honored government tradition, we conducted a study while knowing the outcome we desired. Once the report was in hand, Secretary Gates ordered the establishment of US Cyber Command under US Strategic Command. CYBERCOM was to be formed at Fort Meade with NSA and led by the NSA director, since NSA was the center of expertise and had all the resources and capabilities for operating in cyberspace. Making CYBERCOM subordinate to STRATCOM and giving the NSA director another hat were intended to be temporary provisions until CYBERCOM could take its training wheels off and operate independently. On May 21, Keith Alexander pinned on his fourth star and added another hat as the first CYBERCOM commander. Keith already had served for five years as NSA director, and I observed that his primary institutional instincts remained with NSA. His successor, Admiral Mike Rogers, put on both hats simultaneously, and his focus seemed to be more evenly balanced.

The second notable event of that summer was the appointment of Tish Long as the third director of NGA (fifth, counting my NIMA predecessors). I had always assumed that I'd been named the third director of NIMA in 2001 because DOD wasn't ready to name a woman—namely Joan Dempsey—as director of one of the five intelligence agencies. By

2010, we *were* ready, and more important, Tish was the most qualified and talented individual available to lead NGA. She'd served as the first chief information officer at DIA when I'd been director, and then had replaced Joan as the director of the GDIP staff; she'd also served as deputy director of naval intelligence and in a key leadership position with the USD(I) before moving to DIA as deputy director in 2006. I considered Tish a protégée, and in one of life's happy coincidences, she took her oath of office as NGA director the same day I did as DNI—August 9. That's getting a little ahead of the story.

My confirmation hearing was finally scheduled for July 20. I'm still not sure whether to consider it fortunate or unfortunate that July 20 was day two of the *Washington Post* series "Top Secret America." The articles were a collaboration between Dana Priest and William M. Arkin. Priest had won the Pulitzer Prize for Beat Reporting in 2006 with her work about CIA "black sites," and had received acclaim again in 2007 for exposing the conditions veterans were enduring at Walter Reed. She and Arkin had spent two years doing research, and the *Post* was billing this series as her next big blockbuster. It was not. Its primary premise was that the combined US counterterrorism, homeland security, and intelligence enterprise was massively bloated. It reported that 1,271 government organizations and 1,931 private companies worked in 10,000 locations across the United States, with an estimated 854,000 people holding security clearances. This revelation was met with a collective yawn.

The original plan for "Top Secret America" was for the *Post* to put an interactive website online, on which anyone could see Google Street Views of places that Arkin and the *Post* believed were intelligence sites, alleging that an undisclosed, covert spy facility could be in any reader's backyard! Without confirming to the *Post* whether any of their assessments were correct, intelligence officials, including Denny Blair, convinced the editors that publishing those addresses would invite attacks at those locations, and that the paper could be held criminally liable. The *Post* wisely decided not to publish actual addresses, and what they were left with was breathless reporting from Dana Priest, who recounted sitting at a table with an actual intelligence contractor (one of hundreds of thousands, according to her own reporting) and trying to access the DNI's headquarters building unannounced, prompting "men in black" to "jump out of nowhere, guns at the ready." By the afternoon of July 19, the first "Top Secret America" article had fallen to second place on the Post's website of the most-read stories, behind a commentary on people not giving up their seats on the Metro to people with disabilities.

Day two of the series focused on how, in this huge enterprise, there were so many gosh darn contractors—people who worked for private companies hired by the government to perform jobs that it couldn't fill with federal employees. After 9/11, when national security leaders assessed what the peace dividend had wrought, they realized they would have to pay private companies to quickly reconstitute the capabilities they'd lost through downsizing. By 2010, the pendulum had not swung back far enough toward hiring government employees with the necessary skill sets, but we were well aware of that fact. In a very narrow sense, the appearance of the *Post* series was fortunate for me, because it made the line of questions at my confirmation hearing predictable and generally within my knowledge wheelhouse, thanks to my time as USD(I).

On the morning of the hearing, President Obama called to wish me luck—the first of only two direct phone calls I got from him. I told him I didn't have a feeling for how the hearing would go, and he assured me it would be fine.

Sue, Jennifer, Jay, my brother, Mike, and my sister, Chris, sat directly behind me, sending positive energy my way for the hearing and, I hoped, making the senators more reticent to publicly flog me in front of them. When it was my turn to speak, I acknowledged their support on the official Senate record, noting I'd had Sue's for forty-five years at that point, and I observed that their seats were "more comfortable" than my small chair behind a small table with a thin microphone jutting toward my face. The senators were on a raised dais that extended in a U shape around me. Throughout the confirmation hearing, Senators Feinstein and Kit Bond, the senior Republican and committee vice chair, remained at the center of the dais, directing the action, while the other senators customarily took their seats only when it was their turn to ask questions, at which point the camera would cut to them.

I think the morning's theme was best captured by an off-microphone comment from Bond to Feinstein that did not make it into the official record or media reporting: "Welcome to our *annual* DNI confirmation," which was indicative of a good bit of the cynicism held toward the very concept of the DNI, whether it could work, and whether I was up to the job, particularly as they seemed to view me as too beholden to DOD. Senator Bond noted that the Armed Services Committee had endorsed me, and that the Intelligence Committee didn't regard that as necessarily to my benefit.

After Senator Bond's remarks, I greatly appreciated Senator Mikulski's speaking up. In an exception to protocol, she took the microphone for several minutes before my opening statement, taking Feinstein and Bond to task: "I know we've been through four DNI confirmations, four DNIs," she acknowledged, "and if there is a failure in or questions about the authority and the functionality of the DNI, then it's incumbent on Congress to look at the legislation, but not necessarily fault the DNI nominee for the failures of the legislative framework." She then preempted much of the criticism I'd receive that morning with a rousing defense, which I truly appreciated:

> One of the things in working with Mr. Clapper as head of the NGA was, again, his candor, his straightforwardness, his willingness to tell it *like it is*—not the way the top brass wanted to hear it—I thought it was refreshing and enabled us to work very well.
>
> I think that in this job he will be able to speak truth to power—which God knows we need it—and he will speak truth about power, which we also need. I would hope that as we say, oh, gee, we don't know if we want a military guy chairing or heading the DNI, Mr. Clapper left the military service in 1995. He's been a civilian. He doesn't come with the whole extensive, often military staff that people bring with them when they take a civilian job. And I think in my mind he's probably the best qualified to do this job, because he's not only been a nighthawk standing sentry over the United States of America, but he's actually run an intelligence agency and he's actually had to run a big bureaucracy. And he's had to run with sometimes very inadequate leadership at the top.
>
> So, we ought to give him a chance and I think we ought to hear what he has to say today.

None of Senator Mikulski's statement made it into the press reporting on the hearing, but a quote from Kit Bond, taken completely out of context, made it into *every* piece of media coverage. After a wonky exchange about comments I'd made a decade earlier that the Senate Intelligence Committee—instead of the Senate Armed Services Committee—should have authority over the Military Intelligence Program (MIP), Senator Bond talked about the problems inherent in having the two Senate committees divide oversight duties. I wanted to respond that the 9/11 Commission had judged congressional oversight of intelligence to be dysfunctional for precisely this reason, and that while the Intelligence Community had worked hard to reform itself in that regard, Congress had taken no such steps. I also felt that the single best thing Congress could do to strengthen the DNI and to make post-9/11 intelligence reform successful would be to separate the National Intelligence Program from Cabinet budgets and make it a self-standing appropriation. I didn't say *any* of that; I couldn't, and he knew it. Still, Bond pressed me to agree that his committee should take oversight of the MIP. Out of a sense of self-preservation, I declined to advocate for either of the two committees, both of which I'd be reporting to if confirmed. Bond understood and laughed. Of the fight for budget control between the two committees, he said, "You have, as anyone around here knows, entered into the most deadly minefield in Washington, DC." All of the headlines instead referred to the DNI post itself as "the most deadly minefield in Washington."

I survived the hearing, and the committee advanced my name to the full Senate. Before a vote could happen, though, two committee Republicans—Bond and Tom Coburn—each put a hold on my nomination, saying they wanted the administration to give them classified reports on the dangers posed by releasing Guantanamo Bay detainees. When they released their holds the first week of August, Senator McCain put another hold on me, asking for something else with no relation to me. The Senate was scheduled to adjourn for recess on Friday, August 6, for the rest of the month, and it looked as though they would leave without voting on my appointment.

National Security Adviser Jim Jones told me that if they didn't hold a vote, President Obama would make a recess appointment. I warned Jim that because the DNI's authorities were already ambiguous, an appointment without Senate confirmation would only further weaken the position.

I told him that if the Senate adjourned without voting on me, I would withdraw. On Thursday night, August 5, I attended a social event at which C-SPAN was on in the background—it was that kind of party. Well into the evening, Senator Harry Reid was presiding over votes on the floor. We watched as he called for a vote on measure 1019, my nomination. None of the senators present (if there were any, since C-SPAN is not allowed to pan the gallery) opposed my nomination. As they moved onto the next measure. I simply shook my head and stared at the screen. Just like that, after all that drama, I'd been confirmed.

On Friday I finished packing my office in the Pentagon, and on Saturday morning, I arrived at my new office at Liberty Crossing in McLean, Virginia, which everyone just calls LX, to find Brigadier General Linda R. Urrutia-Varhall, "General UV," my senior military assistant at USD(I) and one of just two people I brought along from the Pentagon, already there with her husband, Greg, setting up my new office. The painting of a ship that had hung at my desk when I'd been the military assistant at NSA in 1972 was now behind what would be my desk as DNI. Across an embarrassingly large stretch of carpet, the portrait of General Patton given to me by the USD(I) staff hung beside a small, circular conference table. As I watched UV and Greg lay out my other memorabilia from the past forty-seven years, seeing my stuff in that office suddenly made the job feel very real—much more so than had the anticlimactic confirmation vote.

On Monday, August 9, I first went to see Tish sworn in as NGA director in a big, formal ceremony at the new NGA headquarters building in Springfield, Virginia—the facility I'd fought so hard for in 2005. The building was still a year from being open for business, but the scale and the vision for the campus were evident, and the ceremony that morning was a proud moment for me. After the ceremony, my new security detail drove Sue and me back to Liberty Crossing, where ODNI chief management officer Mark Ewing met us at the office and swore me in at an informal gathering, making me officially the DNI.

I started on the job the next day with what would become my morning ritual. The protective detail picked me up at 5:45, and I began reading the overnight intelligence reporting in the back of the secure, armored SUV. I changed into workout clothes in my office and hit the small but complete gym in the basement of Liberty Crossing. My office had an adjoining shower, and once I was back in a suit, I tried to finish reading the previous night's reports. Then I met with Pat Rohan, my personal briefer for the President's Daily Brief. Star analysts normally take one-year tours as briefers, but because Pat, who had been my briefer as USD(I), and I had a terrific rapport, I managed to persuade the PDB staff to let him come to Liberty Crossing. When he completed that assignment, he took a one-year rotation as my executive assistant.

The PDB is the IC's daily (well, six days a week) dialogue with the president to address global challenges and opportunities related to national security. Its existence dates back to the Kennedy administration, and today it's among the most highly classified and sensitive documents in all of government, and perhaps one of the most expensive daily publications in the world. Although the CIA still generates the lion's share of the articles in the PDB, all seventeen intelligence components can and do contribute, and then the PDB staff works with the authors to edit their writing and analysis in a grueling process that can take place over several weeks or several days, depending on the urgency of the subject. Working in shifts, the PDB staff compiles the analytic articles and graphics overnight, sometimes making edits on new information or even switching articles completely in the early morning hours. The PDB briefers assigned to national security Cabinet members and a handful of other senior officials, like USD(I), all come to CIA headquarters in the predawn hours each morning. There they meet with the staff and the articles' authors, read the PDB, get a briefing on the intelligence sources behind the articles, and ask any questions they think each principal they brief might ask. The process is as much a final check on the soundness of the articles and the validity of sources as a chance for the briefers to prepare. After the prep session, briefers scatter in the dark across Virginia and Washington with the PDBs, which when I became DNI were hard copies in faux leather loose-leaf binders.

On that first Tuesday morning, after briefing with Pat, my detail took me to the White House. I met with Jim Jones, and we went to the Oval for the president's PDB session. At the time, President Obama had two PDB briefers: Jim Danoy from DIA and an analyst from CIA. Jim was the first non-CIA briefer ever assigned to the president, a distinction that isn't as curious as it sounds, since the PDB was a CIA-only operation until 2005, and I sat with him on the couch in the Oval as the president and vice president listened to him briefly review each of the articles in that day's book. The president paid attention and nodded politely, but clearly he had already read and digested its contents. I wasn't slated to actively participate, but at one point, I interjected on a topic Pat and I had discussed at length that morning. The president and I spoke for maybe four minutes out of a total eight or nine minutes we spent with him, and as we left, Jim told me that was the most conversation he'd ever witnessed at a PDB session with the president. I was amazed and felt we clearly could do better. I wanted to address the situation right then and there, but I was already due to be in a Principals Committee meeting in the Situation Room about Guantanamo Bay detainees. I made a mental note and pressed on with my day, gaining a deeper appreciation of why John Negroponte, Mike Mc-Connell, and Denny Blair felt it was hard to get things done in the post.

For reference, while both the Principals Committee (PC) and National Security Council (NSC) are composed of Cabinet members leading national security–related departments, PC meetings are chaired by the national security adviser, and NSC meetings are chaired by the president. Each took up a huge amount of my time during the next few years, both in preparing for and attending them. The National Security Council staff would typically send over a read book the night before, which I was supposed to digest and be ready to discuss the next day. Meetings almost always started with an intelligence briefing, which I led, or I'd moderate, if CIA, NSA, NCTC, or any other specialized IC entity was there to brief. We'd then discuss a series of questions, always more than we could possibly get through. Early on I grew accustomed to spending long hours with President Obama, Vice President Biden, National Security Adviser Jim Jones, Secretary of State Hillary Clinton, Secretary of Homeland Security Janet Napolitano, Attorney General Eric Holder, Homeland Security Adviser John Brennan, and Secretary of Defense Bob Gates, and their successors, often a few times a week. Over the next six and a half years, the only NSC participants not to change were the president and vice president. I'd see three national security advisers, four defense secretaries, two secretaries of state, two DHS secretaries, and two attorneys general, not to mention three CIA directors, and Michael Morell as acting CIA director—twice.

In Bob Gates's book, he wrote about friendly, competitive dynamics within NSC meetings, particularly his perceived rivalries with Vice

President Biden and Secretary Clinton over policy decisions that affected DOD—a dynamic I can validate. But because of unwritten rule of intelligence number one—leave the policy making to policy makers—I never personally felt that sense of rivalry with any NSC member, including any of the CIA directors. I do think that during President Obama's second term, John Brennan and I had the model relationship for how a DNI and CIA director should work together, presenting a united front on intelligence issues. Even when briefing covert actions, for which I always deferred to the CIA director, I knew what John was going to say. That was partly preparation together and also decades of experience. What we were able to accomplish reinforces why it's better to have intelligence professionals in those positions, rather than politicians or military line officers.

I made it a practice to stay out of the policy fray during NSC meetings, although I recall a conversation I had with the president at a PDB session the morning after a particularly contentious NSC meeting on Afghanistan. In the calm of that morning brief time, I told him that I'd served as an intelligence officer in Vietnam early in the war and in headquarters offices as the war progressed and finally concluded. I said that the conversation at the NSC meeting had eerily reminded me of conversations as that war ground on, with the generals arguing that they just needed a few thousand more troops, a few million more dollars, a little more time, and they could win it. I explained that I wasn't advocating for a particular Afghanistan policy but felt he should know that the language we were using was haunting to me. Irritated, he asked why, if I felt this way, I hadn't spoken up at the NSC meeting. If I'd made that observation during the NSC discussion, I replied, it would have been perceived as my weighing into the debate, and I did not want to compromise my credibility as an impartial, unbiased bearer of intelligence truth. He nodded, agreed, and said that he appreciated my bringing up my observation.

Because of the nature—and unrelenting frequency—of NSC and PC meetings, I never felt I had to take extra steps to cultivate a kinship with the Cabinet secretaries. When Susan Rice became national security adviser, I was one of the few people—perhaps the *only* person at PC meetings—who could get away with jokes at her expense. (Remember that PC meetings do not include the president.) I recall one Situation Room gathering during which UN ambassador Samantha Power was participating via secure video teleconference from New York. (Hello,

JWICS!) That morning, I'd been fitted at Walter Reed military hospital with new hearing aids, which had Bluetooth capability. At the start of the meeting, Samantha complained that she couldn't hear my intelligence briefing very well. I quipped, loudly, that she should get hearing aids like my new ones and pulled out a remote control to demonstrate. "I can turn the volume down," I said, pushing a button, and then, "I can turn the volume up," pushing another. "And finally, there's a special button here that just says, 'National Security Adviser—off.'" I pretended to push an imaginary "silence" button reserved for Susan, and then I sat back and smiled, pretending I couldn't hear Susan—and *then* everyone else—laughing.

On Wednesday, after working out and discussing the PDB with Pat, I met with the four deputy DNIs, trying to get a sense of their concerns. It was obvious that most of them had genuinely liked and respected Denny Blair, and their biggest apprehension was not knowing what would change—yet *again*—with their fourth director in five years. Having led DIA and NIMA/NGA during times of transition, I'd developed in my own head a concentric circle approach to prioritizing relationships. I needed to focus first on making ODNI work, then on relationships with IC agency and component leaders, then on the DNI representatives across the world, representatives of foreign intelligence partners, law enforcement and first responders at the federal, state, local, and tribal levels, and finally on the community workforce around DC and deployed around the world. Similarly, in my head, I had organized circles for the world external to intelligence: the White House, then Congress, the media, and finally the US public. Of course, this was simply an organizing approach, and in practice I had to engage all the circles simultaneously. Reflecting back, the only relationship I could never make work consistently was the one with Congress.

On Thursday of my first week as DNI, I flew with DIA director Ron Burgess to Scott Air Force Base, Illinois, where the intelligence staff of US Transportation Command was to dedicate a conference room named for me. More important, it gave me a chance to get out of Washington and talk to intelligence analysts and customers. Over the next six and a half years, my staff consistently expressed concern for my stamina in taking as many trips as I did, but the truth was, the only way for me to recharge was to get out of the capital to meet with intelligence officers in the field, whose sense of mission energized me.

Thinking of my concentric circles approach, I also had an ulterior motive for this trip. On the flight out, I talked with Ron about the organizational change I wanted to make within the ODNI staff, that while the law said the DNI could have four deputy DNIs, IRTPA didn't say that the DNI *had* to have that many. I intended to tell the staff that we would have only one, the DDNI for intelligence integration. The collection and analysis organizations within ODNI would merge; integration would be ODNI's core mission, and all other ODNI components would be integration enablers. I explained that the ideal person to fill this role was Robert Cardillo, the civilian whom Ron had sent to the JCS to fill in as the senior intelligence officer. Robert had replaced Tish Long as Ron's deputy at DIA only two days earlier, so I understood that moving him wouldn't be convenient. Ron, to his credit, said, "If you want Robert, you've got him."

A big lesson from my DIA and NGA experience was not to leave the staff in suspense when making changes, so I announced what I called "tweaks" to the organization at the senior staff meeting that first Friday morning. Anticipating resistance, I said that I'd already informed the president of my decision—which was true, as I'd written about reorganizing the ODNI in the letter I'd sent him in May. There were some reservations but no real resistance, and everyone seemed to relax and get on with business.

During my second week on the job I focused on concentric circle number two—the leaders at the IC agencies and their components. Because I already had good relationships with the directors of NSA, NRO, NGA, and DIA, and because Leon Panetta wanted to repair the rift that had recently opened between the CIA and ODNI, I started with the CIA. Leon invited me to lunch with the agency leadership on Wednesday, at which I made it clear that while I did not intend to control their work, I did need to know what was going on in the agency. We talked a lot about presenting a united front to the White House and Congress, and in the media if necessary. This wasn't a question of "getting our story straight" when in trouble; it was about being on the same page from the start. I repeated the Air Force expression I'd shared with Leon before my confirmation: "If you want me around when the plane crashes, make sure I'm around when the plane takes off." The agency, to its credit, abided by that rule of thumb for my entire tenure.

My formal swearing-in ceremony took place on August 24. Some of my family had flown in for the event, and a little crowd gathered in the Eisenhower Executive Office Building, about a hundred feet west of the White House. Sue and I stood in the hallway, waiting on Vice President Biden to arrive to officiate at the ceremony. When he appeared, I took a couple of steps forward, preparing to shake his hand, but without making eye contact with me, he went straight to Sue, thanking her for the sacrifices she'd made, for her service, and for letting me come back to government. *What a classy thing to do!* I thought. In that moment I knew that he understood how difficult life can be for families, who also serve, and who often see when we're frustrated, sad, or angry—or sometimes, elated—but can't always be told the reason why.

Robert Cardillo became the deputy DNI for intelligence integration about a week later, and we quickly addressed the president's morning briefings. While the PDB staff had adapted the content for President Obama, we were still conducting Oval briefings modeled for President Bush, who wanted to have the articles briefed in detail, absorb the material, and ask briefers questions at the same session. President Obama preferred to read and digest the material ahead of time. There was almost a mystical aura around the PDB, with people apparently reluctant to make changes to it, but I knew we could make better use of the president's precious time.

Robert and I explained to him that we wanted to stop sending PDB briefers to review what he'd already read. Instead, we would present what we called "walk-ons," short briefing items we'd find to supplement what was in the formal PDB book, or new intelligence reporting that had arrived during the night. We would periodically bring in subject-matter expert analysts from throughout the community to discuss specific topics in depth. The president seemed to appreciate that the PDB, with its four to six articles daily, could not address the entire range of issues that confronted him and that our approach would be a valuable supplement. He agreed, saying we needed to "be able to walk and chew gum at the same time." I proposed that Robert and I rotate attending the briefings, explaining, "This may come as a surprise to you, Mr. President, but I don't lust for Oval Office rug time." He laughed and responded, "Me neither!"

Once we set that process in place, we didn't change it much over the next six years, except that Robert began bringing a secure iPad to play video clips and show imagery. Because President Obama was extremely comfortable with digital technology, we converted the PDB "book" to a digital form in 2012, after which they were delivered on secure iPads. Being old and old-fashioned, I still liked to bring hard copy of maps, charts, photos, and imagery to the meetings, both to enrich the intelligence picture and show off the capabilities of the IC. Because those sessions normally included the vice president, chief of staff, national security adviser, and deputies, I'd have to bring a stack of copies of anything I wanted to present, each stack held together with a paper clip.

In 2015, when President Obama came to Liberty Crossing to help us celebrate the tenth anniversary of ODNI's launch, he gave a speech to the staff, telling them with an air of modesty, "I don't know how astute a consumer of information I am, but I can tell you I sure do rely on it. And those who come and brief me every single morning do an extraordinary job." Then, with a look of concern, he glanced over at me and continued, "I will say that the only flaw, generally, in what's called the PDB that I receive is that when Jim provides it, some of you may have heard, he leaves paper clips all over my office." He smiled, and the staff laughed as he continued. "They're in the couch, they're on the floor. He's shuffling paper." Another pause, with more laughter. "And so, because I knew I was coming over here, one of the things I did was return them all." With that line, he pulled out a jar filled with paper clips. The staff roared and applauded. He placed them on the podium and, addressing me, added, "DNI's budget is always a little tight; we can start recycling these. That's going to be critical." That signed jar of paper clips became a treasure of mine, and it sat prominently on my desk for the rest of my tenure.

Conceptually, changing the President's Daily Briefs was pretty simple, but merging two of ODNI's larger offices into a single force for leading the integration of the intelligence production cycle across seventeen agencies and elements was more complex, to say the least. Fortunately, this was yet another area in which I was very fortunate to have exemplary work on which to build. In ODNI's first year, John Negroponte had established "mission managers" to focus on leading community approaches to difficult intelligence problems—initially North Korea and Iran. In 2010, the Iran mission manager was Norm Roule, who had turned his office into a coordination center, pulling together intelligence from around the community, piecing together the overall picture on everything from the nuclear reactor at Bushehr to political opposition to President Mahmoud

Ahmadinejad. His group was lining up the human and signals intelligence with overhead reconnaissance and defining gaps in collection—things our sources couldn't tell us. Social media became an important component of understanding Iran after the 2009 elections and the "Green Movement" protests, which were the largest demonstrations in the thirty years since the Iranian revolution. Norm's office wasn't running an operation or doing any collection on Iran. It was simply helping the agencies understand each other's work and coordinating so they could work together more effectively.

Robert and I wanted to use that model to create seventeen national intelligence managers, some whose geographic areas of responsibility would be roughly analogous to the DOD combatant commands—like NIM-Europe and NIM-Africa—and others functional—like NIM-Cyber and NIM-Counterterrorism. Using what Norm's office was doing as a template, each NIM would create a strategy to make the most of the IC's collection and analysis capabilities and to identify where we should invest in new ones. We envisioned, given a year or more for all seventeen NIM offices to establish themselves and the unifying intelligence strategies for their areas of responsibility, that they would be able to work together to put rigor behind the compilation of all the government's intelligence needs, the top tier of which was made up of the president's priorities.

Increasingly my own time was consumed with requests from the White House and Congress. On Monday, December 20, I visited Capitol Hill to answer questions from senators who were about to vote on New START—the updated Strategic Arms Reduction Treaty between Russia and the United States, which was up for ratification. I sat in a small room from 1:00 P.M. to 3:30, and Pat Roberts was the only senator to stop by. When the designated time was up, I went straight to my SUV, and my protective detail drove me to the Eisenhower Executive Office Building to participate in an interview with Diane Sawyer of ABC News, along with John Brennan and Janet Napolitano. I'd been out of communications for almost four hours, and I didn't bother to check my BlackBerry during the short ride, a mistake I came to regret and tried never to repeat.

On camera, Ms. Sawyer opened with "First of all, London—how serious is it? Any implication that it was coming here? Director Clapper?" I didn't have a clue what her cryptic question referred to. She looked at me until I finally asked, "London?" John jumped in and explained that the

UK had just made a series of arrests of suspected terrorists. I'd been following the surveillance in and around the London area but hadn't known about the arrests. Sawyer smelled blood, and came back to the subject a little later, commenting, "I was a little surprised you didn't know about London." I was a little irritated at that point and realized I was in trouble, but responded, "I'm sorry, I didn't." John, to his great credit, complained to Sawyer about her stunt after the interview.

ABC waited twenty-four hours to air the interview and recut it to make me look completely out of touch. As was the reflexive response in Washington, some members of Congress called for me to be fired. After an NSC meeting, the president asked me to walk with him back to the Oval Office. He assured me that I had his confidence and enjoined me to learn a lesson from the experience, which I did: Always know what's in the headlines going into any interview. I got a very nice note from Secretary Clinton, which closed with the sentiment, "Finally, as a longtime observer—and sometimes victim—of the press 'gotcha game,' don't let the First Amendment get you down! All the best, Hillary."

In contrast to that bad day, February 18, 2011, was an extremely happy one for me, when Stephanie O'Sullivan was confirmed and became the principal deputy DNI—the PDDNI—which she pronounced as "P-Diddy." Before Stephanie's arrival, I could assign big tasks to tremendously talented staff members and know they'd get done, but I still felt obligated to keep track of all the things I'd delegated. Stephanie stood beside me and helped shoulder the entire load. We approached problems from very different viewpoints: me as a political science major and former Air Force officer who'd spent a career in the defense intelligence ecosystem, she as an engineer who'd started her career designing and building marvelous technology projects and then gone on to build teams of engineers and eventually—as CIA's director of science and technology—lead an organization of some of the most brilliant scientists and technologists in the world. Although we approached intelligence challenges from widely contrasting perspectives, I can't recall a time when we *ever* disagreed about priorities or how to respond to them. More than once, I publicly adapted a line I'd first heard from Bob Gates: "Stephanie speaks for me, even when we haven't spoken."

While Stephanie could speak for me, I was still less than comfortable speaking publicly for the community. A few weeks after she arrived, I managed to cause yet another distraction, this one during our annual series of worldwide threat assessment hearings. Every year between February and April, the DNI, accompanied by selected IC agency directors, appears in open hearings before the intelligence and armed services committees to discuss the threats to the United States and our allies around the world. These open hearings are fraught with potential pitfalls. One, of course, is the risk of compromising sources, methods, and tradecraft. Another is unintentionally offending another country—on at least three occasions, one of our ambassadors got summoned by a head of state to answer for something I said during testimony as DNI. A third pitfall is that the televised hearings could turn into a game of "stump the chump," in which congressional members asked about parochial interests or obscure happenings in the far corners of the world, or about classified programs they knew I couldn't discuss in open sessions. This led me to lament, years later, that talking to Congress publicly about classified intelligence matters while trying to protect vital intelligence sources and methods is one of my *favorite* things to do—ranking right up there with undergoing oral surgery and folding fitted sheets. I was often struck by the contrast in how congressional members would often seem to play to the camera in open session, but when we'd adjourn to a closed, secure room to talk about the classified details, discussions were more businesslike and less frequently polemical. I can validate what Bob Gates wrote: When "the little red light went on atop a television camera, it had the effect of a full moon on a werewolf."

In March, I got into trouble on camera—again—when Senator Joe Manchin of West Virginia asked me, in an awkwardly worded question, which nation-state posed the greatest threat to the United States—not a threat to US interests, but to the United States. I tried to clarify the question, and then responded that only Russia and China, with their nuclear arsenals, posed a "mortal threat." I added the caveat that I was talking about "capability," and that "intent" was an entirely different matter. I also said that my biggest immediate concern was still non-nation-state terrorism. I wound up offending Russia and China, and once again the "fire the DNI" refrain arose.

While all this was taking place, I was brought in on an extremely closely held intelligence project. Since September 11, 2001, the United States Intelligence Community had one mission that surpassed all others, at least emotionally: to find, and capture or kill, Osama bin Laden. In early 2011 we finally had a promising lead on his whereabouts. Truly stellar intelligence work by some dedicated analysts from CIA, NSA, and NGA had tracked him to a small compound in Abbottabad, Pakistan, near the Pakistan Military Academy. Collecting intelligence on the compound was a particularly difficult problem, because the site was a hundred miles from the Afghanistan border. Pakistan was a key ally in the Afghan war, and the bulk of our supply lines traversed it, yet we didn't trust the Pakistani Inter-Services Intelligence agency—at all. In fact, they had a history of tipping off targets (targets for us, proxies for them) ahead of raids. At the same time, the Pakistanis were very suspicious about US intelligence, which made it difficult to conduct human intelligence work. It was hard not to wonder if some of the Pakistanis knew bin Laden was in Abbottabad and were protecting him.

Bin Laden himself went to extreme lengths to minimize his exposure to prying eyes and cameras that might see into the compound's garden. While we had glimpses of a "tall man in white" strolling there, intelligence analysts were unable to identify any communications that would verify his presence, given his meticulous communications-security discipline. In the end, while CIA experts led the effort to confirm that the man was in fact bin Laden, it was really superb teamwork and intelligence integration that built the case. The CIA has rightly received a great deal of credit for their incredible work, but the ensuing raid would not have happened without the efforts of NSA and NGA as well.

As spring approached, the briefings to National Security Adviser Tom Donilon became more intense, urgent, and frequent. Two questions consumed those meetings: How certain were we that bin Laden was there? And what would be the best way to capture or kill him? Each senior member of the national security team, including me, had different perspectives and levels of confidence in the intelligence we had. By March and April, we were meeting regularly with the president and vice president and discussing four options: obliterate the compound with an air strike (in a suburban setting, in a nation we weren't at war with), use a remotely piloted drone to perform a more surgical strike, conduct a special operations raid, or continue to gather more intelligence. Other accounts I've read discount option four, but without confirmation that bin Laden was in the compound, doing nothing and continuing to watch was a perfectly valid response. It risked losing bin Laden again, but didn't risk jeopardizing Pakistani support. The analysts who had been tracking him, some for years, felt sure it was bin Laden, and though the CIA tried several innovative approaches to obtain confirmation, by April we hit the point at which we feared doing more would tip either bin Laden or the Pakistanis that we were wise to his whereabouts. The longer we waited, the more concerned we became about an inevitable leak. Sometimes, speaking difficult truths means admitting what we don't know for certain and leaving the decision maker with a tough call to make.

The final interagency briefing occurred on Thursday, April 28. The analysts presented their best case and concluded that, short of bin Laden's slipping up by taking a stroll outside the compound, the intelligence we had was as good as it was going to get. The president went around the table and asked each of us for our opinion on what course of action to take. Most felt the intelligence was sufficient enough to act upon, and most favored the raid. Bob Gates, who was personally responsible for any troops who would be put at risk, preferred the drone strike option. Vice President Biden had low confidence that the intelligence warranted the risk, and he preferred maintaining vigilance and taking no direct action. When it came around to me, I told the president that, because this was a policy decision, I was speaking as Jim Clapper and not as the DNI. I said that I preferred the idea of the raid, because special operators on the ground were rational actors, who could change the plan if they discovered that bin Laden wasn't there or that the compound was something other than what we thought it was. I told him I felt confident in the intelligence, because the experts most intimately involved had a high degree of confidence. As was the president's practice, he did not make a decision at this meeting, preferring to contemplate it further outside the Situation Room. Again, I thought of the quote from General George Patton: "The time to take counsel of your fears is before you make an important battle decision. That's the time to listen to every fear you can imagine. When you have collected all the facts and fears and made your decision, turn off all your fears and go ahead."

The following day I was told the president had made the courageous—and what proved to be correct—decision for elite Special Operations Forces to conduct a raid on April 30. As has been well documented, he and several others of the group planned to be at the White House Correspondents'

Dinner that Saturday night, which would have meant our all quietly slip-ping out to monitor the progress of the raid, but because the weather in Pakistan turned bad the raid was postponed until Sunday.

The president was in rare form at the Correspondents' Dinner, which took place just a few days after the state of Hawaii had released his long-form birth certificate, putting an end to the conspiracy theory that he was born in Kenya. Halfway through his eighteen-minute comic monologue that night, the president turned to Donald Trump, sitting three tables away from me, who had been leading the "birther" conspiracy charges. The president said, "Now, I know that he's taken some flak lately, but no one is happier, no one is prouder to put this birth certificate matter to rest than 'The Donald,' and that's because he can finally get back to focusing on the issues that matter, like: Did we fake the moon landing? What really happened in Roswell? And where are Biggie and Tupac?"

President Obama spent two and a half minutes poking fun at Trump, drawing laughter and applause throughout. He closed the bit with, "Say what you will about Mr. Trump, he certainly would bring some change to the White House," and the screens around the room showed a Photo-shopped image of the White House turned into a tacky hotel with "Trump" emblazoned across the front in neon lights. Trump smiled and waved, but after the cameras turned away, I could tell he was seething. The president remained calm, cool, and collected throughout the eve-ning; he must have realized that anything he said at the dinner would likely be overshadowed within twenty-four hours.

On Sunday morning, we gathered again in the Situation Room. Ad-miral Bill McRaven was in Afghanistan controlling the mission, although given its nature, the operation was conducted as a covert action under CIA authorities, and so Leon Panetta was nominally in charge at CIA headquarters. Much to Leon's credit, he made no effort to foster the optic that he was in command or to interfere with Bill's leadership.

Remembering stories of President Nixon ordering air strikes in Viet-nam, Tom Donilon was concerned that we not convey the image that the White House was micromanaging the raid, and so we started out in the Situation Room, all staring at a blank screen. As Bob Gates notes in his memoir, *Duty*, Air Force Brigadier General Marshall Webb was in a small adjoining "breakout" room, monitoring a video feed of the compound, and we eventually all drifted in and crowded around him. President

Obama refused to take the seat at the head of the table. After losing my seat to Denis McDonough when I took a bathroom break, I wound up standing behind Hillary Clinton to watch. That's where we were when White House photographer Pete Souza snapped the famous photograph, not in the Situation Room, but in a breakout room, just across the hall.

Given the historical importance of that photo, I would make two observations. One: Robert Cardillo, who was sitting to Vice President Biden's right, was literally cropped out of history. Two: I want to take a rare opportunity to correct Bob Gates. In his memoir, he notes that the photo was later famously Photoshopped to portray everyone as superheroes. Bob writes, "Obama was Superman; Biden, Spiderman; Hillary, Wonder Woman; and I, for some reason, was the Green Lantern." No, Bob. Biden was the Flash, and you were the Martian Manhunter. My comic-book collection may have been lost to antiquity, but I remember. Denis McDonough was Photoshopped as Green Lantern, and that would have been me if he hadn't taken my seat.

To answer the other question often raised about the photo—yes, it *was* that tense in the room. As Bob notes, we watched as the first helicopter crashed. Bill McRaven came over our link to reassure us that the raiders would go to a backup plan, which they did, but we still worried about the mission and egressing the compound. When the team went into the house there was nothing but silence for what seemed like an eternity. Finally we heard "Geronimo—EKIA." "Geronimo" was the code word for Osama bin Laden, and "EKIA" meant "enemy killed in action."

I think everyone in that room appreciated what a courageous decision the president had made in ordering the raid. We'd all played out the scenarios for what might happen if the attack went wrong, either by the Pakistanis being alerted to the plan, by American forces encountering resistance on the ground, or by their inability to get access to the compound—or if the intelligence had been wrong.

The public history of US intelligence traditionally reads as a narrative of failures and shortcomings, certainly dating back to the US misadventure in Southeast Asia. These include our virtual nonparticipation in Grenada, our failure to foresee precisely the collapse of the Soviet Union, not serving General Schwarzkopf well with imagery during the Gulf War, and our having very little foundational intelligence for Somalia and later Afghanistan. Errors were made that led to massive tragedies, such as allegedly not "connecting the dots" to prevent 9/11, and then connecting dots that weren't really there, which helped to lead us into Iraq. And there were mistakes that could have ended in tragedy and didn't, like Umar Farouk Abdulmutallab boarding a flight on Christmas Day 2009 with explosives in his underwear.

When we get it right, though—when we stop someone from boarding a plane bound for the United States or when we prevent dangerous materials from being shipped across borders—we almost never discuss it publicly, mostly because we don't want to lose our ability to repeat our success. And here's the interesting point about intelligence officers and special operators working together on that particular raid: On almost any given night, similar raids built on similar partnerships were almost certainly occurring somewhere in Afghanistan. We were having success after success, devastating al-Qaida and the Taliban leadership, and not revealing our achievements or the operations that led to them—unless the operation went wrong, which meant a tragedy that required a public accounting. In planning the Abbottabad raid together, our communities had certainly discussed our hope that within Osama bin Laden's house, we'd find the intelligence that would enable operations to put the final nail in the coffin of al-Qaida in Afghanistan.

An intelligence failure in Abbottabad would have had major diplomatic repercussions and might have endangered Pakistani support for the fight against the terrorists, a potential outcome we were all aware of and dreaded—I suspect no one more than the president. But on May 1, 2011, the intelligence had been right and the raid a success. After more than a decade of searching, we'd found the mastermind of the 9/11 terrorist attacks and had removed him from the battlefield. But there was no immediate celebration, no shouting, no fist pumping, no high-fiving. We only breathed a collective sigh and glanced around at one another before smiling—not in jubilation, but in relief.

Of course, the mission wasn't over, and we didn't leave the breakout room until the team had gathered up all the hard drives, cell phones, thumb drives, books, and anything else they thought might have intelligence value, and left the compound, and no one left the Situation Room until the team was safely in Afghan airspace. Admiral Mike Mullen drew the short straw to place a phone call to Pakistani Army Chief of Staff General Kayani to inform him of the raid, before President Obama announced bin Laden's death to the American public. Based on the surprised reaction he got, Mike was confident that the Pakistanis hadn't realized that bin Laden was in Abbottabad. I visited Pakistan a month and a half later, after accompanying Hillary on a trip to India, and the hostility with which I was treated confirmed in my mind that they had indeed been unaware of bin Laden's whereabouts and considered our raid an egregious affront to their national sovereignty.

I was still at the White House at 11:35 P.M. when President Obama strode to the microphone and announced, "Tonight, I can report to the American people and to the world, the United States has conducted an operation that killed Osama bin Laden, the leader of al-Qaida and a terrorist who's responsible for the murder of thousands of innocent men, women, and children." By the time he spoke, people had already heard rumors that the CIA and SEAL Team Six were involved in the raid. That, of course, was an oversimplification of both the intelligence and special operations efforts. The incredible contributions from NSA and NGA never really made it into public awareness, but that night, our Intelligence Community got a public win.

I will never forget hearing the crowd that had gathered across the street in Lafayette Park, chanting "USA, USA!" (Leon later claimed they were chanting "CIA, CIA!"). For days and weeks after the raid, the CIA public phone lines rang with callers who just wanted to offer their gratitude. It gave long-awaited closure to the nation, to the Intelligence Community—especially the CIA—and, for that matter, to me personally. I had been DNI for just nine months, and I wondered if I'd just realized what would be the high point of my tenure.

CHAPTER SIX

Benghazi

Four and a half months before the raid at Abbottabad, a fruit vendor in the small town of Sidi Bouzid, located near the center of Tunisia, reached the end of his fuse. Something close to one third of the locals were unemployed, and Mohamed Bouazizi had tried for years to get a job—any job. The only way he could support his family was by selling fruit from a cart, while dealing with regular harassment from police and government officials who couldn't cite any actual laws he was violating. On December 17, a local bureaucrat, accompanied by a few other officials, approached him and announced she was confiscating his fruit, his scale, and his cart. He resisted, and in front of the crowd that had grown to watch the drama, she slapped him, or perhaps she asked for a bribe before the confrontation got physical. Witness accounts vary on the details. Afterward, Bouazizi, perhaps injured, walked to the local governor's office and demanded compensation for his loss, or demanded return of his scale, or just demanded to be heard. When the governor refused to see him, Bouazizi procured a can of gasoline, or maybe paint thinner, walked back to the middle of the street in front of the governor's office, poured the liquid over himself, and set himself on fire. Witnesses agree that less than an hour passed from the time of the initial confrontation to his self-immolation. Bouazizi lived another eighteen days before slipping away on January 4. He never regained consciousness and never learned what his action had triggered.

The Intelligence Community had been warning about potential instability in Northern Africa and Southwest Asia for many years. Factors like food and water shortages and poor living conditions—increasingly driven by climate change—oppression of political freedoms, corruption by autocratic governments and rulers who had been in place for decades, massive unemployment leading to a breakdown in social structure, and a large population bubble of young, single, disaffected men in those parts of the world made them extremely unstable—and a fertile recruiting ground for al-Qaida. By 2010, the group had three major "franchises" in Africa and the Middle East: al-Qaida in the Islamic Maghreb, operating in Northern Africa, primarily Algeria; al-Qaida in the Arabian Peninsula, operating in Yemen and Saudi Arabia; and al-Qaida in Iraq, which had rebranded itself as the "Islamic State in Iraq" in 2006 after a falling-out with al-Qaida in Afghanistan, partly over the Iraqi group's use of brutal terrorist tactics against fellow Muslims. Of course, the other factor leading to the formation of al-Qaida in Iraq was the US invasion in 2003 and the resulting anti-US insurgency, in which the organization took a lead role. But in December 2010, the same destabilizing factors that led to terrorists gaining a hold in its neighbors had dramatically different results in Tunisia.

Tunisia is much smaller than its neighbors—Algeria and Morocco to its west, and Libya and Egypt to its east—but it has a long coastline on the Mediterranean Sea, including Africa's northernmost point, less than a hundred miles from Sicily. Algeria is about the size of the entire US South, from Texas and Oklahoma all the way to Delaware. Libya is about the same size if you take out two thirds of Texas. Tunisia is a little smaller than Florida, but because of its long, more densely populated coastline, its population tops 11 million people—almost twice that of Libya. Still, Western society hasn't thought of Tunisia as a major power in the civilized world since Carthage was destroyed by Rome in 146 BC. Two millennia later, a fruit vendor in a small, central-Tunisian city sparked a fire that would engulf North Africa and the Arabian Peninsula.

Just a few hours after Mohamed Bouazizi's dramatic action, protests began in Sidi Bouzid. Demonstrators shared pictures and video on Facebook and Twitter, and the unrest soon spread to other cities. Tunisian president Zine El Abidine Ben Ali had been in power since 1987, twenty-three years of quickly quelling disturbances with violence. However, even as police cracked down, injuring and killing demonstrators, the strife continued, with riots erupting nationwide. On January 14, 2011, Ben Ali fled Tunisia for Saudi Arabia, resigning the presidency en route. Protests continued until March 9, when Ben Ali's political party was dissolved and all its members removed from power. Tunisia would struggle for another three and a half years to establish an accepted, functioning, elected government, but the people eventually took control of their destiny.

This "Arab Spring," which did not actually start on the Arabian Peninsula, spread across North Africa and into the Middle East. By February 10, when I testified in my first televised congressional hearing as DNI, presenting the Intelligence Community's annual worldwide threat assessment, protests were under way in Egypt, Algeria, Sudan, Djibouti, Oman, Yemen, Jordan, and Saudi Arabia, with the situation in Egypt the most tense and violent. In the previous few weeks, my schedule had been shuffled repeatedly to attend Principals Committee and National Security Council meetings. At each, I was required to give an intelligence update, which mostly consisted of noting the new protests and military crackdowns, along with briefing any intercepted communications that gave us insight into how specific leaders planned to respond to what was happening in their respective countries.

I always cautioned the president and secretaries that intelligence work was about acquiring and assessing foreign secrets, not predicting events or reading minds. In the case of Egypt, for example, unless and until Hosni Mubarak decided for himself and then informed someone of his intentions, we didn't have much insight on when he might step down as president of Egypt or whether he would order troops to fire on the protesters in Tahrir Square. My role was to offer the Intelligence Community's assessment, for instance, that President Mubarak was unlikely to hold power for long, and that when he stepped aside, the Egyptian military would likely take control of the government, at least in the short term. If Egypt held elections within the next few months, we assessed that the Muslim Brotherhood was the only political party well enough organized to win a majority of seats in the country's parliament. While in 2011 the Brotherhood in Egypt was mostly focused on secular concerns of Egyptians, as opposed to Muslim Brotherhood groups in other nations that were encouraging terrorist acts, the Egyptian Brotherhood did have its roots in jihadism, and its hardline and moderate factions were fighting for control. The Egyptian Muslim Brotherhood was unlikely to be friendly to American interests, but we could probably work with them if they came to power.

There were other scenarios, both better and worse. If there was a significant delay before Egyptian elections, other political parties could get organized and have a better chance of holding or sharing power, although there was a chance that the Egyptian military could maintain control indefinitely, a situation no one wanted. With those assessments on the table, I left the discussion to Secretaries Gates and Clinton, and Vice President Biden, who typically led the debate on what to do. After a meeting on February 1, President Obama had reached out to President Mubarak, asking him to step down peacefully, "now."

In getting ready for the February 10 threat assessment hearing with the House Intelligence Committee, I hadn't participated in any specific preparatory sessions on what was happening with the Arab Spring, partly because I was reading a lot about it for White House meetings, and partly because the situation was changing so quickly that studying a week in advance would mean absorbing facts that would have changed by the hearing. But the Arab Spring wasn't the only "worldwide threat" concern, and so, between January 25 and February 8, I specifically brought experts in to help me study the specifics regarding North Korea, China, Russia, Iraq, Iran, Yemen, Africa as a whole, Afghanistan and Pakistan, counterterrorism, proliferation of weapons of mass destruction, cyberspace, Latin America, Guantanamo Bay, WikiLeaks and counterintelligence, intelligence information sharing, and transnational threats. I also went through three "murder boards," at which my senior staff played the roles of senators and representatives and tried to stump the chump. I quickly learned that I wasn't easily tripped up by trivia or "clever" questions; instead, I had more trouble with questions that *seemed* to be about intelligence matters but were really about partisan or personal politics to which I wasn't attuned.

In my opening statement on February 10, I cited international terrorism and the proliferation of weapons of mass destruction as the threats of most concern to the IC. Of the Arab Spring, I said that we'd consistently reported on tensions and instability in the Middle East and Africa, but when it came to predicting the specific triggers that could lead to regime collapse, "We are not clairvoyant."

During the hearing, Representative Sue Myrick asked me about the threat that the Muslim Brotherhood posed to the United States. I tried to explain that there really was no transnational "Muslim Brotherhood" organization, and, at the moment, the political party by that name in Egypt was more concerned about the day-to-day concerns of Egyptians than threatening America, but unfortunately that came out as "The term Muslim Brotherhood is an umbrella term for a variety of movements. In the case of Egypt, a very heterogeneous group, largely secular, which has eschewed violence and has decried al-Qaida as a perversion of Islam." I believe rather than "secular," the word I'd meant to use was "pragmatic." Regardless, I was skewered in the press as being out of touch with reality—how could the Brotherhood be considered secular when the word "Muslim" was right there in their name? For two hours we'd discussed serious threats to the nation and to US interests around the world, but the media coverage focused on my "gaffe," which I found both irritating and distracting.

The following day Vice President Omar Suleiman announced Mubarak's resignation as president of Egypt, and the Supreme Council of the Egyptian armed forces took control of the government. On Saturday, February 13, Arab Spring–related protests began in Iraq, where the United States was negotiating with the Iraqi government over the expiring status-of-forces agreement that governed the 47,000 troops still in the country. On February 14, protests started in Bahrain, home to the US Navy's Fifth Fleet and another 7,000 US troops. On February 15, protests in Benghazi, Libya, were put down by military force. On February 16, I testified at the Senate Intelligence Committee's televised threat hearing—for once not saying anything that prompted Congress to call for my resignation. In late February and March 2011, with the military Supreme Council in stable control of Egypt, our focus on the Arab Spring uprisings shifted to Libya.

As a quick geospatial and historic orientation—which becomes *very important* shortly—looking eastward from the northernmost point of Tunisia, the African coastline falls sharply to the south to the border with Libya, where it curves eastward. The capital city of Tripoli is about halfway along the two hundred miles or so of Libyan shoreline running to the east before it dips southward again at the western shore of the Gulf of Sirte. On the eastern shore is the port of Benghazi, Libya's second largest city. Benghazi and Tripoli are about four hundred miles apart. About 85 percent of Libya's population lives near the coastline, which has been the case stretching back for millennia. "Libya" didn't really exist as a nation until 1951. Before that, the three regions of Libya—Cyrenaica and the city of Benghazi to the east, Tripolitania and Tripoli to the northwest, and Fezzan to the southwest—had for centuries mostly been sequentially governed as separate colonies of various empires. Then, in 1951, eight years after seizing the colonies from Italy in 1943, the Allies put King Idris I on the Libyan throne. In 1969 Colonel Muammar Gaddafi led a military coup to overthrow the only Libyan king to ever exist, and Gaddafi officially took control as the "brother leader" in 1977, ruling Libya as an "Islamist socialist" state.

Gaddafi governed with particular animosity toward the United States, the United Kingdom, and Israel. He sponsored terrorist organizations in Syria and Palestine and was responsible for both the 1986 West Berlin nightclub bombing that targeted US service members and for the 1988 Lockerbie bombing, the in-flight destruction of Pan Am Flight 103. Since the 1970s he had also sought to make Libya a nuclear power by attempting to buy weapons or production equipment—sequentially from China, the Soviets, Pakistan, and India. He hadn't succeeded in doing so, but Libya did launch a large chemical weapons program. After 9/11, President Bush purportedly warned Gaddafi to either abandon his chemical weapons and his nuclear program, or the United States would destroy them. After the American invasion of Iraq in 2003, whether from fear of a similar incursion or as an effort to mend his diplomatic relationship with the West, Gaddafi did give up his nuclear program and asked for international assistance in ridding Libya of chemical weapons. By 2011 much of his stockpile had been removed, but large amounts of mustard gas and the chemicals to make sarin were still under Libyan military control, along with bombshells configured to deliver chemical weapons. We didn't know if Gaddafi would use those remaining weapons to quell protests in his country.

On February 17, 2011, groups opposed to Gaddafi's government in Tripoli declared a "day of rage," quickly seizing Benghazi. Libyan army and police forces either stood aside or joined the cause. Gaddafi's country had effectively split: He maintained control of Tripoli, its population of more than 1 million, and territory to the west, while the opposition—a mix of civilians, police, armed forces, and Islamist militias who'd found a common cause—held Benghazi, its population of seven hundred thousand, and the territory to the east. As the opposition pushed west as far as the port of Misrata, it looked to many observers like another North African strongman would fall, one the United States government truly despised. But Gaddafi had no intention of going quietly. His loyal military units fired into public demonstrations in the capital city, and other military units pushed eastward to retake territory. Along with most other nations, the United States closed its embassy in Tripoli and evacuated as many of its citizens as it could. The international team working on destroying the country's chemical weapons also left the embattled country.

In Washington, we continued to hold contentious National Security Council meetings with the president. The intelligence I presented pointed to Gaddafi's having all the military advantages, including control of the Libyan air defense structure, which was the second largest (after Egypt's) in the Middle East. The Libyan government had thirty-one major surface-to-air missile (SAM) sites, a radar complex focused on protecting the coastline, and a large number of portable SAM systems. Its air force had a few hundred aircraft, and although not very many were operational, they'd used both fighters and helicopters to attack opposition forces and protesters. Further, the 32nd Libyan army brigade and the 9th regiment were robustly equipped with Russian equipment: air defense, artillery, tanks, and mechanized equipment. They were disciplined and loyal to Gaddafi, and I gave the US intelligence assessment that, without outside intervention, they would regain ground and eventually prevail.

At those meetings Hillary Clinton pushed for military intervention in pursuit of regime change, while Bob Gates pushed back, pointing out that we already had two Middle East wars to prosecute, and because of Gaddafi's formidable air defenses, setting up a no-fly zone would require extensive strikes, drawing resources from the other wars. I could see the reasoning on both sides of that argument, and I could tell that President Obama did, too. I didn't envy his having to decide on a course of action.

On March 3 the president addressed Libya in a public statement: "The United States and the entire world continues to be outraged by the appalling violence against the Libyan people. The United States is helping to lead an international effort to deter further violence, put in place unprecedented sanctions to hold the Gaddafi government accountable and support the aspirations of the Libyan people." He committed US military planes to help refugees return home, particularly Egyptian citizens who'd fled west into Tunisia, and he pledged humanitarian assistance. Later in his remarks, he said, "The violence must stop. Muammar Gaddafi has lost legitimacy to lead, and he must leave. Those who perpetrate violence against the Libyan people will be held accountable. And the aspirations of the Libyan people for freedom, democracy, and dignity must be met." He stopped just short of committing the US military to make that happen. The following week, with the United States and NATO still on the sidelines, Gaddafi's forces pushed east toward Benghazi as Libya became entrenched in a full-blown civil war.

On March 10 I again gave televised testimony in presenting the IC's worldwide threat assessment to the Senate Armed Services Committee. I knew that the intelligence update on Libya was going to be controversial. While the president had called for Gaddafi to step down and the press and public supported the forces that opposed him, we still weren't *doing* anything. The day before the hearing, French president Nicolas Sarkozy had officially recognized the National Transitional Council in Benghazi as the true government of Libya. We had not.

During the hearing, when I was asked whether the United States should officially acknowledge the government in Benghazi, I demurred, saying that that question was in the policy lane, not intelligence. But congressional questions about the status of the civil war in Libya and how the opposition to Gaddafi was faring did require "truth to power" answers. I couldn't deflect them or paint the picture as rosy—neither for Congress nor for the American people. So, in response to Chairman Carl Levin's and Vice Chairman John McCain's opening questions, I replied, "Gaddafi is in this for the long haul. I don't think he has any intention—despite some of the press speculation to the contrary—of leaving. From all the evidence we have, which I'd be prepared to discuss in closed session, he appears to be hunkering down for the duration." Later in the hearing, in response to a question from Senator Joe Lieberman, I went further in assessing what might happen without outside intervention. "It's a stalemate back and forth, but I think, over the longer term, that the regime will prevail." I was again lambasted in the press for speaking intelligence truth that went against the more appealing narrative that policy makers in Congress and executive departments were pushing. That afternoon, National Security Adviser Tom Donilon undercut my assessment, calling it a "static and one-dimensional assessment," and Senator Lindsey Graham called for me to be fired. That night, back at the office, I took a call from John McCain, who said that I had his support to keep "telling it like it is." He offered that, while he and his close friend Lindsey often agreed on issues, he thought Senator Graham had "shot from the lip" on this one.

Nine days after the hearing, with a UN resolution in hand, the US military began taking out Libyan air defenses, first with cruise missiles, and then with escorted bombing runs. With help from the British, French, and Canadian air forces, and drawing on targets identified by multinational intelligence efforts, the US military established a safe no-fly zone in four days and turned the mission over to NATO control. Gaddafi pleaded for the United States and then NATO to stop the attacks, citing his cooperation with weapons inspectors, his voluntary disarmament of his nuclear program, and his restraint from using chemical weapons in his current civil struggle. It was far too late, and no one in the West paid attention. However, I believe North Korea and Iran took careful note of what happens when you give up your nuclear program, and Bashar al-Assad in Syria saw what happens to dictators who show restraint.

Under the NATO airspace umbrella and with some limited close-air support, the opposition forces in Libya took the initiative. In June, realizing he could no longer prevail, Gaddafi offered a cease-fire to hold elections, promising to step aside if he didn't win. The war continued, and on August 22, the opposition penetrated Tripoli. By then Gaddafi had escaped the city and was nowhere to be found. Within days the opposition announced they had control of the capital. However, no one was in charge, and pro-Gaddafi troops still roamed the streets, firing on fighters and demonstrators alike.

On October 20, the last of Gaddafi's forces was pinned down in the port city of Sirte as the opposition closed in, unaware that Gaddafi was with them. Attempting to flee, Gaddafi raced out of the city in a convoy of seventy-five cars, but was spotted and fired on by NATO aircraft. He took shelter in a storm-water culvert, where he was found by opposition fighters. The jubilant group dragged him off, and within hours, the National Transitional Committee announced his death, although they couldn't agree on how he died. One member said he was captured alive and executed. Another claimed he was caught in crossfire and found dead. Soon, several cell-phone videos posted on the internet told a different story. In one, his captors slowly tortured him with a bayonet as he screamed and pleaded for his life. For US intelligence, it was a chilling reminder that we had no idea who or what was going to replace Gaddafi in Libya. At the moment, no one was in control.

Despite sporadic fighting as mercenaries and pro-Gaddafi groups continued to clash with the new government's forces in the shadows of the capitol, the United States had reopened its embassy in Tripoli on September 22. Violence was prevalent throughout the country, as massive numbers of people tried to return home. Tunisia and Egypt reported that they had received some five hundred thousand Libyan refugees in 2011, and many more had gone south or been evacuated via flights and ferries into Europe. The UN High Commissioner for Refugees estimated *another* two hundred thousand people were displaced internally, having abandoned their homes without leaving Libya. In a nation of just six million people, those were huge numbers.

The National Transitional Council nominally remained the national governing body, but its focus was on drafting a national constitution and preparing for elections, not governing. The Libyan people hadn't governed themselves in 2,800 years, and in the six decades since the Allies had made Libya its own kingdom in 1951, they'd had one king and then forty-two years of autocratic rule. Self-governance was a novel idea, and while representative democracy seemed, through an American lens, to be the obvious, best end-state, the Libyan people weren't united behind the council's efforts. In January 2012, its headquarters in Benghazi was attacked by protesters who wanted the country to become an Islamic caliphate, governed by Sharia law. No one was hurt, but the incident demonstrated that the council was not in control.

On Friday, April 27, I met with Chris Stevens, who was slated to replace Gene Cretz as the US ambassador to Libya. Chris had an affinity for the Libyan revolution. When during the worst of the war—from March until November of 2011—the United States had closed its embassy in Tripoli and evacuated its diplomats, including Ambassador Cretz, Chris had been the US special representative to the National Transitional Council in Benghazi. During our brief meeting, he struck me as an American patriot and a true believer in democracy. He was elated that he would be present for Libya's first free elections.

Before he left my office, we discussed the deteriorating security situation in Libya and the very real dangers posed by local militias, some of which held extreme Islamist ideologies. Security was reliable for the embassy in Tripoli, but he could not be as certain about conditions else-where in the city or around the country. He had no illusions about the danger he was going back to, but he indicated that he felt a US presence could make a difference to the birth of democracy in this new, indepen-dent nation, and so it was worth calculated risks. We talked about work-ing with the CIA and about where to draw the line between intelligence and diplomacy. My last words as he was heading out the door still haunt me. As he glanced back I told him, "Stay safe."

Chris arrived in Tripoli on May 22, 2012. Libyan national elections were held on July 7, and the National Transitional Council handed power to the General National Congress on August 8 in a ceremony on Martyrs' Square. Intelligence reports noted that the government still had little con-trol of the security situation, and that al-Qaida was attempting to estab-lish a foothold in the country, which they'd been unable to do while Gaddafi had ruled. Local militias with heavy military equipment, rem-nants from the war, controlled the streets, particularly in places like Benghazi, where a dozen or more militias were rivals for power. Some supported the government; others didn't. In June a group called Ansar al-Sharia had paraded through Benghazi with artillery, demanding the National Transitional Council abandon the planned elections and instead impose Sharia law. We in the IC knew that Chris was facing an uncertain and dangerous situation.

Meanwhile, US policy focus had shifted back to Egypt, where the Muslim Brotherhood had—as we'd assessed they would—taken control of the government through elections and appointed Mohamed Morsi as president. We were also watching Syria, where the International Com-mittee of the Red Cross had declared that Arab Spring hostilities had devolved into a civil war. Opposition to Assad grew as he exhibited no restraint when attacking protesters, but the situation was much more complicated for US intelligence and diplomacy than Libya had been un-der Gaddafi. Syria shared borders with Israel (a close friend), Turkey (a NATO ally), Iraq (where 47,000 US troops were still fighting an insurrec-tion), Jordan, and Lebanon. Assad was backed by Iran's government and Russia. The Russians certainly wouldn't allow the UN Security Council to pass a resolution authorizing the use of force in Syria, and—apart from the cost and risk attached to it—establishing a no-fly zone wouldn't nec-essarily enable the resistance to take Assad down.

Because 2012 was an election year in the United States, politicians were weighing in with calls to "arm the rebels" in Syria, particularly Senators McCain and Graham. The Republican narrative held that President Obama simply refused to do the "right thing" and support the opposition to Assad. But from an intelligence standpoint, there were simply no good choices. There wasn't a united opposition force, and many of the resistance fighters were as unsavory as Assad. Some were even affiliated or allied with the Islamic State in Iraq—not exactly whom we wanted to arm.

On Tuesday, September 11, the eleventh anniversary of the attacks on the World Trade Center and Pentagon, a local militia attacked a low-security diplomatic facility in Benghazi, Libya. In the course of the next several hours Ambassador Chris Stevens and three other Americans lost their lives. It took weeks to record many eyewitness accounts—which varied wildly—and acquire, analyze, and correlate video from security cameras, intercepted cell-phone transmissions, and an unarmed Predator drone that arrived on scene an hour and a half after the initial attack. The Predator filmed the buildings burning and the final escape of the survivors from the diplomatic facility. In the coming months, NCTC director Matt Olsen and I briefed what happened that night again and again, to all of our congressional oversight committees and several of the eight—*eight*—congressional investigations. In the course of all those briefings, I became intimately familiar with the consolidated intelligence picture of what we knew, what we thought, and what we didn't know.

At about 9:40 P.M., a group of men, some affiliated with Ansar al-Sharia and some armed, pushed past the main gate of the compound and ran into it, firing guns into the air. The local militia that had been hired as guards immediately fled or dropped their weapons, or both. On the security tapes I've seen, the invaders run right past the building in which most of the Americans are hiding, gleefully skipping around the compound. They don't hunt for hostages. They don't secure diplomatic materials or posts. They don't take up military positions to secure the compound. Instead, they start looting and vandalizing, spray-painting graffiti and stealing Xboxes, clothes, and anything of value they can find. One guy is seen running out of a building with a bottle of ketchup. Other random people stroll in through the gate, joking around or trying to take part in the looting while they could. At some point, the intruders stumble onto cans of gasoline beside a generator. They spread the gasoline around and light the main building on fire.

As soon as they realized there had been a security breach, Chris Stevens, information management officer Sean Smith, and a security officer locked themselves in a safe room in the main building. When looters couldn't break into the room, they moved on to areas more easily accessed. The Americans were safe until the building was set on fire, at which point the security officer said they needed to leave. He became separated from Chris and Sean as they evacuated and, after reaching safety, went back in for them several times, diving through windows with black smoke pouring out.

Calls for help went out from the compound to other local militias, who served as security from time to time. None of them responded, either because they didn't want to incite a militia turf war, as some claimed, or because Ansar al-Sharia had placed its own calls to other militias, claiming the ongoing riot had started because the Americans had fired on protesters at the gate. Accounts vary. Either way, help was not forthcoming from the militias. However, there was a small, covert CIA compound half a mile away that *did* respond. The CIA operatives geared up, armed themselves, and were ready to go within five or ten minutes, and then waited another five or ten minutes while their boss was on the phone and radio, trying to determine precisely what kind of situation he was sending his men into. Those minutes must have been agonizing. Finally, they boarded two trucks and headed out the gate of the CIA annex, just twenty or twenty-five minutes after the gate of the State Department facility was first stormed, and eighteen minutes after they'd been notified. Knowing they would be outmanned and outgunned, they stopped several times, either in an attempt to recruit formerly friendly militia members to join them or to avoid those appearing hostile. It took thirty minutes to travel a little more than a mile, and they were unable to enlist any help.

The handful of CIA officers hit the compound as hard as they could, exchanging gunfire and scattering the looters. They quickly rallied the State Department security officers and began to search for Chris Stevens and Sean Smith, the only two people not accounted for. They found Sean inside the main building, having succumbed to smoke inhalation, but couldn't locate Chris. After about an hour of searching, they came under gunfire again. Recognizing they could be overwhelmed quickly and that they were unlikely to find Chris alive, the CIA and State Department officers all left to return to the CIA annex. It was then about 11:30, not quite two hours after the incident began. When the Americans left, the looting and vandalism resumed. At some point, a few of the Libyans came across Chris, who had also succumbed to smoke. They rushed him to a hospital, where he was pronounced dead.

At around 10:30 Benghazi time, less than an hour after the gate was breached and about when the CIA annex team was reaching the State Department facility, the first word of what was happening in Libya reached Washington, where it was approximately 4:30 in the afternoon. At 5:00 P.M. Washington time, as the CIA team in Benghazi was searching the State Department facility for Chris Stevens and Sean Smith, President Obama met with Leon Panetta, who'd replaced Bob Gates as secretary of defense, and JCS chairman General Marty Dempsey—a meeting that had been previously scheduled. At that point, buildings at the State Department facility were on fire, but the gunfire had stopped, and it seemed that the attack was over. The president and his two top DOD leaders discussed options for military intervention if violence resumed or escalated. Back in the Pentagon after the meeting with the president, Leon would order Special Operations teams to stage in Italy and Spain and be ready to go.

I was at a dinner banquet to receive an award from an industry association when my security detail pulled me aside to take an urgent phone call from Matt Olsen. I knew there had been a series of demonstrations across the Islamic world that day, related to the release on YouTube of an amateurish film that mocked the prophet Muhammad, the founder of Islam. With all the terrible content out there on the internet, I will never understand how this particular YouTube video gained so much traction and caused so much unrest. The US embassy in Cairo had been overrun by protesters of the film, who'd hauled down and burned the US flag and vandalized the facility. The CIA had warned the American ambassador in Cairo of the impending protest, and she had evacuated the embassy, so while there had been some damage, no one had been hurt. Thinking the phone call might be related to that incident, I stepped away to take it. Matt told me that a US diplomatic facility in Benghazi had been attacked, and that Chris Stevens was missing. That was all the information he had at the time. I recalled my meeting with Chris just four months earlier, and I wondered what in the world he was doing in Benghazi on the anniversary of 9/11 while anti-American protests were taking place all over the Middle East. Matt said he'd update me if he received more substantial information, but I didn't hear from him again that night.

Around midnight in Benghazi, the CIA team arrived back at their annex just as a group of attackers began shooting there. They took cover and returned fire. Over the next hour, they intermittently exchanged fire with unknown parties. The shooting stopped around 1:00 A.M. on Wednesday, September 12.

Soon after that a CIA security team from Tripoli, composed of six former Special Operations troops, including former Navy SEALs Glen Doherty and Tyrone Woods, landed in Benghazi. Heavily armed and on foot, they had no way to get to the CIA annex from the airport. Over the next several hours, they tried to cajole or bribe local militias to take them there. Finally, they persuaded someone with a few trucks to give them a ride, and they reached the annex about 5:00 A.M. Doherty and Woods took up sniper positions on the roof just as a mortar attack commenced. The first two shells missed the building, but the final three hit the roof, killing both of them. With the Americans pinned down, the attackers simply left. We don't know precisely why they did so, although I agree with the theory former CIA acting director Michael Morell offered in his account of the Benghazi attack: the attackers probably just happened to have only five mortar shells and left after firing them all.

That morning the Americans left Benghazi for Tripoli, and the four deceased Americans, along with several wounded, were flown out of Libya later in the day. The response teams Secretary Panetta had ordered to prepare couldn't reach Libya before the fighting was over, although a Marine Corps counterterrorism unit did make it to Tripoli later that day.

This narrative describes essentially what took place in Benghazi on September 11 and 12. Others have published much more detailed accounts of that night, notably David Kirkpatrick in his series "A Deadly Mix in Benghazi," in the *New York Times,* and Michael Morell in his book *The Great War of Our Time.* What I've outlined is the consensus intelligence view of the events of that night, which we have compelling physical evidence to back up, including video from the Predator, from security cameras, and from the cell phones of looters and vandals, including a recording of Chris Stevens being pulled from the burning building and the efforts to save him. While we have a great deal of information about the incident now, it's very important to me to note that we knew very little immediately after the attack.

On Wednesday I saw a trickle of information reporting that there had been a series of firefights at the State Department facility and at the CIA annex, identifying who had been injured and who had died, and the security implications of what had been left behind in Benghazi. The first real intelligence analysis attempting to assemble a coherent narrative indicated that there had been a protest outside the State Department facility, similar to the one that had overrun the Cairo embassy, and that extremist elements within the group had, with little or no planning, used the event as an opportunity to attack the facility. As it turned out, there had been no protest in Benghazi. In the years since then, many have asked how we could have gotten that point wrong. Avoiding citing classified sources, I would direct them to Kirkpatrick's series, in which he notes that some of the people who'd actually been doing the looting and vandalizing that night had believed the whole incident started as a protest outside the gate.

Two decades before all of this took place, when General Colin Powell was JCS chairman, he famously advised his intelligence briefers, "Tell me what you *know*. Tell me what you *don't know*. Then tell me what you *think*. Always distinguish which is which." If we fell short in briefing the White House and our oversight committees in Congress on what had occurred, it was as a result of failing to heed that advice, particularly when it came to our analysis that the attack had begun as a protest. That was definitely something we *thought*, not something we *knew*. Also, in my interactions with senators and representatives in the days after the attack, I reported that our analysis was based on the first reports, and first reports are never entirely accurate.

On Thursday, David Petraeus, who'd succeeded Leon Panetta as CIA director, briefed the Senate Intelligence Committee in a closed-door, classified session, and on Friday morning, September 14, he briefed the House Intelligence Committee. The House committee asked him if CIA could put together a set of unclassified "talking points" that they could use for the Sunday news shows over the weekend, which he agreed to have the agency prepare. Washington is a strange place. I can't help but wonder how it would have changed the course of US history if Dave had counter-offered, "We won't write talking points, but if your staff writes something, we'll check it for facts and classification."

I didn't become aware of the talking points until Saturday, when the CIA sent them around for interagency coordination with State Department, DOD, my office, and others. My gut feeling was that the IC's offering any talking points for politicians was a mistake. For us to tell them what they should say about the attack—and how they should say it—was crossing the line of intelligence's leaving the business of policy making to the policy makers. But I judged that by Saturday afternoon, when congressional and public affairs offices in different Cabinet departments and the White House were already squabbling over nuances like whether the State Department facility was a "consulate" or a "diplomatic post," it was too late to gracefully retract Dave's promise to provide something to Congress. That was a mistake on my part. In the end, the IC consensus for the talking points was short and simple:

- The currently available information suggests that the demonstrations in Benghazi were spontaneously inspired by the protests at the US Embassy in Cairo and evolved into a direct assault against the US diplomatic post and subsequently its annex. There are indications that extremists participated in the violent demonstrations.

- This assessment may change as additional information is collected and analyzed and currently available information continues to be evaluated.

- The investigation is ongoing, and the US Government is working w/ Libyan authorities to help bring to justice those responsible for the deaths of US citizens.

The following morning I turned the TV on and found that it wasn't just the House Intelligence Committee members who were using the talking points on Sunday morning shows. Susan Rice, the US ambassador to the United Nations, who everyone presumed was going to replace Hillary Clinton as secretary of state, was also relying on them. I wasn't even aware that Susan had received an intelligence briefing on what had occurred. (She hadn't.) On each of the shows, she discussed how "opportunistic extremist elements" had taken over a protest at the Benghazi facility gate, in what was "initially a spontaneous reaction to what had just transpired hours before in Cairo." She spoke of protests throughout the Middle East, saying, "This is a response to a hateful and offensive video that was widely disseminated throughout the Arab and Muslim world." I watched Susan's appearances with growing unease. It was true that everything she said reflected what we believed at the time. While the talking points from the CIA didn't mention the YouTube video, they did say that the demonstration in Benghazi was a spontaneous reaction to the Cairo protest, which was undisputedly a response to the detestable video. Susan's grasp of what the CIA had provided was fine. In fact, her presentation didn't bother me at all.

What did bother me was the context. It was less than two months before Election Day, and President Obama's campaign had been pushing very hard to argue that his policy decisions had led to significant progress against al-Qaida, while his opponent was claiming that the president was "soft on terrorism." Within hours of the attack, Mitt Romney, the Republican nominee for president, had accused President Obama of responding to the Benghazi attack by apologizing for the video, mistakenly referencing a statement from the Cairo embassy condemning it, hours before protests had occurred there. His facts were incorrect, but they fit the narrative, and so the accusation was effective politically.

Wearing my DNI hat, I would observe that the truth regarding the global terrorism threat in 2012 was complicated. Years of drone strikes and commando raids had decimated al-Qaida in Afghanistan, and the bin Laden raid had provided us with valuable intelligence that the CIA and Defense Department had exploited to put the network that remained on the decline. But the ideology that al-Qaida exemplified didn't need bin Laden or even al-Qaida itself to spread. The same unrest and instability that had led to the Arab Spring had provided al-Qaida "franchises," many other al-Qaida "affiliates," and even more militant groups "inspired by al-Qaida" plenty of impressionable potential recruits. Worse, the Arab Spring had deposed many of the fascist dictators who'd kept the terrorist groups in check. Notably, Muammar Gaddafi had never permitted al-Qaida to get a foothold in Libya, and of course, Saddam Hussein had largely kept it out of Iraq, though it wasn't the Arab Spring that removed him. The autocracies were in many ways like chemotherapy—they poisoned their countries and caused pain to their people, but at the same time kept the cancer of terrorism at bay. I think a reasonable discussion could be had about whether the affliction or the cure was worse. Either way, when the Middle East stopped its chemo, al-Qaida metastasized.

Taking off my DNI hat briefly to address the big question of the 2012 presidential campaign, I believe that calling President Obama soft on terrorism was ludicrous, but it was very legitimate to ask if terrorist ideologies were on the rise. In fact, with my worldwide threat assessment testimony that spring, I'd indicated that the latter was indeed the case. Did this represent an Obama policy failure? I think it's about as fair to hold the Intelligence Community to the standard of omniscience—knowing a fruit vendor's suicide would lead to the overthrow of long-standing governments throughout the Middle East—as it is to hold the president to the standard of omnipotence—having the ability to stop it. While both are completely unfair and unreasonable expectations, Congress, and to a lesser degree the public, demanded both of the administration in 2012.

So here's what bothered me. Dave Petraeus had agreed to write talking points for the House Intelligence Committee, and the CIA properly coordinated them through the interagency process. As that happened, the White House *political* team saw the talking points, added a political spin, and then sent out Susan Rice to five Sunday shows. Rather than merely sharing the intelligence perspective, Susan was using the talking points to defend the policy of the sitting US president against his opponent in the final stretch of an election. The Intelligence Community had effectively and unwittingly written campaign materials.

We suddenly found ourselves open to attack and to having our motives questioned. On the same day that Ambassador Rice appeared on TV, Senator John McCain was out rebutting her, claiming that the attack had been planned months in advance. He found a pithy line and repeated variants of it several times: "It was either willful ignorance or abysmal intelligence to think that people come to spontaneous demonstrations with heavy weapons, mortars, and the attack goes on for hours." There are two factual errors with his statement. One: There were three short attacks, one on the State Department facility, another on the CIA annex a couple of hours later, and a third on the annex after four hours or more of silence, not one sustained attack lasting all night. And two: No one brought heavy arms to the first attack. Rocket-propelled grenades came into play hours later, and the attackers didn't bring mortars into play at the CIA annex until seven hours after someone had first stormed the gate at the State Department facility. So he was wrong.

Unfortunately, we discovered we'd gotten a critical fact wrong in *our* initial assessment: There had been no protest outside the gate in Benghazi. It was a reasonable mistake, given that a crowd had gathered at the gate before rushing inside. But because the original talking point fit the narrative from President Obama's campaign, when we updated our assessment, we were accused of initially lying for the political benefit of the president. I grumbled to my staff that if we were going to be held to the standard of perfection in our initial assessments, then Congress would simply have to wait until investigations were complete before receiving any information from us from then on.

On Thursday, September 20, just nine days after the attack, Secretary Clinton, Deputy Secretary of Defense Ash Carter, JCS vice chairman Admiral Sandy Winnefeld, FBI special agent Mark Giuliano—who had just become the special agent in charge of the FBI Atlanta Field Office after serving as the head of the FBI's National Security Branch—and I briefed all the House members and then all the senators on what we had learned. By that point, we had seen the security camera video from the State Department facility and could say for certain that the incident lacked all the hallmarks of a carefully orchestrated terrorist assault. It was very hard to tell initially who were the actual attackers and who had then walked onto the compound to join in. The attackers had wandered around haphazardly and didn't seem to know the ambassador was on the compound. We laid out in great detail what we knew, what we thought, and what we didn't know. I stressed that, while there were *many* things we didn't know, we could say with certainty that the Benghazi incident was not a carefully orchestrated terrorist attack, planned months in advance.

Even after our briefing, though, some Republican lawmakers continued to insist that it *had* been a coordinated terrorist assault, similar to the 2008 attack in Mumbai, in preparation for which the gunmen had trained and coordinated for months to execute a precise, lethal mission. Their narrative was that the Americans in Benghazi had been under siege from heavy artillery and mortars for hours as al-Qaida–led terrorists assassinated the ambassador. Senator Saxby Chambliss told me afterward that it was the worst intelligence briefing he'd ever attended. Senator Bob Corker said that he'd spoken to witnesses who'd been on the ground, and that we'd gotten it wrong.

That day Secretary Clinton announced that she was appointing an Accountability Review Board, led by Ambassador Thomas Pickering and Admiral Mike Mullen, both recently retired, to investigate what led to the September 11, 2012, tragedy. I designated a recently retired senior career CIA officer who had led the Directorate of Operations—the HUMINT collection service—as the IC's representative on the board. I knew from my experiences investigating the attacks on Khobar Towers and at Fort Hood that determining the precise conditions that led to the attack was impossible. I also knew the board would have an even more difficult task than we'd had in 1996, because it could obviously not interview Chris Stevens, who'd made all the decisions that had placed him and his team on the ground in Benghazi that night. Still, I felt we had assembled a board of public servants with rich experience and whose integrity was beyond question. We just needed to give them room to investigate.

I spent the final week of September in Australia, meeting with my counterparts from the Commonwealth nations—the UK, Canada, Australia, and New Zealand—and being honored with a rare award from the Australian government for my more than two decades of promoting the intelligence relationship between our two nations, recognition that was both touching and humbling. On the plane back to Washington, I caught up with what was happening in the States, reading media clips about the hapless, hopeless, helpless, inept, incompetent DNI who'd acknowledged publicly that the Intelligence Community didn't instantly have a "God's eye, God's ear" certitude about the events in Benghazi. I considered turning the plane around and going back to Australia.

On October 9, I spoke to the 2012 GEOINT Symposium in Orlando. I had no desire to insert myself even further into the politics of the situation, but I felt I couldn't avoid saying something about Benghazi. Instead of sharing my own thoughts, I referenced an article Paul Pillar had just published on NationalInterest.org. Paul had been the deputy chief of the CIA's Counterterrorism Center, and we'd taught together at Georgetown. As I told the symposium in Orlando, "Paul's article so resonated with me, and so succinctly captured the balance and perspective, that I believe all three institutions of our system—the executive, the legislative, and the Fourth Estate, the media—need to bear in mind." I went on to quote his article at length, noting first and foremost, "The seemingly endless public rehashing of the attack in Benghazi that killed the US ambassador and three other Americans is not taking a form that serves any useful purpose. . . . The loss of the four public servants was a tragedy. The rehashing does not alleviate that tragedy."

I highlighted the four main points he'd stressed. The first was "Diplomacy—parenthetically, like military and intelligence service—is a dangerous line of work. . . . There is an inherent tension for diplomats between doing their duties well, with everything it entails regarding contact and exposure in faraway places, and living (and working) securely."

Second: "Hindsight is cheap. . . . One always can construct an after-the-fact case that any one such incident was preventable. This is not the same as saying that such incidents in the aggregate are preventable."

Third: "Resources are limited; threats are not. Even if US diplomats consistently opted for living securely over doing their jobs well, total security cannot be bought. Second-guessing about how more security should have been provided at any one facility rather than any of dozens of others elsewhere that did not happen to get attacked this time is just another example of hindsight."

Paul's fourth and crucial point: "Information about lethal incidents is not total and immediate. The normal pattern after such events is for explanations to evolve, as more and better information becomes available. We would and should criticize any investigators who settled on a particular explanation early amidst sketchy information and refuse to amend that explanation even when more and better information came in. A demand for an explanation that is quick, definite, and unchanging reflects a naïve expectation or in the present case, irresponsible politicking."

As we approached Election Day, the attack had morphed into "the Benghazi scandal." By then the conspiratorial narrative on cable networks and internet-driven news sites held that President Obama and Secretary of State Clinton had knowingly left the State Department vulnerable to a plot by al-Qaida and had then called off the rescue teams. Further, it claimed that the IC was complicit in a cover-up. I ascribed all of this to desperate political maneuvers and hoped it would go away after the election. On Tuesday, November 6, President Obama won reelection handily. On December 18 the Accountability Review Board released its report, finding flaws in State Department security decisions and assigning fault without demonizing anyone. It also lent no credence to any of the conspiracy theories that had been circulating. In February 2013, Clinton, as long planned, resigned as secretary of state and was succeeded by Senator John Kerry. Susan Rice, who had unjustly become a favorite political punching bag after her television appearances the past September, anticipating that a confirmation hearing would become a circus, had pulled her name from contention for the post, and President Obama named her to replace Tom Donilon as national security adviser.

In a sane world, the House and Senate might have each quietly conducted an investigation to review the State Department Accountability Review Board's conclusions. But Washington post-Benghazi was no longer a sane political world. Over the next four years, investigations were undertaken by the House and Senate intelligence committees, the Senate Homeland Security and Governmental Affairs Committee, the House Committee on Oversight and Government Reform, the House Committee on Foreign Affairs, the House Committee on the Judiciary, and the House Committee on Armed Services. Finally, in May 2014, twenty months after the attack, Speaker of the House John Boehner commissioned the House Select Committee on Benghazi. Each of these Republican-led committees attacked Hillary Clinton, who everyone assumed would be the Democratic nominee for president in 2016. The House Benghazi Committee released its report on June 28, 2016, less than two weeks after Clinton secured the nomination.

Matt Olsen and I spent a great deal of time briefing these various committees, describing what happened that night based on the garbled and contradictory accounts of eyewitnesses, and evidence from the security camera, Predator, and cell-phone videos. NGA produced three-dimensional depictions of the State Department facility and the CIA annex, including the routes between the facilities along which the State Department and CIA people had fled. Our presentation, particularly the security-camera video of the looters and vandals, was compelling. When we shared it with the president, he felt it both debunked the myths surrounding the attack and helped him visualize what had actually happened. I urged that we declassify the presentation, publish it, and publicly answer any questions it raised, but the White House and Justice Department pushed back, fearing it might jeopardize future prosecutions. In 2014, US Special Operations Forces captured Ahmed Abu Khattala, the leader of Ansar al-Sharia. In November 2017, he was found guilty of providing material support to terrorists and of three other charges and acquitted on fourteen others, including counts of murder. I hope that people who are interested in the truth will one day have a chance to see our presentation, including the security and Predator videos, NGA graphic projections, and our reconstruction of events.

None of the congressional committees ever rose above political narratives to objectively and dispassionately investigate what had happened at Benghazi. Matt and I were always asked if the attack was terrorism, and we always answered yes, it fit the definition, but that that was a very low bar to clear. Terrorism is an ideologically motivated attack on civilians, intended to intimidate or coerce them into a certain course of action. The attacks on the State Department facility and the CIA annex fit those parameters, which is why President Obama referred to them as an "act of terror" when he spoke about them publicly on September 12. But defining them as terrorism is not the same as saying that al-Qaida was behind the attack. I don't believe there was any real connection between Ansar al-Sharia and al-Qaida before September 11, 2012, although al-Qaida was all too eager to claim them after they struck a blow against the infidel Americans. Beyond that, the mere fact that it was an act of terrorism does not justify the need for eight separate congressional investigations. During President George W. Bush's administration, twelve separate incidents met the same definition of terrorist attacks on US diplomatic facilities. More than sixty people died in those instances, and none of them generated much congressional interest. So I have a hard time believing the investigations were ever really about getting to the truth of what happened in Benghazi.

And there's another reason I don't think the investigations were about discovering the truth or, just as important, about determining what should be done to keep anything like Benghazi from ever happening again. At no point in any of these congressional briefings were decisions made by Chris Stevens questioned. Given the circumstances of his death, Chris effectively became beyond reproach. While I admired Chris, I still have some serious questions about the decisions he made at that time: Why did he remain in Benghazi hours after the US embassy in Cairo had been overrun? Why did he go there on 9/11 in the first place, and why didn't he realize his security was completely inadequate? Confidence in oneself and one's team is admirable, but had he become too complacent? If Stevens had survived, those questions would certainly have been raised if the committees were serious about arriving at the truth—and if the committees were really interested in the truth, they'd have asked those questions anyway.

The events of that night were absolutely tragic. There is only one reason the intelligence account of the events remains controversial, and I still feel angry as I write this, five years after the attack. The singular reason we, as a nation, haven't been able to learn from the tragic events of September 11, 2012, and move forward, wiser and safer, is that a skewed version of the events perfectly suits a particular political narrative that arose at the end of a contentious presidential election, because one political party realized they could continue to benefit from manipulating the facts, and because certain people valued politics over objective truth. All of that became possible because, on a Sunday morning, five days after the attack, the sitting president's campaign opened the door to politicizing intelligence, and because those who should have known better—senior intelligence officials like me—didn't recognize what was happening in time to stop it.

CHAPTER SEVEN

Consumed by Money

The 2004 law that established the DNI outlined three primary tasks for the position. The DNI was to be the senior intelligence adviser to the president and the default leader of the Intelligence Community. My work in those two roles garnered the most public attention, but I and the ODNI staff put a great deal of time and energy into the DNI's third job—determining the budget and resources that went to the intelligence agencies through the National Intelligence Program.

Federal spending on national security tends to grow or shrink based on how threatened we feel at any moment. The same year I became DIA director, 1991, the Soviet Union dissolved, and the defense and intelligence enterprises began to reap the peace dividend. I've written about how I was asked to cut DIA's budget and workforce by 20 percent over a period of five years, how the trend of percentage cuts extended beyond my time as director, and how those reductions were affecting every agency and military service, as well as the secretary of defense and director of central intelligence. After September 11, 2001, the cash-flow valves reversed, budgets surged, and what defense services and intelligence agencies and elements didn't receive in their base budgets, they got from "overseas contingency operation" funding. OCO is "above the line" war funding and not subject to the normal budgetary processes.

Every type of funding was expanded each year, which we can now discuss because Denny Blair and then I declassified the IC's top-line annual budget number. By fiscal year 2007—the government's fiscal year runs from October 1 until September 30—the (strategic) National Intelligence

Program, determined by the DNI, had reached $43.5 billion, and the (operationally focused) Military Intelligence Program, determined by the USD(I), had reached $20 billion, for a total of $63.5 billion spent on intelligence. By fiscal year 2011, the first full budget year of my tenure as DNI, the NIP and MIP had jumped to $54.6 billion and $24 billion respectively—$78.6 billion in total—which was more than was allocated to all but two or three Cabinet departments. (By way of comparison, the overall *defense* budget jumped from $335 billion in Fiscal Year 2001 to $625 billion in Fiscal Year 2007 and $717 billion in Fiscal Year 2011, more than doubling in a decade.)

Considering those two decades of intelligence budgets—or at least, what I can say about them in an unclassified context—I would point to a fiscal reality that makes some people in Washington uncomfortable. According to the federal Office of Management and Budget, in 1992, the fiscal year of the Soviet collapse, the US government spent $290 billion more than it received in taxes—a deficit the government had to address by borrowing through issuing bonds. With the peace dividend we spent less on defense, and as the national economy came out of recession, the deficit fell each year of the 1990s. By 1998, the federal government was actually collecting more from taxes than it was spending, and in 2000, it had a budget surplus of $236 billion—meaning it could afford to pay off some debt principal without borrowing more.

After September 11, 2001, as defense spending rose and markets fell, the federal surpluses became deficits again—reaching $464 billion by 2008. Then, as illustrated brilliantly by Tim Geithner in his memoir, *Stress Test,* driven by the subprime mortgage crisis and financial institutions' lack of liquidity to use for recovery, the US financial sector and US economy collapsed into the worst recession since the Great Depression of the 1930s. In 2009, President Obama inherited President Bush's commitment of $700 billion to bail out the financial sector and rescue the economy through the Troubled Asset Relief Program—TARP. The deficit for 2008 more than tripled in 2009, to $1.41 trillion, as the federal government brought in far less money and spent far more on defense, bailouts, and protecting people who were losing their jobs and their homes. No other government on earth spent as much as $1.41 trillion total in 2009. The magnitude of what the federal government was borrowing had become so large that by 2010, when I became DNI, Mike Mullen, then chairman of the Joint Chiefs of Staff, characterized our national debt as *the* most prominent threat to our national security.

During President Obama's first year in office he faced a situation in which he desperately needed to inject money into the US financial system to prevent a second Great Depression; at the same time, almost as desperately, he had to scale back federal borrowing. It was a time in which we needed to address the fiscal realities we faced removed from the mire of partisan politics.

Unfortunately, in 2009 Congress was still populated by many of the kind of people who had, six months earlier, staged a juvenile walkout in protest of the briefing DNI Mike McConnell and I had given on President Bush's changes to Executive Order 12333, which redefined intelligence authorities after the establishment of the DNI. Also unfortunately, when approaching cuts, many members of Congress felt strongly and uncompromisingly that while the budget did need to be slashed, the programs *they* supported should be protected, whether those were allocated to defense (largely supported by Republicans) or to domestic programs (largely supported by Democrats).

Despite the fact that the federal budget makes headline news constantly, few people know how the process actually works, so it's worth taking a few pages here to present what I hope will clarify some of the intricacies of how the budget cycle is supposed to work. During the first week of February, the president presents his budget request to Congress. In a functional world, after receiving this request, House and Senate budget committees draft a budget resolution that offers broad guidelines for the rest of Congress to use in constructing the actual budget. Then, congressional oversight committees spend the next few months critiquing the president's requests, checking items of particular interest to their committees or to their individual members, making backdoor deals, and marking up the request to become House and Senate "authorization" bills—literally authorizing federal departments to run their programs. Committees also use these authorization bills to conduct oversight. In the wake of the Iran-Contra scandal, Congress made the passage of intelligence authorization bills contingent on the CIA's informing the chairs and vice-chairs of the House and Senate intelligence committees of any covert actions it was conducting. In my time as DNI, Congress extended this oversight to micromanagement levels, which included informing me of the precise size and makeup they wanted for the Office of the DNI staff, caps on staff pay and promotions, skill sets, and how many desks in Liberty Crossing could be occupied by contractors.

Between April and June, committees hold budget hearings, at which executive branch secretaries and directors—like the DNI—defend the budget requests they submitted in February. Intelligence budget briefings are conducted behind closed doors to allow discussion of the details of classified programs. In June or July, the committees release their draft authorization bills to the executive departments for comment. Typically, when Congress sends over the authorization bills, executive departments only have a few weeks to respond, so budget and programmatic experts typically read the draft bills in late-night sessions over delivery pizza on the day they're released. Department headquarters' offices send the draft bills, with specific questions, around to staff experts to get feedback on what provisions and budget lines they can and can't live with. Their responses are then submitted to Congress. Sometimes, departments feel strongly enough about their objections that they recommend the president veto the bill unless changes are made to it. A vetoed authorization bill can have serious consequences for a department, including not being able to start *any* new programs if a bill never gets passed. So in the organizations I directed, we always took recommending a veto very seriously.

Again, in a functional world, committees consider the feedback and objections they've received from executive departments, and the House and Senate counterpart committees come together to meld their bills into mutually agreed-upon legislation, which they send to the president's desk for signature. When the president signs the authorization bill, it becomes law—the "authorization act" for that fiscal year. That's not quite the end of the process. Once oversight committees authorize federal departments to run their programs under a specific budget, the appropriations committees—one each in the House and Senate—appropriate money to be spent. That appropriation is the actual federal budget. There are twelve appropriations subcommittees, so the budget can be doled out as twelve separate appropriations acts, or several can be rolled up into an "omnibus" act.

That budget cycle process is the basis for all federal spending, and for the Intelligence Community, it's even more complicated. IC equities get spread out into two authorization bills—intelligence (for NIP equities) and defense (for MIP equities)—but its appropriation comes through just the defense appropriations subcommittee. There's a reason for this odd arrangement. After congressional investigations determined that the CIA had spied on Americans and engaged in other illegal actions during the Watergate era, Congress decided it required better oversight of intelligence activities. It therefore created select intelligence oversight committees in both the Senate (1976) and the House (1977) to oversee the national-level intelligence program. At the same time, in the Senate, it left oversight of intelligence work that supported military operations in the Armed Services Committee. That's how we ended up with a National Intelligence Program (NIP), determined by the DNI and authorized by the Intelligence Authorization Act each year; and a Military Intelligence Program, overseen by the USD(I) and rolled into the National Defense Authorization Act for all military activities. To further complicate matters, the Senate committee oversees only the National Intelligence Program, while the House committee also has jurisdiction over DOD's Military Intelligence Program.

So every year that all three bills passed, we received three sets of instructions/guidance from Congress, and every year, the priorities of the appropriators differed from those of the authorizers. The IC can't spend money unless it's both appropriated and authorized, which caused annual headaches. If we didn't get an appropriation act, we'd shut down. If we didn't get an authorization act, they'd send us the draft bill from each committee and tell us to consider what they would have passed if they'd agreed to pass it. This is how I learned that Excedrin pairs well with martinis.

Intelligence budgeting is also more complex because of the types of things we have to budget for. If we want to develop, build, and launch a satellite system with new capabilities in ten years, we have to plan in which years the development will require more or less funding to stay on track. If we're growing an online capability, we have to plan for when additional staff will be needed to make it work. We need to know whether that funding will come from the NIP or the MIP, and have to trust that congressional appropriations will be stable and support our careful plans. Much of our effort at USD(I) and DNI was accordingly focused on study and planning for years in the future, rather than what we were currently executing.

With all of that as background, I took my oath of office as DNI on August 9, 2010, and as a general indicator of just how well Democrats and Republicans were working together on Capitol Hill, when October 1, 2010, rolled around, it marked the start of the sixth consecutive year that the Intelligence Community would operate without an authorization act. It also marked the fifth consecutive year that Congress failed to appropriate a government budget by the beginning of the fiscal year. Starting in 2007, Congress had started each fiscal year by passing a "continuing resolution," which essentially was the legislative branch telling the executive branch departments to continue operating, temporarily, at the same funding level as the previous year until Congress could see its way clear to actually fund the government. For each of those previous four years, Congress passed either a series of continuing resolutions or, eventually, an appropriations act. As much as congressional members complain any time the Intelligence Community comes up short on anything, Congress consistently failed to do its one primary job—fund the government.

The 2010 elections were marked by the rise of the Tea Party faction within the Republican Party, which was a backlash to Obama's presidency. Driven by their victories, the Republicans took control of the House of Representatives, and the newly elected Tea Party members made it a point of pride to be even more purposefully disruptive than the previous Congress.

The bright spot for the Intelligence Community, amid so much dysfunction on the Hill, was the January 2011 appointment of representatives Mike Rogers and Dutch Ruppersberger as, respectively, the chair and ranking member of the Intelligence Committee in the House. They were determined to set aside partisan politics and do what they believed best for the IC and for the nation, even if their actions drew the ire of their respective parties. When in 2015 I presented an award to them on behalf of an intelligence industry association, I said I'd been told that sometimes on a single issue, Ruppersberger, the Democrat, would be taking heat from the Obama White House at the same time that Rogers, the Republican, was under attack for supporting the White House.

Rogers and Ruppersberger introduced an authorization bill for 2011 in February—nearly halfway through the fiscal year—and worked with Senate Intelligence Committee chair Dianne Feinstein and Vice Chair Saxby Chambliss to get it to the president's desk. President Obama signed it on

June 8. Subsequently, Rogers and Ruppersberger worked with the Senate
Intelligence Committee to pass authorization bills for each of the next
four years, which they served together. Thanking them on behalf of the
IC in 2015, I joked, "In their *four* years as HPSCI leaders, they passed *five*
intelligence authorization bills—*five* annual authorization bills—in *four*
years. That really only works with congressional math."

On the appropriations side, however, the math was not working. Democrats and Republicans seemed to concur that federal spending was un-
sustainable, but couldn't agree on much else. So in 2010, for the fifth
straight year, they failed to pass an appropriations bill by October 1. On
September 29, two days before a potential shutdown, Congress passed a
continuing resolution, funding the government through December 3. The
next CR went through December 18, with successive ones coming on December 21, March 4, March 18, April 8, and then April 15. None of those
continuing resolutions was passed with more than two days to spare before the previous resolution expired, and some were passed only a few
hours before the government would have to shut down. Because agencies
in the executive branch required days of preparation for a shutdown, across
the government we had to prepare, again and again, to close up shop.

Seven times between December 2010 and April 2011, we canceled
training and called people back from travel. Seven times, we started procedures for closing down infrastructure systems. More than once, we got
so close to shutdown that NSA prepared to phase down some nonurgent
systems related to signals intelligence. Seven times, we notified employees
they were hours from being furloughed, sent home without pay for as
long as the government remained unfunded. Instructions from the Office
of Personnel Management complicated the situation, as we were required
to divide employees into two groups: those whose work was "essential" to
keep the government from actually collapsing (which included such positions as security guards protecting our facilities, analysts monitoring terrorists trying to board airliners, officers deployed to combat zones in
support of warfighters, and, of course, people who could answer whatever
questions Congress had as they debated passing a budget), and those
whose work was allegedly "nonessential" (including, for example, acquisition professionals who made sure satellites were delivered on time and
within budget, officers who coordinated with foreign intelligence services, recruiters who hired new intelligence officers, and the human

resources folks who made sure we all got paid). The actual policy document uses the words "excepted" and "nonexcepted," but it was all communicated to employees as "essential" and "nonessential."

It was demoralizing for intelligence professionals to be characterized as nonessential and then threatened with the possibility of not being paid. Media headlines repeatedly asked: If those people were nonessential, why did we employ them in the first place? The news for essential employees was actually worse, as they would have to work without pay. After previous government shutdowns, Congress had passed a bill retroactively remunerating people for time they missed, but the Tea Party Republicans indicated publicly they would now block any retroactive payments.

At the end of the workday on Friday, April 15, 2011, Congress hadn't reached a deal to pass a budget or a new continuing resolution, and we expected to shut down at midnight. We informed people definitively whether they were "essential" or "nonessential." We told the nonessential employees to take home any medication they had at work, or anything else critical to their personal lives. By some miracle, though, Congress managed to pass an actual appropriation for the remainder of the fiscal year, and we remained open. In fact, we needed our chief financial officer and her staff to come in to work on the weekend to figure out how the enacted appropriations affected the Intelligence Community. It was actually good news for the NIP, which was given a $1.5 billion increase—our last up-year in the post-9/11 streak—but the MIP saw a $3 billion reduction for its Fiscal Year 2011 funding. Because April 15 was more than halfway through the year, and we'd been told to operate under the assumption of the previous year's funding levels, programs funded under the MIP had the remainder of the year to absorb the $3 billion cut, rather than a full year. So instead of an 11 percent cut over a full year, it was a 24 percent cut over five and a half months. As my dad would've said, "This is no way to run a railroad."

This was just the start of the 2011 drama. The United States is one of only a handful of nations that sets a limit on how much money its government can borrow, and other nations that do either fix their debt ceiling as a percentage of their GDP, so that it naturally rises over time, or set a hard limit so high that they don't worry about ever reaching it. In contrast, the US Congress regularly has to raise the ceiling for the amount of money the US Treasury is allowed to owe in bonds. After 9/11, Congress quietly raised the debt ceiling in 2002, 2003, 2004, 2006, 2007, twice in 2008, twice in 2009, and again in 2010, to $14.294 trillion. Shortly after Congress passed a budget on April 15, 2011, all eyes turned to August 2, which the US Treasury had identified as the date when it would reach the debt ceiling limit and be unable to issue more bonds.

The Tea Party Republicans in the House, in particular, saw this as another opportunity to "play chicken" with the federal government in pursuit of their agenda. Republicans wanted cuts to domestic entitlements, particularly social safety-net programs like welfare, food stamps, and Medicaid. Democrats wanted to raise taxes on wealthy Americans. Republicans were set against *any* increases in taxes and wanted to protect national security equities. Treasury Secretary Tim Geithner pointed out the real absurdity of the debate: If the government didn't raise the ceiling to borrow more money, it would default on government bonds. Then, almost certainly, the international credit indexes would downgrade the United States' credit rating, and the interest rates the government paid on bonds would go up. If neither side swerved before Tuesday, August 2, not only could we see a government shutdown, but annual federal spending would increase hundreds of billions of dollars just to cover interest payments, with no tangible benefit for taxpayers.

On Monday, August 1, with this national theater of the absurd playing out in Washington, the Intelligence Community leadership left town for the day. Stephanie and I met the directors of the "Big Six"—CIA, NSA, NRO, NGA, DIA, and FBI—along with USD(I) Mike Vickers and key members of each agency staff at an "undisclosed location" to discuss what *we* were going to do. Regardless of what happened with the debt ceiling that week, our days of ever-increasing intelligence budgets were probably over.

Heading into that meeting, I believed that, to most IC agency heads and to most of our workforce, my oft-repeated phrase "intelligence integration" meant coordinating across agency lines to bring tradecraft from all the intelligence disciplines together. Three months earlier, to the day, outstanding intelligence work by CIA, NSA, and NGA had led to the raid in Abbottabad, Pakistan, and the death of Osama bin Laden. That was intelligence integration built on work that had been under way long before I became DNI.

In the summer of 2011, facing decreasing budgets across the board, IC leaders realized we needed to extend the same spirit of integration to our business processes because we were staring once again into the abyss of a potential shutdown and the certainty of losing resources across the community, which would potentially impact the safety and security of the nation, its citizens, and our allies.

In a somber room, we discussed the realities we faced. Our budgets had increased at a somewhat similar rate to the defense budget since 2001, but our mission imperatives had expanded at the same rate. We'd not only discovered and disrupted terrorist plots around the world; we were supporting active wars in Iraq and Afghanistan, protecting troops from insurgent attacks and IEDs, and giving them intelligence to go on the offensive. At the same time, China and Russia still challenged us, and North Korea and Iran both were pushing to become internationally recognized nuclear states. That spring, I'd told our congressional oversight committees that we must "sustain a robust, balanced array of intelligence capabilities to cope with the wide variety and scope of potential threats." Despite these expanding requirements, the direction from Congress and the public was for us to "trim the fat."

At our off-site, the agency directors and their chief finance officers opened their books to each other to an unprecedented degree. They revealed— in real numbers—how much they were spending on specific missions and programs. It quickly became apparent that each agency had already spent the past year or more identifying efficiencies within their own systems, and that there was very little overlap between two agencies performing similar enough functions that we could feel safe eliminating one and allowing it to be covered by another. I know that skeptics won't buy this, but while many IC programs were very expensive, almost all served a unique purpose within our expanded mission, and there was almost no fat to trim.

I finally spoke out loud what I believed everyone was thinking: We *weren't* going to be able to, as the cliché goes, "do more with less." Saying we could accept these cuts without significant impact would be intellectually dishonest, misrepresenting the facts to our stakeholders and policy makers. So, I told the group, we would "do less with less." That did not mean salami slicing—taking a percentage cut from every program, so that we continued doing the same things but with impaired capabilities— so we agreed to plan as a community to prioritize resources according to the strategies the national intelligence managers in ODNI had been co-ordinating. We would make hard choices and kill off entire programs and capabilities, and we'd keep funding critical programs at the levels they needed to function properly. As Stephanie deftly put it, "*Flat* is the new *up*." We also agreed that "sunk costs" are lost costs—we'd only keep a program because it met mission needs, not just because we'd already invested a large sum of money in it.

As I write this, I can imagine readers thinking that making necessary adjustments in response to cost-cutting measures sounds remarkably obvious. At the time, however, seriously considering intentionally killing a government program to save money felt pretty radical. One of my favorite quotes, which I used again and again over the next few years, was from a New Zealand physicist, Ernest Rutherford, who once remarked, "We're running out of money, so we must begin to think." Later, Stephanie revised Rutherford's quote to say, "So we must begin to think together."

We decided first and foremost to protect our future. That meant, as we froze—and perhaps later even cut—the overall size of the IC workforce, we'd keep a hiring pipeline open to bring in new people with fresh ideas and experiences. It also meant we'd protect our investment in science and technology. Under Dawn Meyerriecks's leadership from ODNI, the chief scientists and research directors of the IC had already formulated how to manage research investment. In some areas, like cryptanalysis, we would continue to lead the world, while in others we would support industry research to ensure we could use their resulting products. In many, many other areas, we would have to leverage what industry was already producing, using "adapt" or "adopt" as our primary principles.

We also agreed to coordinate any cuts we made to the NIP with cuts made to the MIP, so that we could avoid inadvertently creating a serious vulnerability, what could be called "programming fratricide." For that reason, it was crucial that USD(I) Mike Vickers was at the table, and I was grateful when, a month later, Mike invited us to a similar MIP-focused off-site. We'd come a long way from the turf battles of a few years before.

The final—again rather obvious—principle we agreed to was favoring capabilities for conducting intelligence over support functions. Marilyn Vacca, the person most responsible for executing the DNI's authority to determine the NIP, told the group that 20 to 25 percent of our budget request was coded for information technology. IT was so expensive because each of the agencies had developed its own separate and secure infrastructure, network, email system, support services, and user experience. Their respective IT leaders and chief information officers had built interagency bridges to connect the archipelago, but each maintained its own island. I asked Al Tarasiuk, a deeply experienced CIA senior officer on rotation as the ODNI chief information officer, to develop an approach on how we could first bring all the agencies, and eventually the smaller intelligence components, into a single, united "IC IT Enterprise." Al's first contribution was to pronounce "IC ITE" as "eyesight." No program has any cachet in Washington until it has a catchy acronym.

On Tuesday, August 2, the day after our off-site and—once again—the last possible day to avert disaster, Congress passed the Budget Control Act of 2011, and the president signed it into law. The act raised the debt ceiling by $900 billion and cut spending by $917 billion total over ten years, almost all of it back-loaded to the final few years—again kicking the can down the road. It also established a "supercommittee" of six Republicans and six Democrats tasked with cutting *another* $1.5 trillion. To show how serious Congress was about this supercommittee, the act carried a provision that if the supercommittee didn't agree on a way to cut at least another $1.2 trillion, it would trigger a "sequestration" cut, indiscriminately slashing the domestic programs the Democrats cared about and the national security programs the Republicans cared equally about—$600 billion from each side. The law was deliberately cast to make these cuts as painful as possible. Triggering sequestration would not only result in these mindless, draconian, automatic cuts, but would specify that departments and agencies would have to take the cuts to *all* their programs, leaving directors and secretaries no discretion to move around money to save vital systems and capabilities. Essentially, Congress wrote the Budget Control Act of 2011 to force the supercommittee to negotiate, because in their minds, literally anything the supercommittee might come up with would be better than triggering sequestration, which they described as "unthinkable." As we read about this deal, Stephanie correctly observed that much of what we'd accomplished with our off-site meeting would be completely undone if sequestration took place.

After August 2, 2011, the noise of Washington political chaos quieted enough for us to focus on the chaos of the rest of the world for a while. The Libyan civil war was reaching its endgame. The battle of Tripoli began on August 19, Gaddafi was captured and killed on October 20, and NATO ended its mission on October 31. The Iraq War officially ended (or so we thought) with the final withdrawal of US troops on December 18. Almost immediately, the insurgency forces in Iraq regenerated.

Before that, on October 17, I rolled out IC ITE at the 2011 GEOINT Symposium in San Antonio, and in December, Al Tarasiuk presented us with the plan he and the agency CIOs had come up with. The agencies had competitively agreed to lead individual efforts for IC ITE. CIA and NSA won separate bids to provide cloud computing power. DIA and NGA had bid together to provide desktop hardware and a virtual desktop and interface. In addition to hosting a cloud, NSA would make computing accessible and powerful by making available thousands of mission applications through an "app mall." Later, agencies would bid again to lead the longer-term challenge of consolidating IT network infrastructures with all of the associated issues of fiber, routers, and switches. To implement this plan, the agencies agreed not to cut their IT budgets through fiscal years 2012 and 2013. Over the following months, Al Tarasiuk would lead the technical effort, and Stephanie would lead the agency deputies committee to address systemic challenges and overcome the inevitable passive-aggressive resistance that such change inevitably engenders among agencies.

Unfortunately, as IC agencies were integrating in new ways, Congress was reaching new levels of disintegration. On November 21 the cochairs of the bipartisan congressional supercommittee published a statement that began, "After months of hard work and intense deliberations, we have come to the conclusion today that it will not be possible to make any bipartisan agreement available to the public before the committee's deadline" of December 31. Still, no one panicked, for while sequestration had technically been triggered, it wouldn't start until January 1, 2013, not 2012. Congress had another year to find a way out of the trap it had set for itself.

On December 23, 2011, Congress actually passed an omnibus appropriations act, funding the government for the next nine months. The fiscal year 2012 National Intelligence Program was cut $700 million to $53.9 billion, and the Military Intelligence Program was cut another $2.5 billion to $21.5 billion, after having $3 billion cut the previous year. On January 31, 2012, the ill-fated supercommittee dissolved, leaving us in limbo for figuring out future intelligence budgets, all while dealing with operational challenges like the Arab Spring and the tragic attack in Benghazi in September.

That October I addressed the 2012 GEOINT Symposium in Orlando, updating the audience on IC ITE and explaining exactly what was at stake if sequestration came into effect on January 1—less than three months away. I explained that with no latitude on how to take cuts, the sequester "could mean significant reductions in our most valuable asset, our people. And every major systems acquisition program in the NIP is in jeopardy of being wounded. So we can only hope that the lame-duck Congress, which returns after the election, will do something to avert this train wreck." I concluded my remarks with a thought that felt ominous even as I said it: "And the worst part is that if it happens, it would occur during the time of the most diverse and demanding array of threats I've seen in almost fifty years in this business. And I can assure you that to the extent that I have any influence, for as long as I have any influence, I'll do my damnedest to minimize the damage."

The next crisis didn't wait for Congress to return after the election. On the evening of Tuesday, November 6, as I watched the election returns, it looked as though President Obama would be reelected. If he asked me to stay on as DNI, and I had no reason to believe he wouldn't, I planned to tell him I would *only* stay if Stephanie also agreed to stay as PDDNI. The final item on my calendar for the day was a meeting with Sean Joyce, the FBI's deputy director under Bob Mueller. Sean had been promoted to that position after serving as the director of the FBI's intelligence component, so I already had a close working relationship with him. I was told he wanted to brief me on a sensitive cybersecurity issue, so I asked Stephanie to join us.

Sean began laying out a case of cyberstalking between two women in Florida, one of whom had published a biography of CIA director David Petraeus earlier that year. He explained that the FBI had gotten involved after one of the women had filed a report with the Tampa FBI Field Office, and I began to wonder precisely how this seemingly petty civil issue had risen to a level that the FBI's deputy director became involved. Then Sean's tone shifted as he revealed that, while investigating the biographer, they discovered that she was having an extramarital affair with Petraeus, and Dave had been improperly sharing classified material with her. I was stunned, and perhaps for the only time I can recall, Stephanie looked genuinely surprised. Sean said that not only did agency people know about the affair, but at least two congressional offices were aware of it as well, which meant it wouldn't stay a secret for long.

The next morning, I called Dave privately and shared what Sean had told us. He didn't immediately seem to grasp how dire the situation was. I pointed out that if a midgrade government employee had provided classified material to a girlfriend, he would have his clearance suspended, and I asked Dave to consider that in determining his course of action. At one point in our conversation, I reminded him that unlike me he was an international icon, and as one retired general officer to another, I suggested he take control of the situation while he still had some control to exercise by informing his family and explaining the situation to the president before the story went public. By the end of the conversation, he understood the urgency of the matter. I spoke with him twice more on Wednesday and tried to offer support. Appropriately, if belatedly, he took responsibility and did the difficult and right thing by telling his family and the president, and by resigning.

On Thursday, I met with Attorney General Eric Holder and White House counsel Kathy Ruemmler, bringing my superb general counsel Bob Litt with me. The Justice Department chief of staff shared the same information Sean had given to Stephanie and me. Since Dave was presidentially appointed and Senate-confirmed, the White House was dismayed that Sean had briefed me before he had them, and Kathy reminded me I didn't have authority to ask Dave to resign, as only the White House could do that—a reminder I didn't need.

On Friday afternoon, Sue and I flew to North Carolina to spend the weekend with my sister, Chris, and her husband, Jim, a retired Army intelligence officer. President Obama accepted Dave's resignation, the story broke, and I spent the entire weekend on the phone with congressional members, explaining what had happened.

This sequence of events led to my third meeting alone with the president. The first had been my interview for the DNI position. The second had been shortly after April 28, 2011, when I was surprised by the president's announcement that Dave would become the CIA director, succeeding Leon Panetta, who was in turn following Bob Gates as secretary of defense. The 2004 IRTPA legislation explicitly states that the president would nominate the CIA director based on the recommendation of the DNI. Shortly after the appointment was announced, Bob Litt politely reminded the White House counsel about the specifics of the law. That second private meeting with the president appeared to be a hastily scheduled "whoops" acknowledgment, during which he assured me he would seek my recommendation if he ever needed to appoint another CIA director.

Not to be outdone, I used the occasion of Leon's departure from CIA to have my own "whoops" moment—publicly and spectacularly. I was the fifth person to present Leon with an award onstage, and I recycled a joke I'd been using for years, that speaking fifth reminded me of the apocryphal line ascribed to Elizabeth Taylor's eighth husband when he supposedly said, "I know what I'm supposed to do, but how do I make it different?" The line got a laugh, as it always did. After the ceremony, as I was walking off the stage, NGA director Tish Long walked up, smiled, and rhetorically asked, "Guess who's here?" I knew immediately she meant former senator John Warner, one of Elizabeth Taylor's ex-husbands; heart sinking, I scanned the rapidly dispersing crowd for the senator. No luck. I resolved to call him as soon as I could, and I went with my detail to my preplanned exit. There, I encounter none other than Senator Warner, standing on the curb, waiting for his ride. I figuratively fell on my knees, babbling an apology for my insensitive gaffe. He laughed and said, "No, no. It was a great line. I laughed too." Getting in his car, he added, "By the way, I was number six."

Eighteen months later, President Obama met with me alone for what turned out to be the final time to ask for my recommendation on whom to nominate as the next CIA director. I knew he favored John Brennan for the job, and I felt that John would be a terrific agency director and that we could work well together. I told the president that I could endorse two people: either John or Deputy Director Michael Morell, who had served as acting director before Dave, and who assumed that position again after Dave resigned. He ultimately chose John.

Between Benghazi, Dave's resignation, and wondering if Congress would do *something* before its latest self-imposed deadline of New Year's Day, I spent a good deal of time during the fall of 2012 on the phone with congressional members and shuttling back and forth to Capitol Hill. I was deeply concerned that sequestration would take effect, and I felt compelled to let our committee members know—again—that while we accepted that we were not exempt from cuts, sequestration would damage intelligence capabilities indiscriminately. In fact, all of Washington was already up in arms about sequestration. At midnight on December 31, it would kick in at the precise moment the tax cuts passed during President Bush's tenure would expire, and six other economically bad pieces of legislation would all be triggered, along with the debt ceiling being reached again. The government would inexplicably raise taxes and cut spending simultaneously, a move the Congressional Budget Office warned would throw the nation into immediate recession. With all the drama Washington could muster, this impending event had been dubbed the "fiscal cliff."

I was also concerned about another potential legislative disaster—the renewal of what's awkwardly called the Foreign Intelligence Surveillance Act of 1978 Amendments Act of 2008. FISA grants the Intelligence Community much of its authority to conduct intelligence against threats overseas, and this provision of FISA was slated to expire at the end of the year and required reauthorization. Particularly of concern for the Intelligence Community was Section 702, which gave the IC authority, under court supervision, to intercept communications of non-US persons, such as suspected terrorists overseas. When people think of the Intelligence Community "listening to calls" and "reading emails"—actually gathering the content of communications needed to interrupt terrorist plots and target terrorists overseas—Section 702 is a critical tool we rely upon heavily to do so. Understandably, some members of the legislative branch were concerned that we never use this authority for foreign surveillance against the American people, so Congress required under Section 702 that we could only "target the communications of non-U.S. persons located outside the United States for foreign intelligence purposes," a restriction with which I strongly agreed.

That fall I led teams, which at various times included FBI director Bob Mueller, NSA deputy director Chris Inglis, and ODNI general counsel Bob Litt, among others, to meet with key congressional members to explain the importance of Section 702, the procedural safeguards that had been installed to prevent its abuse, and the roles that all three branches of government played in oversight. As the deadline for its renewal approached, these meetings became more frequent—and more intense. In November and December, I briefed our oversight committees, the Senate majority and minority leaders, and the House Speaker and minority leader. I explained how Section 702 works and how the foreign intelligence we collected under its authority contributed to thousands of reports and dozens of articles in the President's Daily Brief, and I described the accesses we would lose, particularly against foreign terrorist networks, without its reauthorization.

I also described what happened when we were monitoring phone or internet communications of a non-American overseas but then realized the person speaking with the target was an American or was located within the United States—the so-called "incidental collection" of a "US person." In those cases, analysts first determined if there was foreign intelligence value to the intercepted communication. If there wasn't, our policy was to delete the communication forever. If there *was* intelligence value—for example, a terrorist's talking to someone in the United States about a terrorist plot—we would "minimize" the protected American's name with the designation "US person #1," or "US person #2," etc., in any signals intelligence reporting.

On November 27, I, along with Bob Litt and Chris Inglis, participated in a particularly contentious discussion with Senators Jeff Merkley, Tom Udall, and Ron Wyden on the details of minimization procedures and the measures we took not to target Americans with this authority. Senator Wyden pressed us for the number of Americans whose communications we had "incidentally" collected since 2008, when Section 702 was enacted. We did our best to alleviate his concerns, but we had a particularly hard time getting him to understand why we couldn't provide the precise number.

Essentially, the IC doesn't have the time and resources to fully process every communication we intercept, and we wouldn't even know if we'd incidentally intercepted a US person unless we went to great lengths to identify every participant on a call or every address on an email. We didn't—and couldn't—use minimization procedures for names if we never identified the names. It's *possible* that we'd unwittingly intercepted a significant number of communications in which our targets were talking to Americans, but the only way to get a precise count of how many times this had happened would be to listen to, read, and analyze *every* communication we'd *ever* intercepted and then try to determine the nationalities of all its participants, which might require a lot of research regarding their identities. Paradoxically, such an effort would mean we'd need to be more comprehensively intrusive in the lives of innocent US citizens, because we would have to approach the problem by intentionally attempting to find and identify Americans. It would even mean looking for Americans in intercepted communications we'd never examined, which, beyond its intrusiveness, would require vast analytic resources we simply didn't possess. We did our best to explain all this, but Senator Wyden, in particular, wasn't interested in our explanations.

After many more discussions and much more hand-wringing, Congress passed the FISA Amendments Act renewal on Friday, December 28—again at nearly the last minute, but with comfortable voting margins—and President Obama signed it into law on Sunday, December 30.

The focus then returned to the drama around the fiscal cliff. On Monday, December 31, House Democrats rejected a deal brokered by the White House and Senate to enact new, smaller tax cuts, which would have effectively allowed taxes to increase by only a small amount, and would have kicked the sequestration can down the road to March 1. Speaker Boehner threatened to derail the whole plan by adding billions in spending cuts, in addition to delaying the sequester. The House threw a tantrum, until 10:45 that night, when he finally allowed a vote, and the compromise bill passed. The Senate didn't approve the compromise and send it to the president's desk until *after* the midnight deadline.

Before the New Year's Eve showdown, it seemed as if the entire government had been energized to prevent leaping off the fiscal cliff into a self-imposed recession. With a compromise bill passed and signed, Washington shifted its attention to the next crisis—the debt ceiling—again. In January 2013 the government exceeded the Treasury Department's borrowing limit, but somehow Treasury took "extraordinary measures" and kept the government open, still needing to reconcile the ceiling with Congress. Regardless, no energy was left to stop or even mitigate the damage from sequestration, which would go into effect March 1. We pleaded with Congress to at least give us some flexibility to manage the budget cuts, but we were consistently told any measures that touched sequestration were "poison pills," meaning, if they were slipped into any bill, they would kill the entire bill. In this case, mitigating sequestration would compromise any chance for getting past the current debt-ceiling crisis and—after that—the expiration of the continuing budget resolution in March. Congress had tied its own hands—quite the magic trick—but was subsequently unable to extricate itself.

On January 29, I took a call from Deputy Secretary of Defense Ash Carter. As a way to absorb sequestration costs, DOD proposed furloughing each of its government civilians once a week, thereby cutting their salaries by 20 percent. This would both lower DOD's budget *and* attract Congress's attention, since DOD civilians were employed in just about every congressional district in the nation. He was informing me of this proposal because it would include all the civilians in the DOD intelligence agencies—NSA, NRO, NGA, and DIA. I shared my concern that putting people with access to top secret, compartmented intelligence in potentially dire financial straits could result in a huge counterintelligence vulnerability, but Ash was determined that DOD would press ahead.

I asked my senior staff to start assessing my authorities under law and executive orders to see if I could stop DOD from furloughing intelligence employees. We determined that Section 1018 of the 2004 IRTPA—the last-minute addition to the act that created the DNI, which stated that the DNI was to exercise his authority in a manner that "respects and does not abrogate the statutory responsibilities of the heads of the departments"—effectively blocked me from stopping a DOD furlough. However, ODNI's new chief financial officer—Rich Fravel, who'd succeeded Marilyn Vacca—pointed out that the whole exercise was about absorbing cuts to the budget, and while the secretary of defense determined the Military Intelligence Program through the USD(I), the DNI alone determined the National Intelligence Program. I could simply state that NIP-funded jobs would be fully funded, and people who worked in those jobs would not be furloughed. I told Rich to draft a diplomatically worded letter I could send to Ash.

The world continued its crazy spiral; on February 12, North Korea conducted its first nuclear weapons test under the regime of Supreme Leader Kim Jong-un. And Washington continued its astounding dysfunction; on February 14, Republicans in the Senate made former Republican senator and two-time Purple Heart recipient Chuck Hagel the first defense secretary nominee in our nation's history to have his confirmation filibustered, mostly for political reasons or, more absurdly, to demand more information about the 2012 attack on the diplomatic compound in Benghazi.

During a visit by a delegation representing the San Antonio Chamber of Commerce, I took the opportunity to complain about our typical government approach of making the same mistakes again and again. I said, "It reminds me of the ancient tribal wisdom that goes, 'When you're riding a dead horse, the best strategy is to dismount.' Well—in Washington—we sometimes do things differently." I explained:

> When *we* find ourselves riding a dead horse, we often try strategies that are less successful, such as: buying a stronger whip, changing riders, saying things like: "This is the way we've always ridden this horse," appointing a committee to study the horse, lowering the standards so that more dead horses can be included, appointing a tiger team to revive the dead horse, hiring outside contractors to ride the dead horse, harnessing several dead horses together—to increase speed— attempting to mount multiple dead horses in hopes that one of them will spring to life, providing additional funding and training to increase the dead horse's performance, declaring that, since a dead horse doesn't have to be fed, it's less costly, carries lower overhead, and therefore, contributes more to the mission than live horses, and my favorite—promoting the dead horse to a supervisory position.

The Chamber of Commerce loved the comedy bit. So did I. It was cathartic, and I believe I repeated it every time I traveled away from Washington for the rest of my tenure. It never failed to draw a laugh or to confirm what people have always suspected about Washington.

The situation in February 2013 was not funny. On February 20, DOD informed Congress of its revised proposal that, unless we avoided sequestration, it would furlough DOD civilian employees for one day of each two-week pay period, starting in April through the remainder of the calendar year, effectively cutting everyone's salary by 10 percent. On the same day, I met with the agency directors to affirm our plans to manage sequestration, now that it was upon us. Among the topics we discussed was that I would exclude employees in NIP-funded billets from the furlough. The challenge we had been working through was figuring out which billets and which individuals were covered by which program. In many offices, an employee paid with NIP funds might be sitting next to someone paid with MIP funds. No one in a given office knew or cared about this distinction, including the two employees—although if I got my way, they would, very soon. We agreed it would be hard to sort out, and that the people funded by the MIP—who would be furloughed—would likely resent the situation, but it was the best I could do under the law, and so I signed and sent Rich Fravel's masterful letter to DOD, which made what I felt was a compelling case that we could cover NIP-funded salaries, still absorb our share of the mandated (and mindless) cuts imposed by Congress, and not have to furlough those employees.

I had a series of phone calls with DOD officials over the next few days, including with Ash Carter on February 26—the same day that Chuck Hagel was finally confirmed as secretary. On February 27, between White House meetings, Ash and I met in the Eisenhower Executive Office Building—neutral turf. Not surprisingly, DOD had a different interpretation of my authorities than I did, and Ash challenged my decision to protect as many employees as I could. Ash and I had served together in the Pentagon in the early 1990s, and had great respect for each other, but the IC had made a commitment to protect our people at the off-site in August 2011, and I said we would honor it. I'd decided this was an issue on which I couldn't and wouldn't compromise, even if our differences would have to be settled by the White House.

On March 1, 2013, two days after this meeting, sequestration became the law of the land. And on that day—not much happened. Instead of plunging off a fiscal cliff, we slowly started slipping down a hill that just kept getting steeper. Congress didn't grant us an exception to allow us to decide how to take cuts, so our resources would definitely be affected. I didn't know yet if I'd managed to protect NIP-funded employees, but MIP-funded staff would take a cut in salary from mandatory furloughs, and they would still have the same workload with 10 percent fewer days to complete it. Our hiring pipeline would slow, as the perpetual backlog of security clearance investigations would balloon. Our ability to replace technology-based collection sources that became compromised or were overcome by the technological progress of the world would be severely undercut.

On Tuesday, March 12, I participated in the first worldwide threat assessment hearing of 2013, this one with the Senate Select Committee on Intelligence, chaired by Senator Feinstein. Feinstein truly was a trailblazer for women in government. She was the first woman to be elected mayor of San Francisco, the first to serve as senator from California, and the first to preside over a presidential inauguration. She was also the first woman to preside as chair of the Senate Select Committee on Intelligence, and she was proud of her legacy. In the summer of 2011, NGA director Tish Long, NRO deputy director Betty Sapp, and PDDNI Stephanie O'Sullivan were present to testify at a hearing, when Feinstein called a halt to it. She couldn't let the moment go unnoted, and said on the official record, "I have never seen a panel sitting in front of me that was all women, all senior women in the IC." Senator Feinstein and I had had some tense exchanges over the years, but I always felt I could work with her. In fact, I had grown to have great respect and affection for her.

She opened the hearing by cautioning, "As members know, we will immediately follow this session with a closed one, and I'll ask that members refrain from asking questions here that have classified answers. This hearing is really a unique opportunity to inform the American public, to the extent we can, about the threats we face as a nation and worldwide." She welcomed new CIA director John Brennan to his first threat assessment hearing and thanked Bob Mueller for appearing in what was likely his last after twelve years on the job.

She then yielded the floor to Vice Chairman Saxby Chambliss, who had been very angry about Benghazi and felt we were hiding something when Matt Olsen and I had briefed him, but we had all moved on since then. In his statement he focused on terrorism, advocating that we stop giving Miranda warnings to captured terrorists and start sending them to Guantanamo Bay for interrogations. I'm sure he realized that was a policy decision and not mine to make, because he didn't bring it up later as a question.

Chairman Feinstein then turned the floor over to me to speak on behalf of John, Bob, and the other witnesses. First, I shared my personal feelings on doing televised hearings at all. I'd tried earlier that year to get us out of answering questions on camera and failed because John McCain, ranking member of the Senate Armed Services Committee (which held its own threat hearing), had responded that if I didn't appear voluntarily, he'd subpoena me. Senator McCain and I had a lot of notable televised exchanges during which he was typically irascible, but we developed a mutually respectful, if sometimes testy, relationship when the red light above the camera wasn't on, mostly because we were both old and crotchety Southeast Asia veterans.

In my opening statement on March 12, I noted that our foreign partners and adversaries watched these hearings, too, and warned, "While our statements for the record and your opening statements can be reviewed in advance for classification issues, our answers to your questions cannot. And our attempts to avoid revealing classified information sometimes lead to misinterpretation, or accusations that we're being circumspect for improper reasons." In fact, we had submitted a highly detailed written statement that laid out the extent of global threats in as many specifics as we could possibly publish in unclassified form. The 2013 statement was somewhat historic, as "cyber" had displaced "terrorism" as the first threat topic addressed.

Having expressed my reservations, I turned to the impact sequestration would have on national security, noting that the associated budget cut was "well over $4 billion, or about 7 percent of the NIP," and that the way the cut was structured compounded its damage because it restricted our ability to allocate deductions in a balanced and rational way. Explaining that I would discuss the subject in greater detail in the classified session, I laid out examples in a carefully constructed script, explaining how sequestration would force the nation to accept unnecessary risk to our security as the IC scaled back global coverage, and because it would force us to restructure contracts, it absurdly would end up costing us more money in the long run. I talked about protecting the IC workforce, and that we recognized we were not immune to cuts, but that we needed the ability to manage cuts, rather than being forced to absorb them on a pro rata basis. I drew on my experience:

> Unfortunately, I've seen this movie before. Twenty years ago, I served as director of the Defense Intelligence Agency, the job that Lieutenant General Mike Flynn has now. We were then enjoined to "reap the peace dividend" occasioned by the end of the Cold War. We reduced the Intelligence Community by 23 percent. During the mid- and late '90s, we closed many CIA

stations, we reduced HUMINT collectors, cut analysts, allowed our overhead architecture to atrophy, and we neglected
basic infrastructure needs, such as power, space, and cooling,
and let our facilities decay. And most damaging, most devas-
tatingly, we badly distorted the workforce.

I concluded with the ominous note that people wouldn't appreciate
the extent of intelligence losses from sequestration until they resulted in
disaster: "Unlike more directly observable sequestration impacts, like
shorter hours at public parks or longer security lines at airports, the deg-
radation to intelligence will be insidious. It will be gradual and almost
invisible—unless and until, of course, we have an intelligence failure."

I then turned to the threats we'd cited in our statement for the record.
I explained why "cyber" had been moved up to lead the report. I talked
about how we'd added global shortages of food and water, along with
disease and pandemics—all influenced by climate change—as drivers of
instability in our list of threats. I spoke on how the terrorist threat had
evolved, no longer driven by al-Qaida in Afghanistan, but was now more
diversified, decentralized, global, and persistent. I discussed the fragile
new governments in the Arab world, whose intentions we were still trying to understand. I talked about the proliferation of weapons of mass
destruction, including the ambitions of North Korea and Iran to achieve
nuclear state status and the huge volumes of chemical and biological
agents in Syria, and how the civil war there had already turned into a
humanitarian disaster unlike anything we'd seen since World War II.
After describing the global picture, I turned to specific threats by region.

Over the next two hours, I answered questions on North Korean prov-
ocations, on the Benghazi attack and the talking points used by Ambassador Susan Rice, about cyber, about sanctions on Iran, about Iran and
North Korea purportedly sharing ballistic missile technology, about
Egypt and the Muslim Brotherhood, Egyptian unrest, the state of the
opposition forces in Syria, the role of Iran in Syria, several more takes on
the effect of Iranian sanctions, and more about politicization of the Benghazi talking points. I answered Senator Chambliss's question on sequestration with "I am not, and none of us are suggesting that we won't take
our fair share of the cuts. All we're asking for is the latitude on how to
take them, to minimize the damage."

Senator Mikulski asked to speak out of turn, as she was hurrying to the Senate floor, in her role on the Appropriations Committee, to introduce a continuing resolution to keep the government running. She said to me, "In terms of the flexibility that you've just asked for, that the Chair has spoken pretty firmly with me about, along with other members, we will not have that in our bill. We were told that was a poison pill," meaning that any attempts to protect the IC would cause the government to shut down. I always appreciated Senator Mikulski's candor about congressional dynamics, and that she always had both the IC's interests and the big picture in mind.

When all committee members had used their allotted five minutes, Chairman Feinstein opened for a second round of questions on camera before we'd adjourn to the closed hearing. Only Senators Feinstein, Angus King, and Ron Wyden had "round two" questions, hers on Hezbollah and Senator King's on extremism in North Africa. Senator Wyden's seemed to come out of left field:

> And this is for you, Director Clapper—again, on the surveillance front. And I hope we can do this in just a yes or no answer, because I know Senator Feinstein wants to move on. Last summer, the NSA director was at a conference and he was asked a question about the NSA surveillance of Americans. He replied, and I quote here, "The story that we have millions, or hundreds of millions, of dossiers on people is completely false." The reason I'm asking the question is, having served on the committee now for a dozen years, I don't really know what a dossier is in this context. So what I wanted to see is if you could give me a yes or no answer to the question, does the NSA collect any type of data at all on millions, or hundreds of millions, of Americans?

After nearly two hours in the "hot seat," I was tired, and annoyed that, months after we'd settled the FISA Section 702 reauthorization, Wyden was bringing it up again at this particular hearing, and on television. I'd explained to him in November that I couldn't give him a number of incidental collections, but he and I both knew it wasn't "hundreds of millions." Also, his question specifically mentioned "dossiers"—collections

of multiple reports on an identified person or topic—not single inadvertent intercepts on someone whom we hadn't identified.

I flipped the microphone on. "No, sir," I replied and then flipped it off.
"It does not?" he asked incredulously.

We *did* have "dossiers"—although that's not the word I would have
chosen—on spies and suspected terrorists in the United States. The Foreign Intelligence Surveillance Court issued us approximately two thousand warrants for domestic surveillance every year, amounting to twenty
thousand or so since 9/11, a number that was classified at the time. The
number of foreign persons *overseas* we collected on was much, much
larger—and definitely classified. As I'd explained in November, I didn't—
couldn't—know the number of inadvertent, "incidental" intercepts without the IC intentionally trying to identify Americans in intercepted
communications, and every other number I knew relating to surveillance I couldn't reveal publicly. In ten minutes, we'd be in a secure hearing room, and then, without having to tap dance around classification
while our adversaries were watching me on TV—something we knew
they did—I could once again explain 702 procedures. On camera, I put
my fingertips to my forehead, a gesture my staff says is a "tell" that I'm
getting aggravated.

I flipped the mic back on and, controlling my voice, replied, "Not wittingly. There are cases where they could inadvertently perhaps collect, but
not wittingly."

Wyden again looked incredulous and responded, "All right. Thank
you. I'll have additional questions to give you in writing on that point, but
I thank you for the answer."

An hour or so later, after the classified follow-on hearing, as our car
was crossing the Potomac on our way back to Liberty Crossing, Bob Litt
brought up Senator Wyden's question. Bob said that he knew what I had
been thinking in my response, but explained that Senator Wyden's question wasn't about FISA Section 702 authorities. What he had actually
been asking about was Section 215 of the Patriot Act, and in that context,
Bob said I'd answered incorrectly.

After taking a moment to recall what, precisely, the Patriot Act Section 215 was, I pushed back. I replied that Wyden's question made zero
sense to me in the context of Section 215. NSA used the authorities under
Section 215 to keep a database of phone call records that consisted only of

metadata—phone numbers and times, not even the names associated with the numbers, much less the content of the calls. The rationale for the NSA database was that, if we discovered a terrorist was calling into the United States and knew the phone number he was calling *from,* we could look at the phone records to see what numbers he was calling *to,* and how long the connection had lasted. If the call records indicated something worth investigating, obtaining caller identities and actually listening to the content of the calls would require requesting a warrant from a court under a different authority than Section 215. In short, you can't create a dossier on someone if you don't know who the phone number belongs to or what was said on the call. In any case, because the NSA program under Section 215 was highly classified, Senator Wyden wouldn't—or shouldn't— have been asking questions that required classified answers on camera. He hadn't even attended the closed briefing where we could have discussed the Patriot Act Section 215 in detail.

When I asked Bob if he was certain that Senator Wyden had been talking about Section 215, he apologized and said that he knew that Wyden's question concerned Section 215, because the senator's office had sent over a note just the day before that *said* he was going to ask about that subject. It was one of hundreds of questions the ODNI staff had planned to prep me for, but—between sequestration and the North Korea nuclear test—we hadn't gotten to this particular obscure one in our limited time and on such short notice. I replayed Senator Wyden's question in my head. He'd used the word "dossiers" several times, but his last sentence— the sound bite, the critical question at the end—was, "Does the NSA collect any type of data at all on millions, or hundreds of millions, of Americans?" When I walked into the office, my administrative assistant, Stephanie Sherline, asked how the hearing had gone. "I screwed up," I told her and followed that up with stronger language.

Months later, after my mistake had become a scandal, Bob would write letters to the *New York Times* and the *New Yorker,* reporting that I looked "surprised and distressed" when he'd told me my answer was incorrect. I was. Over the years I'd given plenty of answers that committees didn't like, but I had never intentionally misrepresented the facts—which is precisely what this looked like.

A few days after the hearing, Bob spoke with John Dickas, a member of Senator Wyden's staff, on a secure phone call and explained my mistake.

Dickas asked Bob to have me correct the mistake on the public record, but Bob pointed out that I could not, because making a public correction would mean revealing a classified program. He said that my error had been forgetting about Section 215, but even if I had remembered it, there still would have been no acceptable, unclassified way for me to answer the question in an open hearing. Even my saying, "We'll have to wait for the closed, classified session to discuss this" would have given something away. Looking back, I think Senator Wyden phrased his question in the obscure way he did because *he* was trying to avoid revealing the classified program himself. For the time, our offices let the matter drop. I ought to have sent a classified letter to Senator Wyden explaining my thoughts when I'd answered and that I misunderstood what he was actually asking me about. Yes, I made a mistake—a big one—when I responded, but I did not lie. I answered with truth in what I understood the context of the question to be.

I didn't have time to focus on our exchange in the hearing, as I was immediately consumed again by world events and sequestration. On Thursday, two days after the hearing, I met with Ash Carter and several other DOD officials in White House chief of staff Denis McDonough's office to finally settle the issue of furloughs, with Denis as the arbiter. Denis wasn't ready to make a call after hearing our arguments, and I think each of us walked out thinking he had presented the stronger case and would prevail.

By this point, DOD had determined that its furloughs wouldn't start until July, and both Ash and new Secretary Chuck Hagel had announced they would voluntarily lower their own salaries to match the losses by furloughed employees. It was a gracious gesture, and I followed suit, although I also recognized that by voluntarily cutting my salary, I only demonstrated that I made enough money that I could afford to lose 10 percent of it and still be able to pay my mortgage, something a GS-10 or GS-12 living in Washington might not be able to manage. I had no illusions that voluntarily lowering my salary made anyone feel better.

On Tuesday, March 26, Denis called to say that, based on the recommendation of the Office of Management and Budget, he agreed that the DNI could determine whether employees in NIP-funded jobs would be furloughed. Ash accepted Denis's decision, and we moved on. With that settled, the agency directors and I started April with a clearer idea of how to deal with the sequestration cuts, which were quickly getting steeper as we slid down that hill.

On the afternoon of April 15, as crowds cheered the runners finishing the Boston Marathon, two homemade bombs exploded at the finish line, killing three people and injuring almost three hundred, including sixteen survivors who lost arms or legs. Amid all the confusion, the perpetrators of the attack walked away unscathed.

By 2011, the ODNI had established "domestic DNI representatives" within the United States, similar to the intelligence leads abroad who maintain cognizance of all intelligence activities occurring in their country or field of influence. The twelve regional domestic DNI reps were senior FBI assistant directors or special agents in charge of field offices, and the representative with purview over the New England area was based in Boston. He immediately tapped resources in the National Counterterrorism Center, the DOD agencies, and CIA, as well as all the Justice Department resources available to the FBI. Within twenty-four hours the IC had determined that no international terrorist network was involved, and no groundwork had been laid for successive attacks.

On April 18 the FBI released pictures of two brothers who had been seen by witnesses and caught on security cameras carrying and setting down the bags that had contained the homemade bombs. In the massive manhunt over the next two days, the brothers shot and killed a police officer, stole a car, and took a hostage. The hostage escaped, and large sections of Boston were placed on lockdown. The brothers, cornered, engaged in a violent gun battle with Boston police. Making his escape, the younger of the two, nineteen-year-old Dzhokhar Tsarnaev, ran over his wounded older brother, twenty-six-year-old Tamerlan Tsarnaev, with a stolen car. Tamerlan died, and Dzhokhar was later found hiding in a boat in a local backyard. He was wounded in the resulting confrontation, and was finally taken into custody, ending the crisis.

In many ways, this incident was a nightmare scenario for US intelligence. Two brothers who had immigrated to the United States as minors in 2002—one a citizen, the other's citizenship application pending—had found instructions for making homemade bombs out of common kitchen pressure cookers in the online magazine *Inspire,* published by al-Qaida in the Arabian Peninsula. They weren't in contact with AQAP or other international terrorist organizations and had come up with their plot for indiscriminate slaughter on their own. They had made no phone or email communication that we could have intercepted, and there was no human source whom we could have exploited to learn of and thwart their plan. In fact, this was one of the few prominent times I can remember NSA's using the Patriot Act Section 215 authorities that Senator Wyden had intended to ask me about and was later so critical of. We plugged the brothers' phone numbers into the database to see if they had placed or received international phone calls, or if there was a pattern in their calls that would indicate a broader conspiracy to commit further acts of terror. If there had been, we would have had to quickly obtain warrants to find out whom they were talking to and what was said. Fortunately, we determined there was no coordinated plan for further bombings, so in this case, Section 215 didn't enable us to prevent an attack but did reassure us there was no broader conspiracy involved, which allowed us to focus on finding and apprehending the brothers.

We learned that the FBI had interviewed Tamerlan in 2011—two years before the bombing—but had concluded he wasn't a threat at the time. When that fact was made public, the FBI and IC were excoriated in the press for not more aggressively surveilling the brothers. After Jim Comey became FBI director five months later, he would lament that this unfair criticism meant that the FBI was no longer merely being held to the standard of "finding a needle in a haystack," but instead to being able to identify "a strand of hay that might one day become a needle."

In the weeks after the attack, I felt the practical frustration that Jim would later give eloquent voice to. Even more strongly than frustration, I felt the philosophical conflict in which we were embroiled, as the public, media, and Congress chastised us for not having monitored Tamerlan's internet usage after he had been cleared by the FBI. It was the same feeling I'd had after the Fort Hood shooting, when Congress had asked why we weren't reading Nidal Hasan's emails. Technically, we could do so. It would have required a significant investment in technology and massive changes to US law to allow the Intelligence Community to get intrusive with the personal business of Americans, but it was feasible. However, I didn't think that's what the US electorate wanted, and moreover, using the US intelligence apparatus to look inward at Americans would require us to override what I believed was an inherent right to privacy, implied if not explicitly stated in the Constitution and Bill of Rights. Some ODNI senior staff members recall us breaking out pocket editions of the Constitution after the Boston Marathon—going right to the source. I don't specifically remember doing that, but it does comport with the kinds of discussions I remember having.

But in the spring and summer of 2013, not even questions as fundamental as balancing national security with inherent civil liberties could be my dominant focus for long. On Tuesday, May 14, DOD announced its final sequestration plan. It would furlough its civilian employees, without pay, for eleven days over the following twenty-two weeks. Certain employees would be exempted from this mandatory furlough—for instance, those deployed to war zones and intelligence employees whose jobs were funded by the National Intelligence Program, as determined by the DNI. I think it's a measure of just how personally employees took this announcement that within weeks, job listings in the IC clearly indicated whether the position was NIP funded or MIP funded. I even saw one advertisement describing how to "Make a career in the NIP." I laughed, but I also understood the sentiment that inspired it.

Suddenly, and somewhat embarrassingly, I was unofficially declared a hero for the IC workforce. Coincidentally, that same day, legendary Marine Corps General Jim Mattis visited Liberty Crossing. He had just retired from active duty on March 22, ending his career as commander, US Central Command, a position in which he'd overseen operations throughout the combat theater and all the nations affected by the Arab Spring for the previous two and a half years. After Jim and I had lunch, he addressed the ODNI and IC workforce for an hour of remarks and spirited conversation. He opened by observing that he was delivering his first-ever speech in a suit instead of in a uniform. He said that he'd chosen to speak to the Intelligence Community as his first audience after his retirement because he owed a great debt to its practitioners, and "a Marine never forgets his debts."

I felt a lot of pride in our community that day, and in my connection to both the Intelligence Community and the Marine Corps. It felt as if we had more positive energy flowing than we'd had in quite a while. I knew that budgets would continue to be cut, but we now had a clearer vision and a plan for how to compensate. I hoped that the month of May would mark a turning point for IC fortunes, and that we could refocus on our mission without all the distractions that had plagued us for the past few years.

CHAPTER EIGHT

Snowden

The same week that DOD announced it would not furlough NIP-funded employees, an IT administrator on contract at the large, and very important, NSA facility in Hawaii told his supervisor he was taking medical leave to fly to the US mainland for treatment. Edward Snowden gave a completely different story to his girlfriend, with whom he shared a home, explaining that he would be away for a few weeks and couldn't say where he was going, conveying the implication that he was off on a secret mission for NSA. On Monday, May 20, 2013, he flew to Hong Kong carrying a bag of laptops holding hundreds of thousands—maybe millions, as we had no idea of the actual number at the time and still aren't certain—of intelligence documents and communications, many not just classified but compartmented to protect sensitive sources; cleared employees are read into compartmented programs only when they have a need to know about them. Tapping into what he thought he knew about maintaining cover, he checked into a plush hotel and began subsisting on room service.

Over the next two weeks, as Snowden divulged gravely damaging secrets about how the US Intelligence Community operated, he wrapped his every action in mystery, using signals and secret code phrases to rendezvous with reporters and give them his stolen information. If we had been looking for him, I believe we would have found him. But we weren't. Snowden's lies to his supervisor and girlfriend were credible enough that neither questioned them, and so the US Intelligence Community was blissfully unaware that, in an exotic port city of mainland

China, we were hemorrhaging intelligence capabilities through a trusted insider turned traitor.

Looking back, there's a coincidental timing to all of this that makes our naïvete in not preparing for the possibility of insider treachery and actively monitoring for it inexcusable. On June 3, in Washington, DC—literally as Edward Snowden was meeting with two reporters and a documentary filmmaker in Hong Kong—the military trial of Private First Class Bradley Manning was getting under way. (We knew Manning was a transgender woman in June 2013, but she didn't become Private Chelsea Manning until after her sentencing in August.)

Manning had been a low-level intelligence analyst in Iraq from late 2009 into 2010, when she became disenchanted with intelligence reports she was reading, which she felt showed a moral ambiguity not apparent in the public narrative of the war. She felt obligated to reveal that prisoner abuses were still taking place, nearly six years after the Abu Ghraib scandal, and she was disturbed by combat reports and video that indicated that US soldiers—some of whom had deployed on repeated combat tours—had a casual attitude toward killing. For Manning, the line defining which side was "in the right" had blurred until it ceased to exist. Envisioning it a form of citizen activism, she swept up all the classified and sensitive materials she could acquire—half a million military documents and a quarter million diplomatic cables—and gave them to the online organization WikiLeaks in January 2010. This single massive theft and release made everything else WikiLeaks had published, combined, pale by comparison.

On April 5, 2010, at the National Press Club in Washington, WikiLeaks publisher Julian Assange released the most incendiary material he'd received from Manning—a gunsight video from an Apache helicopter, complete with the audio from its radio transmissions and cockpit internal-communications circuit. The video showed the gunship firing on a gathering of men on a town square in New Baghdad, Iraq, on July 12, 2007. Later in the video, the Apache fires again, this time on a van that pulls up to the scene, after its occupants get out and begin to move casualties. What differentiated this footage from other combat videos is that, during the series of firefights, two Iraqi correspondents who were covering the war for Reuters were killed, and two children who were in the van were injured and later evacuated by US troops. DOD had shown the video to Reuters soon after the incident occurred but hadn't released it publicly, despite Reuters having filed a Freedom of Information Act request. With that information as the backdrop, Assange staged the April 5 event as a way of announcing that his organization could and would publish leaked materials that governments did not want released. He pitched WikiLeaks as an organization with no agenda, other than shining a bright light into the dark places that powerful governments and international organizations didn't want the world to see.

In fact, WikiLeaks did have an agenda, which was apparent in its editorial choices, even at that early point. The video opens with a quote from George Orwell, white letters on a black screen: "Political language is designed to make lies sound truthful and murder respectable, and to give the appearance of solidity to pure wind." Over ominous garbled voices and clicks and buzzes of military radio microphones being keyed, the screen cuts to a title card reading "Collateral Murder," with a website address, www.collateralmurder.com. The video then provides this context:

> On the morning of July 12th, 2007, two Apache helicopters using 30mm cannon fire killed about a dozen people in the Iraqi suburb of New Baghdad.
>
> Two children were also wounded.
>
> Although some of the men appear to have been armed, the behavior of nearly everyone was relaxed.
>
> The U.S. military initially claimed that all the dead were "anti-Iraqi forces" or "insurgents".
>
> The stories of most of those who were killed are unknown. But among the dead were two Reuters news employees, Saeed Chmagh and Namir Noor-Eldeen.

The footage cuts to photographs of the deceased Reuters correspondents and of their families in anguish, interspersed with quotes from friends and coworkers. It then cuts to a black screen with the words:

The U.S. military claimed the victims died in a battle that took place between U.S. forces and insurgents.

"There is no question that coalition forces were clearly engaged in combat operations against a hostile force."
—Lieutenant-Colonel Scott Bleichwehl, spokesman for U.S. forces in Baghdad. (New York Times)

The implication of the introduction, running two minutes and forty-six seconds in a video with a total runtime of seventeen minutes and forty-six seconds, was unmistakable: WikiLeaks and Assange intended to demonstrate that the US military was covering up its extreme wrong-doing with lies.

After the introduction, the video cuts to the black-and-white gunsight video. As the helicopter crew attempts to discern what's happening in the town square, an arrow inserted by WikiLeaks points to "Saaed w/ camera," and as one of the pilots says on the internal circuit, "That's a weapon," another arrow identifies "Namir w/ camera." A moment later, the pilot says, "He's got a weapon, too." No arrow appears to identify another man holding an AK-47, nor the man holding an RPG—a rocket-propelled grenade. The helicopter crew requests and receives permission to engage, and the ensuing fire kills or disables everyone on screen. Arrows identify "Namir's body" and "Saaed trying to escape." The video fades out and back in. On the internal cockpit circuit, the pilot handling the flight controls congratulates the pilot who had done the shooting, and they discuss the incident in a manner indicating they are comfortable with what had just occurred. The pilots acknowledge one person as being still alive, which a WikiLeaks-inserted arrow indicates is Saaed. Once the pilots identify him as being disabled and unarmed, they report on the radio that they will hold fire, but they keep the helicopter's gun trained on the wounded man. On the internal circuit, one is heard saying, "Come on, buddy. All you gotta do is pick up a weapon." The helicopter continues to circle as a van pulls up near the wounded man, and one pilot transmits, "We have individuals going to the scene, looks like possibly picking up bodies and weapons." As the van drivers carry Saaed, the pilots repeatedly request permission to engage. Finally, given the go-ahead, they fire

on the van. When they cease firing, an arrow identifies Saaed's body, and
the video cuts to a black screen, reading:

> Eight minutes after the attack, ground troops arrive on
> the scene.

> "We pulled up and stopped and I could hear them over
> the intercom say they couldn't drive the Bradleys [tanks] in
> because there were too many bodies and didn't want to
> drive over them."
> —Captain James Hall, Army chaplain. (Washington Post)

The remainder of the video shows a Humvee driving over a body as it
arrives on scene, to the apparent amusement of the pilots, fades out and
then cuts to soldiers pulling the two wounded children from the van and
running with them in their arms. After several moments, one pilot is
heard on the internal circuit saying, "Well, it's their fault for bringing
their kids into a battle." The other replies, "That's right."

I believe the early parts of this video could prompt Americans to contemplate and discuss how years of war have produced a generation of
soldiers who were callous about inflicting death. However, the selective
editing and editorializing done by WikiLeaks encouraged a different narrative, one that seemed to recall the My Lai Massacre in Vietnam. In
1968, an angry US Army platoon entered a Vietnamese village and wiped
it out, killing 347 men, women, and children indiscriminately. The massacre was a monumental turning point for American public tolerance for
the Southeast Asia war. But New Baghdad was not My Lai. The Apache
pilots may have been more comfortable with taking life than we'd like,
but they were not indiscriminate killers.

This would have been even more apparent if the "context" inserted by
WikiLeaks had made any attempt to portray the military perspective. At
no point does the "Collateral Murder" video indicate that the AH-64
Apaches were providing cover ahead of the troops in Humvees and on
foot who are shown at the end of the video—soldiers who, just before the
video begins, had been attacked by insurgents with AK-47s and RPGs just
a few miles down the road. And what the video revealed, at least to my

ears, is the shift in tone in the final lines of dialogue between the pilots. When the pilot manning the guns blames the children's injuries on the men who'd driven the kids into a firefight, I hear, as I've heard in many similar circumstances, a service member taking his first steps toward trying to live with the reality of an action carried out in battle—something he already regrets.

The video quickly became a sensation in the media and online. Along with continued publication of the documents provided by Manning, it and the April 5 release event put WikiLeaks on the map and brought the idea of activism through massive leaks into the public consciousness as a means of ostensibly making political statements. Assange was elevated in the press to celebrity status, and he traveled the world, promoting himself and his organization, as Manning remained anonymous. Six weeks later, in an online chat on May 20, Manning revealed to semifamous former hacker Adrian Lamo that she was WikiLeaks' source. Lamo contacted the FBI, and on May 27, 2010, the Army Criminal Investigation Command arrested Manning.

Before Manning's apprehension, WikiLeaks had been releasing small caches of classified and sensitive US documents onto the internet, appearing at least not to intend to put lives in danger, although not taking sufficient care to actually accomplish that goal. After Manning's arrest, Assange seemed intent on dumping as many classified documents onto the internet as he could, as quickly as he could. In my last few months as USD(I) and my first few months as DNI, on top of dealing with the confirmation process and starting work as the fourth DNI in five years, my time and attention were also taken up by the efforts at DOD and CIA to deal with these document dumps. Teams were on standby in both places to sort quickly through whatever was exposed in an effort to find names and identifying details for people in Iraq and Afghanistan who were helping the US war effort, and then to try to rescue them before the Taliban or Iraqi insurgents could find and kill them. In the midst of this, some young action officer with a sense of humor snuck an in-joke past CIA leaders, calling the CIA team the "WikiLeaks Task Force," abbreviated as "WTF."

Then Julian Assange made a personal mistake. In August, two women in Sweden alleged to police that, in separate incidents, what had started as consensual sex became nonconsensual, and in both instances, Assange didn't stop. Sweden issued an arrest warrant, and in December, Assange turned himself in to British police. His attorneys fought extradition for the next year and a half, but in May 2012 the British Supreme Court ruled that the Swedish extradition order was valid. In disguise as a delivery-man, Assange snuck into the Ecuadorian embassy in London, claiming that he was the victim of a US-led conspiracy to get him to Sweden, where the CIA could whisk him away to stand trial for political crimes in the United States. (In fact, the US justice system doesn't work that way, and the United Kingdom, where Assange was living, was our closest partner for both military and intelligence operations, while Sweden was *more* likely to resist if the United States asked for Assange.) The Ecuadorian embassy granted him asylum, and he took up permanent residence there, fearful that leaving it would lead to his immediate arrest. The result of this bizarre series of events is that the director of WikiLeaks hasn't set foot outside the Ecuadorian embassy since May 2012. Grotesquely to me, much of the international media glamorized him, establishing a new archetype of "long-suffering leaker-activist under self-imposed house arrest" for others to follow. I'm in agreement with CIA director Mike Pompeo's 2017 characterization of WikiLeaks as a "non-state hostile intelligence service."

In December 2012—at the very time I was trying to explain to law-makers on Capitol Hill why intelligence collection under Section 702 of FISA was so important to security—Edward Snowden sent encrypted emails to Glenn Greenwald, a reporter for the UK daily newspaper the *Guardian,* holding out the offer of classified documents that he claimed revealed NSA spying on US citizens. According to Greenwald, Snowden's first approach to him was so wrapped in code names and backdoor communications channels that he initially didn't take the offer seriously. Snowden then contacted Laura Poitras, a documentary filmmaker who had been the subject of a feature Greenwald had written in April 2012, and asked her to help him recruit Greenwald. Once she convinced Greenwald to give Snowden an opportunity, they began exchanging encrypted communications and Snowden transmitted some of the documents he'd stolen. By the time Snowden fled to Hong Kong in May 2013, Julian Assange had been ensconced in the London Ecuadorian embassy for only eleven months.

Poitras, Greenwald, and a second reporter for the *Guardian,* Ewen MacAskill, flew to Hong Kong to meet Edward Snowden. In a piece for the *New York Times,* Peter Maas somewhat famously captured the cloak-and-dagger feel of that first meeting:

> Snowden had instructed them that once they were in Hong Kong, they were to go at an appointed time to the Kowloon district and stand outside a restaurant that was in a mall connected to the Mira Hotel. There, they were to wait until they saw a man carrying a Rubik's Cube, then ask him when the restaurant would open. The man would answer their question, but then warn that the food was bad. When the man with the Rubik's Cube arrived, it was Edward Snowden.

Over the next several days, blocking cracks around doors with blankets and pillows and covering his laptop, Snowden spilled the US government secrets he'd stolen to the two reporters, as Poitras recorded the sessions. By each of their accounts, Snowden eventually gave them the massive files of highly classified documents he'd smuggled out of Hawaii. On Wednesday, June 5, the *Guardian* published Glenn Greenwald's first story from the Snowden leaks. The article began:

> The National Security Agency is currently collecting the telephone records of millions of US customers of Verizon, one of America's largest telecoms providers, under a top secret court order issued in April.
>
> The order, a copy of which has been obtained by the Guardian, requires Verizon on an "ongoing, daily basis" to give the NSA information on all telephone calls in its systems, both within the US and between the US and other countries.
>
> The document shows for the first time that under the Obama administration the communication records of millions of US citizens are being collected indiscriminately and in bulk—regardless of whether they are suspected of any wrongdoing.

I've said many times in private, and even a few times publicly, that what transpired next would have played out very differently if, in September 2001, someone—Secretary Rumsfeld, DCI Tenet, or even President

Bush—had come out and publicly stated, "We need to be able to track whom the terrorists overseas are talking to here in the United States. So we're going to save call records, and we're going to treat them like the FBI treats its fingerprint files: We'll hold them in reserve, and if we discover a plot to conduct a terrorist attack, we'll get a warrant to see who the terrorist is communicating with." If someone in authority had announced that, I believe both Congress and most Americans likely would have judged such actions to be reasonable, and we could have had an open discussion about how to execute them while protecting civil liberties. Instead, seven years after the phrase "enhanced interrogation techniques" had become part of the public lexicon, and many Americans had begun questioning what their Intelligence Community was doing in their name, a UK daily paper published a report that we were collecting intelligence, "indiscriminately and in bulk," on millions of Americans. We appeared as if we'd been caught doing something terribly wrong.

Greenwald's story also implicated me personally. Near the end of that first article, he wrote, "The court order appears to explain the numerous cryptic public warnings by two US senators, Ron Wyden and Mark Udall, about the scope of the Obama administration's surveillance activities." Very quickly, the internet dredged up video of the March hearing in which Senator Wyden and I had our exchange, and cable networks began to air it. Leaving off Senator Wyden's long and confusing preface about "dossiers," which complicated the narrative and didn't fit into a sound bite, the clip merely showed the final back-and-forth.

> *"Does the NSA collect any type of data at all on millions, or hundreds of millions, of Americans?"*
> *"No, sir."*
> *"It does not?"*
> *"Not wittingly."*

The media narrative immediately solidified into the simple assertion that the DNI had lied to Congress under oath to cover up NSA wrongdoing. Missing from the ensuing discussion were two honestly inconsequential facts: I wasn't under oath at the worldwide threat hearing, and the *Guardian* story concerned a court order from April, after my testimony. I describe these details as "inconsequential" because at the time I testified, there were other programs collecting metadata under Section 215 authorities, and because I always have an obligation to tell the truth to Congress, whether I'm under oath or not.

However, the accusation also left out three very *consequential* details that put my answer into context. First, Senator Wyden had asked me about "dossiers" on Americans, using that word twice in his question, and dossiers are impossible to build from telephone metadata. Second, my answer "not wittingly" only makes sense in the context of intercepting the communications content of bona fide foreign targets without knowing Americans were on the other end of the line. We absolutely knew we were collecting metadata. We were "witting," very aware of that, as was the committee. Third, and foremost in my mind, the accusation held that I had lied to the Senate committee dedicated to oversight of the IC, a committee whose members had access to and already knew the facts about each of the programs in question. My reputation on Capitol Hill was that I consistently spoke truth, often at the expense of politics and propriety. I'd stated, for example, that China and Russia were the greatest threats to US national security, when the State Department and White House really would have preferred I not. I had testified dozens of times over the two and a half decades since my DIA confirmation in 1991, and I'd never lied and never been accused of lying, but the accusation was that—just this once, for a change of pace—I'd chosen to lie, and I'd done it on live television before the Senate committee who had both the authority and ability to check my answer immediately, and that I'd done it ten minutes before a closed, classified hearing at which we could lay out all the details of the programs in question and discuss them freely. Really?

I recognize, of course, that this explanation may sound defensive and as if these accusations bother me a great deal. If I'm going to continue speaking truth, I have to acknowledge that it is and they do. I'm bothered, because, as an intelligence officer, I depend on my customers, which in 2013 included the president and Congress, to take it as a given that I will *always* speak truth to power. The media members who pressed this narrative that I'd lied sought to undermine that trust. I'm also angered because the narrative was purposefully blind. Later that summer, ODNI public affairs director Shawn Turner invited journalists from two national publications, separately, to discuss the March hearing, and why I'd answered the way I did. Both journalists, again separately, gave Shawn

the same answer: The explanation he gave to them sounded plausible—
even believable—but reporting that the DNI lied under oath sold newspaper copies and drove internet clicks, and their editors would never let
them change that narrative. So in writing that I'd lied, at least some jour-
nalistic publications were shirking their own obligation to the truth.

In June 2013, however, we had much bigger concerns than my personal
reputation. While we couldn't publicly confirm or deny the existence of
a top secret court order forcing Verizon to turn over its call records, after
June 5, our adversaries certainly knew to stop using Verizon for their
communications. Then, on June 6, the *Guardian* published another article that began:

> The National Security Agency has obtained direct access to
> the systems of Google, Facebook, Apple and other US internet
> giants, according to a top secret document obtained by the
> Guardian.
>
> The NSA access is part of a previously undisclosed pro-
> gram called Prism, which allows officials to collect material
> including search history, the content of emails, file transfers
> and live chats, the document says.
>
> The Guardian has verified the authenticity of the docu-
> ment, a 41-slide PowerPoint presentation—classified as top
> secret with no distribution to foreign allies—which was appar-
> ently used to train intelligence operatives on the capabilities
> of the program. The document claims "collection directly
> from the servers" of major US service providers.
>
> Although the presentation claims the program is run with
> the assistance of the companies, all those who responded to a
> Guardian request for comment on Thursday denied knowl-
> edge of any such program.

Revealing the existence of PRISM was no longer merely exposing a
program that aggregates metadata. PRISM was how we collected content
from terrorists, adversarial governments, and hostile intelligence services. This and subsequent articles said PRISM gave us access to "email,
video and voice chat, videos, photos, voice-over-IP (Skype, for example)
chats, file transfers, social networking details, and more." Included in the

Guardian's feature were images purported to be PowerPoint slides from NSA marked as top secret and compartmented, which would give our adversaries not only an overview of a powerful US intelligence tool, but also clues as to how to avoid surveillance. Worse, the level of specificity in the article, combined with the fact that the *Guardian* had published details of disparate classified programs two days in a row, and that the *Washington Post* published its own PRISM story, left no doubt that NSA wasn't just leaking, but had its own version of PFC Manning, one who was disclosing secrets far more dangerous to national security. This riveted the attention of the entire national security enterprise, and galvanized our counterintelligence and security apparatus to identify and locate the traitor. (The *Washington Post,* at least, ran an acknowledgment a few days after its PRISM article retracting the allegation that NSA had "direct access" to the company servers. The retraction received almost no notice.)

On Friday the *Guardian* published an article alleging that President Obama had asked the IC to draw up a "target list" for overseas cyber-attacks, and included a copy of a purported presidential memo issuing the order. That day the *Washington Post* also featured two new pieces from leaked documents.

On Saturday the *Guardian* published their fourth article:

> The National Security Agency has developed a powerful tool for recording and analysing where its intelligence comes from, raising questions about its repeated assurances to Congress that it cannot keep track of all the surveillance it performs on American communications.
>
> The Guardian has acquired top-secret documents about the NSA datamining tool, called Boundless Informant, that details and even maps by country the voluminous amount of information it collects from computer and telephone networks.
>
> The focus of the internal NSA tool is on counting and categorizing the records of communications, known as metadata, rather than the content of an email or instant message.
>
> The Boundless Informant documents show the agency collecting almost 3 billion pieces of intelligence from US computer

networks over a 30-day period ending in March 2013. One document says it is designed to give NSA officials answers to questions like, "What type of coverage do we have on country X" in "near real-time by asking the SIGINT . . . infrastructure."

Images attached to the article, marked as top secret and compartmented, revealed, not surprisingly, that much of our signals intelligence collection was taking place in active combat zones, but it also indicated that signals intelligence was a global enterprise. However, while the reporters framed this as a revelation that the US Intelligence Community was spying on poor and irrelevant nations of the world, our more astute adversaries could use the leaked information to discern how we were spying on them, using back doors around the globe.

We were hemorrhaging capabilities, and because we didn't know the source of the leaks, we couldn't stop them. Then, on Sunday, the *Guardian* posted a video filmed by Laura Poitras. After an establishing shot of marine traffic moving about Hong Kong harbor, the camera cuts to the face of a young man, wearing an open-collared shirt and glasses, with mussed hair and a slight, uneven stubble. His head and shoulders fill the right side of the frame, and a mirror reflects the back of his head, out of focus. A still frame from this video became the iconic image of Snowden, his "Che Guevara T-shirt" shot, featured on his Wikipedia page and whenever a story about him runs on TV. He glances at the camera and then away again as he says, "My name's Ed Snowden. I'm twenty-nine years old. I work for Booz Allen Hamilton as an infrastructure analyst for NSA."

Over the next twelve minutes, as edited by Poitras, Glenn Greenwald interviews Snowden on camera, describing how Snowden had moved from working at CIA to Dell to Booz Allen Hamilton in a series of information technology–related jobs. Greenwald asks what led Snowden from "thinking about being a whistleblower to making the choice to actually become a whistleblower." Snowden answers:

When you're in positions of privileged access, like a systems administrator for these, sort of, Intelligence Community agencies, you're exposed to a lot more information on a broader scale than the average employee, and because of that, you see things that may be disturbing, but over the course of a normal person's career, you'd only see one or two of these instances. When you see everything, you see them on a more frequent basis, and you recognize that some of these things are actually abuses.

When you talk to people about them in a place like this, where this is the normal state of business, people tend not to take them very seriously and, you know, move on from them, but over time, that awareness of wrongdoing sort of builds up, and you feel compelled to talk about it, and the more you talk about it, the more you're ignored, the more you're told it's not a problem, until eventually you realize that these things need to be determined by the public, not by somebody who was simply hired by the government.

His answer was chilling. Here was someone, a kid—yes, at seventy-two, everyone was a kid to me—who, like Manning, believed he had unique access, was someone who could "see everything." Like Manning, he had appointed himself as judge over what he had seen, and then, without conducting an investigation or calling out wrongdoers, was going to bring about justice in ways that multiple executive branch agencies, Congress, and federal courts—which were all aware of and conducted oversight of the very programs that concerned him—apparently were unable or unwilling to do. Unlike Manning, however, Snowden had unique IT accesses and had acted methodically to steal secrets, continuing to collect them for a full six months after first communicating with the person to whom he planned to leak, tricking his coworkers into giving him their passwords, even changing to a new job with different accesses to get at other files he wanted to leak. The materials Manning had leaked were embarrassing; the secrets Snowden was releasing were revealing to our adversaries and international terrorist groups how to avoid or thwart our surveillance. By the time the video was published online, Edward Snowden had bid farewell to Greenwald, Poitras, and MacAskill and gone to ground in Hong Kong with Sarah Harrison, Julian Assange's most trusted aide and someone who actually knew how to disappear.

In Washington and at NSA headquarters in Maryland, the IC scrambled to learn what they could about Edward Snowden. By all accounts he was a high school dropout who'd later earned a general equivalency diploma and was a capable software engineer. He'd enlisted in the Army and had suffered stress fractures in his legs from unaccustomed exercise during basic training. His Army records indicated that, instead of recycling him to a later training class to allow him to heal, they'd simply discharged him. He'd gotten work as a security guard for a publicly acknowledged NSA facility at the University of Maryland in 2005, and then applied for and got an IT job at the CIA. After a six-month training course in 2006, the CIA stationed him in Europe, where his supervisor and coworkers considered him difficult to deal with. Fearing he was going to be fired because of an incident in 2009, he resigned, listing his girlfriend's health issues as his reason for leaving.

And here's where an IC security vulnerability became glaringly evident. The CIA hadn't attached any alerts to his background profile, and when Snowden applied to become an NSA IT administrator, contracted through Dell Technologies, NSA supposedly never verified his references. NSA assigned him in Asia, then back to Maryland, and then to Hawaii in March 2012, where he worked on IT systems in the agency's information-sharing office. In that role, he had access to a vast array of NSA systems, programs, and data. In March 2013, he left Dell to work for Booz Allen Hamilton in a similar role, still at NSA Hawaii, and he continued to steal classified material. Because of his frequent job-hopping, his employment history was difficult to reconstruct, but by late Monday, we knew where he'd worked and generally what information he'd had access to, and we knew he'd used his system administrator privileges to get to many things he should *not* have had access to.

We learned later that he had begun copying and stealing classified material across multiple systems almost as soon as he arrived in Hawaii in March 2012. Our security programs were not designed to monitor users' electronic behavior across multiple systems and domains, and NSA couldn't distinguish what he'd actually copied and stolen from what he'd merely examined. He'd skirted security safeguards by accessing information through the accounts of coworkers, one of whom lost his job and career for giving his login information to Snowden, who claimed to need it for his system administrator work.

Also tellingly, when retracing his steps, NSA found that he'd applied to work in the agency's Tailored Access Operations office as one of its truly elite "hackers." The TAO qualification test is notoriously difficult—as one would expect—and about 50 percent of applicants fail. Snowden took the test, passed, and was offered a job in TAO as a general schedule government employee, though he believed he should have been graded as a senior executive service officer. (SES officers make up less than one half of 1 percent of the government workforce, and I don't know of anyone who was promoted to that position in his twenties.) He turned the position down, citing his larger salary as a contractor. When reconstructing his steps in 2013, NSA discovered that he had used his IT administrator privileges to access the account of the person in charge of administering the TAO qualification test and had stolen and viewed the test before taking it. Cheating on a test to become a spy is an amusing premise for Dan Aykroyd and Chevy Chase in *Spies Like Us*. It's obviously not acceptable in the real world of US intelligence.

On Tuesday morning I entered the Oval Office with a sense of foreboding; a day and a half after Snowden had been identified publicly, I would have to brief the president on what we knew. My trepidation wasn't just because the news was bad, but because I simply had so little information to report. In the anteroom outside the Oval, I mentally ran through the questions we didn't have answers for: Was Snowden recruited by or working with a foreign intelligence agency? Did he have help? Where was he in Hong Kong? Why did he go to China? What was he going to do with whatever he took? And most critical, what exactly did he steal? I knew this would be an entirely different "truth to power" moment than I'd ever had in the Oval Office before. This time I wasn't asserting an intelligence hard fact that went against my principal's worldview, but instead was about to inform the president of the United States that we'd potentially had one of the worst thefts of US secrets in the history of intelligence—and that I couldn't tell him much for certain beyond that fact. This wasn't exactly the IC's—or my—finest hour.

I could usually tell how an Oval session was going to go by what the president was doing when I arrived. If he was walking around, standing at the credenza by his scheduler's desk scanning the newspapers, or standing outside the office chatting with the White House staff, it would probably go pleasantly. That morning I found President Obama already in his seat, studying his iPad with a grim look. He didn't glance up when I walked in.

Since my days of briefing signals intelligence intercepts of the Vietcong to General Westmoreland, I've always felt more comfortable having the aid of some sort of graphic depiction, as both a memory crutch and a security blanket. For this meeting I came equipped with printed graphic depictions of all the NSA and IC systems Snowden had had access to, where he'd been stationed in Hawaii, the hotel where he'd first gone in Hong Kong, and the progress of his seven-year IC career.

When the president finally looked up, I held out a chart showing Snowden's job-hopping career. As he scanned the graphic I started to discuss the very little that we knew about Snowden. President Obama held up a hand to stop my talking, glanced over the page one more time, and waved it away too, saying, "We'll get more detail later." There was a pause—I have no idea how long—and then he shook his head, incredulous. Everyone else was very still and silent, trying to avoid being noticed.

The president never raised his voice but turned his frustration on me. "How could you people allow this guy to jump around like this and not see that he was a problem child?" My fifty years of experience, mostly as the "junior guy in the room," told me not to answer, just let him vent. He described what he'd seen of this as "bush league." My job was supposed to be getting the agencies to talk to one another, and yet NSA officials had no idea that they were hiring someone the CIA considered problematic and untrustworthy. Worse, that failure had happened on Obama's watch, during his first year as president. He fumed about all the ways this was going to hurt his relationships with foreign leaders—a ramification I'd certainly considered—and he complained how it was going to distract from and set back other agenda items, like health care, climate change, and legalizing same-sex marriage, just when our nation was making progress—things I hadn't fully considered. He didn't yell. He didn't call me names. But for the ten minutes or so we had allocated for the intelligence session that morning, he released the steam of his slowly boiling anger at me. I left the Oval that morning feeling like an omega dog slinking away from a confrontation with the alpha, not quite sure if he's actually hurt or just feeling that way. We had badly let down the president, and for that matter, the nation. I wanted to disappear into the woodwork.

Leaks continued to drip through the *Guardian* and the *Washington Post*, and on Thursday, June 13, Snowden gave an interview to the *South*

China Morning Post, claiming that NSA was hacking computers in Hong Kong and mainland China and that, while he felt the United States was bullying China to extradite him, he had no intention of leaving and would fight extradition in Hong Kong's court system.

The following day, the US Justice Department brought formal charges against Snowden under the 1917 Espionage Act, and the UK government took steps to prevent him from traveling through their airspace. Perhaps in retaliation, on Sunday the *Guardian* dragged the UK into the fray with an article saying the GCHQ—their NSA equivalent—had spied on global leaders during the 2009 G20 Summit in London.

More stories and more leaks spilled out every day. One claimed that the GCHQ tapped fiber-optic cables belonging to the communications companies to gain access to the world's emails, Facebook posts, and internet histories, and that they then shared all of that information with NSA. Another said that the US courts were complicit in enabling NSA to use "inadvertent" collections against Americans. Many—if not all, but who could keep track?—of these stories were inaccurate, misleading, or incomplete in how they characterized intelligence activities. Still, many did reveal vital secrets, and we watched as our intelligence advantage eroded. There wasn't much we could do about the factual errors, as attempting to correct them would mean revealing *actual* intelligence sources and methods that weren't in the leaks.

As I dealt with the fallout within official channels, I was grateful for former intelligence officials like Mike Hayden, who could appear on TV and say things I couldn't say as DNI. On Friday, June 14, in a conversation with Fareed Zakaria on CNN, Mike laid out how the publication of the leaks was undermining national security:

> We've reminded our enemies how good and comprehensive we are at this. We will punish American businesses that have cooperated—under US law and at the direction of a US court. This is bound to be bad news for them, in terms of their international business. And then, finally, globally, a country or a source that might be thinking of cooperating with the United States should have almost no confidence in our discretion or in our ability to keep a secret.

Over the next year and more, Mike would be an IC surrogate for many of the difficult conversations to come, including debates about balancing civil liberties protections against security. At several points he spoke about the metadata program, explaining what it was and wasn't. Noting other actions we as citizens take for the common good, like following traffic laws and submitting to searches before boarding planes, he posed the reasonable question: What are we willing to let our Intelligence Community do in the name of public safety? I didn't consider that to be a rhetorical question, and wished we as a nation could arrive at a reasonable consensus answer.

Two weeks into the deluge of Snowden stories, the entire IC was constantly on edge and on the defensive. We issued statements explaining the procedural steps that prevented NSA analysts from doing the kind of surveillance Snowden said they were engaged in. We published papers discussing how the oversight process involved all three branches of government and how everyone was checking everyone else's work. Those publications were ignored, disregarded, or scoffed at by the skeptical media and by politicians with axes to grind. What bothered me the most was that in the public discussion of intelligence, there seemed to be an implicit, nearly universal narrative that the IC's workforce was filled with people scheming to spy on their friends, neighbors, and citizens at large. That story simply did not describe the Intelligence Community people or mission I knew and believed in. The fact that we had neither the inclination, authority, nor resources to actually do what we'd been accused of didn't seem to matter.

IC service starts with swearing an oath to uphold the Constitution of the United States—the same oath the military takes. Intelligence officers of all types have the same dedication to public service that our uniformed troops do, and they make the same sort of sacrifices. IC people do shift work, keeping watch through the night. They toil long hours, staying until the job is done, because they can't bring classified material home to finish after dinner or bedtime stories. And when they do get home, they don't get parades, and they aren't able to boast to their parents or children, "I did that"—I made this research breakthrough, I brokered a partnering agreement with a foreign power, or I broke up this terrorist plot. IC service means toiling in anonymity and not getting public recognition for achievements. It means accepting less pay to serve. And for many members of the IC in the summer of 2013, it meant enduring government-mandated furloughs and trying to pay bills with 10 percent less income.

Intelligence officers deploy to dangerous places, away from their families. Some lose their lives, and some of them will never have their sacrifice publicly acknowledged—even in death. In the lobby of CIA headquarters, 125 stars are carved into the white marble wall, one for each CIA officer who died in service. In the book at the base of the wall, only 91 names are listed. The other 34 stars have no names associated with them, because public disclosure of the officers who lost their lives, or public discussion of their missions, would mean revealing national security secrets. NSA has a similar display honoring an even greater number of people who've paid the ultimate price. Those officers knew what that sacred trust meant when they took on the missions that cost their lives. And in June 2013, one of their own—a former CIA employee who became a contractor with NSA—had betrayed that trust and revealed many damaging secrets about how the IC did its job.

On June 21, for the first time, we took the extraordinary step of declassifying a major program—the metadata storage governed by Section 215 of the Patriot Act. Snowden had made public the mechanics of how the program worked, and the media had run with the story, stating as fact that anything IC employees physically *could* do with this program—and honestly, many things we physically couldn't do—we *were* doing. In declassifying it we went to great lengths to defend its utility. Looking back, I think it was a mistake to oversell Section 215. At one point NSA asserted that its authorities had led to the disruption of fifty terrorist plots, when in fact those plots turned out to have been thwarted through a combination of surveillance authorities. Section 215 was actually a rarely used safety net, but one we were reluctant to live without. If an incident like the Tsarnaev brothers blowing up two pressure cookers filled with shrapnel occurred, or if we uncovered another active plot, we used Section 215 authorities to quickly check if further attacks were imminent. We should have just explained that. We had had serious discussions of whether the metadata storage program governed by Section 215 was even an "intelligence" database, since it really functioned as a reference to confirm or refute a potential domestic terrorist nexus—a need identified by the 9/11 Commission. It might have been more appropriate for the database to be held by the FBI or DHS, rather than NSA.

Regardless, the upshot of declassifying the Section 215 program for me personally was that I was able to send a letter to Senate Select Committee on Intelligence chairman Feinstein. That letter explained that during the unclassified hearing three months earlier, when questioned by Senator Wyden, I was thinking only about the *unclassified* FISA Section 702 program when I'd answered, and not about the then-classified Patriot Act Section 215 program. Our declassification of the 215 program finally allowed me to correct the record. As I wrote, "I have appeared before congressional hearings and briefings dozens of times, and have answered thousands of questions, either orally or in writing. I take all such appearances seriously and prepare rigorously for them. But mistakes will happen, and when I make one, I correct it." My letter did nothing to change the public discussion about me, but it felt good to admit publicly to a mistake I'd made publicly. I'm not sure anyone noticed.

As I was sending that letter, all eyes and all cameras were again focused on Hong Kong. After bringing charges against Snowden, the US government had suspended his passport, which should have prevented him from leaving the city. However, on June 23, Hong Kong authorities allowed him, accompanied by Sarah Harrison, to board a flight to Moscow. His plan was to eventually get to Ecuador, the same nation that was protecting Julian Assange in its London embassy. China waited until the flight had cleared its airspace to announce that Snowden had left. Hong Kong authorities said the United States had made a mistake with paperwork, one that invalidated our invalidation of Snowden's passport. I suspect China and its new president, Xi Jinping, were happy for any excuse to remove themselves from this awkward diplomatic situation.

Vladimir Putin held a different worldview. For him, Snowden's arrival was an opportunity to slowly torment his old adversary—the United States—one that could be available to him for as long as he desired. So the Russian government officially recognized the US revocation of Snowden's passport and refused to let him board a transfer flight. Snowden and Harrison were left stranded in the Moscow airport, unable to pass through customs into Russia and not permitted to board a flight to anywhere else. A group of journalists, who either didn't know or didn't believe Moscow was keeping Snowden from traveling, figured out that the next leg of his planned trip to Ecuador would be a flight to Havana the following morning, June 24. They bought all the remaining tickets for the flight and boarded with cameras and notepads, ready to capture the story of a lifetime. When the plane left without Snowden, the journalists took turns tweeting pictures of his empty seat.

For the next forty days, Snowden and Harrison lived and slept in the no-man's-land of the Moscow airport, unable to leave or enter Russia, as the world's diplomats decided their fate. On Tuesday, June 25, Secretary of State John Kerry asked the Russian government to extradite Snowden. On Wednesday, Putin refused. Under pressure from the United States, the government of Ecuador revoked its offer of safe passage and asylum. A host of other nations followed suit, and many more skirted the issue by declaring that he'd have to be present on their soil before they'd consider the matter. On July 3, based on a false tip that Bolivian president Evo Morales was smuggling Snowden out of Moscow, France, Spain, and Portugal refused to let his plane transit their airspace. It landed in Vienna, where it was held overnight for a fruitless and embarrassing twelve-hour search. Several Latin American nations showed their displeasure at this insult by offering Snowden asylum. He instead requested asylum in Russia. Putin responded that before he'd grant it, Snowden would have to stop "harming American interests." I got the feeling Putin was really enjoying this. Snowden rescinded his appeal. On July 8, the *Guardian* posted more of Greenwald's interview with him, during which he predicted that the US government would "say I have committed grave crimes; I have violated the Espionage Act. They are going to say I have aided our enemies." Finally, on August 1, Snowden was granted temporary asylum by Russia. He walked out of the airport and into his new life in Moscow.

The media reporting on the leaks had continued during Snowden's time at the airport. The *Guardian* and the *Washington Post* published stories claiming, among other things, that the US government had bugged the offices of the European Union in New York, Washington, and Brussels; that we were spying on thirty-eight foreign embassies; and that we were reading millions of emails and text messages of innocent German citizens, at which point the German magazine *Der Spiegel* joined in printing the leaks. Together, the three media outlets released stories claiming the United States was spying on the citizens of Brazil, Venezuela, Colombia, Argentina, Panama, Ecuador, and Peru. On July 10, the *Washington Post* published what was purported to be an NSA graphic showing how the agency gained physical access to fiber-optic cables. I couldn't fathom how this supposed revelation could benefit anyone except adversarial intelligence services. Other stories claimed the intelligence services of Australia, New Zealand, and Germany were complicit in the US crimes, and that the United States paid GCHQ in the United Kingdom to conduct activities that were illegal under US law. On July 20, when UK authorities came to the *Guardian* offices with a warrant to seize the electronics given to them by Edward Snowden, the paper dramatically destroyed all of its equipment, saying they had copies of all the files safely somewhere outside the UK.

I spent a great deal of time in classified briefings on Capitol Hill and on secure phone lines with my foreign counterparts, refuting many of these claims from the leaks, while Stephanie O'Sullivan continued to focus on the IC workforce. At an event largely attended by IC employees, Stephanie captured what we were all feeling about Snowden:

> It's been clear that neither he—nor the reporters he gave these to—understood what they were looking at. A story early this month claimed that we had collected seventy million French telephone calls in a month. Those seventy million calls were in fact collected by the French intelligence service, outside of France, in furtherance of mutual counterterrorism and force protection concerns, and provided by the French intelligence service to us. But until the truth was leaked to the *Wall Street Journal*, we couldn't correct this publicly, because we'd damage sensitive intelligence relationships.
>
> That's the kind of problem we face. Most of the stories that have sprung from the leaks have focused on our considerable raw-technical capabilities. They lay out our sources and methods; and what the *Washington Post* reports, al-Qaida knows. It's gotten to the point where, I pick up the paper in the morning, and I read an article with details that would have horrified me eight months ago. And now, I think, "Well, this isn't—so—bad."

By the end of June we'd decided we would respond to the leaks as an integrated community, much as we'd responded to the first round of budget cuts. In doing so we would add a new word to the Intelligence

Community lexicon—"transparency." As someone who had been in or around the intelligence business for the better part of seven decades, transparency felt "genetically antithetical" to me. But we knew we couldn't continue to counter the narrative just by reflexively saying, "No comment," or "That's not true," particularly because—and this apparently comes as a shock to some people—we *did* conduct surveillance, both on hardened adversaries and sometimes on our friends. We knew they collected on us too, as that's what sovereign nations do to protect themselves and their interests.

As the summer wore on, I became fond of quoting Captain Renault from the movie *Casablanca,* when he walks into the casino and declares, "I'm shocked—shocked—to find that gambling is going on in here!" Yes, we were spying, but we were complying with US law, with the full visibility of all of our oversight entities.

Through July and the first part of August, we worked through how we would be transparent about the matters we could be transparent about, and how we'd protect our sources and methods in a more targeted way. On August 9, President Obama announced at a White House press conference the four steps we were taking "to strike the right balance between protecting our security and preserving our freedoms." First, he called for "reforms to Section 215 of the Patriot Act," explaining, "This program is an important tool in our effort to disrupt terrorist plots, and it does not allow the government to listen to any phone calls without a warrant. But given the scale of this program, I understand the concerns of those who would worry that it could be subject to abuse."

Second, he promised to "work with Congress to improve the public's confidence in the oversight conducted by the Foreign Intelligence Surveillance Court." Third, he called for more transparency, saying, "I've directed the Intelligence Community to make public as much information about these programs as possible. We've already declassified unprecedented information about the NSA, but we can go further." At the end of this set of initiatives, he noted, "The Intelligence Community is creating a website that will serve as a hub for further transparency. And this will give Americans and the world the ability to learn more about what our Intelligence Community does and what it doesn't do, how it carries out its mission and why it does so."

His fourth announcement, "forming a high-level group of outside

experts to review our entire intelligence and communications technologies," went almost unheard in DNI's public affairs office, as our social
media manager, Michael Thomas, realized the president had just announced live on national television the Tumblr site he was in the process
of building. He gaped at the TV screen, as Public Affairs Director Shawn
Turner patted him on the back, asking, "So, how's that website coming?"

We launched the Tumblr site, IC on the Record, on August 21, and by
the end of September had declassified and published eighteen hundred
pages of FISA court opinions. This wasn't simply a pile of unclassified
documents we'd been sitting on, or a collection of improperly overclassi-
fied papers, but actual classified court opinions, including requests for
surveillance warrants. We knew our adversaries would see them, and that
making them public, to some degree, posed a risk to national security.
But we judged that if we didn't take drastic steps like this, national security could be undermined more by the erosion of trust of the American
public and its elected representatives.

The site went on to become a clearinghouse for all the agencies to
publish declassified documents and to show whatever work they were
doing that they could discuss, specifically that of our oversight committees and courts. Much of the success of that website is the result of a decision we made in late June that we weren't going to release only documents
that made us look good. Many of the first court opinions we published
were highly critical of our surveillance requests, forcing the IC to reconsider or significantly revise warrants before they'd issue them. A year and
a half later, Tumblr featured the IC's site as one of a select few "Big in
2014" websites in their annual review. Michael Thomas noted that we
were right up there with "Lil Bub," which led me to publicly observe what
an honor it was for me, personally, to share the stage with a famous internet cat: "That's how you know you've arrived."

On August 21, as we were still scrambling to deal with the intelligence
leaks, we obtained evidence that Syrian president Bashar al-Assad's government had launched rocket shells loaded with the chemical weapon
sarin gas into the Damascus suburb of Ghouta, a community where some
people had expressed support for the opposition. Hundreds, perhaps
thousands of civilians—many of them children—had died horrifically.
Assad had learned from the mistakes that led to Gaddafi's downfall and

was keeping dissent in Syria in check with brutal force, in violation of international law and all standards of human decency.

The Intelligence Community's response reflected lessons we'd learned in the decade since the Iraq WMD national intelligence estimate. We red-teamed the evidence, questioning our assumptions and assessing the limits of our analysis. When we presented our assessment, we clearly stated our confidence levels. We gave alternate explanations and highlighted the things we didn't know. All the contributing "INTs"—SIGINT, GEOINT, HUMINT, and open-source—were validated and cross-checked.

Our assessment differed from the Iraq WMD report in another significant way. In 2003, the IC seemingly succumbed to pressure from the White House to find evidence of chemical and biological weapons sites. Because President Obama had previously declared that any use of chemical weapons would warrant US military action, in 2013 the White House would much rather we *not* announce we had proof that Assad and Syria had crossed President Obama's famous "red line." National Security Adviser Tom Donilon seemed to keep raising the evidentiary bar we needed to meet before he believed our reports, and we kept meeting each new challenge until I finally told his deputy, Denis McDonough, in a sidebar meeting at a Principals Committee meeting that we could no longer avoid telling Congress about what had become an elephant in the living room.

Everyone—Congress and even the UN—found our evidence to be compelling. Foreign ambassadors who were in attendance at Colin Powell's 2003 speech on WMDs in Iraq told our analysts that the information the IC made available on Syria, the degree of transparency we afforded the international community, and our candor regarding the limitations of our data far exceeded what was provided in the run-up to Iraq.

At a Friday evening National Security Council meeting, DOD laid out the plans for a Tomahawk Land Attack Missile attack on Syria. When the meeting broke, the president went for a walk around the White House grounds, asking Denis to join him. That evening I got a call that President Obama would not order the attack without congressional authorization. I was surprised, but again, it wasn't my place to agonize over such policy decisions, which are ultimately the president's to make. His decision was widely panned by all sides, but cooler heads prevailed, and diplomacy accomplished what a TLAM strike could not.

As the flood of leaks continued I began to worry that sources and methods we might need for the next crisis were being exposed. In Snowden's initial interviews, he'd said he'd personally reviewed all the documents he was giving to the reporters, and that they would only expose NSA's abuses of Americans' civil liberties. He then amended that to extend to the privacy rights of the world's citizens. He finally acknowledged that the scope of the material he'd leaked went beyond those parameters, but repeated he'd personally reviewed them all to make sure no sources would be revealed that would compromise US security. It says a lot about Snowden that he thought he knew enough about how sources and methods were being used across the community that he could— unilaterally—decide what exposures would or wouldn't cause damage.

On August 29, the *Washington Post* published an article and a leaked document that demonstrated Snowden had not, in fact, made an effort to protect intelligence sources. The *Post,* to their credit, called ahead of publication to inform us that they had the entire 2013 IC Congressional Budget Justification Book. As I've explained, the CBJB is the annual report to Congress that describes in detail the full extent of intelligence capabilities, essentially detailing what we'd done with the money that had been allocated to us and justifying our requests for the following year. It went into specifics about many programs—how they worked, what results they produced, and the effect they had on national security. It covered how we protected our forces from insurgent attacks and how we assessed adversarial leaders' intentions. It explained how we monitored proliferation of weapons of mass destruction, including in Iran, North Korea, and Syria. It contained, in short, the full expanse of how the US conducts intelligence.

The *Post* contacted my office, they explained, because they intended to publish this document and wanted to confirm that it would not cause grave damage to national security. In the conversations that followed, I learned that the editors at the paper had a very different understanding of "grave damage to national security" than the practitioners of national security did. Their focus was short-term and tactical; ours was long-term and strategic. While they didn't want to release material that might directly and immediately result in someone's death, they didn't seem concerned about exposing programs that would cause us to lose our ability to collect and exploit intelligence over the long term. After a short negotiation, which mostly involved my pleading from the national security perspective, the *Post* published most of the CBJB. The accompanying article included subheadings including "High-tech surveillance," "Counterintelligence," and "Critical gaps"—areas we'd identified to Congress as being where our collection capabilities were lacking and where adversaries could operate with little opposition.

Snowden changed his story yet again, saying that he'd given materials he knew could be damaging to reporters, not to WikiLeaks, because he trusted that as journalists they'd serve as curators and would release only information that related to civil liberties and not that involved security functions. The *Post*'s publication of the CBJB revealed just how naïve that notion was, if he ever actually believed it. Months later, in January, the *New York Times,* with which the *Guardian* had decided to partner, displayed another way in which trusting journalists to protect secrets was naïve. The *Times* published a story with a highly classified document that they'd redacted to protect the names of human sources in Iraq and the method we used to surveil al-Qaida in Mosul—the group that would become the Islamic State. The problem was that the *Times* did such an amateurish job of redaction that the internet very quickly figured out the actual names and the technical methods. I can't reveal what happened to the human sources, but that method of surveillance was gone to us.

There were many losses we never publicly acknowledged, but I want to point out a particularly important one. In February 2014, Glenn Greenwald started his own online publication, *The Intercept,* to capitalize on the Snowden leaks. That spring *The Intercept* staff called to say they were working on an article about how the United States was sweeping up every cell-phone call in two nations, the Bahamas and Afghanistan. We asked them not to publish either, but gave them a compelling enough reason to not release the Afghanistan information. On May 19, *The Intercept* published "Data Pirates of the Caribbean," which merely mentioned that there was another country in which all cell calls were being collected. Almost immediately Julian Assange and WikiLeaks announced they knew what the other country was and demanded that *The Intercept* divulge its name. When Greenwald refused, Assange published through WikiLeaks on May 23 that the second country was Afghanistan.

At the time I couldn't reveal what program we'd lost as a result, but in

September 2015, I declassified it and said in a public speech that what they'd exposed was what the US Command in Afghanistan regarded as "the single most important source of force protection and warning for our people" there. Specifically, I explained that it provided warning of impending IED attacks, and "the day after he wrote about it, the program was shut down by the government of Afghanistan." Intelligence losses are typically experienced as second- and third-order effects, such as an intelligence gap that didn't enable us to put two pieces of information together. The loss of the Afghan program had more immediate consequences.

Those first few months of leaks—June through September—were among the most difficult of my career. Not only were we witnessing our intelligence advantage erode and losing valuable sources, but we were also being vilified by the press and experiencing the people we served turn on us. In the meantime sequestration was not only eroding our capabilities but restricting us from using funds in ways that might have helped blunt the damage from Snowden.

At the same time, nations we considered our friends were concerned that we were spying on their citizens—which we weren't—and our closest intelligence partners were questioning whether we could still be trusted with their secrets, or if more Snowdens were poised to expose their activities to the world. By the end of the summer, the companies we'd relied on for help—particularly in telecommunications—had decided that, no matter how dire the situation was, they had to make a choice between patriotic duty and what would happen to their bottom line if customers believed their data or conversations were no longer secure, an issue some believed impacted the viability of their company.

As the cherry on top of this misery sundae, Congress failed to pass either an appropriations act or continuing resolution, and the government shut down from October 1 through October 16, 2013. Our "nonessential employees" were sent home, and our "essential employees" worked without pay.

Through all of those tribulations, I'm proud of how the IC responded with creative solutions to keep programs functioning and to quickly fill gaps by pivoting collection platforms whenever a publication exposed our capabilities. Agencies admitted their losses and looked to one another for help filling intelligence gaps. At the same time, our counterintelligence and security professionals put new procedures and online programs in place intended to thwart other potential leakers and to detect any attempts to repeat what Snowden had done. Finally, the people of the IC also opened their files and vaults to a review of their work, including by Congress and by a team appointed by the president.

My greatest personal disappointment through all this was that my exchange with Senator Wyden in the March testimony continued to be a distraction, one we apparently could not move beyond. On December 19, seven Republicans from the House Judiciary Committee—James Sensenbrenner, Darrell Issa, Trent Franks, Raúl Labrador, Ted Poe, Trey Gowdy, and Blake Farenthold—wrote to Attorney General Eric Holder, demanding that he investigate me for "knowingly and willfully" lying to Congress under oath. When I spoke to Eric about the letter, he dismissed it as frivolous and political, and I responded that I thought he *should* take them up on their request. Having been convicted in the court of public opinion, I would have preferred a formal investigation rather than dealing with the accusations and innuendos of reporters selling papers and politicians making political hay. Eric said he didn't want to dignify their allegations. I always thought it telling that the Senate Intelligence Committee itself never saw fit to make a referral to the Justice Department.

On January 17, 2014, President Obama addressed the nation to discuss the results of the Intelligence Community review he'd ordered and some changes he was making. I was in the audience in the auditorium at the Justice Department—a location specifically chosen to emphasize the importance of oversight and the rule of law—when the president both delivered a rousing defense of the Intelligence Community and described specific steps for reforming how we did business, aimed at regaining the trust of the American public. He began by saying that he'd come into office skeptical of intelligence overreach, and as president he'd put additional protections and oversight procedures on programs that could feasibly be abused. But he clarified:

> What I did not do is stop these programs wholesale, not only because I felt that they made us more secure, but also because nothing in that initial review and nothing that I have learned since indicated that our Intelligence Community has sought to violate the law or is cavalier about the civil liberties of their fellow citizens.

To the contrary, in an extraordinarily difficult job, one in which actions are second-guessed, success is unreported, and failure can be catastrophic, the men and women of the Intelligence Community, including the NSA, consistently follow protocols designed to protect the privacy of ordinary people. They're not abusing authorities in order to listen to your private phone calls or read your emails. When mistakes are made—which is inevitable in any large and complicated human enterprise—they correct those mistakes, laboring in obscurity, often unable to discuss their work even with family and friends.

I later said publicly that President Obama understood where his intelligence came from better than any of his recent predecessors—even George H. W. Bush, who had served as CIA director for almost a year. I just wished he'd gained that understanding for a better reason. The president continued:

If any individual who objects to government policy can take it into their own hands to publicly disclose classified information, then we will not be able to keep our people safe or conduct foreign policy. Moreover, the sensational way in which these disclosures have come out has often shed more heat than light, while revealing methods to our adversaries that could impact our operations in ways that we might not fully understand for years to come.

He said that "regardless of how we got here, though," we had serious work ahead of us "to protect ourselves and sustain our leadership in the world while upholding the civil liberties and privacy protections our ideals and our Constitution require." He laid out a series of major reforms in quick succession. First was "a new presidential directive for our signals intelligence activities both at home and abroad," which in many ways provided that we treat ordinary foreign citizens with the same protections we had for Americans—something no other nation on earth would consider. Second was putting concrete programs in place "to provide greater transparency to our surveillance activities and fortify the safeguards that protect the privacy of U.S. persons," particularly regarding the Section 702 foreign intelligence program and the Section 215 metadata program. Third, he asked the attorney general and me to "place additional restrictions on the government's ability to retain, search, and use in criminal cases communications between Americans and foreign citizens incidentally collected under Section 702." Fourth, he placed time limits on the secrecy of court warrants known as "national security letters," under which a suspected terrorist or foreign spy is investigated or surveilled without being notified. Fifth and last, he addressed the controversial Section 215, beginning with why it had come into existence, after "one of the 9/11 hijackers, Khalid al-Mihdhar, made a phone call from San Diego to a known al-Qaida safe house in Yemen. NSA saw that call, but it could not see that the call was coming from an individual already in the United States."

He noted that his "review group turned up no indication that this database has been intentionally abused," but that he believed "critics are right to point out that without proper safeguards, this type of program *could* be used to yield more information about our private lives," and that while the courts and Congress did exert oversight, "it has never been subject to vigorous public debate." He then made an announcement that shocked many people: "For all these reasons, I believe we need a new approach. I am therefore ordering a transition that will end the Section 215 bulk metadata program as it currently exists and establish a mechanism that preserves the capabilities we need without the government holding this bulk metadata."

The new program, embodied in the USA Freedom Act, took another year and a half to pass in Congress, but it required telecommunications companies to hold their own data and the IC to obtain a warrant referencing a specific threat in order to be able to access the companies' records. In practice, this wasn't significantly different from what we'd been doing, but people seemed to trust the commercial providers holding and protecting their data more than they trusted the US government to do so. President Obama concluded his speech with this thought:

> It may seem sometimes that America is being held to a different standard. And I'll admit the readiness of some to assume the worst motives by our government can be frustrating. No

NEWARK PUBLIC LIBRARY
121 HIGH ST.
NEWARK NY 14513

one expects China to have an open debate about their surveillance programs or Russia to take privacy concerns of citizens
in other places into account.

But let's remember, we are held to a different standard precisely because we have been at the forefront of defending personal privacy and human dignity. As the nation that developed
the internet, the world expects us to ensure that the digital
revolution works as a tool for individual empowerment, not
government control. Having faced down the dangers of to-
talitarianism and fascism and communism, the world expects
us to stand up for the principle that every person has the right
to think and write and form relationships freely, because individual freedom is the wellspring of human progress.

Six days later the German TV network ARD interviewed Snowden,
who was, unsurprisingly, unimpressed with the president's speech and
the new initiatives. I didn't watch the interview when it aired, but some
colleagues clipped one specific question and answer and sent it to me. The
interviewer asked Snowden, "You were working until last summer for the
NSA, and during this time you secretly collected thousands of confiden-
tial documents. What was the decisive moment, or was there a long period of time or something happening, why did you do this?" Snowden
replied, "I would say sort of the breaking point is seeing the Director of
National Intelligence, James Clapper, directly lie under oath to Congress." I was, to say the least, incredulous at the level of cognitive disso-
nance it must have taken for him to give that answer. Snowden had been
stealing US intelligence secrets—copying them and removing them from
secured spaces—for a full year by the time I testified in March 2013. Four
and a half months before my testimony, he had contacted Glenn Greenwald and offered these classified documents, and by the time I'd testified,
he'd already leaked them to Greenwald and Laura Poitras through encrypted emails, as well as contacted Bart Gellman, offering to leak to the
Washington Post.

When my friend Loch Johnson—whom I'd known since we attended
high school together in Germany, and who had been a staff member on
the Church Committee when they'd investigated intelligence abuses in

the 1970s—invited me to the University of Georgia that April, to make up the Charter Lecture that I'd been forced to cancel because of the shutdown in October, I knew I would have to address Snowden to the student body. In my speech, I talked to them about politics in Washington, and how we don't always follow "ancient tribal wisdom" about dismounting "dead horses." I talked about the vast array of threats we faced as a nation, and about the damage done by the leaks. I then spoke about how what Snowden had done affected me personally, which I hadn't done before publicly.

> A few weeks ago, I saw an article in the *Washington Post* detailing college admissions. An admissions officer from George Washington University told the *Post* that for the admissions essay question, "Who's your personal hero?," this is a quote: "She's seeing a lot of Edward Snowden citations."
>
> The idea that young people see Edward Snowden as a hero really bothers me. So I felt that I needed to talk about Snowden here. First off, I get it. I understand that some people see Snowden as a courageous whistleblower, standing up to authority. I personally believe that whistleblowing takes an incredible amount of courage and integrity. But Snowden isn't a whistleblower.

Of course, by April 2014 most government executives were comfortable with saying that Edward Snowden wasn't a whistleblower. We'd pointed out how Snowden had failed to use the legitimate whistleblowing avenues open to him: senior officers at NSA, criminal investigation units, NSA's or the IC's inspector general, the civil liberties protection officer in my office, the Justice Department, or Congress. We had also laid out how irresponsible he'd been with releasing hundreds of thousands of documents relating to the full spectrum of lawful intelligence activities all over the world, but I understood that it was very easy to talk about what someone has done wrong, to tell people what they *shouldn't* do, and whom they *shouldn't* emulate. It's more of a challenge to point out examples they *should* look up to and emulate. We couldn't expect the next generation of selfless, patriotic young people to join the Intelligence Community if our

pitch was going to be, "Come here, and *don't* be like Edward Snowden." I
wanted to offer the students at UGA something different.

> If you want a whistleblowing role model, look at Sergeant Joe
> Darby. He was an Army reservist stationed at the Abu Ghraib
> prison in Iraq in 2003. One afternoon, one of the prison guards
> handed him a CD. Joe stuck the disk into his computer and
> was shocked when he saw graphic images of guards abusing
> prisoners.
>
> Those guards were friends of his, some since high school.
> He agonized, thinking of his friends and his superiors, whom
> he'd be implicating. And he worried that those people could
> come after him for retribution. It took him three weeks of tor-
> ment before he turned the disk over to a special agent with the
> Army Criminal Investigation Command. You know about the
> global uproar when the pictures went public.
>
> For Joe, it was more personal. His fellow soldiers at Abu
> Ghraib shook his hand and thanked him. But back home,
> people called him a traitor and threatened his life. The Army
> needed to give his family an armed escort for six months. That
> act of whistleblowing took courage and integrity. In 2007, Joe
> Darby told the BBC, "I've never regretted for one second what
> I did when I was in Iraq, to turn those pictures in."
>
> I think he makes a great role model. I'd like to read an
> admissions essay on him. And I want people working for me
> who have the same sense of right and wrong, and the courage
> and integrity to speak up.

I then introduced Sean Curran, a University of Georgia graduate with
a double major in mathematics and geology who was now working for
DOD, helping develop the cryptanalytic capabilities the IC relies on for
its foreign intelligence mission. Before turning the microphone over to
Sean to talk about his experience, I gave the students a recruiting pitch:

> We need people with the talent and dedication of Sean Curran
> in the IC, and we absolutely welcome people with the courage
> and integrity of Joe Darby. Being an intelligence officer means

A favorite picture of my dad, taken in Germany when he was a major.

Fort Wayne, Indiana, probably 1943. I'm showing my early interest in communications intelligence.

Around the time I was twelve years old, when I "hacked" my grandparents' TV set to listen to the Philadelphia Police Department dispatcher.

Marine Corps Base Quantico, Virginia, August 1961. I'm wearing the helmet liner with an *X* in this photo of my training platoon. At left and right in the front row are drill instructors Sergeant Stiborski and Gunnery Sergeant Fowler, and in the middle is our platoon commander, Second Lieutenant Badolato.

July 16, 1963. My first official portrait.

Goodfellow Air Force Base, Texas, August 1963. Standing in front of my spiffy 1963 Corvair convertible. I was on what was called "casual status" while awaiting my security clearance.

Nakhon Phanom, Royal Thai Air Base, June 1971. On the occasion of my "fini" flight (my seventy-third and last flying mission) over Laos and Cambodia in an EC-47. I would rotate back to the States the next day.

Fort Meade, Maryland, circa early 1973. The promotion list for major had just come out and I was promoted to the rank a year early. From left to right are NSA director Lieutenant General Sam Phillips, Sue, and yours truly.

, June 1987. An honor
rd ceremony in Korea on
e occasion of my departure.
o my left is General Bill
Livsey, commander US Forces
Korea, and to his left, Brigadier General Charlie Bishop,
who replaced me as director of
intelligence for USFK.

Offut Air Force Base, Nebraska, March 1989.
Celebrating the occasion of my thirty-seventh
and last "Looking Glass" mission—the airborne
command post for the Strategic Air Command.
I was the deputy chief of staff/intelligence for
SAC at the time.

Bolling Air Force Base,
Washington, DC, circa January
1992. Bob Gates, in his role as
director of central intelligence,
visits Defense Intelligence
Agency headquarters, where I
was director.

Bolling Air Force Base, September 1, 1995.
With Sue right after my retirement
ceremony. After thirty-two years, my
career in the Air Force was over. Right
after this we got our retirement ID cards.

Wreckage of the Khobar Towers in Saudi Arabia after a bombing on June 25, 1996, killed nineteen American airmen.

September 11, 2001. Smoke rises from the southwest side of the Pentagon after the worst terrorist attack in our nation's history. The ensuing war on terror became the driving force behind our push for intelligence integration, and I would be sworn in as director of the National Imagery and Mapping Agency three days later.

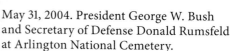

May 31, 2004. President George W. Bush and Secretary of Defense Donald Rumsfeld at Arlington National Cemetery.

February 5, 2003. Secretary of State Colin Powell addresses the United Nations Security Council, citing "irrefutable and undeniable" evidence that the government of Saddam Hussein continued to conceal Iraq's WMD program. CIA director George Tenet is seated behind him on the left.

Tallil Air Base, Iraq, June 2003. The use of unmanned aerial vehicles like the Predator pictured here provided unprecedented real-time persistent imagery intelligence, which revolutionized warfighting.

After footage of a 2007 airstrike in Baghdad was leaked to the website WikiLeaks, Army intelligence analyst Chelsea Manning was detained and later tried for violations of the Espionage Act. President Obama commuted Manning's sentence in January 2017.

April 2007. Secretary of Defense Bob Gates administers the oath of office as undersecretary of defense for intelligence to me in a hastily arranged ceremony after my confirmation.

June 5, 2010. Just before President Obama's rollout of my nomination as the fourth director of national intelligence in the Rose Garden. Pictured from left to right are me; Sue; my grandson Ryan; my son-in-law, Jay; my daughter, Jennifer; my grand-daughter, Erin; and President Obama.

Far left: My deputy director of national intelligence for intelligence integration, and later director of the National Geospatial-Intelligence Agency, Robert Cardillo.

Left: My principal deputy director of national intelligence, Stephanie O'Sullivan.

September 9, 2010. A President's Daily Brief in the Oval Office. Clockwise starting from far left are Robert Cardillo, Tom Donilon, Rodney S., John Brennan, James Jones, me, and President Obama.

September 13, 2011. With David Petraeus, testifying on "The State of Intelligence Reform 10 Years After 9/11" in front of a crowd of protesters at a joint hearing of the House and Senate select committees on intelligence.

February 1, 2011. Secretary of State Hillary Clinton and Homeland Security Secretary Janet Napolitano conferring on human trafficking as I look on.

May 1, 2011. The now-iconic picture of President Obama's national security team tracking the progress of the mission to apprehend Osama bin Laden.

The compound in Abbottabad, Pakistan, where Osama bin Laden was killed by US Special Forces in a daring strike.

Watching President Obama deliver a statement on the bin Laden mission in the East Room alongside Tom Donilon, Leon Panetta, Mike Mullen, Hillary Clinton, and Joe Biden.

September 11, 2012. This image was taken inside the US consulate in Benghazi on the night of the attack that took the lives of four Americans.

Ambassador Christopher Stevens delivering a speech in Tripoli in late August 2012.

October 22, 2015. Hillary Clinton testifies before the House Select Committee on Benghazi in what was to become a marathon eleven-hour hearing.

March 12, 2013. With FBI director Robert Mueller, presenting the worldwide threat assessment before the Senate Intelligence Committee. My exchange with Senator Ron Wyden during this briefing would later be the source of much controversy.

WikiLeaks founder Julian Assange in London, where he has helped to coordinate the ongoing leaking of government, corporate, and personal secrets from the Ecuadorian embassy.

Edward Snowden pictured during an interview in Hong Kong in summer 2013.

August 2014. The crash site of Malaysia Airlines Flight 17 near Donetsk, Ukraine. The entire chain of events leading to the Russians' firing on the plane was reminiscent of the 1983 Soviet attack on Korean Air Lines Flight 007.

North Korea, November 8, 2014. This photo was taken on the grounds of the state guesthouse in Pyongyang. Pictured with me are my executive assistant, Neil K., and Allison Hooker from the National Security Council staff.

An exterior shot of the state guesthouse in Pyongyang.

February 2015. Testifying to the Senate Armed Services Committee with Lieutenant General Vincent Stewart, director of the Defense Intelligence Agency, and pretending not to see the camera in my face.

Sharing a word with Michael Flynn during a hearing of the House Intelligence Committee. CIA director John Brennan is at left.

April 24, 2015. President Obama addresses the Office of the Director of National Intelligence on the tenth anniversary of its founding and uses the opportunity to return all the paperclips I've left in his office over the years.

August 2, 2016. With Sue in the receiving line before a state dinner for the prime minister of Singapore.

May 2017. With Sally Yates, testifying before a subcommittee of the Senate Judiciary Committee. After the 2016 election, she had warned the White House about contacts between former national security adviser Michael Flynn and Russia that might make him vulnerable to blackmail.

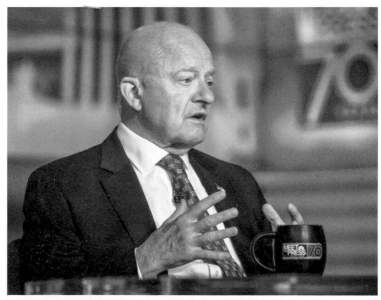

In the wake of Russia's unprecedented campaign of active measures to influence the 2016 presidential election, I felt it was my duty to speak out in media appearances like this one about the threat the Russians and their enablers continue to pose to American democracy.

December, 2016. One final Clapper family gathering in the Oval. From left to right are my oldest grandson, Ryan; me; President Obama; my son, Andy; my grandson Colin; my daughter-in-law, Kim; and my grandson Mac.

that sometimes you are the most junior person in the room, and you still have to voice an unpopular truth, to speak truth to power, because, at the end of the day, it's our job to give useful intelligence to decision makers and policy makers, not just to tell them what they want to hear.

I think most of you really would like working in intelligence, but if that's not your cup of tea, I hope you can serve our country in some other way, at least for a few years. We need bright young men and women like you everywhere in government. Serving is better than making a ton of money or skating through a life of leisure. It really is. And I do believe that so many of you already know that.

CHAPTER NINE

Not a Diplomat

When I went back to Capitol Hill in January and February to present the IC's 2014 Worldwide Threat Assessment, I felt like a man who had traversed mountains and rivers through hostile territory only to find himself back at the spot where he'd started, now surrounded by adversaries on all sides. In less than a year we'd lost some of our most important intelligence collection capabilities to a traitor from within our own ranks; we'd lost much of our capacity to replace those capabilities due to sequestration cuts, along with shedding thousands of contractors we could no longer afford to pay; we'd lost access to a lot of telecommunications information, as many companies resisted helping us, sometimes even with active terrorist investigations; we'd lost the trust of some foreign governments, which were truly surprised we were surveilling them, not to mention many more who *feigned* surprise, because, as we both knew, they were also surveilling us; we'd lost the trust of some foreign intelligence partners, who questioned our ability to keep their secrets as they lost their own capabilities to Snowden's leaks; and most disturbing, we'd lost the trust of the American public, which questioned what we were doing globally on their behalf and what we were doing domestically to them. We were being far more transparent than I would have imagined possible just a few years earlier, but it felt as though we had barely made a dent in dampening the public anger.

Also, as I sat for the 2014 hearings, I felt a new, *personal* antagonism from some congressional members, which had nothing to do with performing for the red light over the camera. Attorney General Holder had not answered the House Judiciary Committee's request to investigate me in December, and he had not replied to their follow-up letter in January asking why he hadn't begun an investigation. I hadn't done myself any favors, repeatedly trying to oversimplify an explanation for my mistake into something that could be expressed in a sound bite. That was particularly true of an interview with MSNBC's Andrea Mitchell just days after the Snowden leak, when I'd tried to explain what I'd been thinking when answering Senator Wyden's yes or no question months earlier, which I'd misunderstood at the time he asked it. I still couldn't clarify what my answer should have been for Mitchell, as the Section 215 program was still classified even after being leaked. On camera, I'd told her something incomprehensible about "no" being the "least untruthful" of the two answers I could give.

My statement had been widely recognized as the best Washington "doublespeak" of that month and had earned me the *Washington Post*'s "Worst Week in Washington" award on June 14. Whatever else happened, there was no way to get that moment back. I'd sent an email to Denis McDonough, offering to resign. I will never forget Denis and his perceptive and compassionate leadership. He called me less than fifteen minutes later to say my resignation was not accepted and to tell me to focus on my duties. This, I came to learn when Denis became chief of staff, was typical of him. For the rest of the administration, I witnessed countless examples of Denis reaching out to people at just the right time with just the right dose of encouragement. Six months after receiving Denis's timely support, continuing my duties meant going to the Hill again.

Complicating the 2014 hearings, just before I briefed our threat assessment to the House Intelligence Committee on February 4, President Obama gave an interview with CNN in which Jake Tapper asked him about my exchange with Senator Wyden and my "least untruthful" answer to Andrea Mitchell. The president responded:

> I think that Jim Clapper himself would acknowledge, and has acknowledged, that he should have been more careful about how he responded. His concern was that he had a classified program that he couldn't talk about and he was in an open hearing in which he was asked, he was prompted to disclose a

program, and so he felt that he was caught between a rock
and a hard place. Subsequently, I think he's acknowledged that
he could have handled it better. He's spoken to Mr. Wyden
personally.

His answer was an attempt to paint what had happened in a constructive light and move on, and I might have been okay with it had the president or I ever spoken directly about my exchange with Wyden. We had
discussed and moved past other questionable comments I'd made in
hearings, as well as my "London?" gaffe with Diane Sawyer, but we never
talked about this one. After the Tapper interview, I remarked privately to
a group that included USD(I) Mike Vickers that since I was "so far under
the bus, I might as well change the oil while I'm down here." Later, I
learned that Mike never forgets anything.

If appearing publicly on Capitol Hill felt like walking into "a field of
fire," to borrow an Army expression I'd learned in South Korea, the situation in no way affected my obligation to speak intelligence truth to
power, and I had no intention of being cautious or taking a diplomatic
course with Congress. So, to the great distress of the National Intelligence
Council, instead of having them write the first draft of my opening statement, I wrote it myself, broad-brushing the threats around the globe and
focusing on how leaks and sequestration were causing us to lose our ability to collect intelligence on those threats. Long-tenured NIC chairman
Chris Kojm urged me to take a more traditional approach, and I eventually gave in to his argument that Congress and the public deserved to
hear more actual details of the threat picture, and I let the senior analysts
on the National Intelligence Council edit and expand the opening
statement.

Still, parts of my first draft survived, including referring, during the
February 11 hearing with the Senate Armed Services Committee, to the
confluence of sequestration, leaks, and loss of partnerships as "the perfect
storm." I told them that we would, as always, meet the threat to the best
of our abilities, but sequestration with its drastic cuts and arcane rules
was a self-imposed handicap forcing the nation "to accept more risk."

After speaking truth to power on how all of this was clouding the
threat picture and making the world more dangerous, I highlighted the

few specific crises we considered the most pressing, one being the civil war in Syria, which by then was creating a threat to the US homeland.

> The strength of the insurgency is now estimated at some-where between 75,000 to 80,000 on the low end and 110,000 to 115,000 on the high end, who are organized into more than 1,500 groups of widely varying political leanings. Three of the most effective are the al-Nusrah Front, Ahrar al Sham, and the Islamic State of Iraq and the Levant, or ISIL, as it's known, whose numbers total more than 20,000. Complicating this further are the 7,500-plus foreign fighters from some 50 coun-tries who have gravitated to Syria.

Unlike in Libya in 2012, there was no unified resistance in Syria, and despite what Senator McCain had said in 2013, we had a very difficult time identifying the "good guys." Mixed in throughout the Syrian resis-tance were al-Qaida operatives and Iraq insurgency veterans, all of whom hated America. Our biggest concern was that, eventually, the fighters who had traveled from abroad—particularly those coming from Europe, but a growing number from the United States—would return home, having been radicalized by the terrorists they were fighting alongside and having learned new skills in war they could now apply against their fellow Euro-peans or Americans. Adding to this nightmare, refugees were pouring across Syria's borders, and its border with Iraq was merely notional. There was very little stopping transit between the two countries, as we saw when the Islamic State of Iraq changed its name to include both Iraq and Syria (the Levant) as its territory.

The one piece of positive news in Syria was that after the US Intelli-gence Community had presented such a compelling case to show Assad's use of chemical weapons the past fall, he had admitted to having about a thousand tons of mustard gas, sarin, and the nerve agent VX, and an international team had destroyed the equipment for producing the chem-icals. By February, they were well into destroying or removing Syria's existing stockpiles. It was, however, difficult to destroy chemical weapons in a war zone, and we had no illusions that Assad couldn't reconstitute his chemical weapons program quickly if he decided to.

At the hearings, I continued my tradition of adding a year to the count of how we were "facing the most diverse set of threats I'd seen in my now more than five decades in the intelligence business." In the televised SASC hearing, I cited:

> The growth of foreign cyber-capabilities, both nation-states as well as non-nation-states; the proliferation of weapons of mass destruction; aggressive nation-state intelligence efforts against us; an assertive Russia; a competitive China; a dangerous, unpredictable North Korea; a challenging Iran, where the economic sanctions have had a profound impact on Iran's economy and have contributed to the P5-plus-1 joint plan of action; lingering ethnic divisions in the Balkans; perpetual conflict and extremism in Africa: in Mali, Nigeria, Central African Republic, and South Sudan; violent political struggles in, among others, the Ukraine, Burma, Thailand, and Bangladesh; the specter of mass atrocities; the increasing stress of burgeoning populations; the urgent demands for energy, water, and food; the increasing sophistication of transnational crime; the tragedy and magnitude of human trafficking; the insidious rot of inventive, synthetic drugs; the potential for pandemic disease occasioned by the growth of drug-resistant bacteria.

"I could go on with this litany," I said, looking up from the script, "but suffice it to say, we live in a complex, dangerous world." The events of the past year had made the world so much harder to keep track of, and not just because some of our capabilities had been compromised. No matter how good they were, imagery and signals intelligence would only get us so far in understanding the reality on the ground in the far-flung areas of the world, and CIA only had so many operatives in a relatively limited number of places. To assess the situation in a remote nation in Africa or island in South Asia, we relied on the governments and intelligence services of the regional powers that were invested there. Over the past eight months, I'd spent a lot of time on secure, long-distance calls and traveled many thousands of miles trying to repair and restore those relationships. In November, I'd been to Europe and Asia, and was soon scheduled for a trip to Norway and Sweden, and then to meet with our close "Five Eyes" English-speaking partners: the UK, Canada, Australia, and New Zealand.

Overseas travel was not glamorous. I flew with my executive assistant, one or two subject-matter experts, the three-star general who led ODNI's "partner engagement" (successively Mike Flynn, Ted Nicholas, and then John Bansemer), and a travel coordinator, along with the aircrew, security, protective-detail, and communications teams, on a large Air Force transport plane, inside a secure box with no windows. In whatever country we'd landed, we'd ride to a hotel in a caravan of SUVs, typically eat dinner with our hosts, and prep for the next day, which would be filled with meetings—both with foreign government counterparts and with the US intelligence officers stationed there. We packed as much personal interface time into these trips as possible, typically across a conference table, never a putting green.

At meetings of the Five Eyes partners, which we held twice a year and rotated among each of the five nations, we dwelled on how we could collectively mitigate the damage we were all incurring from the publication of the leaks. Those were the serious discussions. During breaks, all four of the other national intelligence leaders took turns—and great joy—in asking pointed questions about our American political processes. "Sequestration and debt ceilings. We don't have those; what are they like?" And, "So tell me again about how the greatest democracy on earth works." More than once, the United Kingdom's intelligence chief observed that it had been a grave mistake for the United States to declare independence, but that Queen Elizabeth was willing to welcome us back into her good graces, once we were willing to admit to our error. I never was able to come up with an appropriately witty retort. Our mutual challenge had drawn us closer than ever, and a year later, I would publicly make the—seemingly outlandish to the archconservatives in the US IC—suggestion that dual-citizenship privileges and obligation should be extended to all the Five Eyes partners whenever we found ourselves in one another's intelligence footprint, with full access to each nation's networks. This is an idea whose time hadn't come before I retired, but I'm convinced it will happen someday.

For most of the other parties mentioned in the Snowden leaks, I'd developed a script for how to get past the awkward first few minutes of our meetings. The delegation leader would start with some version of

"We've read all the shocking media reporting about your collection on our government through NSA's capabilities." Without acknowledging the specific allegation, I'd respond, "The president has tasked us to study this with an intent to reform how we conduct intelligence." We would all nod and then get on with business, leaving unspoken any understanding of how *their* intelligence services were spying on us. Everyone wanted insight on what US leaders were thinking—in general and in relation to their parochial issues and their government, and on the state of technology in America. Every national delegation I met with also needed US intelligence insights, particularly on terrorist threats, to keep stability in their sector of the world. Outside the Five Eyes circle, Norway and Japan understood our mutual dependencies best and did the most to minimize damage from public discussion of the leaks and what they revealed. Not surprisingly, those two nations have moved into the next concentric circle of partnership with US intelligence in the years since, to their credit and our mutual benefit.

I can say, however, that without a doubt, the 2014 bilateral meeting I had with a delegation from Brazil—the nation where Glenn Greenwald kept his residence—was one of the ugliest and nastiest of my career. Most nations sent their intelligence leaders to these gatherings; some, to make a point, sent their diplomats. Brazil sent its attorneys. President Dilma Rousseff was furious with the United States for purportedly spying on her, her government, and her citizens—at least according to Greenwald—and so dispatched her lead attack dog, Antonio Patriota, who had once been Brazil's ambassador to the United Nations and was specifically named by Greenwald as someone we'd surveilled. He was backed up by a large contingent from Brazil's Ministry of Justice. Without exchanging pleasantries, Patriota began reading aloud twenty-eight pejorative questions—charges, really—that he demanded the United States answer. Each was intentionally insulting, either to the United States or to the US Intelligence Community. I sat and listened, and when he was halfway through his list, I politely interrupted and asked if he would give me a copy of it, so we could provide him with formal, interagency-coordinated responses. That only seemed to infuriate him more, as my attempt to cooperate had broken his rhythm.

But even that enmity was short-lived. Two years later Brazil hosted the 2016 Summer Olympics, and the US Intelligence Community supported their efforts in a major way, deploying people and teams from several IC components. We provided them with intelligence that was not only timely enough for them to act, but was specific enough for them to make preemptive arrests. There were no attacks on any Olympic venue or event. Debriefing the success of the Olympics in 2016, after Rousseff's exit, I recounted for the DNI representative in Brazil what had occurred with Antonio Patriota in 2014. He suggested it would be an opportune time to visit Brazil, and I did. That was one of the most pleasant and most productive foreign trips I ever took.

Another key strategic ally with whom our relationship was very publicly damaged was Germany. When *Der Spiegel* joined the *Guardian* and the *Washington Post* in publishing leaks, its citizens' ire turned inward at the nation's intelligence services, particularly the Federal Intelligence Service—the BND. *Der Spiegel* portrayed German intelligence as an American pawn, doing our bidding at the sacrifice of German sovereignty. Chancellor Angela Merkel publicly expressed her shock and dismay at reports that we'd surveilled her. I believe that, unlike probably all the other politicians who expressed their outrage in 2013 and 2014, Merkel's anger was genuine, and she honestly didn't know the extent to which Germany was spying on the United States, including surveillance of our national leaders.

I also had sympathy for her personal position. Angela Merkel had been a young girl in Brandenburg, in the East, when I'd attended Nuremberg American High School and the University of Maryland in Munich. She was still living in East Germany when the Berlin Wall went up in 1961, and she remained there until it came down in 1989, an event that prompted the start of her political career. So, for her, the Stasi wasn't a mythical boogeyman. She had grown up under its oppression, and for that reason, I believe she *never* trusted intelligence organizations—hers or anyone else's. She didn't know and didn't want to know what her intelligence services were doing, and the reports from *Der Spiegel* that said the BND was helping NSA spy on her and on German citizens recalled the real-life experiences of her childhood and young adult life all too well. Even worse, her experiences and biases were not—and are not—outliers among German politicians. The truth was, many *Der Spiegel* stories had come from reporters, wittingly or unwittingly, misreading data Snowden had leaked from Boundless Informant statistics, believing the

numbers represented one thing—such as collecting on German citizens—
when they actually accounted for efforts such as German intelligence
collecting on the Taliban and al-Qaida. Unfortunately, Merkel was, I
think, predisposed to believe *Der Spiegel,* and the reports struck a painful, personal nerve.

As someone with very little diplomatic skill—to say the least—I came
to appreciate Susan Rice's considerable dexterity as a negotiator. After the
political fallout from her recitation of the Benghazi talking points in 2012,
she had moved to the senior-most White House national security position that did *not* require confirmation. In a twist of fate, she succeeded
Tom Donilon as national security adviser just weeks after the first
Snowden story appeared. As bad as the timing was for Susan, having her
talents in that job at that very difficult time was a good thing for our nation. Within the National Security Council, she was known for being a
bit rough around the edges and for suffering no fools. While abroad, however, she patiently listened and then, with a unique combination of good
humor and sharp intellect, turned very difficult and sensitive discussions
back to our need to work together and focus on the way ahead instead of
dwelling on the past. In early 2014, the scandals and political skirmishes
between Germany and the United States were far from over, but we were
warily working together to take stock of the situations in Afghanistan,
Iraq, and Syria, and without Susan, I'm not sure that would have been
the case.

If we had not had that cooperation from Germany and other European nations, I honestly don't know how we would have responded to
what happened in March. The IC had been closely watching the ongoing
political protests in Ukraine, which began in November 2013 when
Ukrainian president Viktor Yanukovych suddenly backed out of a deal
that would have brought Ukraine a desperately needed infusion of cash
from the European Union in exchange for aligning itself more closely
with EU policies. We were aware of the unrest but did not have the clairvoyance to predict a Russian invasion, which I remain convinced
stemmed from Putin's spur-of-the-moment opportunism, rather than
being a long-planned operation.

Before the fall of the Soviet Union, Ukraine had been a crucial Soviet
state to Moscow, hosting strategic air bases, the strategic intelligence sites
I visited in 1993 as DIA director, and—more important—the Soviet Black

Sea Fleet on the Crimean Peninsula. When the Soviet Union collapsed in 1991, Ukraine became the largest wholly European nation. Ukraine was—and is—extremely poor, which is why the government invited me behind the former Iron Curtain in 1993 to see the most sensitive of its intelligence sites. It desperately needed foreign investment if it was going to be independent of Russian influence and was eager to have the United States subsidize its operations. Unfortunately, its massive SIGINT sites—like so much else in Ukraine—held no practical value to the United States in 1993, so it fell back under nominal Russian control. For Russia, Ukraine remained strategically important, because it buffered Russia's border from EU nations, and because Crimea was still home to its critically important Black Sea Fleet.

Ukraine is also starkly divided ethnically, with the population of its center, west, and north identifying as and speaking Ukrainian, and the population to the south and east identifying as and speaking Russian, particularly in Crimea and in the territories in the far east, bordering Russia. The capital city, Kiev, sits squarely within the Ukrainian-identifying population. So when President Yanukovych backed away from EU money and alliances in November 2013, Kiev and the surrounding areas protested—not just the cancellation of the deal, but also the huge levels of corruption and cronyism in the national government. After student protesters were attacked by police and government forces at the end of November, the volume of demonstrators swelled into the hundreds of thousands—by some reports, a million. In many ways, it reminded me of the Tiananmen Square protests of 1989.

When I briefed the worldwide threat assessment to Congress in February 2014, there were still massive numbers of protesters enduring brutal weather in Kiev, but the demonstrations had largely calmed, and interactions with police were less violent. That changed on February 18, when police came to take down barricades, and protesters held their ground. Five days of deadly clashes followed, during which the opposition gained control of Kiev, and Yanukovych fled to Russia. What remained of the parliament voted unanimously to remove him from office the same day.

This whole series of events was reported very differently to the citizens of Ukraine who spoke Ukrainian than to those who spoke Russian. Russian media described the uprising in Kiev as being orchestrated by the United States to put either Jewish or fascist elements—or absurdly, both—in control of the Ukrainian government. Backing up the fictitious media reporting was an army of Russian internet trolls pretending to be Ukrainians in the east who were afraid their country was falling to fascist elements in Kiev. They created internet memes that associated the capital with sympathy for Nazi Germany and wrote false eyewitness accounts of how the new government in Kiev was organizing to wipe out the ethnically Russian population.

On February 27, Russian special forces—without insignia—took control of the building occupied by the Supreme Council of Crimea. Then, on March 1, as Russian-stoked protests against the new Ukrainian government raged across its Russian-speaking areas, Yanukovych sent a letter to Vladimir Putin, asking for Russian troops to stabilize Ukraine for the safety of its citizens. Putin asked Russia's parliament to sanction the use of Russian troops, and immediately put this authority into action, marching Russian troops—also without insignia—up from the naval base and across from mainland Russia into Crimea. Any pro-Ukrainian forces were immediately overwhelmed without shots ever being fired. By the end of the following day, Russia had complete control of Crimea, although Putin denied having any forces anywhere in Ukraine, apart from what was allowed on its naval base. He spoke approvingly of "little green men"—troops wearing Russia's newest military uniforms and outfitted with Russia's newest military equipment—who he claimed were ad hoc Ukrainian militias. Russian-language social media, driven by Russian intelligence, began a lovefest with these "little green men," whom it portrayed as loving guardians of the Ukrainian people.

On March 4, still denying the presence of Russian forces in Crimea, Putin declared that Russia had no intention of annexing the peninsula, and at the same time, floated the idea that secret polls in Crimea indicated the people there supported annexation by Russia. On March 16 the Crimean Supreme Council issued a referendum, nominally asking if the people of Crimea wanted to be part of the new Ukrainian government or secede to the Russian Federation. On March 17 they announced that 95 percent of voters had opted to join Russia. On March 18 Putin made a show of reluctantly bowing to the will of the Crimean people and graciously accepted the strategically vital peninsula on the Black Sea as the newest Russian state. What surprised leaders in the West the most wasn't that he would lie about his intentions or actions, or even that he would move to annex a former Soviet territory, but rather the relative ease and speed with which he achieved it.

I believe this whole episode illustrates how Western observers, particularly diplomats, completely misread Putin. He's not an idealist, and he doesn't care about communism or want to follow in Lenin's or Stalin's footsteps. While he's a former KGB officer, he's *not* a callback to the Soviets. He's more of a throwback to the tsars, and wants to restore the greatness of the Russian empire. In his mind, with this particular episode, he was simply correcting the injustice done to the Soviet republic of Russia in 1954, when Khrushchev handed Crimea to the republic of Ukraine.

In March 2014, I was excoriated—again—by national leaders and the media for not seeing all of this coming. In fact, we'd been warning for several days in February about Russian soldiers without insignia positioning themselves around Crimea and Russian troops massing near the border, but we never expected Russia to actually seize control, much less formally annex the peninsula. Of course, it's extremely difficult to assess Putin's intentions. As a former KGB officer, he understands US intelligence capabilities well enough not to send an unsecured email saying he plans to take control of Crimea on March 2. And even if we had some insight into his plans and intentions, it would still have been impossible for us to predict all of the external issues and random occurrences that would have factored into what would actually happen.

Back under the metaphorical bus for my lack of clairvoyance, I took some solace in an article that Will Inboden, who was teaching at the University of Texas at Austin, published in *Foreign Policy* magazine on February 18, before events in Ukraine began to unfold. Titled "The Seven Impossible Demands Policymakers Place on Intelligence," it cited as one of them, "Give me accurate and precise forecasts about the future, but don't make any mistakes," with the apt example: "Consider an intelligence forecast that 'In Moscow on April 1, 2015, Vladimir Putin will rise at 6:47 am, eat a poached egg for breakfast, and order yet another missile test in violation of the INF treaty.' Pity the poor analyst if it turns out that Putin does all of the above—except eats oatmeal that day instead."

The morning after Putin annexed Crimea, my security detail drove me from Liberty Crossing to NSA headquarters to give a speech that had nothing to do with Ukraine, or Congress, or Snowden's leaks. Nevertheless, I flipped through the pages of my script, underlining certain phrases to stress and making edits to more precisely capture what I was thinking. With all the professional challenges and world events going on, this event suddenly felt unusually personal, a reminder that leading the community wasn't just about responding to the daily churn of overseas threats and Washington politics. General Keith Alexander greeted me at the door. Keith had been NSA director since 2005 and had met the Snowden leaks head-on, sometimes to the dismay of the White House, as when he'd spoken the previous fall at the annual Black Hat convention of hackers in Las Vegas. I had first known Keith as a bright, up-and-coming Army major in the late 1980s, but we had more recently bonded behind the witness table at congressional hearings, particularly at the worldwide threat assessments, and I was glad to see him. I stepped to the lectern with my speech to address the "IC Pride" group at its Lesbian, Gay, Bisexual, Transgender, and Allies Summit. Here I was, a seventy-three-year-old white, straight, cisgender man, and I hoped I might have something worthwhile to say to them. Their warm applause helped calm my nerves. I opened my text, adjusted the microphone, and began.

> I thought I should start by explaining to you why I'm here speaking to you, and why I wanted to be here to speak to you. It has to do with my own personal history, my own "journey," I guess you might call it. This began for me about fifty years ago, when I was a very young lieutenant in the Air Force, on my first assignment after technical training as a SIGINT officer, at what was then Kelly Air Force Base in Texas.

Over the next twenty minutes, I told them the story of the two Russian linguists, the airmen I'd processed out of the Air Force on less-than-honorable discharges for being homosexual. I told them about Admiral Inman restoring a security clearance on the condition that an NSA crypto-mathematician out himself, and how I'd similarly restored an Air Force civilian's clearance in 1989. I didn't name him then, but Mark Roth was there, sitting in the front row, and when I glanced at him while telling his story, I saw that he was quietly weeping. I almost lost it right then, but looked away and pressed ahead, describing Admiral Mike Mullen's testimony in 2009, when he'd explained why Don't Ask, Don't Tell was so wrong.

So, let me come back to why I wanted to speak to you here, at this summit. I always try not to take myself, or the position I occupy, too seriously. But I do realize that I can, should, and must use the position as a "bully pulpit" when the occasion calls for it. And this occasion calls for it. I need to set the example in the Intelligence Community, and be part of the change that we all want to see take place. There's no way that I can ever really know what members of the LGBT community have gone through. But I can absolutely proclaim myself as an Ally. And I'm proud to be one.

They applauded and then stood and applauded more. I looked down at the next line of my speech, but they wouldn't let me go on, so I just stopped and drank the moment in. These were people who had each, for years or even decades, kept their secrets about who they were, who had suffered through repeatedly being told that people like them didn't belong or that their personal identity was a clinical personality disorder. While giving that speech was a great personal catharsis, divesting myself of a burden of fifty years, the event meant more to me than even that. The whole auditorium, the whole event, was an outpouring of unconditional love and acceptance, an expression of joy from the audience in finding a community in which they didn't have to hide who they were. And just like that, they made it very clear that they'd accepted me into that community. I'm sure they had no idea just how much that meant to me at that moment.

Eleven months later, during a social event in Paris, an IC employee took me aside and said she had been in the NSA auditorium when I gave that speech. She told me it had come at a critical time for her, and that hearing me talk about my experience had made an impact on her choice to stay in the IC and in her chosen profession. It struck me later that the roles were reversed from my encounter with President Kennedy, as I had become the public figure, but the impact on me was the same. I don't know if that woman ever thought about our conversation again, but I will never forget it.

Back in the outside world, the IC was in for another surprise just a few weeks later. The Islamic State of Iraq and the Levant had, through a series of uprisings, taken control of several cities in western Iraq, including

Fallujah and Ramadi. They had also made gains in Syria and were fun-
neling captured weapons across the border. It appeared they were massing forces to try to capture Mosul, Iraq's second-largest city, which was
an entirely different and more ambitious undertaking. We estimated that
somewhere in the range of a thousand ISIL fighters were preparing to
drive into Mosul in their 4x4 trucks, armed with machine guns and some
artillery. We fed that intelligence to the Iraqi government, which positioned itself to meet the challenge with about thirty thousand army
troops, backed by tens of thousands of members of the police forces, all
armed with modern US-provided equipment in up-armored Humvees.
The Iraqi troops outnumbered the ISIL fighters by at least thirty to one
and were better equipped, fed, and positioned.

If I were to say that on June 4, thirty thousand Iraqi troops caught
sight of a truck bearing a black flag, threw down their weapons, and
ran, that would be an exaggeration, but not by much. Over the next six
days, the ISIL fighters killed approximately sixty-five hundred Iraqi
troops, four thousand of whom were prisoners they summarily executed;
captured almost all of the US equipment the Iraqi troops abandoned,
including hundreds of Humvees; and gained control of large caches of
paper money in Mosul's banks as well as a steady source of funding from
the oil refinery in the town of Baiji. Shortly after, ISIL declared a caliphate, and its leader, Abu Bakr al-Baghdadi, named himself as the religious
successor to the Islamic prophet Muhammad and descendant leader of
the world's Muslim community. This declaration was a call to all Muslims to join the Islamic State and defend Muhammad's nation.

Once again, the US Intelligence Community's lack of clairvoyance left
us looking inept. I told the president and Congress, and even said publicly, that intelligence analysis is very good at evaluating capabilities—
orders of battle, armament, positioning—but assessing "will to fight" was
frustratingly difficult. We had underestimated the North Vietnamese and
Vietcong and overestimated the Army of the Republic of Vietnam. We'd
been surprised in 1991 when the US-led coalition quickly took back Kuwait from the Iraqis with very little bloodshed. To many policy makers,
that explanation simply wasn't good enough, and once again, the IC was
dragged through the gauntlet of the cable-news networks and political
talk shows.

Of all the people I worked with who were affected by the Islamic

State's victories and its declaration of a caliphate, and by subsequent video postings of war atrocities on the internet, the group I felt the most sympathy for was the American Islamic community. After 9/11, they'd been targeted for violence by angry fellow US citizens, who found them a convenient target. Muslim groups around the nation had largely responded with equanimity and attempts at dialogue. Some were willing to work with the US Intelligence Community, developing relationships with the FBI and DHS. Things had, for the most part, reasonably settled down for American Muslims in the years since 9/11, but with the rise of the Islamic State, anti-Muslim sentiment in the United States was again on the rise.

As the summer wore on, we continued to deal with another negative public narrative—this one comparing US intelligence officers with the East German Stasi. This image had become so entrenched that we surprised people when we expressed support of the USA Freedom Act, the draft legislation proposed to end NSA's bulk storage of phone call metadata as governed by Section 215 of the Patriot Act. With that legislation, NSA would destroy its database and be required to obtain a court order for a specific phone number to run a search against the records held by the telecommunications companies, which were already storing the data for business purposes. NSA could request that companies provide data on what other numbers the target was in contact with. We needed to work out the details for how this would actually function, particularly how we would gain physical accesses to quickly search phone number databases across multiple providers in an emergency, but in broad terms, the act met our foreign intelligence needs. We wouldn't be burdened by either the physical requirements or the social and political stigma of holding the data, and when we did need it, we would have a much more complete and useful record to search, since the USA Freedom Act included cell-phone data as well as landlines.

A year after Glenn Greenwald began publishing stories from Snowden's documents, the internet was full of stories about how we were spying on ordinary citizens, trying to ascertain if they were cheating on their spouses, growing weed in their basement, or pirating Hollywood movies. None was true. We were—and are—looking outward at the threats that could harm or threaten our nation or our friends and allies.

In the summer of 2014, that meant trying to contain the Islamic State to the no-man's-land between Iraq and Syria, as the Iraqi Army continued to fold at the least resistance. It meant monitoring the sudden influx of foreign fighters who answered the call of the caliphate, particularly from Northern Africa and Europe and even from the United States, as well as trying to keep what remained of Syria's chemical weapons stockpiles out of the hands of this terrorist group. It meant more closely following what China was doing in the South China Sea, where they were dredging sand over coral reefs to create new "Chinese" islands—eight hundred miles from the mainland—so that they could claim what had been international waters as their territory. It meant turning the geospatial-intelligence enterprise, led by NGA, on to West Africa to monitor the Ebola outbreak, which had spread to major cities in Guinea, Liberia, and Sierra Leone, and posed a danger to the entire world. It meant ongoing tracking of Iran's and North Korea's nuclear weapons programs. And it meant watching "little green men" from Russia slowly invade eastern Ukraine, bringing heavy weaponry across the border in what Vladimir Putin claimed were humanitarian aid convoys.

The Russian military truly broke new ground in social media use that summer, both helping and harming their case. While their brigade of internet trolls churned out false stories about the humanitarian successes in eastern Ukraine, bolstered by tricks like causing a town's electric power to go out and then entering the town and restoring it, the regular Russian Army soldiers were posting pictures of themselves by recognizable Ukrainian landmarks with their armored personnel carriers and antiaircraft weapons. Heavy Russian military equipment was positioned all around eastern Ukraine, and on July 17 the tense situation led to tragedy.

Malaysia Airlines Flight 17 was en route from Amsterdam to Kuala Lumpur, and despite myriad warnings about combat operations taking place on the ground, the flight was routed over eastern Ukraine. Russian soldiers, operating a Buk surface-to-air missile system well inside Ukraine's border, mistook the civilian airliner for a military target, engaged it, launched a missile, and brought it down, killing 298 civilian passengers and crew. Those are the facts, as determined by the Dutch Safety Board, except that they did not specify that Russian soldiers were operating the SA-11, only that the surface-to-air system had been brought across the border from Russia and was returned there shortly after the airliner was destroyed. Of course, this wasn't a weapons system available to the Russian-speaking Ukrainian rebels. More to the point for US intelligence, while it took the Dutch Safety Board more than a year to reach its conclusions, we had the Russians dead to rights in just a few hours, fusing data from our so-called "national technical means satellites," intercepts, and open-source reporting—particularly social media.

For me, our ability to pinpoint attribution for this tragedy to an overly aggressive and trigger-happy Russian military was particularly gratifying, because I'd lived through the downing of Korean Air Lines Flight 007 in 1983. This time we had systems in place that were designed to collect the relevant information, systems that would allow us to show precisely what happened. Not only did those systems work as advertised, but we also had the means in place to integrate data from several different sources to reconstruct the event in great detail. Our ability to speak intelligence truth to the world contrasted starkly with my experience with KAL 007.

The Russian response, however, was remarkably consistent. Despite overwhelming evidence, they simply denied responsibility. They first claimed that ethnically Russian Ukrainian separatists had shot down a Ukrainian Air Force plane, which the Russian SA-11 team initially genuinely believed they'd done. Then, when it became impossible to deny it was a civilian airliner, they claimed that it had been the Ukrainian military that had shot it down from central Ukraine, not the separatists. The Russian government–sponsored television network in the United States, RT America, even said the United States IC had cleared them of wrongdoing, running the headline US INTELLIGENCE: NO DIRECT LINK TO RUSSIA IN MALAYSIA PLANE DOWNING. RT then reported that Ukraine had shot down the plane in an attempt to assassinate Vladimir Putin, and even went so far as to falsify imagery, publishing a composite photograph of a Ukrainian fighter firing on a Malaysian airliner, an image so obviously fake that I pointed out that there really was no system owned by anyone that could have taken such a photo. When that story fell apart, they claimed Ukrainian air traffic control had directed the plane to execute maneuvers similar to what a military flight would do—precisely the same excuse they'd used with KAL 007 in 1983.

Unfortunately, technology had brought about another major shift in how the world interacts with information. The internet enabled Russian trolls to bring their conspiracy theories directly to the types of people who believe airline contrails are a government plot to poison everyone on the ground. Even as early as 1983, Russia knew that they didn't have to prove their case or even present a viable theory to discredit known facts. All they had to do to raise doubts was throw out enough contradictory theories to obscure what really happened, and people who didn't have the time or education to research the issue on their own would conclude they'd never know "what really happened." Putin, particularly, understood how effective that strategy could be when carried out through the pervasive enabler of the internet. In 2007, Edelman, one of the largest marketing firms in the world, published a groundbreaking "trust barometer" study showing that—by far—people trusted "someone like me" over anyone else—more than "experts" and certainly more than "government officials." In 2014, Russia was effectively putting the theory behind that study into practice, with their intelligence operatives going online and pretending to be everyday Ukrainians, sharing and retweeting fake news stories with "people like them."

At the same time that we were coming to grips with the new reality of Russian online deception, we were still taking fire in the press and in Congress for allegations originating from the Snowden leaks. In September, at a meeting of the Armed Forces Communications and Electronics Association and the Intelligence and National Security Alliance—the two largest professional organizations relating to the intelligence and national security arena—I rolled out the 2014 National Intelligence Strategy, which included the "Principles of Intelligence Ethics," a positive statement about what intelligence professionals stand for, which we consciously wrote to be similar to the ethics principles that doctors try to uphold. While this unfortunately had the appearance of being a response to the Snowden affair, we'd in fact first tried to publish these principles in September 2012, but that effort had been sidelined by the Benghazi attack, and then world events and Washington politics; damage-control efforts had pushed off the publication for another two years. By the fall of 2014 the world felt so dark that I tried to make the most of the opportunity to inject some levity into our circumstances, at one point in the speech summing up the situation the IC had found itself in:

> We are expected to keep the nation safe and provide exquisite, high-fidelity, timely, accurate, anticipatory, and relevant intelligence; and do that in such a manner that there is no risk; and

there is no embarrassment to anyone if what we're doing is publicly revealed; and there is no threat to anyone's revenue bottom line; and there isn't even a scintilla of jeopardy to anyone's civil liberties and privacy, whether US persons or foreign persons.

We call this new approach to intelligence: "immaculate collection."

The audience of intelligence professionals appreciated the remark. I also presented an update on IC ITE, noting that it had taken us about two years to lay the foundation to begin building the systems, that CIA and NSA had delivered their promised cloud storage and cloud computing capabilities, and that NGA and DIA had begun to supply common desktop interfaces. Combining a serious point with a gibe about how difficult my work had become, I said, "Making sure IC ITE sticks is one of the biggest reasons my principal deputy Stephanie O'Sullivan and I agreed to stick around for—*maybe*—another 122 weeks, or 855 days. But who's counting?" For the first time in what seemed many years, I got some positive media coverage for something I'd said—not for the content of the ethics principles, but for my self-deprecating humor.

Those good feelings lasted all of ten days. On September 28, I was at home, watching Sunday football games, when during a break I flipped the station to President Obama's interview on *60 Minutes*. When asked about how the Islamic State had succeeded in seizing so much territory so quickly, he responded, "Well, I think our head of the Intelligence Community, Jim Clapper, has acknowledged that, I think, they underestimated what had been taking place in Syria." Well, that's not exactly what I remembered saying. I'd commented that we had a difficult time assessing the "will to fight," and that no one—myself included—predicted the Iraqi Army's folding overnight in the manner it did.

A few days later, I was in the Pentagon for meetings and stopped by the USD(I) section for a visit with the staff. Holding something behind his back, Mike Vickers announced that he had a presentation to make. He said he'd caught the president's interview with *60 Minutes,* and that, since I was once again under the bus, he thought I should look the part of someone who changes oil. With that, he placed a Jiffy Lube ball cap on my head. I wore it proudly.

By the fall of 2014, we had all fallen into a rhythm of working, trying to ignore what was being said about us in the media, and taking on each new crisis as it occurred. On November 3, I boarded an Air Force plane and flew north to discuss business with my counterparts in Canada. I was eager to have some time outside Washington, and so I'd planned to spend successive days in Boston and New York after the meetings in Ottawa. That Monday night, I was getting settled and preparing to attend a dinner hosted by the Canadians when I got an urgent call from Susan Rice: "Come home *now.*" North Korea was holding two US citizens as prisoners in hard labor, she explained, we finally had a small window to secure their release, and President Obama was sending me as his envoy.

Some aspects of our relationship with North Korea had changed since I'd served under General Livsey from 1985 to 1987. There had been a brief period when both sides began to trust each other. In 1994, Kim Jong-il signed an agreement that would provide food and economic assistance to his starving nation in exchange for stopping plutonium production. But Kim didn't live up to his side of the deal, and in 2006 and 2010, North Korea conducted increasingly successful nuclear tests. After his death, his son Kim Jong-un presided over another in 2013. North Korea also continued to test increasingly longer-range missiles capable of carrying nuclear warheads. By 2014 it had demonstrated it could reliably fire a missile as far as Japan and possibly launch something toward the United States West Coast. With everything else going on in 2014, the United States was treating North Korea as a noisy aggravation, and neither side had anything resembling diplomacy with the other. Unfortunately, that meant American citizens were caught between two nations giving each other the silent treatment.

Kenneth Bae was a naturalized US citizen born in South Korea, with children in Arizona and Hawaii. He had been living in China with his wife and stepdaughter and running a tourism service into North Korea, which the North Koreans later claimed was a Christian missionary program. In November 2012, while escorting five tourists into North Korea, he was arrested by the DPRK government, which charged him with "hostile acts against the republic." American and South Korean press speculated that he'd taken pictures of starving North Korean orphans whom he wanted to help. Bae had a number of health issues, including diabetes and high blood pressure, which likely wouldn't be treated in North Korea. In April 2013, despite intercession from the Swedish embassy in Pyongyang, Bae was sentenced to fifteen years of hard labor. For two years, the US government had tried to free him, but to no avail. After visiting Pyongyang and meeting the Supreme Leader, former NBA star Dennis Rodman even tweeted out that he'd asked his friend Kim Jong-un to "do him a solid" and let Bae go, but basketball diplomacy didn't help Kenneth Bae.

Matthew Miller was a California native who'd traveled to South Korea in 2010 and had taken a job there teaching English. He appeared to have lived a somewhat solitary life, and in April 2014 had traveled unaccompanied to North Korea as a tourist. Several reports said that upon arriving in the Pyongyang airport, Miller had promptly ripped up his visa, loudly asked for political asylum, caused a scene, and was arrested. In September he had been sentenced to six years of hard labor. Based on his erratic behavior, US officials were concerned about Miller's mental health and, through Sweden, had asked for his release.

In October, North Korea had quietly released a third American, Jeffrey Fowle, to a quiet, lower-level American delegation who'd flown him out of Pyongyang. Fowle had been convicted of bringing a Bible into the country after it had been found, with his name and contact information written inside the cover with pictures of him and his family, in a North Korean nightclub where he'd left it. After Fowle was freed, the government in Pyongyang had said they would only release Bae and Miller to a Cabinet-level US official who was an active member of the US National Security Council and who came bearing a letter from President Obama to Supreme Leader Kim Jong-un.

Even today, whenever the subject of this mission to North Korea comes up, I'm asked, "Why you?" Why on earth would the president send the director of national intelligence—especially *this* DNI—on so delicate a diplomatic mission? The truth is, the operation had been in the works for quite a while, and the White House knew I had a long history of working Korea issues. When they put my name forward as the president's representative, I think we were all surprised when the North Koreans agreed. That's the official story, although Mark Sanger of the *New York Times* may have had the best explanation: "Gruff, blunt-speaking and seen by many in the Obama administration as a throwback to the Cold War, the retired general is an unlikely diplomat but, in the words of one American official, 'perfect for the North Koreans.'" That's about the nicest thing the *New York Times* has ever written about me.

Complicating the mission was the fact that President Obama was scheduled to arrive in China on Monday of the following week. To avoid "distractions," the White House wanted me in and out of North Korea before then, which left me six days to reach Pyongyang, secure Bae and Miller, and get out. If I failed, it was not clear if we'd have another opportunity to free them. Not only would that be bad for the two Americans, but it could be an embarrassing backdrop for the president's China visit. So—no pressure.

I hastily canceled dinner plans and flew back to Andrews. My security detail drove me to the White House, where a half dozen or so hastily assembled Cabinet deputies and NSC staff members had gathered in the Situation Room. Susan chaired the meeting, and Wendy Sherman, the undersecretary of state for political affairs, connected by secure video.

We were under an additional time crunch because the longer we took to secure the Americans, the likelier it was news of the mission would leak, which could scare off the skittish North Koreans. The agenda for that late-night meeting was to discuss the trip itself, review my talking points for discussions with North Korean interlocutors, and, importantly, to cover diplomatic "dos and don'ts": Don't bow, don't smile, don't accept flowers, and generally, avoid any appearance of obsequiousness toward the North Koreans, particularly if photographers are present. The amount of information I had to process was overwhelming, and I was asking myself if I was really the right choice when Wendy spoke up. "I think we can trust Jim to do the right thing." If she'd have been physically present, I would have hugged her.

After the meeting, my security detail drove me home to repack. Sue, who had spent so much of her life being discreet and flexible, was unfazed when I told her where I was headed and that I wasn't sure when I'd be back. At Andrews I boarded a specially modified Air Force 737, accompanied by a small personal security detail; a specially trained Air Force security detail to protect the aircraft; communications specialists; a medical doctor; NSC Korea director Allison Hooker; my executive assistant, "Neil K"; and a couple of other staff officers with special skill sets I won't go into. It was, in short, a dream team.

We left Andrews at 2:00 A.M. on Tuesday, November 5. After stopping in Hawaii for repairs, losing a day to the international date line, and swapping to a less-broken plane in Guam—a testament to the resource-fulness of Air Force and Navy maintenance crews coping with sequestra-tion and budget cuts—we launched on the final leg of our trip on Friday afternoon. Thanks to the professionalism of our armed services and In-telligence Community, no news of our mission had leaked to the press in the almost three days since we'd left Washington.

Once airborne, I checked that we had the all-important letter from President Obama to Kim Jong-un, which simply stated that I was the president's envoy and that it would be considered a positive gesture if Supreme Leader Kim Jong-un released our two citizens to me. I re-viewed the talking points the White House had given me. The first was uncompromising—the United States would not negotiate on *any* other issue until North Korea agreed to denuclearize. I knew that was a non-starter, so the rest of the points were somewhat academic.

It was well past sunset when we landed at Sunan, the major airport for the capital city of Pyongyang. The scene outside my window made me think of the famous satellite picture of the Korean Peninsula at night. In the photo, the DMZ demarks a sharp line between the electric com-motion of the South and the impenetrable darkness of the North, broken only by a small spot of light emanating from Pyongyang. As we landed, I wondered where the lights of Pyongyang were, because the city was dark. On the ground, even the runway and taxiways were sparsely lit and so rough that we damaged a tire while taxiing. The only real source of illu-mination was a floodlight behind a small spray of DPRK press cameras.

For security and logistical reasons, the aircraft would remain occu-pied, and Air Force regulations on crew rest stated that the flight team could only sit in a "ready" state on the plane for the next twenty-four hours. With the clock in mind, I stepped out onto the eerily silent tarmac in a land intelligence officers only talk about visiting, the first Cabinet-level US official to visit North Korea since Secretary of State Madeleine Albright in October 2000.

A smiling, uniformed officer greeted me with a quick handshake; we posed briefly for the cameras (*Don't smile, don't show deference*), and then I was whisked into a 1990s-vintage Mercedes limousine and seated in the place of honor—the right rear, next to General Kim Won-hong, then the minister of state security and commander of the notoriously brutal state secret police. (In 2017, the general would fall out of favor with Kim Jong-un, be purged from leadership, and removed from public view.) Sitting on a jump seat in front of General Kim was a younger Korean man, a translator who spoke flawless English with an incongruous British accent. My senior protective detail officer sat in the front passenger seat next to the North Korean driver. A glass partition separated us, and we could not hear each other—which made both of us uneasy.

Through the translator, General Kim got right to business. He said that the DPRK government expected my visit would constitute a "breakthrough" in its stagnant relations with the United States and that it further expected that it could dispatch a comparable senior envoy to the US. This, perhaps, would lead to negotiations culminating in a peace treaty to end the sixty-year-plus armistice. He barely waited for the translation and spoke glowingly about what we would accomplish. When I finally got a chance to respond, I said that, while I hoped for a productive dialogue, my principal objective was to secure the release of our two citizens. The atmosphere darkened, even in the dim back of the limo, and I wondered if I'd blown it already.

We rolled along slowly—maybe twenty-five miles per hour—as General Kim continued to hold forth on the unique opportunity we had to bring peace to our nations. I searched for ways to engage him on safe conversational ground—touching on my long-standing interest in the peninsula, my experiences as the senior intelligence officer in South Korea, even my seventy-two combat reconnaissance missions in Southeast Asia during the Vietnam conflict—but it was like talking to a television screen; he just continued with his monologue.

Glancing out of the window into the pitch blackness, I asked where we were, where we were going, and when we might get there. The general was busy lecturing me about the great place I'd have in history if I could bring about a peace, and how history would consider me a failure if the United States didn't take advantage of this great opportunity. This disjointed discourse, every word of which was translated back and forth with a British accent, continued for what seemed a lot longer than the forty-five-minute drive. We finally stopped at an attractive, pagoda-style building, set back in a park beside the Taedong River. General Kim announced we'd arrived at the state guesthouse, clearly disappointed in me and in our lack of a "breakthrough." We shook hands perfunctorily and parted company.

The exterior of the guesthouse was impressive, imparting a sense of stately Korean history and hospitality. Inside, the foyer, stairs, and wide hallways were dominated by a garish green rug patterned with large, intertwining, bright red roses—the kind of rug I wouldn't want to encounter the morning after heavy drinking. The rooms were clean, but the furnishings were spare and left me with the same sense of heaviness I'd experienced in Eastern Europe. I was assigned a two-room suite with an elaborately decorated bed in ersatz French Provincial style, but the thin mattress lay on plywood. The phone next to the bed had no dial tone. I also had a bookcase filled with volumes and volumes of English translations of the writing of Kim Il-sung, the founder of the DPRK.

We had just enough time to unpack before the Mercedes limo returned with the British-accented translator, at around 8:45 P.M. Greeting me this time was another General Kim, Kim Yong-chol, the head of what the North Koreans call the Reconnaissance General Bureau, the RGB, which is an organizational amalgam of intelligence and special operations that conducts missions ranging from clandestine activities to cyberattacks to overseas intelligence collection. I judged he was just a few years younger than I, and his demeanor comported with his reputation as a "knuckle-dragger"—more relentless than bright. He introduced himself as my DPRK counterpart, which wasn't precisely right, but I thought of Bae and Miller and tactfully did not correct him.

We rode slowly through the desolate and dimly lit streets, devoid of much vehicular or pedestrian traffic, to downtown Pyongyang. The RGB chief had clearly been ordered to host me and made it clear he was only enduring the experience. His whole demeanor was accusatory and pejorative, and anti-American sentiment rolled off his tongue as North Korean hate translated and filtered through a British accent. When he paused his diatribe, I tried to lighten up the conversation by describing my first trip to the DPRK in the errant Huey, some twenty-nine years earlier. Looking constitutionally incapable of amusement, General Kim continued to berate my country and everything it stood for. I decided I could, in return, grit my own teeth and suffer this "turret head," as I used to call Soviet interlocutors, for a few hours if it meant Bae and Miller got to come home.

The limo turned a corner, and I saw an enormous neon sign shaped like a bowling pin—the only bright light I'd seen since the floodlight at the airport. I asked General Kim through the translator if bowling was a popular pastime in the DPRK. General Kim paused for the first time to give me a strange look. I was surprised when the limo came to a stop in front of the storefront bowling alley. We all debarked, and I could see through the windows that there were bowling lanes inside, but no one was bowling.

We went through a side entrance, took an elevator to the second floor, and were ushered into a private dining room dominated by a semicircular table with elaborate place settings and a beautiful spray of flowers as a centerpiece. It was a reasonable facsimile of an upscale restaurant in South Korea.

General Kim and I took our seats at the center, with the translator to his left, followed by silent functionaries and note-takers. Seated to my right were Allison, Neil, and a few other US staff officers. Over the next several hours we were treated to a thirteen-course meal—one of the best Korean dinners I've ever experienced. Each dish was prepared and served to the highest standards of Korean cuisine and hospitality. The conversation, in contrast, remained tense. As the first course was being served, General Kim made it clear to me that Americans generally were criminals, warmongers, and posed a threat to the very existence of the DPRK. Our joint exercises with the South Korean military were aggressive, threatening, and provocative. Our B-52 missions were particularly menacing and threatened the "peace-loving people" of the DPRK. General Kim seemed especially consumed with B-52s, implying that my visit should somehow mark an end to these missions, and if I wasn't there to discuss terminating these dangerous, provocative flights, he questioned why I had come to the DPRK at all.

I explained that the expectation of my government, and specifically our president, was that the first priority was the prompt release of our two citizens. If they were freed, other steps could follow to move toward relaxing tensions on the peninsula. I then reiterated US talking point number one: Before we could begin any sequence leading to better relations, the DPRK had to agree to a path to denuclearization.

General Kim replied that nuclear weapons were central to the DPRK's survival because the United States was so threatening, particularly (again) with its B-52s. The United States must, he continued, recognize the DPRK as a nuclear power and treat it with the same respect it accorded other such powers, like Russia and China. As the evening wore on, he grew even more strident, asserting that North Korea was under siege from the South, aided and abetted by the United States. Somewhere around the seventh or eighth course, he began pointing at me, charging that the annual joint US and ROK military exercises were a provocation to war. Not being a diplomat, I pointed my finger back at him—a gesture that was not acceptable in polite Korean circles—and pointed out that shelling islands off the west coast of South Korea and sinking an ROK Navy ship weren't conducive to reducing tensions either. It was, perhaps, not my finest moment. It did, however, establish that the overworked translator was giving faithful renditions of my words, as General Kim visibly bristled.

When General Kim and I shifted in our seats to face each other, Neil piped up and suggested, "Hey, boss, I bet you need to make a head call." Neil had earned his keep as my executive assistant many times over, but never as deftly as when he suggested that I take the best-timed restroom break of my intelligence career.

When I returned to my seat, I tried another approach. "The United States has no permanent enemies," I said, citing Germany and Japan as prime examples of how bitter adversaries can become close, stalwart allies. I recounted my 2013 trip to Vietnam and told him how the United States had developed productive diplomatic, economic, and even military relations with a nation we'd gone to war against, and suggested the same could happen with North Korea. We didn't need to be enemies in perpetuity, and the relationship could be quite different if we could find common ground. This was the only exchange we had all evening that did not evoke reflexive pushback from General Kim. We ate in silence for a few minutes before he remarked that I could foster that transformation by negotiating the normalization of relations. I returned to US talking point number one, and we resumed talking past each other.

At the end of the dinner, we still had no specific commitment for the return of Bae and Miller. General Kim soon prepared to leave, giving no indication we'd meet the next day. The only leverage I had was the letter from Obama to Kim Jong-un. Allison and I quickly caucused and agreed that this might be our last opportunity to give the letter to someone in authority who could present it to the North Korean leader. It was a risk, but one we had to take.

Catching General Kim as he was heading to his car, I told him, "This letter is from President Barack Obama to your Supreme Leader Kim Jong-un," making certain I used the appropriate honorific. Without saying a word, General Kim took the letter, got in his car, and rode away.

Back at the guesthouse, I tried unsuccessfully to sleep on the thin mattress. I turned on the TV, hoping to at least see some of the propaganda for which North Korea is famous, but there was no signal on any station. I glanced at the bookcase of Kim Il-sung writings and decided I'd rather be alone with my apprehensions than leave a volume out of place that would let them know I'd picked it up. Outside the window, the dark, distant city skyline was silhouetted against the stars.

The next day, Saturday, was nerve-racking. We were alone in the state guesthouse, except for a cooking staff who didn't speak a word of English, but who I suspected *understood* English just fine. At one point, I mused to Neil that at least we'd gotten a great Korean dinner free of charge. He shrugged and said that, to pay for the dinner the North Koreans had "hosted," he had in fact handed over a great deal of American currency out of the bag of cash he was carrying around.

At some point during the morning, the physician who had accompanied us was summoned to examine Bae and Miller. He returned a few hours later and reported they were both in good physical condition. The North Koreans had given him strict orders only to tell the prisoners that he was checking on their health and welfare, and not to mention there was an American delegation in the country or that there was a possibility they could be freed. We took it as a good sign that he had been allowed to see them at all, although I felt as though we were trying to read tea leaves.

At around 11:00 A.M., a midlevel staff officer from the Ministry of State Security arrived with a message from the DPRK government. He announced that the Great Leader Kim Jong-un had effectively demoted me, as the government no longer considered me a presidential envoy. The citizens of Pyongyang were aware, he continued, that my purpose was not to work toward peace between our two nations, but merely to free the two "criminals." Accordingly, they could no longer guarantee my safety and security in the city of Pyongyang, nor the safety and security of my delegation, since its citizens were "agitated." He left the guesthouse without further comment.

As Neil noted in our debrief, "waiting around" isn't my strong suit, but because we were under control of the North Koreans, we weren't free to just hail a cab and tour Pyongyang. So we sat, paced, and shot the breeze, recognizing, of course, that we were undoubtedly being surveilled. The cooking staff prepared lunch, which we ate more to kill time than out of hunger. Periodically, two or three of us would take short walks in the park surrounding the guesthouse. If we went near the river, a couple of stone-faced minders would appear, seemingly out of nowhere, staying just within hearing range. They didn't object to our taking pictures of one another with the Taedong River as backdrop.

At about 3:30 that afternoon, the staff officer returned. With no explanation, he told us to gather our luggage and check out. We had all traveled light and were already packed, so after more cash changed hands, we quickly piled into a small convoy and were driven downtown to the Koryo, a first-line hotel appointed in traditional North Korean style. We were ushered up to a conference room on the second floor and shown to seats at a large oval table. Five North Koreans, who we learned were prosecutors, sat across from us, four of them in suits and one in uniform. They barely acknowledged our arrival. Behind them, Kenneth Bae and Matthew Miller stood in their prison garb, each flanked by two guards. At the far end of the room was a smaller table with one empty chair. I suspected that whoever sat in judgment would have a bias. No one said a word, and the silence reminded me, oddly enough, of a church just before the service starts.

This was the first time I laid eyes on the two American citizens. Miller looked tired and gaunt, while Bae, who had been in hard labor confinement for two years, appeared rested, even robust. They were both standing unsupported, which was a good sign and comported with our doctor's report, but were impassive and didn't acknowledge our entrance. I wondered whether they understood that we were there for them, or if they thought this was a North Korean trick or a trap to see if they would react inappropriately. We sat, still and silent, for fifteen or twenty minutes, although at the time it seemed a lot longer. Finally the door opened, and the first General Kim, the political four-star who'd met us at the airport, strode into the room. The prosecutors rose; we rose. General Kim sat; we sat. General Kim took a moment to get settled, and then looked up and nodded to the prosecutors.

One of them stood and began reading a lengthy proclamation, recounting the crimes of Miller and Bae against the peace-loving people of the DPRK. He paused after each section to allow a translator to render the proclamation in tortured English. Then he extolled the benevolence of Kim Jong-un, and said that as a gesture of kindness, the Great Leader forgave the crimes and freed the criminals to my custody. General Kim stood; we all stood. Through the translator he told me, "I hope the next time we talk, it will be about something other than your criminals." He crossed the room and left, followed by the prosecutors, guards, and every other DPRK official.

Our physician and a few members of the protective detail took Miller and Bae into a nearby room to help them change clothes and began to acclimatize them to the reality that they were free and about to head home. The rest of my detail hustled me out and downstairs to the limo, where I sat and waited for about ten tense minutes, wondering if this could still go wrong. When Bae and Miller emerged from the hotel, I relaxed for the first time in days. When everyone was accounted for, the mini convoy started toward the airport, wending its way through the city streets.

This was my only real opportunity to see the streets of Pyongyang. Even during daytime on a Saturday, there weren't many cars or people out. The streets had no stoplights, but at the center of several intersections, women dressed in immaculate white tunics with white gloves stood on small raised platforms. They faced us with their arms held out to each side, keeping nonexistent cars from crossing in front of us. I wondered if it was all a show for my benefit, or if they stood and gesticulated on those platforms every day.

We drove past the famous square where the DPRK Army had, over the years, marched in their characteristic unnerving goose step for stage-produced parades in salute of three generations of Kim family leaders. The square seemed much smaller in person than in film footage of those events. I watched out the window as the peace-loving people of Pyongyang swept the streets and sidewalks and walked slowly, almost zombie-like, to . . . I don't know where. The experience was even more surreal than I'd imagined. I had expected the drab clothes and their lack of possessions, and certainly no cell phones, but I was also struck by how no one seemed to show any emotion. They didn't stop to greet one another, didn't nod hello, and no one was conversing or laughing.

As we rode, the staff officer from the Ministry of State Security spoke through the translator with the British accent, whom I was almost glad to see and hear again. The atmosphere and tone were more temperate; even the translations were less formal, more conversational. The MSS officer asked what I thought of the DPRK, and I told him I'd had little opportunity to see much of it. He asked me whether I would be willing to come back. I responded that if I were invited, I would be pleased to return.

During the rest of the drive, he talked about what a shame it was that the Korean people had been divided for so long, tragically separating so many families. He noted that even their language was growing apart, as the dialect of the South changed with the Western influences there. As we approached the airport, he remarked—and I'll never forget this: "I have been to Seoul. I have seen what's there. I would hope that someday we can unify." I suspect this conversation was just as staged as every interaction I'd had since we'd arrived, but I found his comments, demeanor, and tone compelling. I think the intent was to conclude my visit on a more positive note.

Finally, Sunan airport came into view. No aircraft with "United States of America" emblazoned across it ever looked more beautiful. I boarded first and moved to the back of the plane as our two newly freed citizens took seats up front. We'd made the conscious choice to minimize my involvement in securing their freedom, to avoid the appearance that this had been a US intelligence operation, and so I left the direct interactions with them to others in the party.

We flew from North Korea to Guam, Hawaii, and then on to Joint Base Lewis–McChord in Washington State. As Miller and Bae debarked, I walked to the cockpit to watch their emotional reunions with their families. Leaving North Korea with them had given me a sense of relief. Witnessing their embraces and seeing them express the emotion they had been forbidden from showing during their release ceremony in Pyongyang was something much more powerful. When the cameras stopped rolling, a truck towed our plane away to refuel for our last leg to Andrews Air Force Base. As I watched Bae and Miller walk away with their families, I thought how the view from that cockpit sure beat the view from under the bus.

Shortly after we took off, President Obama called to thank and congratulate the entire team on our success, and I passed along his message. Everyone cheered, and we shared some high fives and fist bumps. We landed at Andrews sometime after 2:00 A.M. Monday, and when I finally arrived home about forty-five minutes later, I was tired but still keyed up enough to stay awake into the wee hours to share my adventure with Sue.

Typically, on Monday I conduct an "expanded" staff meeting for senior ODNI leaders. When I walked into the conference room that morning, it was packed. The group stood and applauded, beaming at me with pride, which took me off guard. When we all sat down, I tried to lighten things up by asking, "Anyone go anywhere special this weekend?" I gave them a debrief of the events of the past week, which served as a dry run for a similar account I gave the president a week later, when he returned from China.

The president was in his habitual spot when I entered the Oval Office, in the chair just in front of and on the right side of the fireplace. Susan and the national security team were there, and White House photographer Pete Souza was on the periphery, snapping pictures, as was his official practice. I took my then-customary place on the couch to the president's right and spent the next fifteen minutes describing the trip. When I mentioned the *New York Times* theory of why he'd picked me for the mission, he laughed and agreed with their take. At some point, Pete stopped taking photos and just listened. As I wrapped up, the president said he was grateful to everyone involved and asked me again to pass that on to the team, and not only those who had accompanied me, but to everyone who had supported the trip. Even though we'd had a few rough spots over the past year, I knew that President Obama never took for granted all the "invisible" people who work behind the scenes to make sure missions succeed and intelligence makes it to military commanders in the field and to the Oval Office each morning.

Looking back, perhaps the most impressive aspect of the North Korean mission was that in our post-WikiLeaks world, no one involved had leaked anything to the media. Our success demonstrated that not only is the IC populated by people who can keep secrets, but our profession is filled with creative and dedicated individuals across the globe who can operate in unfamiliar and dangerous places and take on tasks they could never really have trained for. I couldn't have been prouder.

CHAPTER TEN
Unpredictable Instability

While my North Korea trip officially ended November 9, one interaction I'd had in the Hermit Kingdom took on added significance two weeks later. On November 24, a hacker group calling itself the Guardians of Peace published a tranche of personal emails and embarrassing information about the executives at Sony Pictures. Over the next couple of days, the hackers continued to post emails and documents and even yet-to-be-released Sony movies, and they then tried to sabotage Sony Pictures' IT operating systems. They threatened to do more damage if Sony didn't cancel the release of *The Interview*, billed as a comedy about a reporter and a producer (played by James Franco and Seth Rogen) who, before going to North Korea to interview Kim Jong-un, are recruited by the CIA to assassinate him—by the way, not something the CIA does in real life anymore, and hasn't for decades. The IC got involved with the cyber breach, used forensics I can't write about, and at a classified level demonstrated—without a shadow of a doubt in my mind and those of our top cyber specialists—that the Sony hacks had originated in North Korea and that, to do what they'd accomplished, the North Koreans had been on Sony Pictures' systems for weeks, even months.

It was an eerie moment for me, as I thought back to the dinner I'd had on Friday night, November 7—the wonderful food and the hostile company. General Kim, whom I had assumed was my host until I learned we'd actually paid for the meal, was the director of the RGB—the agency that ran foreign intelligence collection, special operations, and cyber operations. So, it was he who ultimately would have ordered the cyber assault against Sony. Reading the intelligence assessments, I realized the hacking operation had been well under way as we were "enjoying" each other's company that night. I would say he kept a good poker face, except that I've never played poker with anyone who just yelled at me for hours on end.

All of the vitriol he spewed over that dinner was genuine. The DPRK really does believe it's under siege from all directions, its people are deadly serious about affronts to the Supreme Leader, whom they consider to be a deity, and there's no room for dissent—not when the favorite management technique of its leader is public executions. It's "super effective." That's why *The Interview* upset them so much.

In Kim Jong-un's mind, allowing this film to be released would mean showing weakness, which might cost him his rule and his status as a deity, not to mention his life. In response, in June 2014, North Korea threatened action against the US government. Sometime between then and November, the DPRK realized that the government doesn't control the American film industry, so it went after the distributor, first hacking and leaking damaging information, and then threatening terrorist attacks on any theater that screened the film. A few independent movie chains, like Alamo Drafthouse, wanted to call the North Korean government's bluff, but for larger theater chains the 2012 shooting at an Aurora, Colorado, movie theater was still too fresh and raw. So Sony Pictures canceled the theatrical release and instead, on December 24, released the film for online rental and purchase, where it still turned a profit. I did my patriotic duty and paid to stream the film, which confirmed two things I already knew: One, Franco and Rogen have a lot of fun making silly movies together. And two, the North Koreans don't have a sense of humor.

In January 2015, I spoke at the International Conference on Cyber Security at Fordham University—the first government official to discuss North Korea as the perpetrator of the Sony Pictures hack. (I was first only because Jim Comey and Mike Rogers were scheduled to speak on the subject later in the day.) After telling them about my interactions with General Kim over dinner, I figured I should offer some insight from our IC cyber experts, since industry was under a constant barrage of cyber intrusions. First, I gave the conference the IC's perspective:

> Taken all together, cyber poses an incredibly complex set of
> threats, because criminals, and "hacktivist" collectives like

Anonymous, are all thrown in together with aggressors like North Korea and Iran, and with the Russians and Chinese, who could do real damage if they are so inclined. Each of those actors has different capabilities and different objectives when they engage in Cyberspace, and all of them operate on the same Internet.

Back in the halcyon days of the Cold War, the world essentially had two large, mutually exclusive communications networks. One was dominated by the United States and our allies, and the other by the Soviets. We could therefore be reasonably sure that if we were listening to someone on the Soviet-dominated network, that person was *not* a US citizen. Today, it's not so clean and easy.

I also offered the conference four pieces of advice from our cyber experts: One: "Patch IT software obsessively. Most Chinese cyber intrusions are through well-known vulnerabilities that can be fixed with patches already available." Two: "Segment your data. A single breach shouldn't give attackers access to an entire network infrastructure and a mother lode of proprietary data." Three: "Pay attention to the threat bulletins that DHS and FBI put out." And four: "Teach folks what spear phishing looks like. So many times, the Chinese and others get access to our systems just by pretending to be someone else and then asking for access, and someone gives it to them." A few months later, I was surprised to find an online article with the headline: "What Law Firms Can Learn from James Clapper." Since most of the time Bob Litt and the other attorneys on ODNI's staff are educating *me,* I succumbed to the clickbait and read the article. A guy named Daniel Lewis, who specializes in firm security, had picked up my four points and applied them to law firm cyber practices. If that resulted in a single firm protecting its systems better, I'm glad he shared it.

Of course, my last piece of advice didn't concern protecting systems from hacking. Spear phishing doesn't require someone to have special coding skills to obtain unauthorized access or control of your computer or network. It's social engineering—tricking people, not systems—and everyone's vulnerable to it. About a year after my speech at Fordham, someone called the phone and internet service provider Sue and I used claiming to be someone he wasn't, and our provider gave them access to

Sue's email account. From there, they got into an account assigned to me that I'd never used, and leveraged that access to play some jokes. It was less of a security issue and more like "griefing"—cyber vandalism—and by then it had become something of a status symbol among the Washington Beltway "elites" to be cool enough to get "hacked." I got to join John Brennan as one of the new initiates in that club.

Later in 2015, our counterintelligence and security team determined that approximately 90 percent of all cyber intrusions start with phishing, because there are always unwitting victims who fall for the scheme. So, when I was giving my four pieces of advice to industry, I was careful not to sound too pious. In January 2015, we hadn't had any massive government losses—at least not that we knew of—on the scale of what had happened to Sony, which was already costing them hundreds of millions of dollars. We did know, though, that the larger federal government wasn't following the advice my security folks had armed me with, and we were just as vulnerable as everyone else.

A few weeks later, when I again presented the IC's annual report, I again opened with cyber. As I told Congress, "Attacks against us are increasing in frequency, scale, sophistication, and severity of impact. Although we must be prepared for a catastrophic, large-scale strike, a so-called 'Cyber Armageddon,' the reality is that we've been living with a constant and expanding barrage of cyberattacks for some time." The first draft of my statement actually called for me to say that we didn't consider a "Cyber Armageddon" to even *be* a real threat, but we decided that having me state that on camera would only be tempting fate, and if, for instance, Russia ever decided to attack our infrastructure, as they'd done on a limited scale to several of their neighbors, a clip of me giving assurances that "Cyber Armageddon isn't a real threat," would be played on loop on whatever media infrastructure was left. So I merely focused on the ongoing cyber onslaught.

Citing cyber first in my presentation didn't mean the terrorist threat had diminished; in fact, the cancer of al-Qaida had made further incursions into the Western world. On January 7, 2015, terrorists who claimed to represent al-Qaida on the Arabian Peninsula had walked into the Paris offices of *Charlie Hebdo,* a French satirical magazine that had pointedly lampooned the Prophet Muhammad. Calling out names of cartoonists and targeting them with gunfire, they killed twelve and wounded another eleven. A massive manhunt and continued violence in Paris followed. On January 10, 2 million people, including forty world leaders, marched in defiance of the violence through the streets of Paris, along with another 1.5 to 2 million in other French cities. I appreciated the show of worldwide solidarity, but I had also seen the intelligence and media reports that Boko Haram had murdered two thousand people in Nigeria between January 4 and 7, and I wished those victims could also have such public attention.

Terrorist violence was, in fact, accelerating around the entire world. I told Congress that while we only had statistics for the first nine months of 2014, in that period some thirteen thousand terrorist attacks had resulted in thirty-one thousand deaths—far more than the twelve-month totals for 2013—and we already knew that 2015 was off to a horrific start. Many of the threats we laid out in our report were getting worse because of one major global trend that I called "unpredictable instability."

I explained that unpredictable instability was both the "new normal" and the driving force behind many of the world's woes: "The year 2014 saw the highest rate of political instability since 1992, the most deaths as a result of state-sponsored mass killings since the early 1990s, and the highest number of refugees and internally displaced persons . . . since World War II. Roughly half of the world's currently stable countries are at some risk of instability over the next two years." What made this instability unpredictable was that so many nations across the globe showed signs of it, and there was no way to predict what sort of event, even something as localized as a fruit seller's self-immolation, might trigger citizens to revolt, a military to seize power, or an aggressive neighbor to grab territory.

My discussion of unpredictable instability made some headlines. What would have truly made national news was the conversations we'd had behind closed doors, that—based on publicly available information, and not on any particular intelligence—the United States had begun to show many of the same characteristics of instability we used to assess other nation-states. First among these was increasing inequality of income and wealth. The Center for American Progress had published a report in the fall of 2014 with some astounding statistics. As it wrote in an analysis of the 2007–9 recession, "Ninety-five percent of all income gains since the start of the recovery have accrued to the top 1 percent of

US households." This was only part of a longer trend. From 1983 to 2010, the top fifth of US families by net worth had increased their wealth by 120 percent and the middle fifth by only 13 percent; the net worth of the bottom fifth had *decreased* in that period.

Looking at the theoretical household at the perfect center of American earnings—50 percent of American families earning more, and 50 percent earning less—they wrote, "The median family saw its income fall by 8 percent between 2000 and 2012." At the same time, they noted that childcare costs grew by 37 percent and health-care costs by 85 percent. "In fact," they added, "investing in the basic pillars of middle-class security— child care, housing, and health care, as well as setting aside modest savings for retirement and college—cost an alarming $10,600 more in 2012 than it did in 2000."

The United States also had an increasingly restive population of young people who couldn't find work, many of them with crushing college debt. Companies had laid off workers of all ages during the recession, and on recovery found that with automation and digital technology advances, they didn't need to hire people back once money started flowing again. Making the situation worse, unemployment was often geographically focused, with some small towns and even larger regions finding the manufacturing jobs that had supported their economies completely dried up. In many ways, there was a growing overlap of the urban versus rural divide and the have versus have-not divide. Those segments of society increasingly looked at each other with resentment, and people who lived in the more rural, less-educated areas of the country no longer felt represented in a government they perceived as dominated by liberal elites.

The state of political discourse in the media and among politicians, meanwhile, had descended to a winner-take-all, scorched-earth mentality. It was a trend that had been developing for decades, but one that Republican strategist Karl Rove turned into a science for the 2000 election, the Tea Party into an art form for the 2010 election, and social media into an epidemic since then. Social networks had siloed people into echo chambers with those who shared similar viewpoints, amplifying their anger. All of this concerned many of us who had watched the Arab Spring lead to uprisings throughout the Middle East and North Africa. We didn't see the United States turning into the next Syria, but what these symptoms *would* eventually lead to was, again, unpredictable instability.

Regardless, as always, our personal concerns remained private, because our professional attention as intelligence officers was always turned outward to understanding the world and helping policy makers work to make it safer.

March presented us with a great opportunity to advance global safety and security. At the end of the month, representatives from the permanent members of the UN Security Council—the United States, the United Kingdom, Russia, France, and China—met in Lausanne, Switzerland, with representatives from Germany, the European Union, and Iran to discuss creating the framework for a deal to stop Iran's nuclear weapons program. Many people, including many politicians and recognizable media figures, misunderstood how narrow and limited this goal was. No deal we could achieve was going to be able to compel Iran to stop sponsoring terrorism, interfering with operations in Iraq and Syria, or menacing its neighbors—particularly Israel. As I said publicly, to me this all boiled down to the question of whether we would rather have a state sponsor of terrorism *with* a nuclear weapons capability or a state sponsor of terrorism *without* a nuclear weapons capability.

Between March 26 and April 2, Secretary of State John Kerry and his team became demanding consumers of intelligence. Their questions came in rapid-fire bursts, and we tasked the intelligence production cycle with responding to them quickly—sometimes within hours—all while meeting similar demands from the president and the National Security Council. It was a stressful eight days, but at the end, the group of foreign ministers announced they had reached "solutions on key parameters of a Joint Comprehensive Plan of Action"—namely, that Iran would give up nuclear materials that could be weaponized, and that it would allow international inspectors access to its nuclear power facilities at a level no other nation on earth had ever permitted. In return, it would regain access to perhaps $100 billion of its assets that had been frozen by sanctions specific to its nuclear weapons program. The April 2 agreement was just a framework for a future deal, a point stressed by Iranian foreign affairs minister Mohammad Javad Zarif, who announced: "No agreement has been reached, so we do not have any obligation yet." That was true, but we knew that the mere fact of arriving at a framework for an agreement validated the work the Intelligence Community had been doing for decades and the power of political and economic pressures we'd worked so hard to support. It also illustrated the value of persistent intelligence over time—often a *long* time.

The announcement of the Iran nuclear deal framework was a terrific high note leading into ODNI's tenth-anniversary celebration. On Friday, April 24, President Obama spoke at our headquarters, opening, as I mentioned earlier, by poking fun at my briefing proclivities and presenting me with a jar of paper clips he said I'd left strewn around the Oval Office. To further laughter and applause, he noted for the crowd, "Today is also special to him because it happens to be his fiftieth wedding anniversary to his wonderful wife, Sue. So we want to congratulate the two of them. And fear not, this is not all he's doing for their fiftieth wedding anniversary." Sue smiled in appreciation.

The president used most of his speech to recognize the effort and impact the IC has had on national security, repeatedly telling the workforce, "You can take great pride in your service." He concluded with specific accomplishments he was grateful for:

> I don't want you or folks across the intelligence community to ever forget the difference that you make every day. Because of you, we've had the intelligence to take out al-Qaida leaders, including Osama bin Laden. Because of you, we've had the intelligence, quickly, that showed Syria had used chemical weapons, and then had the ability to monitor its removal. Because of you, we had the intelligence, despite Russia's obfuscations, to tell the world the truth about the downing of Malaysia Airlines Flight 17 over Ukraine. Because of you, we had the intelligence support that helped enable our recent nuclear framework with Iran. And you're going to be critical to our efforts to forge a comprehensive deal to prevent Iran from ever getting a nuclear weapon.
>
> So you help keep us safe, but you also help protect our freedoms by doing it the right way. And the American people and people around the world may never know the full extent of your success. There may be those outside who question or challenge what we do, and we welcome those questions and those challenges because that makes us better. It can be

frustrating sometimes, but that's part of the function of our democracy.

But I know what you do. We're more secure because of your service. We're more secure because of your patriotism and your professionalism. And I'm grateful for that. And the American people are grateful as well: to you and your families who sacrifice alongside you.

Life has a strange way of keeping my ego in check whenever I'm starting to feel too puffed up about my role in community accomplishments. In April, one of those checks came in the form of a Fairfax County, Virginia, jury duty summons. My assistant, Stephanie Sherline, called the County Courthouse, got in touch with an actual person—a very sweet lady in the County Clerk's Office—and explained who I was, what I did, and that my security detail would have to accompany me into court. The lady considered for a moment and then replied that none of that sounded like a legitimate reason for getting out of jury duty. However, she did note that I was seventy-four years old and that because many "older people" have a hard time sitting through the process, Fairfax County has an automatic exemption for anyone over the age of seventy. I'd like to think Stephanie paused at least a moment before saying, "Yes, we'll take the geezer exemption."

So, life keeps you humble. Sometimes it does so with humor, and sometimes with a jarring sobriety. On May 1, Sue and I left on a weekend trip to Salem, Virginia, to visit our son Andy's family and watch our youngest grandson play in a soccer tournament. After the tournament, we went to a Class Double-A baseball game. As the game progressed, Sue became very quiet. I asked if she was feeling all right, and she answered that she was very tired, so we left. In the SUV, her conversational responses became less and less coherent. Fortunately, the lead security detail officer happened to be a paramedic and conducted an exam. He found the results were more than a little concerning, so our detail driver flipped on the lights and sirens and we sped to the Salem hospital, where Sue was admitted to the emergency room. I stood and watched as the ER doctor in Salem held a video-teleconference with a neurologist in Houston. Between them, they couldn't figure out what was happening, but eventually concluded that she was exhibiting strokelike symptoms, but wasn't suffering a stroke. I mentioned a previous episode she'd had, seven years earlier, in which she'd become quiet and lethargic for a few days, but explained that her current condition was worse by orders of magnitude. We kept watch as over the next few hours Sue fell into a comatose state.

She spent the next three days in a coma in the Salem hospital, and I didn't leave that room. The security detail officers were saints, going far beyond their job descriptions to care for my family and to keep Stephanie O'Sullivan and the other IC leaders updated. I knew that when it came to running the community, Stephanie was every bit my equal—and then some—and my confidence in her enabled me to focus on Sue, holding her hand and talking to her, and visiting with my kids and grandkids in the hospital room. After three days, we hired an ambulance to drive Sue from Salem to Walter Reed National Military Medical Center in Bethesda. On the ride there, she awoke to a semiconscious state, but was not coherent. At midnight, ODNI's lead for personal security met us at Walter Reed's emergency room and helped us settle there. Over the next week or so, Sue gradually returned, although it was six months or more before she felt like herself again. The doctors never really figured out what had gone wrong.

A lot of thoughts passed through my head while I sat in a hospital room holding my wife's motionless hand in the middle of the night. During our fifty years of marriage, I'd spent all but a few focused on service to the nation. I'd thought of it as selfless, but of course, when I'd returned to lead NIMA fourteen years earlier, it had been over Sue's objections and because I'd missed the psychic income—which was, in retrospect, a selfish reason. While I'd served our nation, she'd served our family, raising Jen and Andy, maintaining our house and finances, and living life mostly alone and independent. I really hadn't appreciated the toll those five decades had taken on her. And even without the guilt from recognizing those realities, I had to face the fact that I was seventy-four, and Sue was seventy-one. I suddenly became all too aware of mortality—hers, mine, and others. So, that first night in the Salem hospital, I resolved that whatever Sue's outcome would be, I would resign as DNI and spend the rest of my time focused on her and our kids and grandkids.

That plan didn't last long, not because the community wouldn't have been just fine without me, but because after Sue began to recover, I realized she might not *want* me quite so attentive to her every need, around the clock. She didn't know I knew this, but with the security detail and with Andy and Jen, Sue had nicknamed me Huey, because I was always hovering like a helicopter beside her bed. It went unsaid, but I think she was greatly relieved when I went into the office for a few hours on Friday, May 8. So I didn't resign, but I worked shorter hours for a few weeks, and I came to grips with the reality that I had just twenty months left before I handed off the reins to the next generation, and that, whoever won the election in 2016, I would walk away on January 20, 2017, with no regrets. I envisioned myself sort of tap dancing off stage, preferably to very little fanfare as everyone focused on what was next for our community and nation.

But there were a few things I wanted to do, successes and progress I wanted to make permanent in the time I had left on the job. I started to consider my legacy—not the grade historians might give me on my DNI term paper, but rather the state of the community I'd be leaving behind. I'd stepped into the DNI position honoring the mantra of intelligence integration, and the IC had made very real advances toward achieving that goal since 9/11, which we'd reinforced in the years I'd been DNI. That was one change I wanted to make permanent. With time to reflect, I saw that the second big change we needed to solidify was increased transparency. I'd been saying publicly for nearly two years that transparency was just something we had to achieve, however much it initially felt almost genetically antithetical to me. By May 2015, somewhat to my surprise, I realized that it no longer felt that way to talk publicly about our work.

On May 20, a transparency project we'd been working for four years came to fruition when we released an initial collection of the books, papers, computer files, and documents the special operations team had collected during the Abbottabad raid in 2011, which we had come to refer to as "Bin Laden's Bookshelf." The day we published it, I flew to Tampa to address the annual Special Operations Forces Gala. That evening I told those in attendance, "The materials you took in 2011 from bin Laden's house have been invaluable in our continued fight against al-Qaida, and we've come to understand they're also important to history. I think it's interesting to see what works influenced him, but those who want to see him as a 'supervillain' are going to be disappointed. There was no Sun Tzu, but about half of the thirty-eight full-length English-language books he had—and seems to have read closely—were conspiracy-theory books about the Illuminati and Freemasons. I'm not making that up."

To say there was public interest in Bin Laden's Bookshelf would be an understatement. We got as much web traffic in two days—750,000 site visits and 2 million page views—as our website had received in all of 2013 and 2014 put together. For a while afterward, if someone ran a Google search for "bin Laden," dni.gov was the number-two search result, behind only Wikipedia. Over the rest of my time in office, we continued to update the bookshelf as we cleared documents for public release, and while there was always a group of conspiracy-minded people out there (including a few members of Congress) who believed that we were keeping the "good stuff," we weren't holding back anything of legitimate public interest, unless there were valid concerns with protecting intelligence sources and methods. Another group of like-minded people did figure out what we were holding back, and they continually submitted Freedom of Information Act requests for any pornography collected in Abbottabad. We declined those requests.

Thanks to our Tumblr site—IC on the Record—and to Bin Laden's Bookshelf, our transparency initiatives were running smoothly. Stephanie O'Sullivan and our IC deputies committee were driving intelligence integration, pushing to shift control of the IC ITE initiative away from the information technology leaders to the intelligence mission leaders. As a young engineer, early in her career, she'd spent her free time working as the pit crew chief in an amateur auto racing circuit and had a knack for relating the IC mission to that hobby. During that spring of 2015, she told an audience of collection and analysis leaders that the new IT systems coming out through IC ITE were like a finely tuned race car built by the IT engineers. She challenged them to rethink business applications, rather than just methods for sending emails faster: "If you keep doing the same old things with the brand-new system, that's like saying you really like the new racing car we built for you, but it's too fast, and you're only comfortable driving it if we put on a thirty-five-miles-per-hour governor. Don't do that. Take your game up a notch, or better yet, a whole bunch of notches at once. You have a chance to completely change how you do business."

Given these successes, I naturally began to expect something to go wrong, fitting the pattern of my first five years as DNI. What I didn't expect was to uncover a massive foreign intelligence operation aimed at the people of the IC.

As far back as March 2014, we knew that Chinese hackers were trying to penetrate the Office of Personnel Management, which recruits and manages the 2 million or so employees of the federal workforce, or to hack into the companies it had contracted with to perform security-clearance investigations. OPM believed it had fended off every cyber assault, but in 2015 we found out that wasn't remotely true. While running new software designed to detect intrusions, OPM discovered that they were compromised, and then slowly uncovered just how bad the intrusion was. On June 4, OPM announced that the names, birth dates, home addresses, and social security numbers of 4.2 million current and former federal employees had been stolen. As OPM was sending out notifications to those who were affected, it found another—much worse—intrusion: someone had accessed and exfiltrated 19.7 million security clearance applications. Not only was the applicant information stolen, but the applications themselves revealed information about 1.8 million nonapplicants referenced in the applications, mostly family members. Even worse, they got transcripts of interviews conducted by background investigators, along with the usernames and passwords that applicants had used to fill out forms online, and 5.6 million fingerprint files.

We all but knew from the start that Chinese intelligence was responsible for the theft, and the counterintelligence implications were staggering, not just from what they had, but from what they *didn't* have. OPM didn't conduct security clearance investigations for all of the IC elements, and whoever had the wherewithal to penetrate its systems would certainly know which agencies and departments OPM conducted investigations for and which they didn't. They could therefore also start making assumptions about cover for cleared people whose files they didn't have.

Congress fumed—at me and anyone else who came to testify about the "OPM hack." During a town hall, I noted for the ODNI staff: "I've spent some time up on the Hill talking about the breaches and cyber threats in general. I've heard a lot of outrage over the loss of information and over our apparent lack of response. On the Hill, 'outrage' is now used as a verb. I can even conjugate it: 'I outrage.' 'You outrage.' 'He/she/they outrage.'" In closed briefings Congress demanded I commit to a proportional cyber response against China, which was just ridiculous on a number of levels. First, any response was a policy decision, and I'd made it clear for the previous five years that I don't get involved in those. Second, reciprocity and collateral damage in cyberspace are very difficult to control. NSA and Cyber Command, both still under Admiral Mike Rogers's leadership, had tremendous capabilities, and we felt it was reasonable—but not certain—that if we did decide to attack someone, we would affect only the systems we specifically targeted. But no one else in the world could reasonably be that confident about their abilities, and the infrastructure for the internet was largely independent of international boundaries. So if we attacked someone in cyberspace and they returned fire, Cyber Command and even DOD and the IC might have some level of protection and defense, but the New York Stock Exchange or telecommunications in Eastern Europe or a power grid in Central America might well be taken offline. No one could predict the unintended consequences and potential damage such an assault might cause.

I was particularly attuned to these second- and third-order vulnerabilities because of a discussion at a Principals Committee meeting during President Obama's first term about retaliating for cyber intrusions into Wall Street. After several secretaries shared hawkish opinions, Treasury Secretary Tim Geithner, who by any measure should have been the most aggrieved person in the room, asked a simple question: "Does anyone here know what would happen if there was a serious cyberattack on our financial institutions? Because I don't." That ended the discussion.

In June 2015, I was the Principals Committee member whose equities had been most injured and, like Geithner had been, was most opposed to an aggressive response. In fact, I was much less "outraged" by the Chinese intrusion than almost anyone else, a fact that caused a bit of a stir on June 25 when I publicly discussed the case. After I gave the closing keynote speech at the 2015 GEOINT Symposium, Jim Sciutto of CNN moderated the question-and-answer session that followed. When Jim began the discussion by asking me about the OPM cyber theft, I answered candidly, "You know, on one hand, please don't take this the wrong way, you have to, kind of, salute the Chinese for what they did. If we had the opportunity to do that, I don't think we'd hesitate for a minute." There was a brief pause before Jim gave me an out from being the first government official—without asking for anonymity—to blame China. He asked, "Just to be clear, are you identifying China as the perpetrator behind the OPM attack?" There was some nervous laughter in the crowd. I couched my answer just a little, "Well, I mean, that's the leading suspect."

My security detail drove me from the DC convention center to the White House for back-to-back national security meetings, first with the president, and then another without him. When I returned to the office, I learned that I'd caused a kerfuffle. Apparently, as I'd been naming China the "leading suspect," OPM director Katherine Archuleta had been declining to attribute the attack in testimony before the Senate Armed Services Committee, a discrepancy Congress and the media picked up on. I was honestly surprised that my remarks had made the news, as no one at the White House had been upset about them, including the president. More to the point, I told my staff that we would have looked silly if everyone in Washington was anonymously saying that China did it, if everyone knew China did it, but I wouldn't go on record acknowledging that fact.

More to the point—and maybe this was me being naïve as to what the news cycle cared about—I hadn't thought naming and shaming China would be the controversial part of my comments. To me, the important point—which *wasn't* quickly picked up on—was that I'd said China had hurt us dearly, but that it hadn't done anything outside the bounds of what nation-states do when conducting espionage. They'd exploited a vulnerability in a way not fundamentally different from how, at the age of twelve, I had "hacked" the Philadelphia Police Department. The Philadelphia PD hadn't intended to let me listen in to their conversations in 1953, just as OPM hadn't intended to let China gain access to everyone's security clearance paperwork in 2015. This wasn't just an idle, academic observation. In NSC meetings that summer, I got more involved with policy decisions than I typically would have, arguing that if we responded, we needed to treat what China had done as an act of cyber espionage, not cyber warfare. I warned that how we responded would set a precedent that might come back to haunt us if we ever took a similar opportunity to collect on someone else. In the end, we didn't do much beyond making the symbolic gestures that typically take place after one nation discovers it's been successfully spied on.

For the affected security-clearance holders, the fact that it was Chinese intelligence that had stolen their information was—truthfully—both good news and bad. The good news was that Chinese intelligence was not likely to sell their personal information on the black market, so the employees were less likely to become victims of identity theft than if cyber criminals had perpetrated this breach. The bad news was that elements of Chinese intelligence suddenly had a large body of information they could potentially exploit to compromise our employees professionally or to gain access to the agencies or companies for whom they worked.

The theft did get intelligence leaders to consider what else cyber actors could do to and with our information. As I continued to proselytize the four commandments of cybersecurity, I explained three different ways that that information could be affected. First and most obviously, cyber spies, criminals, and terrorist entities all try to steal our data, undermining *confidentiality,* so that we can't trust that any information is private. Second, when we're the target of denial-of-service operations or someone breaks into our system and deletes data, we're prevented from accessing our own information, undermining *availability.* The hacker group Anonymous seemed to enjoy shutting down government websites by flooding them with automated web traffic. We put safety systems in place to counter this, including some that act like circuit breakers, so that if there's a sudden surge in traffic, the program takes the site off-line. When we published Bin Laden's Bookshelf, we had to warn our cybersecurity officers ahead of time to disable the circuit breakers, because we anticipated a sudden rise in traffic that would otherwise have indicated a denial-of-service attack.

But there was a third potential way to exploit data we hadn't yet seen used. I had started warning public groups that in the future cyber operations would attempt to manipulate information to compromise its *integrity.* In other words, an offensive cyber organization with the skills, technology, and persistence of the Chinese could change our data itself, without doing anything as noticeable as exfiltrating it or blocking our access to it. I urged people to imagine the chaos that could have resulted if the Chinese had actually *changed* people's security-clearance background investigation results. What if a hostile party altered the specs for the construction of an aircraft or spacecraft? How would making even subtle changes to data affect our defense industry, financial sector, or medical record-keepers?

Not only were our vulnerabilities growing, but in some ways, our opportunities were shrinking. As a second- or third-order effect of Snowden's

leaks, encryption technologies sold by commercial industry were proliferating, and even relatively low-tech terrorist organizations like the Islamic State had learned they could frustrate US intelligence surveillance
with encryption applications for sale online. As someone who values privacy, I understood and appreciated making encryption accessible to the
private citizens of the world. At the same time, as President Obama said
in January:

> If we get into a situation in which the technologies do not
> allow us at all to track somebody that we're confident is a ter-
> rorist, if we find evidence of a terrorist plot somewhere in the
> Middle East that traces directly back to London or New York,
> we have specific information and we are confident that this
> individual or this network is about to activate a plot, and de-
> spite knowing that information, despite having a phone num-
> ber, or despite having a social media address or e-mail address,
> that we can't penetrate that, that's a problem.

It was clear to me that applications of digital technologies had fundamentally changed since 2010, when as USD(I) I'd helped establish US
Cyber Command and dual hatted the NSA director as CYBERCOM
commander. Because commercial encryption had made cyber espionage
exponentially more difficult, and the increased capabilities of our adversaries had made both offensive and defensive cyber operations more challenging, I decided to begin pushing to elevate CYBERCOM's status to
equal that of US Pacific Command or US Strategic Command and to
separate it from NSA, preferably before January 20, 2017.

Fortunately, in the middle of dealing with Washington and Pentagon
politics, I had an opportunity to travel, meet with deployed military and
intelligence officers, and see the results of intelligence work. At the end of
June, I went on a whirlwind tour of the Middle East, with a final stop in
Israel, our closest ally in the region, where I was scheduled for a rare personal meeting with a head of state. At the time, Prime Minister Benjamin
Netanyahu was conducting a very public campaign against the impending Iran nuclear deal, even addressing a joint session of the US Congress.
Since I was in Israel as a representative of the president, who, of course,
was in favor of the deal, I neither expected nor received a warm welcome,

and indeed found myself on the receiving end of an hour-long diatribe. Netanyahu gave me very few opportunities to respond to his critiques of the proposed deal, which he felt, among its other shortcomings, neglected to force Iran to recognize Israel's right to exist. When I was able to inter-ject, he was uninterested in my pointing out that the deal would be pur-posefully limited in scope to prevent Iran from developing nuclear weapons, and that diplomatic pressure on Iran for other issues would not stop. While he wasn't as openly belligerent as General Kim had been in North Korea, I understood that I couldn't point my finger at the chest of the Israeli prime minister while making counterarguments.

As our meeting came to a merciful end and we were readying to leave, I mentioned that the paternal grandfather and namesake of one of my staff traveling with us, Jan Karcz, had fought the Nazis as the general in charge of the Polish cavalry, then served with the underground resistance and had died at Auschwitz. Jan's maternal grandfather had hidden two Jewish women in Warsaw, saving their lives, and his mother had served as a squad leader of teenage medics in Poland. Netanyahu's demeanor changed instantly, and he asked us to be introduced to Jan. We soon found ourselves chatting companionably in his small private office and looking through his memorabilia.

One item he showed us that particularly struck me was a thick hard-bound book about the size of *Webster's Dictionary*. In about a six-point font, the word "Jew" was printed six million times—once for each Jewish victim of the Holocaust. For me, it was a powerful reminder of why we do intelligence. Our work isn't just about protecting national security. It's about uncovering and shining a light on evil throughout the world, to prevent a tragedy like the Holocaust from happening again. As we de-parted, the prime minister gave me a cigar from his private stock, a con-solation to end a tough encounter on a pleasant note.

When the final Iran nuclear deal—the Joint Comprehensive Plan of Action—was signed on July 14, I knew that Prime Minister Netanyahu was probably furious, and truthfully, I, too, felt we had given away too much for what we'd gotten from Iran, but at the same time, I still believed the world had just become a lot safer. Iran regained access to their $100 billion or so that had been frozen by sanctions. In return, they shipped out *all* of their uranium that was enriched beyond the 3.67 percent mark that capped "low-enriched uranium," and 15,000 pounds of their low-enriched uranium, leaving just 660 pounds to be used for nuclear power and medical research. They also placed more than two thirds of their first-generation centrifuges into storage monitored by IAEA, along with all of their advanced centrifuges necessary to advance uranium beyond a low-enriched state. They poured concrete into their heavy-water facility in Arak, destroying it, and they allowed unprecedented surveillance—cameras and sensors—into their sole remaining nuclear facility in Natanz. Iran agreed to keep all of these stipulations in place for ten years, a period I wished were longer, but that was not my call. None of this turned Iran into a "shining city on a hill," but that was never the intent. We had taken a potential nuclear weapon out of their hands for at least a decade, and I was proud of the role the IC had played in supporting negotiations in the three months since the initial framework had been settled.

July 2015 also presented an unexpected opportunity to work on protecting our people, when DOD announced that—after taking a brief period to study how best to implement the change—it would allow transgender troops to serve openly in uniform, including those stationed at the intelligence agencies. Given the glacial pace of bureaucracy in the Department of Defense, this announcement came surprisingly fast—less than four years after gay, lesbian, and bisexual service members were first allowed to serve openly. The major forces that made the transgender decision possible were simple: One was that the United States had quickly become aware of its transgender citizens after Caitlyn Jenner's very public, reality-show transition that spring—something the transgender community had very mixed feelings about, at best—and a second was that there was tremendous outside pressure from LGBT groups that were seasoned from fighting for gay, lesbian, and bisexual Americans' rights and had embraced transgender rights as the next battlefield. The third factor was the fact that all the problems the military had expected to encounter when gay, lesbian, and bisexual troops were allowed to serve openly had never materialized.

I would like to think the IC's example also played a part into DOD's decision. We'd shown that it was not only workable, but advantageous to employ openly transgender employees, who brought unique perspectives to mission challenges and contributed to successes. We also had a tremendous model for support. The LGBTA group I'd addressed a year and a half earlier had created a cross-agency, transgender "fly team" that could deploy quickly when an employee decided to come out. They could swoop in, both to help and support the employee through a difficult transition and to normalize the concept of being transgender and candidly answer questions and concerns from coworkers. That was certainly not an application of intelligence integration I had thought of, but I was proud that someone else had.

In just a few years, we had made great strides toward inclusion of our LGBT employees, but as much as we'd made public our business case for diversity, we still fell below the federal government averages in employing black and Hispanic intelligence officers. Those numbers hadn't substantially improved in decades, despite Marine Corps Lieutenant General Vince Stewart's having been sworn in at DIA as the first African American director of a major intelligence agency in January—a long overdue event. Likewise, the high-profile appointments of Tish Long, Betty Sapp, and Stephanie O'Sullivan didn't lead to more women in broader management positions. The annual IC demographics report we submitted to Congress that summer was disheartening, but since it was classified, only the few select congressional members who had taken on workforce diversity as a pet project were tracking the information. So I tasked our equal employment opportunity and diversity chief, Rita Sampson, to find a way to publish an unclassified report in 2016, to hold us—and, more important, future leaders—accountable for our shortcomings.

I don't want to leave the impression that we worked on integration and transparency for a while, then we worked on advancing technology, then provided intelligence to support policy makers, and then focused on protecting people. The truth is, we were doing all of those things, all the time and all at once. We were not, however, as a significant number of Americans seemed to believe in the summer of 2015, conspiring with US Special Operations Command to seize control of states across the southern United States during the Jade Helm 15 military exercises. Radio host and conspiracy theorist Alex Jones, who called Texas home, pushed out daily updates about what was "really" going on, seemingly unbothered by contradicting himself from one day to the next. Some days he seemed to be pushing his own conspiracy theories, and on others, he just reported what he'd read on social media. His only real consistent message was that the president and the liberal elites in Washington were preparing to use military force to impose their will on southern rural conservatives. Some people were so taken by the fear that Obama was going to declare martial law, seize their guns, and impose his agenda that citizens armed with AR-15 assault rifles started showing up at military bases, declaring themselves "citizen observers" of the exercise. Asked about it later, President Obama remarked that Jade Helm was his "favorite conspiracy." I don't know the level to which he was being sarcastic in that interview, but to me, the situation was ominous, and we were very fortunate that heated discussions between soldiers and armed civilians never turned violent.

With the benefit of hindsight, the persistence of the Jade Helm conspiracy theory reminds me—far too much—of Putin's social media campaign to turn the Russian-speaking region of Ukraine against its national government. In both instances, the purveyors of the conspiracy focused on a geographic region whose population viewed itself as physically isolated and culturally different from the people who were running their country. Both conspiracies had their roots in social media, with trolls quickly generating new, outrageous content. Both played on racial and ethnic prejudices and targeted people who were predisposed to believe they were victims of their national government's agenda. In the summer of 2015, it would never have occurred to us that low-level Russian intelligence operatives might be posing as Americans on social media. As far as I know, we've never checked to see if Russia was involved in promoting the Jade Helm conspiracy, but it certainly followed their playbook, and it took place at around the same time that they launched their social media campaign to undermine Democratic candidate for president Hillary Clinton.

On the opposite side of the world, Russia was very open about what it was doing in Syria, and in September, any hopes that the United States held for ridding Syria of Bashar al-Assad's tyranny evaporated. By then Assad's crimes against humanity far outpaced what Gaddafi had done in Libya. Hundreds of thousands of Syrians were dead, including perhaps as many as a hundred thousand civilians, and of Syria's prewar population of 22 million, about a quarter had fled the country, while another quarter were internally displaced. Assad had intentionally targeted civilians, including with chemical attacks, and as bad as the casualties inflicted by the Islamic State were, nine of every ten civilian deaths in Syria could be attributed to Assad's regime. The US government wanted him gone—and said as much—but efforts to oust him had been continuously frustrated by two realities: first, the Russians and Chinese blocked any UN Security Council resolutions with real teeth, and second, no ready options emerged to replace the Assad regime.

By 2015, there were still hundreds of resistance factions in Syria, unable or unwilling to unite. The only group that had managed to seize and hold any real power or territory and who had made any effort—however sadistic—to govern had been the Islamic State. Fighting IS was very difficult, as they blended with the population and used civilians as cover, which made both intelligence targeting and actual strikes difficult to carry out. But the narrative asserting that President Obama was afraid to attack them was simply untrue. According to statistics published by the Council on Foreign Relations, the United States conducted more than twenty-two thousand strikes against the Islamic State and other terrorist groups in Iraq and Syria in 2015, and that number was limited only by the intelligence available to generate targets. Those efforts, as well as US support of Iraqi troops and other Syrian groups, were gradually wearing down the Islamic State.

Then, in September 2015, following a prenegotiated script, Assad's regime formally asked Russia to intervene on its behalf in the civil war, and Russia responded by securing a Syrian air base on the coast of the Mediterranean and flying in fighter jets and attack helicopters. The Black Sea Fleet moved into the Mediterranean, and the Russians went to work, targeting anyone who didn't support Assad's regime. As is the Russian military modus operandi, they publicly claimed almost every strike was carried out against IS, but month after month, Russian air attacks killed more civilians than they did Islamic State fighters. We monitored the strikes and assessed that they were conducting so many that it was impossible that they were operating on credible intelligence for targeting. They were simply blowing up cities and towns whose people didn't support Assad. I'm not convinced these raids made a significant difference against IS, and many were counterproductive, targeting groups who were actively fighting the Islamic State. But Russian engagement in the civil war certainly escalated the pain and suffering of the people of Syria as it accomplished the real goal of keeping Assad in power.

As Russian military intervention in Syria was ramping up, the Syrian migrant crisis in Europe hit a flash point. On September 2, a journalist published a photograph of a three-year-old Kurdish-Syrian boy whose body had washed ashore in Turkey. His family had fled Syria into Turkey and were trying to cross into Europe aboard a tiny inflatable boat, loaded well past its maximum occupancy, when it capsized just offshore. The vests the passengers were wearing turned out not to be flotation devices, and in the chaos, young Alan Kurdi was lost and drowned. The current carried him back to Turkey, and a few hours later the journalist captured the image of him, facedown in the sand. After the picture sparked world-wide outrage, his father told the media that they were ultimately trying to reach Canada. The incident and sympathy for the refugee crisis became major factors in the 2015 Canadian election and helped sweep the liberal politician Justin Trudeau into office as prime minister.

According to records of the UN High Commissioner for Refugees, more than 137,000 people had crossed the Mediterranean in just the first six months of 2015—nearly double the number from the same period in 2014. The vast majority were refugees, fleeing Syria, Iraq, Afghanistan, or North Africa, trying to reach Greece or Italy as entrance points into the European Union. Horrifyingly, in the month of April alone, 1,308 refugees had drowned or gone missing in their desperate attempts to cross. As terrible as the human toll had become, many European nations were wary of harboring those fleeing violence. Fully one third of the refugees were from Syria, and even the combined efforts of US and European intelligence agencies couldn't guarantee that a handful of the hundreds of thousands of people making the crossing weren't sleeper-cell terrorists with the Islamic State or al-Qaida. By the end of 2015, the refugees had become a moral crisis for the entire Western world.

On November 13, the risk the European Union was taking came into sharp focus, as half a dozen suicide bombings and mass shootings occurred almost simultaneously across Paris, killing 130 people and wounding more than 400 at a soccer match, a concert, and in crowded streets and cafés. The Islamic State claimed responsibility, saying the attacks were carried out in retaliation for French targeting of its fighters in Syria. The terrorists came from a prepositioned cell in Belgium and were not refugees, but the attack stoked anti-Islam sentiment across Europe and caused many European nations to halt taking in the "huddled masses" requesting asylum—precisely the Islamic State's goals.

Less than three weeks later, terrorism hit the United States. A married couple in San Bernardino, California—he a US-born citizen and she a Pakistani-born US permanent resident—opened fire at the Christmas party for his office, the county Department of Public Health. In just a few minutes, they killed fourteen people, wounded another twenty-two, and fled. A few hours later, the police caught up with and killed them in a bloody shootout. The Islamic State baselessly tried to take responsibility for these murders before eventually settling for having "inspired" the attack. The incident inflamed tensions with US Muslim communities again, and despite neither perpetrator's having any connection to Syria, Americans began asking their elected representatives about the US policy for resettling refugees.

The response to the shooting demonstrated the real-world effects of commercial encryption on intelligence and law-enforcement work, and it underscored the post-Snowden tension between the US information technology sector and the US government. Fearing that other conspirators could still be at large, the FBI seized the San Bernardino shooter's iPhone 5 but the government was unable to penetrate the device's encryption and security without triggering mechanisms that would delete all its data. So the FBI quietly asked Apple to create a program that would disable the security on the phone, but the company declined. Jim Comey publicly acknowledged the FBI's difficulties in unlocking the device, and publicly requested Apple's help. CEO Tim Cook, in turn, wrote an open letter to Apple's customers, stating that Apple would refuse the FBI's request and reassuring them that it would never do anything to weaken the security features of its products. The FBI filed a court petition, and tensions escalated until, just before the court deadline, the bureau announced it no longer needed Apple's help.

This is an issue that is still unresolved in this country. I certainly understand the imperative for personal privacy, but there has to be a better balance between societal safety and individual privacy. Stephanie attended a series of working group meetings at the White House to try to arrive at a reasonable compromise and way ahead. One proposal I thought had merit was a system of what's called "key escrow," in which as many as three separate, independent entities would hold a part of the encryption key, and a court order would be required to gain access to each of the keys held by the key holders. What I have found frustrating is the unwillingness of industry to apply all its great technical acumen to this problem. But since we were dealing with absolutist positions on both sides, we decided to pass this issue on to the next administration—and we informally knighted Jim Comey to be the continuity, since he had more than six years remaining in his statutory term as FBI director.

Considering that struggle, not surprisingly, technology was a sharp point of focus for the threat hearings during the first few months of 2016—which I happily noted for each congressional committee would be the final time they would hear from me about the "most diverse set of threats I've seen in my more than fifty years in the intelligence profession." I started each hearing by giving a countdown of days until I retired—by then under a year—and then launched into discussing how the same technology advances that were "central to our economic prosperity" would create new security vulnerabilities that we were just beginning to grasp. I talked about artificial intelligence making autonomous decisions and about the ways in which everyday machines were being connected to the internet. "The Internet of Things," I explained, "will connect tens of billions of new physical devices that could be exploited."

I'd publicly illustrated how the internet is both a privacy and security concern with the example of connected refrigerators: "It's not hard to imagine a fridge that knows whether you are stocking it full of fresh veggies and fruit and then reports that information back to your health insurance provider. But if the latest software patch can't distinguish between an apple and an apple pie, your insurance rates could go up." I also noted that, in theory, someone could hack the appliance and alter its temperature while you're at work, producing "maliciously spoiled milk." That typically drew laughs, and then I cited a case from 2015—as reported by the *Register*, a paper in the United Kingdom—in which a security firm had successfully hacked into a refrigerator digitally displaying its owner's Google calendar. Having gained access to the calendar, they then surreptitiously collected the log-in and password for all his Google accounts. With a primary-email log-in, they could easily reset passwords for his bank and credit accounts.

I also briefed Congress on Iran, which continued "to be the foremost state sponsor of terrorism" and to interfere in regional crises. Although the IAEA had announced in January that Iran had dismantled its nuclear-weapons program, as we'd said, that didn't suddenly make the nation a beacon of justice and freedom. I discussed Russia, noting that the annexation of Crimea made Putin "the first leader since Stalin to expand Russia's territory," and that Moscow's military venture into Syria marked its first deployment of significant combat power outside the Soviet space since its foray into Afghanistan in the 1980s. I noted that "Moscow faces the reality, however, of economic recession, driven in large part by falling oil prices, as well as sanctions. Russia's nearly four percent GDP contraction last year will probably extend into 2016."

I updated my warnings about "unpredictable instability," citing much more specific statistics than the year before:

> Violent extremists are operationally active in about 40 countries. Seven countries are experiencing a collapse of central government authority, and 14 others face regime-threatening, or violent, instability, or both. Another 59 countries face a significant risk of instability through 2016. The record level of migrants, more than one million arriving in Europe, is likely to grow further this year. Migration and displacement will strain countries in Europe, Asia, Africa, and the Americas. There are now some 60 million people who are considered displaced globally. Extreme weather, climate change, environmental degradation, rising demand for food and water, poor policy decisions and inadequate infrastructure will magnify this instability.

My survey of cyber technology, artificial intelligence, and the Internet of Things made the most news, although it was the phrase I used to end my opening statement that made all the headlines: "Needless to say, there are many more threats to US interests—worldwide—that we can address, most of which are covered in our Statement for the Record. But I'll stop this litany of doom and open to your questions." Someone at ODNI thought that "James Clapper and the Litany of Doom" would be a great name for a heavy metal band, and by the end of the week, I was presented with a concert T-shirt that featured my likeness, front and center, absolutely shredding on lead guitar as pyrotechnics exploded all around.

I turned seventy-five on March 14 and spent my birthday en route to Australia to meet with the Five Eyes intelligence chiefs to discuss the future of intelligence and security. In Canberra I found one presentation

to be particularly compelling. Dr. Paul Taloni, the director of the Australian Signals Directorate—their equivalent of the NSA director—described
sitting with his seven-year-old daughter and looking at the pictures of
Pluto taken in 2015 when the New Horizons spacecraft made its flyby.

The first image he showed her, and later included in his presentation,
was the now-iconic first color image NASA posted online: a rusty brown
planet with the shape of a white heart covering its lower-right quadrant.
He asked his daughter what it was, and she replied, "Just a photo of Pluto."
Each successive shot was taken at closer range, with more detailed views
of the texture of the dwarf planet's surface. The picture on his third slide
showed sharp ridgelines and peaks on Pluto's surface, casting shadows
into a vast valley, with the nitrogen atmosphere hanging in layers, heaped
above the curve of the horizon. His daughter told him it was "just the
mountains on Pluto, with the air." Then he showed her the best picture
we'd had of Pluto at the time when he was seven—a faint white dot among
many other dots. "Wow, Dad," she observed, "you're old." I didn't bother
to say anything at the time, but when I was seven, we'd only just *discovered* Pluto a few years earlier. His point was that, in just one generation,
technology had leapt from seeing Pluto as a faint dot to actually visiting
the dwarf planet and sending back detailed color images.

While I was in Canberra, a Google team was in Seoul, Korea, putting
its DeepMind artificial intelligence to a unique test. Twenty years earlier,
in 1996, IBM's Deep Blue had shocked the world by defeating the reigning
world chess champ, Garry Kasparov. In 2016, Google's AlphaGo program
took on the Chinese board game Go. Deep Blue had been able to process
all possible chess moves to outmaneuver Kasparov. In Go, there are 10^{90}
times as many possible positions as there are atoms in the universe. So a
computer cannot win at Go by brute processing force. Instead, using neu-
ral network technology, AlphaGo taught itself to play, and in the process
developed what Google's engineers called "an intuition" for the game.
That month, AlphaGo beat world champ Lee Sedol in four of five games.
The biggest moment of the best-of-five match was move 37 of game 2. The
commentator, also a Go grand master, thought AlphaGo had made a
huge blunder, placing its piece far away from the action. Lee took several
minutes to try to understand the move, hoping to capitalize on AlphaGo's
error. Eventually he recognized the brilliance—what he termed the
"beauty"—of the move, one that likely had never been played before and

not one a human would think of making. Lee had to leave the room for fifteen minutes to compose himself. So we have left behind the world of 1996, in which our smartest computers put their speed and brute force behind algorithms written by human programmers. We now live in a world in which machines can learn from their own mistakes and can develop a "beautiful" intuition.

Later that spring, at the 2016 GEOINT Symposium, I recounted Paul Taloni's presentation and Google's victory, and I told the attendees that we could view that pace of technical innovation either as an alarming development that could take away any advantage we had, or as a force that would revolutionize our lives for the better, one that we in the IC could and, I was confident, would take advantage of. But, I said, we needed to stop fighting technology and instead put it to work for us.

I illustrated what I meant with a problem our security folks had recently come across. During a standard sweep of a new facility of which the Intelligence Community was about to take possession, they'd discovered several wireless signals transmitting out into the world. When they located their sources, they were relieved to discover the signals were *not* from foreign intelligence bugs in the facility, but from vending machines trying to inform their distributor that they were empty. Apparently, "phoning home" for refills is a fairly common feature in vending machines, and one we learned to check for and mitigate. But this led to more questions about how the Internet of Things affected us: Where were the weak points that we weren't yet considering? And how would we adapt when even our clothes are connected, or when doctors regularly prescribe wireless monitors for health conditions? I mentioned that I had needed to obtain a security waiver for my hearing aids, which had Bluetooth connectivity. Technology had the potential to revolutionize our business and our lives, but we needed to move past just defending ourselves from drink machines and hearing aids.

I felt that I ought to deliver a suitable valedictory address to close out my final GEOINT Symposium, having spoken as NGA Director, USD(I), and as DNI (although I did threaten to return in 2017 to represent "the GEOINT needs of the assisted living community"). So, I tried to sum up what my fifty-two years in the intelligence profession had taught me, particularly the subjects that had weighed on my mind as DNI while our nation was holding a very public conversation about the IC and how it does its work. What was lost in that public debate was the question of *why* we even do intelligence. Why does any nation-state? I told the GEOINT Symposium that "at its most basic level," we conduct intelligence "to reduce uncertainty for decision makers. That can be anyone, from the president in an Oval Office to a private in an oval-shaped foxhole. We can't eliminate uncertainty for any of them . . . but we can provide insight and analysis to help their understanding and to make uncertainty at least manageable." Appreciating the risks involved, they can make educated decisions, and we and our friends and allies can operate with a shared assessment of the facts and the situation.

I closed with this thought:

> I believe that in this time of change, when we don't know who "Intell Customer Number One" will be a year from now when we hold GEOINT 2017, what our national priorities will be, and what challenges we'll face next, if we keep the truth in front of us of why we do intelligence, our unique accesses and insight will continue to help our national leaders manage the inevitable uncertainty for a long time to come.

CHAPTER ELEVEN

The Election

On December 4, 2011, Russians went to the polls in what would be the most closely contested parliamentary election since Vladimir Putin and his United Russia party came into power in 1999, when Putin succeeded Boris Yeltsin as president and then never left. Putin had served two terms as Russia's second president but was constitutionally prevented from running for a third consecutive term, and so he'd stepped down in 2008, nominating Dmitry Medvedev to stand for United Russia. He helped Medvedev get elected and then served as prime minister—first in succession to the presidency—during Medvedev's term. Few doubted that Putin was still calling most of the shots. Then, in September 2011, Medvedev announced he would not run for a second term. Instead, he nominated Putin to stand as the party's candidate for president in the March 4, 2012, election. Putin accepted the nomination and offered the prime ministership to Medvedev, should he win.

This arrangement met the letter of the law—no more than two consecutive terms—but not everyone in Russia thought it was ethical or in the nation's best interest, and for the first time in twelve years, voices of dissent were widely heard around the nation. People began to refer openly to United Russia as "the party of crooks and thieves," and opposition parties dared to point out government corruption. Three months before the presidential contest, tensions came to a head during the December 4, 2011, Russian parliamentary election. It was a critical test for Putin's party. Maintaining a hold on Russia's parliament wasn't just a matter of being able to run a legislative agenda without opposition; it answered the question of whether or not people with opposing political viewpoints would be able to get away with criticizing Putin.

On parliamentary election day, the US IC and diplomats around the world watched the results with interest. As polls closed and votes were tallied, United Russia received a little less than 50 percent of the vote, but because of the way the elections were structured, it managed to keep a slim majority of seats in parliament—the rest split among the other six registered political parties, with the Communist Party finishing a distant second. As the tallies were rolling in, the opposing parties and independent organizations—Russian and international—began releasing reports of suspected voter fraud and voter intimidation, both at the polls and in workplaces, where employees likely to vote against United Russia were held at work and prevented from voting. Armed men appeared at polling stations and chased off election observers. Then reports came in of people being bused around to vote for United Russia at multiple stations throughout the day. That evening, US secretary of state Hillary Clinton joined other world leaders in expressing unease with the results. She called for an investigation with a statement that read, "We have serious concerns about the conduct of the election."

On the following day, Monday, citizens took to the streets to stage a genuine protest against the election—something else new in Putin's Russia. There had been protests in previous years, but mostly from former Communist retirees whose marches were more nostalgic parades than legitimate threats. But now several thousand angry young people gathered in Moscow, showing their opposition not only to the election, but to the corruption they perceived as pervading Putin's party and Medvedev's government. They disrupted traffic and damaged property, and police couldn't move them along. The demonstrations on Tuesday and Wednesday spread to other Russian cities. Putin seethed at this public embarrassment, coming on the heels of the closer-than-expected party win and just months before he would stand for president. On Thursday, he spoke to the Russian media, describing the protesters as mere "pieces on the chessboard" and claiming they were all being directed by an "unseen hand"—US secretary of state Hillary Clinton, through his old nemesis, the CIA.

Whether he actually believed Clinton was behind the protests or whether the statement was a cynical move designed solely to stoke anti-American sentiments, his provocation worked. Those favoring United Russia galvanized around the American threat, and the state propaganda machine shifted into high gear. Over the next three months, the state media portrayed Putin as the only leader who could stand up to the United States, and Medvedev tweaked election rules to ensure no one who could compete with Putin was allowed to stand. In March, Putin won almost two thirds of the votes in the presidential election, and with new laws extending the presidential term to six years, he could theoretically remain in office until 2024. While it's likely that Clinton's public condemnation of the 2011 Russian parliamentary election actually *helped* Putin to a convincing win in 2012, Putin continued to blame her for Russian unrest, and he is not one to forgive or forget a grudge—ever. So when Clinton announced her candidacy for president in 2015, Putin remembered.

After the 2016 US presidential election, the Intelligence Community investigated, documented, declassified, and published accounts of what Putin and Russia had done to influence the election—in remarkable detail. But that IC assessment didn't capture the experience of actually being on the receiving end of the Russian influence operation in 2015 and 2016—the slowly dawning realization that our primary adversary for nearly all of my half century as a US intelligence professional was, without exaggeration, hacking away at the very roots of our democracy. Before then I'd never seriously considered writing a book about my experiences, even after transparency began to feel more natural. But after Election Day 2016, I felt compelled to share my experience of what had happened to us, to educate the electorate—not because I thought I could stop it from happening again, but because we needed to be able to recognize it when it did. In truth, "again" is the wrong word, because the Russian propaganda didn't stop.

Russian interference in the most recent US elections is not without precedent. The Soviet Union likely tried to influence *every* US election during the Cold War. The Soviet efforts for their favored candidate in 1960 are well documented. Adlai Stevenson had lost both the 1952 and 1956 elections to Dwight Eisenhower, at least partly because he'd made statements against the escalation of nuclear weapon testing and procurement, particularly of hydrogen bombs, and so was seen as "soft" on the Soviets. As documented at the time by *New York Times* Washington bureau chief James Reston and later by Stevenson's biographer, John Bart-low Martin, after Stevenson announced he wouldn't run in January 1960, he was invited by the Soviet ambassador to their embassy on a false diplomatic pretext. There the ambassador read him a letter from Soviet premier Nikita Khrushchev, offering support—including money and propaganda—if Stevenson would enter the race. He declined, went home, documented the conversation, and reported it to Eisenhower's administration—putting the welfare of the nation above his own personal interests. With Stevenson out, Khrushchev favored *anyone* over Richard Nixon, and so, reportedly, the Soviets turned their efforts toward helping Kennedy get elected, without actually colluding with Kennedy's campaign. (I can only wonder if during the Cuban Missile Crisis Khrushchev regretted having backed Kennedy.)

We know the Soviets worked against Nixon again in 1968, and that Hubert Humphrey reportedly declined direct financial support. In the 1976 campaign, they successfully recruited a Democratic Party activist to report inside knowledge of candidate Jimmy Carter's campaign that they could use to influence the new administration after Carter's election. They worked against Ronald Reagan's reelection in 1984, using intelligence services to dig up and promulgate dirt on the sitting president. And those are just the few specific examples already in the public sphere that I can mention. In the IC's report on Russian activities in the 2016 US presidential campaign, we noted that the Soviet Union used intelligence officers, influence agents, forgeries, and press placements to disparage candidates perceived as hostile to the Kremlin until the end of the Cold War, when the Soviet Union collapsed and ceased to exist.

We also wrote that after the Cold War and up until 2016, Russian intelligence efforts focused on undermining US democracy and on collecting intelligence on candidate positions from their campaigns. I know from encounters with foreign intelligence services and governments around the world that both our friends and our adversaries take careful note of every word candidates say. Of course, our adversaries will look for an advantage, an indication of what the candidates are saying behind closed doors, and they understand that campaigns and political parties are softer targets than presidential administrations are later.

In 2012, Russia introduced a powerful new platform for broadcasting anti-American sentiment inside the United States. The Kremlin-funded television network Russia Today had been on the air during the 2008 election, but its name and its coverage were too "on the nose," too obvious, and no one had watched it. In 2009, it rebranded itself as "RT" and positioned itself as an alternative to CNN and Fox News, similar to what Al Jazeera did at the time. It mostly ran straight news, not very different from what was offered by the mainstream media, just with a slightly funky flavor and an occasional story promoting Russian interests. Some pro-Russian policy stories were more subtle than others. Its series warning of the environmental dangers of fracking was a well-masked campaign, designed to protect Russian oil exports from increased US production of oil and natural gas. By contrast, RT's series backing the Syrian regime was more obvious. By the time of the 2012 election it had cultivated viewership and raised its social media presence, with 450,000 subscribers on YouTube averaging one million views a day—more than any other network. By then it was well positioned to run a classic Soviet-era propaganda campaign on its massive American audience.

We didn't take any steps to counter Russian propaganda in 2012, but we did watch their efforts closely, and after the election, the US IC published a report describing how RT had portrayed the US election as "undemocratic" and had urged the public to "take this government back." From August to November 2012, RT ran stories on election fraud and voting machine vulnerabilities, alleging that the election results "cannot be trusted and do not reflect the popular will." RT hosted, advertised, and broadcast third-party candidate debates, and then ran stories supporting the third-party political agendas. Supporting those candidates wasn't inherently un-American at all, but RT's pretense was that "the two-party system does not represent the views of at least one-third of the population and is a sham." In the final days before the election, RT ran a documentary on the Occupy Wall Street movement, linking the political resistance of the Occupy movement to its own frequent call to "take this government back." After President Obama won reelection, RT began running a documentary called *Cultures of Protest,* about violent political resistance.

How Russia used RT during the 2012 election cycle wasn't illegal, and in fact wasn't all that different from how the CIA had employed Radio Free Europe in the 1950s and 1960s to broadcast information into Eastern Europe in an attempt to undermine the Communist regimes behind the Iron Curtain. I would be remiss if I glossed over well-documented

US intelligence efforts to interfere with many foreign elections. In December 2016, Carnegie Mellon researcher Dov Levin published his research indicating the United States had intervened in eighty-one elections between 1946 and 2000, making us, by his count, the most prolific election interferer in the world during that period. I can't verify or refute many of his claims, but we've declassified some of the examples he cites—for instance, the CIA's work in Chile in the 1960s. Levin doesn't include our non-election attempts at regime change, like the successful 1953 Iranian coup or the unsuccessful 1962 Bay of Pigs invasion. Nor does he count the case of two former CIA officers, under orders from the Nixon White House in 1972, breaking into a room in the Watergate Hotel to steal secrets from the Democratic National Committee and Nixon's election opponent, thereby interfering in our own election. In the aftermath of Watergate, the Church Committee uncovered many other events that constituted intelligence abuses or overreach. In the aftermath of the Church Committee's report, new laws and executive orders were put in place to prevent the CIA, FBI, and other intelligence agencies from spying on US persons, infiltrating US political organizations, and assassinating foreign leaders.

Of course, the new laws didn't stop US policy makers from—legally—using information operations, covert action, and even full-scale military conflict to bring about regime changes around the world, some of which I was involved in, such as the Iraq invasion in 2003. Looking back, I've always—at least since I've been in positions to know what was happening and why—viewed our attempts to influence developments in other countries as doing what our policy makers thought was best for the oppressed citizens of those nations, and then, secondarily, what was best for US interests. I believed we've been motivated by a commitment to spread liberal, democratic values throughout the world, and that, I think, has led me to see our efforts as ethical. In other words, simplistically, I always viewed us as the "good guys," with at least noble intentions.

As someone whose fingerprints were on the faulty National Intelligence Estimate that led the United States to invade Iraq, I certainly knew we were fallible, and as someone who'd helped fight the forces of chaos unleashed after we'd removed Saddam Hussein and Muammar Gaddafi from power, I was well aware that the actions we took from initial good intentions could have horrific unintended consequences. Looking back

now, I may have been more than a bit Pollyannaish—being overly generous in my assessment of our motives, intent, and ideals—but that's how I
thought about them then, and while I can reassess views I held earlier in
life, I don't get to remake my decisions after seeing how they turned out.
I can only learn from my choices and keep moving forward. And here's
the hard truth: I can't—and we as a nation can't—let concerns about historical hypocrisy stop us from facing the facts in front of us now. That's
particularly true about confronting what happened in the 2016 election.

The US Intelligence Community first started noticing Russian activity
around the election after Clinton announced her candidacy in April 2015.
This was not a coincidence. For RT, 2015 was already a banner year.
They'd gleefully covered the Black Lives Matter protests, incidents of police shootings, and the March 12 shooting of two police officers by a
young black man in Ferguson, Missouri, as revenge for the police shooting of a young black man in Ferguson in 2014. They'd covered US income-
inequality issues and encouraged minimum-wage workers to strike, and
were set to cover the fast-food worker "walk off the job" rally across the
nation on April 15. Those stories fit perfectly in RT's wheelhouse. They
were provocative and drew viewers with dramatic photos and clickbait
headlines. They were about concrete issues that split the American public
and deepened socioeconomic divisions. And they were mainstream
enough to hide the fact that they served to support the Kremlin's agenda.

They were also perfect for the moment, as RT was helping to frame
issues for the presidential election in a way that, no matter which side of
an issue a candidate came down on, some segment of the American electorate would feel anger and resentment. RT and Russian leaders—up to
and including Vladimir Putin—had learned a lot from RT's work in the
2012 presidential campaign.

Of course, Clinton's candidacy was a given long before she made her
formal announcement, but RT wasn't waiting for that—or those of her
rivals—to get up to speed before they prepared the political battlefield.
On April 10—two days before Clinton announced—they ran an online
story with the lead "Hillary Clinton, a former US secretary of state (and
senator, and First Lady), will reportedly announce her 2016 presidential
run Sunday via social media. Expect these recent Clinton scandals to surface again (and again) for the duration of her candidacy." What followed

was a primer on how to attack Hillary Clinton, with subheadlines for each section: "State Department emails," "Benghazi attacks," "Diplomatic cables published by WikiLeaks," "The Clinton Foundation donors," and "Support for Iraq war, Patriot Act, bank bailouts." Each section laid out the relevant issue and how it made Clinton vulnerable. Each contained an embedded video clip of her that played to her disadvantage, and each linked to previous RT stories with greater detail.

The first section, on her State Department emails, succinctly made this case against her:

> The latest Clinton controversy stems from her use of a private email account and server—which was found to be insecure for at least three months—to conduct official business as US secretary of state. Clinton has said she used her private email account—just as past secretaries of state have done—as a matter of convenience. Then just over a week ago, it was revealed that Clinton used both her Blackberry [sic] and an iPad to email State Department employees from her private account and server.
>
> US Rep. Trey Gowdy (R-SC), who heads the House Select Committee on Benghazi, issued a subpoena for the private server that hosted Clinton's emails as the congressional panel investigates the 2012 attacks on the US consulate in Benghazi, Libya, that killed four Americans, including Ambassador Christopher Stevens. Late last month, he announced that Clinton had failed to respond to the subpoena and had wiped her server clean. In response, the Benghazi committee has formally asked Clinton to answer questions about the server during an in-person, transcribed interview before May 1.
>
> Clinton has said that she deleted 30,000 of about 60,000 emails exchanged during her four years as secretary of state because they were "personal in nature," but that she turned all of her work-related emails over to the State Department.

Within those seven sentences, RT perfectly framed the issue that would haunt Clinton more than any other over the next eighteen months, in *precisely* the way that the Republican candidates would use it against her—with the exception of one aspect I'll get to in a moment that wasn't yet public—and it linked to seven other related RT stories.

Despite RT's labeling the emails as "the latest Clinton controversy," the issue had in fact dogged her since she'd resigned as secretary of state in February 2013. Just a month later, a Romanian hacker with the moniker "Guccifer" published Clinton's email address at the domain "clintonemail .com" and revealed that she'd used it almost exclusively for her duties as secretary of state. The "new" factor in 2016 was that the House Select Committee on Benghazi had discovered that the State Department didn't have a record of all of Clinton's official emails. The committee demanded access to what was missing. Answering public allegations of impropriety from committee members, Clinton tweeted that her attorneys had given all work-related emails from her private server to the State Department—minus, of course, any emails deemed "personal," which her attorneys had deleted—and that she'd asked State to release the emails to Congress. The State Department determined that it needed to conduct a classification review before doing so and that it would take some time to complete—probably not until January 2016. Almost immediately, the Benghazi Committee subpoenaed all of her emails relating to their investigation, furious that she'd let her attorneys delete any emails without an outside review. They insinuated that she could have deleted incriminating emails regarding Benghazi along with those about her daughter's wedding. The committee subpoena was followed quickly by a court order for the State Department to publish reviewed emails on a rolling basis—a new batch every thirty days. This order was unfortunate, both for Clinton and for the State Department, as it ensured it would continually provide fresh news for the media to discuss through the entire election cycle.

Personally, I was a bit baffled by the whole situation—first and foremost, that any committee was still investigating the Benghazi attack two and a half years after the event and after Matt Olsen and I had so painstakingly briefed them and rebriefed them on what had happened that night in Libya. I was deeply saddened by the loss of Chris Stevens and the three other Americans, but in the aftermath, we'd been as open as possible with intelligence assessments, and by 2015, the committee was generating all the controversies it was investigating. At the same time, I was surprised to learn that Hillary had a private server in her basement.

People have asked me, "How could you not *know*?" Well, it's not a question that comes up, and I can't recall ever asking it of any other Cabinet secretaries. Hillary had used the server for Clinton Foundation work before she became secretary of state, so I can understand how she simply may have never thought twice about the matter. Based on my own life experience, it never would have occurred to me to put a server in my basement. Of course, for Russia and for Secretary Clinton's political opponents, that was precisely the point.

The net effect of the seven "scandals" published by RT was that Clinton was portrayed as aloof, selfish, entitled, and corrupt; a member of an overly educated, liberal elite who couldn't relate to and didn't care about Middle Americans and their problems; someone who believed the law and the rules didn't apply to her, who felt she was entitled to the presidency, and who would stop at nothing—whatever it took to get elected. Of course, it was the same narrative her political opponents had been using against her for twenty years or longer, but RT, the Russians, and Putin had sharpened it to a fine point and built the infrastructure to impale her with it.

RT partnered with Radio Sputnik to amplify its stories in another broadcast medium, on the web, and in social media, and backing up the overt stories was an army of secret Russian social media trolls who, years earlier, had established fake accounts with stolen pictures and fictional biographic data, each with a history of posting and accumulating "friends." As RT went live with its traditional anti-American propaganda and newly created anti-Clinton campaign, the covert Russian trolls began reposting RT videos and stories—and similar articles from mainstream media—on YouTube, Facebook, Twitter, and other social media platforms. On Twitter they'd learned to automate their work, using bots to retweet unflattering stories millions of times, flooding the system to make anti-Clinton stories "trend." After the work the Russian troll army had done during the Russian annexation of Crimea, the military intrusions into eastern Ukraine, and the Ukrainian elections of 2014, this was a "battle-hardened" battalion that understood its mission space and was already running at its peak.

Meanwhile, Russia's spy agencies also got involved, particularly in the cyber realm. They ran both spear-phishing and brute-force hacking operations, gaining access to the IT systems of think tanks, lobbying groups, both national parties, primary campaigns in both parties, and some state election networks and voter registration databases. By July 2015, they had penetrated the Democratic National Committee's systems, and they maintained that access for nearly a year, playing off political vulnerabilities they discovered and feeding secrets to RT, Sputnik, and the trolls.

Then, just as Clinton's campaign was getting some traction, her candidacy took a serious blow, from *my* office, of all places. The State Department inspector general had identified a sampling of forty emails sent or received through Clinton's private server to further investigate. Recognizing it was not the ultimate authority to determine classification, the State Department IG's office had given the emails to IC inspector general Chuck McCullough to review. I'm sure this was very close to the last thing in which Chuck wanted to get involved, but he had a professional obligation, and he led the review. On July 23, he reported that four of the forty emails were classified, and he referred the case to the FBI for investigation. Of course, little did we know that would be the start of an ordeal that would continue through Election Day and beyond. At the time, it was just Chuck following the facts and reporting a hard truth.

Secretary Clinton responded to media questions about classified emails passing through her home server the same way she'd responded to questions about why she'd used a personal email for government business, why she'd had her own server at her house in the first place, and why her attorneys had deleted thirty thousand emails deemed to be "personal" without someone from outside her circle reviewing them. She simply asserted there was no scandal and tried to move on. In this case, she insisted that she hadn't sent or received any classified emails through her server, which may be what she thought at the time. Unfortunately, this only served to reinforce the narrative the Russians had established, and to her visible frustration, RT and Sputnik, along with the mainstream outlets, continued to lambast her. I remembered the note she'd sent to me four years earlier after the Diane Sawyer flap over "London," the one reading "As a longtime observer—and sometimes victim—of the press 'gotcha game,' don't let the First Amendment get you down! All the best, Hillary." I'm sure she could have used a similar note just about then, but my official position prevented me from reciprocating with that kind of support to any political candidate.

In August she finally told a press conference that she'd ultimately been responsible for determining which emails to delete, and so she had made the decision. With cameras still rolling, she walked off, yelling over her shoulder to the assembled media, "Nobody talks to me about it other than you guys." Russian trolls pushed the clip, writing that everyday people wanted to talk to Clinton about the emails, but she was sequestered in her ivory tower. In September, she posted on Facebook, "Yes, I should have used two email addresses, one for personal matters and one for my work at the State Department. Not doing so was a mistake. I'm sorry about it, and I take full responsibility." When just a few weeks later on NBC's *Meet the Press* host Chuck Todd asked her about a newly released email, she referred to the whole thing as "another conspiracy theory."

To be sure, not every slight and slander against Clinton posted on the internet came from Russia, but Russia egged on anyone in its sphere of influence who would bash her, particularly the field of seventeen Republican candidates. To use a sports analogy, Putin's attitude through the fall of 2015 was much like that of a University of Michigan football fan on a weekend the Wolverines don't have a game—cheering for whoever was playing Ohio State. Up until December 2015, Putin and Russia simply pulled for whoever was bashing Hillary Clinton. RT and Sputnik ran articles covering the GOP debates and highlighted any GOP candidate who took a swipe at her, no matter who that was. At the same time, the troll army continued to promote all sorts of conspiracy theories, including some about Clinton's health, which had been circulating since 2012, when, sick with the flu, she'd fainted, fallen, and suffered a concussion, which led to a blood clot near her brain and hospitalization. The trolls claimed that she had a brain tumor, repeated strokes, Alzheimer's, Parkinson's, dysphasia, epilepsy, a traumatic brain injury, lupus, and/or HIV. I imagine that someone in St. Petersburg, where most of them were working, received a performance bonus for coming up with the story that Clinton was being slowly and repeatedly poisoned by Russian agents.

I don't want to leave the impression that RT and Sputnik were focused only on bashing Clinton. They would have lost their television viewership and social media followers if they didn't produce some other content, and while Putin had a personal vendetta against Clinton, Russia's primary goal still was to breed distrust of the US government. RT's coverage of Clinton's eight-hour testimony before the House Benghazi Committee on October 28, 2015, is illustrative of how they accomplished both. In one typical RT clip, posted on YouTube under the headline "Hillary Clinton Grilled in Marathon Benghazi Hearing," the anchor leads into the story, stating the hearing was part of "a probe by a select bipartisan committee into what was known by Clinton ahead of a terrorist attack on September 11, 2012, at the US embassy in Libya, an attack that led to the murders of US ambassador Chris Stevens and three other Americans." Having alluded to the conspiracy theory that Clinton knew about the attack beforehand, the clip cuts to a reporter in the Capitol quoting committee chairman Trey Gowdy, who said the hearing with Clinton was necessary because previous investigations were "not thorough enough." So, before getting to any actual video of the hearing itself, RT voiced the most damaging allegation against Clinton and quoted a congressional leader alleging that the seven previous congressional investigations as well as an FBI investigation were all conducted improperly—thus providing a fairly compelling reason for Americans to question the competence of their government.

The reporter continues, "Throughout the day, Republicans in the committee grilled Secretary Clinton on why more wasn't done to provide the necessary security for Ambassador Stevens in Libya prior to the attack that resulted in his death. Now, the irony of this is, when looking at congressional votes, it was actually the Republican-controlled House that voted to cut funding to foreign embassies, leading up to the September 11, 2012 attack." Again, it raises an allegation against Clinton, and another at congressional dysfunction.

Next, the piece reports that the hearing had a heavy focus on the Clinton emails, "the ones that have been recovered from the secretary's private server, particularly those that show discrepancies." The clip cuts to Tea Party Republican representative Jim Jordan questioning Clinton: "You're looking at an email you sent to your family. Here's what you said. At 11:00 that night—approximately one hour after you told the American people it was a video, you said to your family, 'Two officers were killed today in Benghazi by an al-Qaida–like group.' You tell the American people one thing; you tell your family an entirely different story." RT didn't run either Jordan's question or Clinton's answer, just the preceding allegation. The clip simply shows a US representative alleging that Clinton had lied and continued to lie. The reporter observes that was just "one example" of the "nitpicking" of emails, and that the burden was on Republicans to show this wasn't just a "witch hunt" against the Democratic front-runner for president. Again, RT has it both ways, attacking Clinton personally and the institution of Congress generally.

Finally, the clip shows Secretary Clinton as a witness. For eight hours she had answered questions in a cool, calm, collected—some mainstream outlets even described it as "presidential"—manner, never breaking composure, which should have shut down any questions about her health and stamina, but, of course, didn't. Showing any of that footage might have undercut Congress but helped Clinton. Instead, RT aired a thirty-second video clip of Clinton smiling awkwardly while Gowdy and Democratic representative Elijah Cummings, the ranking member, incomprehensibly yell at and over each other about the House rules for releasing transcripts of other hearings. The exchange all too vividly demonstrates why nothing gets done in Washington, and Clinton's expression of discomfort leads the viewer to imagine her as president, still unable to get Democrats and Republicans to work together.

The clip aired on RT, and audio segments on Sputnik. Trolls could link to RT's YouTube channel, targeting either liberals or conservatives with "This is why nothing gets done in Washington," or "This is the truth about Hillary—she's been lying to us this whole time," depending on which demographic their social network and followers were composed of and how Russia wanted to manipulate them.

The US Intelligence Community knew at least as early as 2015 that the Russians had a collaboration of forces working around the clock—literally in shifts—to post and manipulate stories against the US government and Hillary Clinton. We told policy makers, but we didn't have any mechanism to counter RT and Sputnik. We'd been successful in building platforms for being transparent with the American public about US intelligence work, but we didn't have a viable, credible path to reveal to the electorate how Russian intelligence and propaganda were attempting to manipulate them. I was less concerned that they'd picked a particular candidate to attack than that they were so aggressively engaging with the American public and doing so with impunity.

By December, the Russian strategy of merely favoring whoever was bashing Clinton changed, as Moscow developed a clear favorite. Donald Trump had a long history of flirting with politics before the 2016 election, briefly running a campaign as the Reform Party candidate in 2000 and publicly discussing running in 1988, 2004, and 2012, but he was probably better known as a real estate developer and reality TV host when he entered the race in June 2015. His success as a businessman was somewhat mixed. He'd developed a series of structures around the world that bore his name, most notably Trump Tower in New York, and also hotels, casinos, and golf clubs, but his experience was in managing massive sums of money, not large numbers of people, and his businesses had filed for bankruptcy six times. Since the turn of the century, he'd largely shifted his focus to licensing his name for others' projects, and in 2011, he got into a spat with *Forbes* when they valued his brand at $200 million, and he asserted that his name really was worth $3 billion. Whatever the case, the Trump brand stood for wealth and success.

Since 2004, he'd starred in *The Apprentice,* a reality TV series wherein contestants competed for a one-year contract to run a Trump business at an annual salary of $250,000. The show ran for eleven seasons, until Trump declared for the presidency, when he brought his reality TV skills into the political arena: how to make an entrance, how to make headlines, and how to play to his core audience. When his campaign officially kicked off, he didn't just "come out of nowhere," as many people seemed to believe. Prior to the 2012 race he had engaged pollsters about his chances and how to position himself, including Kellyanne Conway, who would help lead his 2016 campaign down the final stretch. In fact, he already was positioning himself with the base of voters that would carry him in 2016 when, in March and April 2011, he'd publicly promoted the "birther" theory that alleged that President Obama had been born in Kenya and therefore wasn't eligible to be president of the United States. The conspiracy snowballed with an allegation that Obama was secretly Muslim, a rumor that somehow coexisted in the same space with the claim that Obama's Christian pastor in Chicago was putting anti-American and antiwhite ideas into the president's head.

All of these anti-Obama conspiracy theories contained transparently racist sentiments, and the right-wing websites complained incessantly about how great the United States "used to be," before progressive ideas about valuing diversity in race, gender, sexual orientation, and religious expression took hold—narratives that resonated with people whose jobs had evaporated in the recession. They'd lost everything, they were angry, and the belief that the situation wasn't their fault—which it largely wasn't—was appealing. They blamed the "educated, liberal elite" and believed that if Washington had exploited them before, it would do so again.

In 2011, Donald Trump understood this anger as well as anyone in American politics, and he knew that no one incited this anger more than Barack Obama, not because he was black—or not *just* because he was black—but because he was seen by some opponents as a smug, overly educated liberal, one who had graduated from Harvard Law School and taught constitutional law at the University of Chicago. Obama was cerebral, seemed to never make a gut call on any decision, and then lectured the public about the decisions he had made and why he'd made them, which they perceived as condescending. When in April 2011 President Obama was heard on tape talking about people who "cling to guns and religion," rural America heard that as mocking them behind their backs.

This is precisely whom Mr. Trump was appealing to when he tested the election waters in 2011, pushing the birther conspiracy and demanding that President Obama produce his "long-form" birth certificate. He was proclaiming that he'd heard the complaints about Obama and was going to reveal that this arrogant, smug, liberal black man was not the legitimate president. It was a bluff, of course, but one unlikely to be called, because Hawaii had been saying for three years that it would not publish the proof he was demanding. Then, in the final week of April 2011— terrible timing for Trump, who became Obama's primary target at the White House Correspondents' Dinner—Hawaii finally released Obama's birth certificate. The president announced the death of Osama bin Laden the next day, and national surveys the following week indicated that believers in the birther conspiracy had dropped from one in four Americans to just one in eight.

Many people have argued that being so publicly embarrassed by President Obama somehow prompted Mr. Trump to run for president in 2016. I think it more likely that he had already decided he wanted to run, and the humiliation at the Correspondents' Dinner helped convince him of what the pollsters were telling him in 2011—that he wasn't yet positioned to run for the 2012 election. So over the next four years, he used his money and fame to legitimize himself as a Republican, first and foremost convincing the 2012 Republican nominee, Mitt Romney, to publicly accept his endorsement, and then working in fund-raising circles to get invited to speak at conservative conferences and to connect with people in the power center of the Republican Party. Still, no one took him seriously as a presidential contender for 2016, because having never been on a ballot, much less won an election, he simply didn't seem to have the political bona fides.

However, Mr. Trump's persona on *The Apprentice* appealed to the disadvantaged rural demographic of Americans in ways no one seemed to understand. He was portrayed as a businessman who worked hard, appreciated others who worked hard, and created opportunities for people who applied themselves and listened to his direction and advice. He was harsh with those who didn't meet his expectations, but he also presented an avenue for someone to *earn* respect and success. The winner of the show didn't get a prize or a handout, but a job—a well-paying, hard-earned job—and the opportunity to become just as successful as the show's host. That, essentially, was his pitch to what would become his core base of voters, when on June 16, 2015, he descended an escalator into the lobby of Trump Tower with his glamorous wife, Melania, and announced that he was running for president.

He didn't use big words or soaring rhetoric, he didn't use GOP-approved talking points, and he didn't discuss the political issues of the day. Instead, he said,

> Our country is in serious trouble. We don't have victories anymore. We used to have victories, but we don't have them. When was the last time anybody saw us beating, let's say, China in a trade deal? They kill us. I beat China all the time. All the time. When did we beat Japan at anything? They send their cars over by the millions, and what do we do? When was the last time you saw a Chevrolet in Tokyo? It doesn't exist, folks. They beat us all the time. When do we beat Mexico at the border? They're laughing at us, at our stupidity. And now they are beating us economically. They are not our friend, believe me. But they're killing us economically. The United States has become a dumping ground for everybody else's problems.

To Washington insiders and political elites, this speech was a disaster, but to the people who would become Mr. Trump's core supporters it demonstrated that, finally, a politician had arrived who was unafraid to voice their concerns. They heard him say: I see you and I hear you. I know what you're going through, and it's not your fault. You just don't have opportunities to put in a hard day's work and get paid for it. You don't have a chance to improve your place in the world, and in fact, you've had the things your parents and grandparents built taken away from you before you could pass those things along to your kids. It's not your fault, and if you elect me, I'll put the country back to the way it was. This sentiment was perfectly captured by his campaign slogan, "Make America Great Again."

The next lines of his speech put the liberal elites into a tizzy. He said, I believe very purposefully, "When Mexico sends its people, they're not sending their best. They're not sending you. They're not sending you. They're sending people that have lots of problems, and they're bringing those problems with us. They're bringing drugs. They're bringing crime. They're rapists. And some, I assume, are good people." He then made his first specific campaign promise: "I would build a great wall, and nobody builds walls better than me, believe me, and I'll build them very inexpensively. I will build a great, great wall on our southern border and I'll have Mexico pay for that wall." While this was racist and xenophobic, that's not what made it appealing to his base. What they liked was that he was flouting convention and had upset—*outraged*—the progressive politicians and the liberal media. In 2017, David Brooks wrote in the *New York Times,* "Trump is not good at much, but he is wickedly good at sticking his thumb in the eye of the educated elites."

Through the summer and fall, he made ever more outrageous and disrespectful statements and issued personal, playground-level insults, and, to the disbelief of other Republican candidates, steadily rode the wave to the top of the polls. He continued to traffic in conspiracy theories, telling a rally in November, "I watched when the World Trade Center came tumbling down. And I watched in Jersey City, New Jersey, where thousands and thousands of people were cheering as that building was coming down. Thousands of people were cheering." This was demonstrably false and had been debunked years before, but it played to suspicions his base harbored. At a rally on December 7, five days after the San Bernardino shooting, Mr. Trump read aloud a statement his campaign had issued that morning: "Donald J. Trump is calling for a total and complete shutdown of Muslims entering the United States until our country's representatives can figure out what the hell is going on." The statement continued, "Our country cannot be the victims of horrendous attacks by people that believe only in jihad and have no sense of reason or respect for human life." A few days later, Trump said that, as president, he would target and kill the family members of anyone who belonged to the Islamic State.

His base ate it up, and the Russians took notice. In the January 2017 IC assessment, we noted that "social media accounts that appear to be tied to Russia's professional trolls—because they previously were devoted to supporting Russian actions in Ukraine—started to advocate for President-elect Trump as early as December 2015." Of course, this was something we could only pinpoint in retrospect. By then, not only did Mr. Trump have a solid lead in the polls, but he'd just begun to promulgate one of Russia's favorite conspiracy theories. Promoting the fiction that American Muslims had cheered on 9/11 and that they were secretly supporting jihad in the United States perfectly aligned with Russian interests. First and foremost, it served to divide Americans—not just Muslims and Christians but also conservatives and liberals. It stirred up long-running conspiracy theories about Clinton, particularly the rumors that she was sympathetic to extremist organizations and that her chief of staff, Huma Abedin, was tied to the Muslim Brotherhood. And inciting anti-Muslim sentiment in December 2015 was very timely for Russia's foreign policy. The Russians had just started their Syria operations in September, and by December they were bombing Islamic State fighters and Syrian civilians alike. Horrific images of Muslim civilians fleeing the Syrian city of Aleppo had less of an impact in the United States if the leading Republican candidate was dehumanizing even American Muslims.

Three days after candidate Trump released his December 7 anti-Islam statement, former DIA director and retired lieutenant general Mike Flynn appeared in Moscow at a gala for RT. He was seated beside Putin at dinner and was paid forty-five thousand dollars to speak. I knew Mike well, and it boggled my mind that he would so knowingly compromise himself. He had more time deployed to war zones than most of his peers—which is saying something—and he understood the psychology of the terrorist threat perhaps better than anyone else. As General Stan McChrystal's top intelligence officer in Afghanistan in 2010, Mike had published "Fixing Intel: A Blueprint for Making Intelligence Relevant in Afghanistan," a paper that described shortcomings in serving forces in the war zone. Mike decried the fact that the US forces in Afghanistan lacked fluency with the microdetails of the political and sociological dynamics in each Afghan village—something under his control as the guy on the ground, not something the national intelligence enterprise could influence. It reminded me of the quote from the *Pogo* comic strip: "We have met the enemy and he is us." Nonetheless, in 2011 I brought Mike to the ODNI specifically to work on how the bigger Intelligence Community engages our partners. That September, I helped pin a third star on his uniform, promoting him from major general to lieutenant general. He served in ODNI for less than a year before USD(I) Mike Vickers and I agreed to recommend that Leon Panetta appoint him as DIA director.

Mike had spent his career, particularly the decade since 9/11, on the tactical edge of battle. He had never directed a large organization before, and he made some of the same mistakes I'd made as a new DIA director in 1991, including not properly engaging the workforce before undertaking a major reorganization. He could have rectified the situation, but he didn't address the civilian workforce's concerns when they were brought to him, and he made matters worse by increasingly demanding that civilians behave like uniformed service members. Stories started leaking out of DIA that he was using analysts to chase down crazy conspiracy theories, which the workforce had dubbed "Flynn facts." He also clashed with his boss in the Pentagon, Mike Vickers, and publicly criticized the president's policy decisions, asserting that the president should refer to terrorists as "Islamic extremists." That made sense from a warfighting perspective, but the president was also concerned with maintaining relationships with Islamic governments around the world that had repudiated the terrorists. For Mike Vickers, Flynn's insubordination became too much to bear; for me, it was his impact on the workforce at DIA that led to our mutual decision to make a change.

In late 2013, we met with Flynn in Vickers's office in the Pentagon to let him know we were ending his tour a year early. He could remain until August 2014, which would allow him to retire with the grade and pay of a lieutenant general. He seemed to take it well and retired the following summer. I had a lot of respect for what Mike had done during his years of service, and I didn't hold it against him that things hadn't worked out at DIA.

So I was taken aback in December 2015 when pictures of Mike sitting at dinner with Vladimir Putin surfaced in the media. From his public statements that followed, I gathered that he felt an affinity with the Russians when it came to dealing with terrorists in a tough way. He even talked about meeting privately with Russian intelligence to discuss fighting the Islamic State, another decision I was uneasy with. When he'd been DIA director, I'd cautioned Mike to be wary of the Russians attempting to woo him, as they had attempted with me when I'd been DIA director. Looking at pictures of Mike sitting with Putin at dinner, I wondered if the Russian courtship had been more appealing to Mike in his retirement. Regardless, he knew that taking Russian government money compromised him personally, particularly since he was consulting with several Republican presidential campaigns at the time. In February, he officially joined Mr. Trump's campaign, bringing his connection to RT and an angry, fiery edge that he'd acquired sometime after retiring in 2014.

Meanwhile, Mr. Trump's campaign interests continued to align more with Russia's, and specifically with Putin's. In the first year of his campaign, Trump boasted many times that Putin was someone he could make deals with, and pointed out that Putin had prior positive experiences working with businessmen turned national leaders, particularly Italian prime minister Silvio Berluśconi and German chancellor Gerhard Schroeder. The two began a public courtship in the media, and in July 2015, Trump announced that if he was elected president, Putin would extradite Snowden to the United States, because Putin respected him but not Obama. In September on Fox News, he said of Putin, "I will tell you that I think in terms of leadership, he is getting an 'A,' and our president is not doing so well." In October, he supported Putin's aggression in Syria, telling the *Guardian*, "He's going to want to bomb ISIS because he doesn't want ISIS going into Russia and so he's going to want to bomb ISIS. Vladimir Putin is going to want to really go after ISIS, and if he doesn't it'll be a big shock to everybody."

In December, as the Russian social media trolls began to focus on helping candidate Trump's cause, Putin seemed to endorse Trump, calling him "a colorful and talented man," and indicating that he would welcome the closer relations with the United States that might come with Trump's election. Shortly after, Trump had an on-air conversation with Joe Scarborough of MSNBC, during which Scarborough reminded him that Putin was someone "who kills journalists, political opponents, and invades countries." "He's running his country and at least he's a leader, unlike what we have in this country," Trump responded. Scarborough reiterated, "He kills journalists who don't agree with him." Trump said, "Well, I think our country does plenty of killing also, Joe."

Then, in January, when a British inquiry found that "the FSB operation to kill [former KGB agent Alexander] Litvinenko was probably approved by Mr. Patrushev and also by President Putin," Trump stated publicly, "He says he didn't do it; many people say it wasn't him. So who knows who did it?"

Getting its target audience to conclude that facts and truth are "unknowable" is the true objective of any disinformation campaign. Climate change deniers aren't trying to convince people that surveys they commissioned are better than those agreed upon by the vast majority of scientists. Antigovernment conspiracy theorists aren't *really* trying to convince people that some towns in the Midwest are governed under Sharia law, or that Jade Helm was an attempt by Obama to come for their guns. If someone actually believes the falsehood, that's a bonus, but the primary objective is to get readers or viewers to throw their hands up and give up on "facts." Do vaccines cause autism? Maybe. Was Senator Ted Cruz's father involved with President Kennedy's assassination? Anything's possible. Is Hillary Clinton running a child-sex ring out of the basement of a DC pizza parlor? Who knows?

In February, Flynn joined the Trump campaign, and on March 1, voters in eleven states went to the primary polls. Mr. Trump won seven states outright and finished a close-enough second in Senator Ted Cruz's home state of Texas. He took a considerable lead in committed Republican delegates just as Secretary Clinton extended her lead over Senator Bernie Sanders in committed Democratic delegates, and the Kremlin decided to fully support Mr. Trump's election bid. Putin didn't formally endorse Trump, which the Russians believed would hurt his chances at election, but RT anchors began full-throated praise, particularly targeting the base of voters most incensed at politicians in Washington. They pushed the message that while Mr. Trump would be the nominee of the Republican Party, he was nonetheless a complete and welcome outsider. That was music to the ears of Trump's campaign, and he quickly returned the favor, repeating at public events and in press interviews that the United

States was paying too much into NATO—the alliance specifically established to counter the Soviets—and that it should reconsider its obligations to defend NATO nations who weren't paying "their fair share." RT jumped on the story, reporting, "Republican presidential candidate Donald Trump slammed NATO on the campaign trail this week, saying he can live with breaking up the military alliance, which he calls 'obsolete.'"

In April, Mr. Trump first used the phrase "lying, crooked Hillary" to refer to his likely opponent in the primary election. RT, Fox News, and paid and unpaid trolls across social media latched on to the moniker. Russia and the Trump campaign seemed to be quite in sync, but that didn't necessarily mean they were colluding—coordinating their efforts behind closed doors. They may simply have had a lot in common: a strong dislike for both the Washington political establishment and Hillary Clinton personally; a proclivity for social media, particularly Twitter, which meant they'd end up sharing each other's ideas on the internet; and a genuine delight in wallowing in conspiracy theories.

As spring turned into summer in 2016—and as Mr. Trump promoted pro-Russian lobbyist Paul Manafort to campaign chairman—the US IC was well aware that Russia was trolling social media networks, and we knew that RT and Sputnik were spouting propaganda to large American audiences, but none of these efforts seemed radically different from what they'd done before. The social media trolling was a new phenomenon but also a tactic that had backfired on Russian interests during the 2014 Ukraine elections, largely because it incited threats of violence that had closed polls in Russian-controlled areas. RT had grown its audience considerably since 2012 but was pushing the same sort of messages and was once again targeting the right as much as the left, hosting a Green Party debate on May 9 and a Libertarian Party debate on May 12, and pushing the agendas of both. That effort served both to undermine the two-party system and to take votes away from Secretary Clinton. So while it looked as if the Trump campaign and Russian propaganda were working in tandem, I didn't see any evidence at the time that there was direct coordination between them. I was, however, convinced that the Russians needed to be confronted about their cyber intrusions into American parties, campaigns, and state electoral databases. On May 18, I announced during a cybersecurity event at the Bipartisan Policy Center in Washington that the IC had indications of Russian hackers targeting presidential campaigns—our first public warning shot at Russia, six months before Election Day.

Beyond being the first to call out Russian interference publicly, I continued to stay away from any involvement in the ongoing election shenanigans. I figured at the time that the last thing our country needed was any appearance that the Intelligence Community was involved in partisan politics. As someone who'd served as a political appointee in both Republican and Democrat administrations, I didn't have a personal dog in the fight. At the same time, I was deeply and personally bothered by the divisive rhetoric that continued to be a hallmark of the campaigning. My biggest concern with the political rhetoric from the Republican campaigns and Russian propaganda was that the demonizing of minority groups in the United States was having a tangible impact on how we treated one another as Americans. In May, Georgetown University published a study on escalating violence against Muslim Americans. They reported that anti-Muslim political rhetoric first escalated in August 2015, and then September saw a surge in violence against Muslims, which kept rising. As the study noted:

> Anti-Muslim attacks surged once more in December 2015. There were 53 total attacks that month, 17 of which targeted mosques and Islamic schools and 5 of which targeted Muslim homes. By comparison, when the presidential election season began just 9 months earlier, there were only 2 anti-Muslim attacks. Attacks on Muslims during this month constitute approximately 1/3 of all attacks last year. In fact, in December 2015, anti-Muslim attacks occurred almost daily and often multiple times a day.

That troubled me professionally, as well as personally, and the rhetoric was only becoming more inflammatory as candidate Trump again called for a ban on refugees from Islamic countries entering the United States, and pondered aloud banning *all* travel to this country from Muslim nations. He and several GOP congressional members castigated President Obama for not referring to terrorist groups as "radical Islamists," as though uttering that phrase would change anything on the battlefield.

At the time, I was primarily focused on leaving the IC positioned for the next generation to take the reins and excel, particularly when it came to technology and the exceptional people of the IC. I was challenging attendees at the Geospatial Intelligence Forum to "not be afraid to fail" in the pursuit of technological breakthroughs. I asked the IC Women's Summit in March and the African American and Hispanic Hiring Summit in May to find ways to encourage diversity. On Wednesday, June 8, I met with the IC Pride group and was again taken with their joy at finding a community within the IC. They were so happy that after years of living under draconian rules, they could finally live openly, honest about who they were, without fear of losing their clearances, jobs, or social standing.

That feeling came crashing down four days later, on Sunday morning, June 12, when the LGBT community was targeted with violence—yet again—when a man opened fire inside Pulse, a gay nightclub in Orlando, killing forty-nine people and wounding fifty-three. No event since 9/11 had affected me as deeply as Orlando did. It was just so unfair for a community that had lived under oppression and fear for so long to be targeted by someone with such hate, and the anguish of the moment was even more intense because I'd just celebrated service with a segment of that community, one I thought of as family, because they were also intelligence officers.

On Tuesday, June 14, I met with the national security team and President Obama in Treasury Department headquarters for an update on the progress we'd made to counter the Islamic State in the ungoverned spaces in Iraq and Syria. After it ended, we walked out to a press conference for the president to talk about the parts of our meeting he could discuss publicly. As is typical, two other leaders (this time Secretary of the Treasury Jack Lew, our host for the meeting, and chairman of the Joint Chiefs of Staff General Joe Dunford) and I stood behind him. In these situations, I always try to do my best "potted plant" impression, standing motionless and expressionless, becoming part of the scenery. Just before we stepped out, the president pulled Joe and me aside and told us he wanted to apologize ahead of time, because he tried never to put us on display for a political statement. As I stood listening while he began speaking to the press, channeling my inner bonsai, I wondered what he had meant.

Halfway through the conference, the president's tone changed as he addressed the criticism that he refused to use the phrase "radical Islam" to label terrorists. "We're starting to see where this kind of rhetoric and loose talk and sloppiness about who exactly we're fighting, where this can lead us," he said. "We now have proposals from the presumptive Republican nominee for president of the United States to bar all Muslims from immigrating to America." He asked, "Where does this stop? The Orlando killer, one of the San Bernardino killers, the Fort Hood killer, they were all US citizens. Are we going to start treating all Muslim Americans differently? Are we going to start subjecting them to special surveillance?"

As he continued to speak, I felt my thoughts carried away from that auditorium. I thought of the Muslim American leaders I'd met with, of their patriotism and their fear of how the country they loved had treated the communities they represented. In the press conference, the president was saying that if we implied we were at war with an entire religion, we'd be doing the Islamic State's work for them, and if we demonized Muslims and other groups in the United States, we'd lose sight of what this nation stood for. We'd regretted the times in our past when we'd given in to fear and lashed out at minority groups of American citizens. If we abandoned our values, the terrorists will have won. He talked about diversity as a great strength of this country, about the outpouring of support in Orlando from all corners and all walks of life. I thought about our IC Pride group. My colleagues had for years hidden their true selves, not for personal gain, but to serve—a sacrifice I couldn't imagine making. America's intelligence force worked, fought, and sacrificed in the shadows, without expecting praise, and these exceptional people had finally gained the ability to live openly as who they really were, and that freedom and joy had reverted to fear again so quickly and so savagely. The president finished with a message about how our military members supported each other regardless of what they looked like or whom they loved. "Those are the values that ISIL is trying to destroy," he said, "and we shouldn't help them do it." Our military had come a long way to arrive at a place where that statement was true and could be acknowledged publicly. I'd been there on that journey.

When the president finished, we retired to an anteroom, and he bid quick farewells to Joe and Jack. When he turned to me, I started to lose it. Tears welling, I managed to babble something about how proud I was of him. He pulled me into a hug for just a moment, and we then went our separate ways back to work. In the car I couldn't help but think about how far the president and I had come since our first meeting in the Oval Office, when we'd chatted about lifting weights and doing cardio on alternating days, which is when I guess he decided I would be okay to hire as his DNI.

I went back to Liberty Crossing, satisfied that I could focus on the community for my final seven months instead of being caught up in the election. On May 26, Donald Trump clinched the Republican nomination, and on June 6, Hillary Clinton clinched the Democratic nomination. I was thinking about how I would dance quietly off the stage on January 20, hoping that no one really noticed I was leaving. Events of the next two months would prove both of those to be extremely naïve wishes.

On July 5, Jim Comey held a press conference to read a statement about the results of the FBI investigation into Secretary Clinton's emails. I didn't know anything about this beforehand, and I consider it a good thing that I wasn't told, as it demonstrates the independence the FBI has with its investigations, particularly when US persons are involved. Calling a press conference was an unusual step, but former president Bill Clinton had complicated the situation on June 27, when he was seen boarding Attorney General Loretta Lynch's plane in Phoenix. When news of the meeting—which both said was unrelated to the investigation— leaked out, Attorney General Lynch appeared to be compromised and therefore unable to make an unbiased decision about prosecuting Secretary Clinton. So rather than quietly passing FBI findings and recommendations to the Justice Department behind closed doors, as would typically be done, Jim Comey opted for a press conference.

By that point I had read the emails in question and come to my own conclusions. None of them was sent to or from anyone outside of government, and none was marked in a way that would indicate it was classified, but several did discuss sensitive intelligence sourcing that shouldn't have been transmitted across open internet connections, where they could be intercepted by an adversary. Secretary Clinton hadn't intentionally disclosed secrets, as CIA director Petraeus had done, but I was surprised that she'd participated in email conversations about such sensitive information. If a line IC employee had done the same, I expect we would have held proceedings to decide if that person should keep his or her security clearance and continue employment. So I didn't know how Jim was going to handle this, and I watched live with as much interest as anyone.

The next fifteen minutes were riveting, starting with Jim's opening assertion that he hadn't coordinated or shared his remarks with the

Department of Justice or any other government organization, and he affirmed, "They do not know what I'm about to say." My entire front office stopped work to watch as Jim laid out the process the FBI had used to investigate the matter. They had come to the conclusion that 110 of the 30,000 emails given by the State Department to the Justice Department contained classified material when they were sent, including 8 email chains that had top secret information. There were another 2,000 emails that had information that was unclassified when they were sent but was later classified. In investigating the servers Secretary Clinton had used, the FBI had also found several thousand work-related emails that were not in the collection of 30,000 that she had given to the State Department. The bureau didn't assess that she'd hidden those, merely that her personal server had no archiving capability, and they'd not turned up in normal recovery procedures.

After nine minutes of discussing the investigative process, Jim changed tone. "That's what we have done. Now let me tell you what we found. Although we did not find clear evidence that Secretary Clinton or her colleagues intended to violate laws governing the handling of classified information, there is evidence that they were extremely careless in their handling of very sensitive, highly classified information." He noted that that included seven email chains with information from "Special Access" programs, protected even more carefully than other top secret intelligence. The FBI had also determined that it was possible that hostile actors had gained access to Secretary Clinton's account, but that the FBI didn't have the capability to know if they actually had.

Finally, he said he was opting for "unusual transparency" in discussing his recommendations to the Justice Department. "Although there is evidence of potential violations of the statutes regarding the handling of classified information," he noted, "our judgment is that no reasonable prosecutor would bring such a case," further stating that previous such cases brought for prosecution "involved some combination of: clearly intentional and willful mishandling of classified information; or vast quantities of materials exposed in such a way as to support an inference of intentional misconduct; or indications of disloyalty to the United States; or efforts to obstruct justice. We do not see those things here." He continued, "To be clear, this is not to suggest that in similar circumstances, a person who engaged in this activity would face no consequences. To the contrary, those individuals are often subject to security or administrative sanctions. But that is not what we are deciding now. As a result, although the Department of Justice makes final decisions on matters like this, we are expressing to Justice our view that no charges are appropriate in this case." He thanked the FBI for its apolitical professionalism, adding, "I couldn't be prouder to be part of this organization," and then left the stage. To me, it was a stunning rebuke of a presidential candidate by the director of the FBI, and what could only have been a difficult decision for my friend and colleague who'd spent his career in service to the nation and to speaking truth to power. In this case, the "power" was the American people. Whatever the consequences would be, he did what he considered to be the right thing and in the best interests of the nation.

The Russians—to be fair, along with everyone else—immediately jumped on Jim's announcement. RT led with video of Clinton's saying, "Nothing I sent or received was marked classified at the time," followed by Comey's acknowledgment that "110 emails in 52 email chains have been determined by the owning agency to contain classified information at the time they were sent or received." A viewer would have had to pay close attention to appreciate the significance of the word "marked." RT, Sputnik, and the online trolls played off one another to portray Clinton as corrupt and the FBI as complicit. Any number of conspiracy theories took root. Some alleged that she'd deleted the emails to cover up crimes. On July 10, Seth Rich—a young Democratic National Committee staff member—was killed in Washington in a botched robbery. Within hours, internet conspiracy theorists, including the Russians, suggested that Rich had been murdered at Clinton's behest to cover up the email leaks. They dragged out the "Clinton body count" rumors, dating back to the 1980s, which claimed that Bill and Hillary had been assassinating political rivals. Leading into the party conventions that summer, the Russians had laid sufficient groundwork to get a subset of American voters to believe nearly anything about Hillary Clinton.

Still, if things appeared bad for Clinton and the Democrats, they were worse for her opponent and his party. Even before it officially kicked off on July 18, the Republican National Convention seemed headed for chaos and animosity between Mr. Trump's team and the old guard GOP. In particular, Trump campaign staff worked behind the scenes to rewrite the party platform, which when it was released noticeably dropped calling for "maintaining or increasing sanctions" on Russia and of promising "lethal defensive weapons" to Ukraine in support of their resistance to Russian aggression. Reflecting deep divisions in the Republican Party, the governor of Ohio, John Kasich, who had run against Mr. Trump for the nomination, refused to come to Cleveland to introduce him as the nominee.

With the Trump team setting the agenda, the convention seemed to revel in pessimism about the state of the nation and the direction it was heading. On Monday, Mike Flynn led the crowd in chanting "Lock her up!" in reference to the Clinton email scandal. He seemed so consumed by partisan anger that I barely recognized the man I'd traveled the world with when he'd still been in uniform. On Wednesday, Senator Cruz, who finished second in primary voting, declined to endorse Trump, and—to raucous boos and jeers—told Republicans to "vote your conscience." On the final night, Mr. Trump delivered a dark speech about how far the nation had fallen, declaring that he was the only person who could "make America great again." Accepting the nomination, he said, "The crime and violence that today afflicts our nation will soon come to an end. Beginning on January 20, 2017, safety will be restored." While RT focused their coverage on Black Lives Matter protesters who had clashed with police in the streets of Cleveland, most media coverage of the Republican National Convention portrayed a broken Republican Party in crisis.

Before most of the media had landed in Philadelphia for the Democratic Convention four days later, Russia launched its big surprise. Russian intelligence—specifically their military intelligence agency, GRU, the agency with which Mike Flynn had met—had quietly gained access to the Democratic National Committee networks in July 2015. Sometime in March 2016, Putin and the Russian leadership decided that it was worth the risk of diplomatic blowback if they were caught, and the GRU went on the offense, exfiltrating emails and large volumes of data. In April, Russia used a third-party "cutout" to send more than nineteen thousand DNC emails and more than eight thousand documents to WikiLeaks and Julian Assange, attempting to cover its tracks and to give WikiLeaks some degree of deniability in knowing the source of the leaks. It took WikiLeaks three months to verify the emails were authentic before it released them, and I find it implausible that Assange, as he claims, didn't figure out during that period that Russian intelligence was his source.

The DNC had actually realized they had a problem in April and hired the cybersecurity firm CrowdStrike to assess the situation and try to save their systems. CrowdStrike detected the Russian activity and did what it could to quietly remediate the damage. On June 14, the DNC went public, acknowledging they'd been hacked by Russian intelligence. The next day, a hacker self-styled as Guccifer 2.0 claimed to have been the perpetrator. The name was clearly a reference to the Guccifer who had first revealed Secretary Clinton's email address and domain information in March 2013. Guccifer 2.0 claimed to be Romanian, just as the original had, although he communicated very well in Russian and not well at all in Romanian. The US IC determined later that Guccifer 2.0 was not, in fact, a single person, but was a persona used by multiple Russian state hackers working in tandem.

On Friday, July 22, the day after Mr. Trump's acceptance of the Republican nomination, WikiLeaks dumped the DNC emails online. The most incendiary of them were between DNC staff members disparaging Secretary Clinton's opponent, Senator Bernie Sanders, saying that he didn't deserve the nomination. In one exchange DNC chair and congresswoman Debbie Wasserman Schultz wrote, "He isn't going to be president." The national media—not without cause—concluded that Senator Sanders's campaign was never given a fair shot at winning the nomination. On Sunday, Sanders called for Wasserman Schultz to resign as DNC chair, remarking in an interview with George Stephanopoulos, "I told you a long time ago that the DNC was not running a fair operation, that they were supporting Secretary Clinton." In the late afternoon of the day before the convention began, Wasserman Schultz stepped down as DNC chair.

In response Mr. Trump published a barrage of tweets late Sunday, including: "The Democrats are in a total meltdown but the biased media will say how great they are doing! E-mails say the rigged system is alive & well!" and "The highly neurotic Debbie Wasserman Schultz is angry that, after stealing and cheating her way to a Crooked Hillary victory, she's out!" The mainstream media outlets seemed to have little time to discuss the DNC's and CrowdStrike's claims that Russian intelligence was behind the cyber theft and leaks, and ironically Mr. Trump seemed to be the only one publicly discussing their source, tweeting, "The new joke in town is that Russia leaked the disastrous DNC e-mails, which should never have been written (stupid), because Putin likes me."

The following day the FBI announced it was opening an investigation into the hacking, and the Democratic National Convention scrambled to cover the absence of the DNC chair. Bernie Sanders supporters protested on the conference floor, and the entire assembly seemed to be in disarray. Just a week prior, the national press had speculated that the RNC might implode while trying to find a way to nominate a more palatable candidate than Donald Trump. In a single day, Russian intelligence and WikiLeaks had completely upended the narrative.

Mr. Trump, for his part, continued to hold rallies as the Democrats tried to pull their convention together. On Wednesday, the day before Secretary Clinton was scheduled to accept the nomination, he was in Miami, gleefully answering questions about the hacked emails. One person asked him if he should tell Putin to stay out of the US presidential race. "Why do I have to get involved with Putin?" Trump replied. "I have nothing to do with Putin. I've never spoken to him. I don't know anything about him other than he will respect me. He doesn't respect our President. And if it is Russia—which it's probably not, nobody knows who it is—but if it is Russia, it's really bad for a different reason, because it shows how little respect they have for our country, when they would hack into a major party and get everything. But it would be interesting to see. I will tell you this . . ." He turned from the questioner to face the cameras, and his next words absolutely chilled me: "Russia, if you're listening, I hope you're able to find the 30,000 emails that are missing. I think you will probably be rewarded mightily by our press." He turned back to the questioner and said, "Let's see if that happens. That'll be next."

Some fifty-five years earlier, I'd first taken an oath to defend the Constitution, and now, in 2016, I was confronted with the fact that our election was under attack by a foreign power—the Russians no less, who'd wanted to destroy the United States for nearly the entire time I'd been alive—and that a candidate for president had just encouraged them to use their intelligence services to help him defeat his opponent. I didn't know what would come next, but I felt I bore some responsibility for protecting America from these threats. I'd grown up in a family devoted to serving the nation. I myself had served in every administration since President Kennedy's and was a political appointee for both President Bush and President Obama. I'd tried to serve apolitically, and yet, hearing Donald Trump ask Russian intelligence to attack his political opponent—in a very specific, direct way—made me fear for our nation.

The following day, July 28, Secretary Clinton's acceptance of the nomination was overshadowed by the earlier remarks of Khizr Khan, a Muslim and Pakistani immigrant, and a longtime US citizen whose Army officer son, Humayun, was killed in Iraq in 2004. With his wife, Ghazala, standing beside him—too emotional to speak—and with Humayun's photo on screens around the convention center, Khan told the assembled delegates about his son's service. He said that Clinton had referred to Humayun as "the best of America," and that "if it was up to Donald Trump, he never would have been in America. Donald Trump consistently smears the character of Muslims. He disrespects other minorities, women, judges, even his own party leadership. He vows to build walls and ban us from this country." Pulling a copy of the Constitution from his coat pocket, he raised it in front of him and addressed the Republican nominee directly:

> Donald Trump, you are asking Americans to trust you with our future. Let me ask you: Have you even read the US Constitution? I will gladly lend you my copy. In this document, look for the words "liberty" and "equal protection of law." Have you ever been to Arlington Cemetery? Go look at the graves of the brave patriots who died defending America. You will see all faiths, genders, and ethnicities. You have sacrificed nothing and no one.

The following day Mr. Trump responded, telling George Stephanopoulos, first, "I think I've made a lot of sacrifices. I've created thousands and thousands of jobs, tens of thousands of jobs, built great structures. I've had tremendous success. I think I've done a lot." And then he "hit back" at the Khans and their religion. "If you look at his wife, she was standing there. She had nothing to say. She probably, maybe she wasn't allowed to have anything to say. You tell me." There was immediate backlash from Republicans, with Senator Susan Collins going as far as to say she would not be voting for Mr. Trump in the general election. For about a week—from the WikiLeaks dump until he publicly attacked a Gold Star family—Mr. Trump had led Secretary Clinton in national popularity polls. After July 29, that would never happen again.

Following the two conventions, by long-held tradition, both candidates were eligible to start receiving intelligence briefings. This seemed to come as a great shock to many elected officials and some of the Washington Beltway media, even though giving classified briefings to candidates was a tradition that began in 1952, when President Truman offered them to both General Eisenhower and Governor Stevenson, and the newly formed CIA conducted them. Truman felt an obligation to provide these because of his own ignorance when he'd taken office. He hadn't known of the existence of the Manhattan Project until twelve days after he was sworn in as president, and he had been Roosevelt's vice president. That practice had continued for every election since 1952, with the CIA handling briefings until 2008, when ODNI assumed the responsibility. (As a point of trivia worthy of note, there have only been three elections in which briefings were offered to candidates from *both* major parties: 1952, 2008, and 2016—the only years in which one of the candidates wasn't already receiving intelligence briefings as the incumbent president or vice president.) Regardless, both candidates gained access to this intelligence by virtue of their nominations, and I had no place in clearing them or not. Further, in our effort to make sure that there was *no* political influence on the briefings, only career intelligence officers gave the briefings, not political appointees like me.

Nevertheless, Republican senators and representatives sent a flurry of communications to my office, insisting we withhold President's Daily Briefs from Secretary Clinton. At the same time some media—including the generally conservative *Foreign Policy,* of all outlets—along with some very senior intelligence officials, insisted that I "withhold PDBs" from Mr. Trump. Senator Harry Reid even suggested publicly that we should give "fake briefings" to the Republican nominee. We, of course, didn't give these suggestions any countenance, and I went out publicly to dispel myths—first, the complete fiction that my office was giving President Obama's President's Daily Brief to *either* candidate. In fact, one team from my office produced and delivered the PDB, and a completely different team produced and coordinated the cross-agency effort to brief the candidates with intelligence on broad global topics that were separate from the intelligence President Obama received on his secure iPad.

As we had in prior elections, we set ground rules months before the briefings started, which the White House concurred with on June 22, and the IC operated independently from that point forward. We had a list of topics that we offered to both candidates, and both could ask for briefings on any or all of them. They could also request briefings on other subjects, although precedent dictated that if we agreed to do so, we'd make sure the other candidate had a chance to receive the same information. We don't tell either the opposing campaign or the public what takes place in those briefings: not what topics each candidate shows interest in or gets briefed on, not how either candidate reacts, and not what questions are asked. I'm sticking to that precedent in this book.

As our teams briefed both candidates in separate sessions, I participated in the first formal meeting between the Obama administration and the transition teams, led by chief of staff Denis McDonough at the White House. I was struck by how sober, professional, courteous, and civil the conversation was. It was so different—both substantively and tonally—from what the campaigns were saying in public, particularly Mr. Trump.

In August, he tweeted out Russian conspiracy theories such as: "Many people are saying that the Iranians killed the scientist who helped the United States because of Hillary Clinton's hacked emails." He implied that if Clinton was elected, the only way to prevent her from taking everyone's guns would be to shoot her: "Hillary wants to abolish, essentially abolish, the Second Amendment. By the way, and if she gets to pick her judges, nothing you can do, folks. Although the Second Amendment people—maybe there is, I don't know. But I'll tell you what, that will be a horrible day." He repeated another absurd conspiracy theory about President Obama: "He is the founder of ISIS. He's the founder of ISIS, OK? He's the founder. He founded ISIS and I would say the co-founder would be crooked Hillary Clinton." After the Russians published fake medical records claiming Clinton suffered from dementia, he suggested she was hiding something and that they should both release their medical records, tweeting: "I have no problem in doing so! Hillary?" And as he fell further behind in the polls, he began repeating the phrase the Russians had already been pushing: "The election's going to be rigged."

In the midst of all this, a new source of turmoil erupted in the Trump campaign, as reports surfaced that campaign chairman Paul Manafort had connections to former Ukrainian president Viktor Yanukovych—the corrupt pro-Russian official who had fled to Russia in 2014 as protesters overwhelmed Kiev. Manafort had received millions of dollars for supporting Yanukovych's interests in Russia and in the United States. Even as the campaign was taking a downturn, Manafort's presence exposed a real vulnerability for Trump. Then, on August 14, the *New York Times* published a ledger revealing just how much Manafort had received. So four days later, Mr. Trump hired Steve Bannon, the chairman of Breitbart News, as his new campaign manager and pushed Manafort out. Breitbart was known for its virulent attacks on Clinton and for promoting conspiracy theories, and Bannon publicly promised to stop trying to bring Trump to heel in a traditional campaign. He would, instead, unleash him.

At the same time, RT began even more aggressively advancing conspiracy theories originating with the social media troll army. They posted a twenty-eight-minute video interview with Julian Assange titled "Do WikiLeaks Have the Email That'll Put Clinton in Prison?" RT's teaser for the video read "Afshin Rattansi goes underground with Julian Assange. We talk to the founder of WikiLeaks about how his recent DNC leaks have no connection to Russia. Plus what are Hillary Clinton's connections to Islamic State, Saudi Arabia and Russia?" It released what would become its most popular Clinton video, with more than nine million views across all social media platforms: "How 100% of Clintons' 2015 'Charity' Went to Themselves." This was particularly galling to Clinton's campaign, as it pulled data from her 2015 tax filings, which showed the Clintons had contributed one million dollars to the Clinton Family Foundation—a legitimate vehicle for their personal charitable giving that was completely separate from the Clinton Foundation. In contrast, Mr. Trump continued to refuse to release any of his tax returns. The heated political rhetoric had become unlike anything I'd ever seen.

I'd like to be able to say the IC was shielded from all of this, but the Intelligence Community is a microcosm of American society, susceptible to the same doubts and anxieties as everyone else. As DNI, I continued to carve out time to meet with the workforce, and as the summer passed, I began to hear concerns about what would happen on Inauguration Day. Most were worried about Mr. Trump's erratic statements and tweets; in addition to his barrage of political attacks on his opponent, he'd asserted that he'd bring back waterboarding, that he'd authorize killing family members of the Islamic State, and that he thought letting Japan, South Korea, and Saudi Arabia build nuclear weapons might be a good idea. At the same time, there were many members of the IC who were legitimately angry that Secretary Clinton had so carelessly mishandled classified information, putting sources and methods in jeopardy, and they didn't understand how she could become president after she'd done something that likely would have cost them their clearances and jobs. I tried to reassure people individually, but felt that perhaps the entire community needed to hear from me.

On September 7, in a speech to a joint conference of the IC's two biggest industry associations, I first laid out my "litany of doom" on the vast array of threats we were facing around the world. I then noted the obvious: "With all this as a backdrop, I think it makes a lot of people nervous that with an election cycle that's been 'sportier' than we're used to, we'll drop a new president with new national security leaders into this situation—in 135 days, but who's counting?" That drew a small laugh. I went on, "I know a lot of people have been feeling uncertainty about what will happen with this presidential transition. There's been a lot of 'catastrophizing,' if I can use that term, in the 24-hour news cycle, and of course, on social media. So, I'm here with a message. It'll be okay." I assured them that that would be the case because "our nation has a great legacy of orderly transition and power, going back to George Washington retiring in 1797, when he turned the presidency over to John Adams. I remember it well." I then spoke about the actual political process, explaining how the IC was briefing the candidates, and reminded them that in times of national transition, the US Intelligence Community was "a pillar of stability."

Apparently "It'll be okay" was a message that the whole nation needed to hear. By that evening that short clip from my speech was airing on the cable news networks, and commentators were stealing my word to lament their own "catastrophizing." The next morning, papers published my reassuring phrase, and *Vital Speeches of the Day* included the speech in their November issue, published a few days before the election. It felt good to—for once—be the calming voice in the room. I wanted to ask the *New York Times* if I was still "perfect for the North Koreans."

Lost in that same news cycle was an interview Mr. Trump gave on RT. Asked about the possibility that Russia was behind the election interference, Trump responded, "Who knows? But I think that it's pretty unlikely."

My calm words on September 7 belied what I was saying and doing behind secure doors. As I believe this chapter shows, the Russians had been actively attacking our election process for a long time, and I—along with the Intelligence Community I was charged to lead—had merely been watching and following along. But as summer led into fall, I'd begun to meet with a small group of national security leaders that included the CIA director, secretary of state, secretary of defense, attorney general, FBI director, homeland security secretary, and a few key White House staff. Collectively, we could draw on the full scope of our national capabilities to understand what was happening, and we all agreed that Russia was behind an unprecedented, aggressive, multifaceted influence campaign, using cyber theft and cyber espionage, propaganda across the broadcast spectrum and all of the largest social media platforms, and an influx of Russian money at least for buying advertisements, perhaps even laundered and funneled into campaigns. The Russians had been probing state and local election IT systems in nearly half the states—that we knew about—and although we saw no evidence of manipulation or exfiltration, they'd accessed and viewed voter registration databases. Jeh Johnson had offered DHS assistance in securing state election systems, but for whatever reason, several states refused his help.

We didn't see any hard evidence of political collusion between the Trump campaign and the Russian government, but as I said at the time, my dashboard warning lights were all lit. We knew there had been meetings between the two, and by August, both the Russians and the Trump campaign were, in parallel, pushing conspiracy theories against Secretary Clinton with three identical themes: she was corrupt, she was physically and mentally unwell, and she had ties to Islamic extremism.

Finally, we all agreed this kind of effort could only be approved at the highest levels of the Russian government, and by September, we knew Putin was personally involved. While others thought a publicity blitz could just feed the fire rather than douse it, Jeh and I felt strongly that we should inform the electorate about the full extent of what was happening. In early September, we brought our concerns and our classified evidence to the White House for a policy decision. I don't think any single piece of what the Russians were doing was a surprise to the president and NSC members outside our small group, but once all the evidence was put together, the scale and scope of the Russian interference in the election—including classified evidence I can't discuss—were very disturbing. The Russians had been working for decades to undermine US democracy and the US government, but by August 2016, the president of Russia was directing intelligence and propaganda efforts specifically to get the Republican Party nominee elected and, in case that failed, to undermine the Democratic Party nominee's ability to govern.

President Obama seemed convinced by the intelligence we presented but felt he should carefully consider his involvement with exposing the Russian interference. He was, after all, a politician who had endorsed the Democratic Party nominee, and he didn't want to be seen as using the Office of the President to influence the outcome. He asked Denis to approach congressional leaders to elicit support for a bipartisan congressional statement acknowledging and condemning the interference, and he confronted Putin directly in person, telling him to stop the interference at risk of serious consequences.

Days later the Republicans, led by Speaker Paul Ryan and Majority Leader Mitch McConnell, said they would not support a bipartisan statement that might hurt their nominee for president. I was disappointed but not surprised. It seemed they had decided by then that they didn't care who their nominee was, how he got elected, or what effects having a foreign power influence our election would have on the nation, as long as they won. Jeh and I continued to argue the case for informing the nation. President Obama said he'd considered his options and felt that if he acted publicly, it could serve to amplify the Russians' message and would give them more fodder to undermine Clinton's authority as president later. I inferred that in the end, he trusted the electorate to see through the conspiracy theories and propaganda, and on Election Day, to do the right thing.

Jeh and I felt that, however unwilling President Obama was to "put his thumb on the scale of the election," Russian president Putin wasn't concerned with fair play, and we weren't as confident the electorate would, on its own, realize what was happening. There were a lot of angry and frustrated people out there, and this was, after all, the same electorate that had been showing signs of political and social instability for years, the same electorate that had bought into Jade Helm conspiracies, and as the fall went on, the same electorate that seemed to believe crazy conspiracy theories originating from Russia.

On September 9, while campaigning in New York, Secretary Clinton was diagnosed with pneumonia. Not wanting to reveal that she was sick—which could give conspiracy theorists an opening to discuss her health again—she'd kept her condition private and pressed on with her schedule. Two days later, at a 9/11 commemoration ceremony, she collapsed and had to be helped into her car. Someone recorded cell-phone video as her Secret Service detail lifted her off her feet to help her into the car. The Russians—and every other troll on the internet—dissected the video as if it were as momentous as the Zapruder film of President Kennedy's assassination, and refused to accept the campaign's statement a few hours later that she was "severely dehydrated." The Russians and Breitbart filled the gap with screaming headlines—Why has the Clinton campaign been silent for hours? When Clinton did reappear later that day, they claimed that she was actually in a coma, and the person appearing in public was a body double. They manipulated pictures to create differences between Clinton's wardrobe precollapse and postcollapse.

Just as those rumors were racing around Facebook and Twitter, amplified by Russian bots, a second surreptitiously recorded tape appeared on the internet. On September 10—the day between her pneumonia diagnosis and collapse—someone recorded Secretary Clinton at a fund-raising event saying, to laughter and applause, "You could put half of Trump's supporters into what I call the 'basket of deplorables.' . . . They're racist, sexist, homophobic, xenophobic, Islamophobic, you name it." Her comments played perfectly into the narrative that she was an elitist. Her response to the leaked tape only made the situation worse: "I regret saying 'half.' That was wrong." RT bounced between the two stories, broadcasting and posting "Democrats and Republicans are now questioning what other health conditions Clinton may be hiding," and then cutting to tweets of people reacting to #basketofdeplorables.

Considering that neither President Obama nor Congress was going to address the Russian interference directly, Jeh and I felt that, not only was saying *something* the right thing to do, but if we did not disclose the information we had, there'd be hell to pay later. We proposed to the small NSC group that we issue a joint statement from the Department of Homeland Security and the Office of the DNI, officially alerting the electorate to Russian activities. The group—and President Obama—assented, and Jeh and I had our staffs carefully push the boundaries of what we could say in an unclassified statement, ensuring that it addressed only the Russian activities and couldn't be misconstrued as a government accusation against, or endorsement of, either campaign. We discussed whether we should name Putin as personally directing the effort, and decided not to be quite so specific. We settled on attributing the attacks to "Russia's senior-most officials."

The short statement, which was issued on October 7, led with the following paragraph:

> The U.S. Intelligence Community (USIC) is confident that the Russian Government directed the recent compromises of e-mails from US persons and institutions, including from US political organizations. The recent disclosures of alleged hacked e-mails on sites like DCLeaks.com and WikiLeaks and by the Guccifer 2.0 online persona are consistent with the methods and motivations of Russian-directed efforts. These thefts and disclosures are intended to interfere with the US election process. Such activity is not new to Moscow—the Russians have used similar tactics and techniques across Europe and Eurasia, for example, to influence public opinion there. We believe, based on the scope and sensitivity of these efforts, that only Russia's senior-most officials could have authorized these activities.

Initial media reports called our joint statement "stunning." And then, within an hour of its being published, two other stories broke: WikiLeaks dumped a massive and controversial collection of emails belonging to Clinton campaign chief of staff John Podesta, and the *Washington Post* released a leaked video from 2005 of Donald Trump bragging about sexual assaults to *Access Hollywood* host Billy Bush. On tape, Trump says, "Yeah, that's her, with the gold. I better use some Tic Tacs just in case I start kissing her. You know, I'm automatically attracted to beautiful—I just start kissing them. It's like a magnet. Just kiss. I don't even wait. And when you're a star, they let you do it. You can do anything." Bush interjects, "Whatever you want." Trump clarifies, "Grab 'em by the pussy. You can do anything." With these scandals exploding, the nation didn't have the attention span to consider our carefully worded press release. Our warning on Russian interference was so effectively buried that, in December, the national consensus held that the Intelligence Community and DHS had failed to provide *any* warning about the Russians before the election.

Just as Clinton's response to the "basket of deplorables" tape made her situation worse, Trump's response to the *Access Hollywood* tape exacerbated the scandal. Instead of admitting that bragging about sexual assaults was wrong, he dismissed his behavior as "locker-room banter," saying he'd "heard much worse" from former president Bill Clinton on the golf course. The right-wing media and the Russians—retweeted by the most ardent Trump supporters—argued that Secretary Clinton was culpable for her silence after her husband's indiscretions. By now I had begun to wonder if Mr. Trump had meant it literally when he'd said, "I could stand in the middle of Fifth Avenue and shoot somebody and I wouldn't lose voters."

At the presidential debate two days later, Trump paced behind Clinton, glaring at her whenever she was speaking. On camera, he looked the part of a predator. Afterward, at rallies, he dismissed the growing number of women coming forward with allegations of sexual assault, specifically naming women he alleged weren't attractive enough to assault. On October 14, he described standing behind Hillary Clinton at the presidential debate, remarking, "And when she walked in front of me, believe me, I wasn't impressed." Outside his base, his popularity was plummeting.

At the same time, the leaked Podesta emails were hurting the Clinton campaign. The Russians had gained access to Podesta's account in March, when they'd faked a Google Alert that gave him a link to open and then prompted him to enter his login and password. Once they had his login information, they'd passively watched his email traffic until a very late stage of the general election campaign, when they assessed it was the optimal time to release his messages, again through WikiLeaks. The most damaging, on its face, was from Donna Brazile, who had replaced Debbie Wasserman Schultz as Democratic Party chair. In the email, Brazile appeared to leak a planned question to Podesta ahead of the CNN-hosted presidential debate; Secretary Clinton had later received a similar question at the debate. Russian trolls—with months of advance notice to figure out how to maximize the damage from the emails—posted about "coded language" in Podesta's emails that proved their favorite conspiracy theories, including Clinton's clandestine support for the Islamic State. They even used the opportunity to revive the bizarre claim that Clinton and Podesta were running a child-sex ring out of a Washington pizzeria. On October 10, Trump announced at a rally, "I love WikiLeaks!"

However, the Trump campaign appeared to be the more wounded party in the dueling scandals. According to polls, he was far behind Clinton before the release of the *Access Hollywood* tape and had since fallen further still. RT remained largely silent on the tape until posting a video four days later of Russian foreign minister Sergey Lavrov making light of the whole controversy with the incendiary remark "There are so many pussies around your presidential election on both sides." But Russia and Putin seemed to have made a judgment that the election was lost for Trump. They shifted their efforts to discrediting the US election in general and undermining Clinton's authority as its next president.

RT began introducing each of its election coverage segments with a Halloween-themed video clip portraying the horrors of a Clinton White House before cutting to the message "Choosing the lesser of two evils." After mid-October, the Russians no longer tried to compare Mr. Trump positively with Secretary Clinton. Instead, they complained that Americans had never been given a decent choice. In the final weeks before Election Day, they continued promoting conspiracies about Clinton corruption and her connections with Islamic extremism. Their video "Assange: Clinton & ISIS Funded by Same Money" received more than a million views on YouTube before the election, and "Trump Would Not Be Permitted to Win" became their most viewed video about him, garnering 2.2 million views. Both featured John Pilger's interview with Julian Assange.

Mr. Trump seemed to make the same shift in tactics to delegitimizing an inevitable Clinton win. He tweeted on October 15, "Hillary Clinton should have been prosecuted and should be in jail. Instead she is running for president in what looks like a rigged election." He insinuated that, unlike all previous candidates, he might not accept as legitimate a clear win by his opponent. At the final presidential debate on October 19, when asked by moderator Chris Wallace if he would honor the election results, Trump responded, "I'll keep you in suspense, okay?" At a rally the following day, he said, "I will totally accept the results of this great and historic presidential election—if I win." On October 27, he told the crowd at a rally, "And just thinking to myself right now, we should just cancel the election and just give it to Trump, right? What are we even having it for?"

The following day, October 28—eleven days before the election—offered one last surprise. While investigating allegations that former congressman Anthony Weiner had sent illicit texts to a fifteen-year-old girl from a laptop he shared with his then-wife, Huma Abedin, Secretary Clinton's chief of staff, the FBI found thousands of *new* emails relating to Clinton's work at the Department of State. Jim Comey, having promised in testimony to keep Congress informed of any updates to the investigation, felt he was obliged to inform congressional oversight of this new discovery. He sent a private letter to the Republican chairs of the eight committees, with copies to the eight senior Democrats, writing, "Although the FBI cannot yet assess whether or not this material may be significant, and I cannot predict how long it will take us to complete this additional work, I believe it is important to update your Committees about our efforts in light of my previous testimony." The chairman of the House Committee on Oversight and Government Reform, Jason Chaffetz, promptly leaked the letter, tweeting, "FBI Dir just informed me, 'The FBI has learned of the existence of emails that appear to be pertinent to the investigation.' Case reopened."

The Russians jumped into action, and because Chaffetz had leaked the letter without having any actual information about the content of the emails, they could claim the emails contained evidence for their favorite conspiracy theories, alleging Clinton's support for the Islamic State and writing that she was paid directly by foreign dignitaries to take meetings as secretary of state. They also used the association with Anthony Weiner illicitly texting a minor girl to reprise the idea that Clinton was involved with a child-sex ring. (This particular theory was so widely shared— including by people associated with Trump's campaign—and so strongly believed that a month after the election, a man drove to Washington with an AR-15 rifle, went into the pizzeria in question, fired shots causing damage to the restaurant, and demanded to see the basement where children were being held so he could free them. The pizzeria had no basement, and the man was arrested without anyone being hurt.)

Again, Russia's aim wasn't to get anyone to actually believe the crazy stories they were publishing. The point of their influence operation was to overwhelm facts, to sow doubt that facts were even knowable. So when Jim Comey sent a second letter to Congress on Sunday, November 6, two days before the election, that read "Based on our review, we have not changed our conclusions that we expressed in July with respect to Secretary Clinton," it made no difference to the Russians or to the those in the US electorate who were susceptible to the Russian campaign.

On Election Day, November 8, no one really believed Mr. Trump had a chance—including the Russians, who had never pivoted back to promoting him, and who, it could be argued, gave Green Party candidate Jill Stein more favorable coverage. On election night, they'd planned a multifaceted campaign to discredit Clinton's win, with the Twitter hashtag #DemocracyRIP.

CHAPTER TWELVE

Facts and Fears

I was eating a quick lunch at 11:31 A.M. in Muscat, Oman—2:31 A.M. on the US East Coast—when the Associated Press declared Donald Trump to be the president-elect. I had only a few minutes to absorb my shock before I'd be closeted in further meetings with the host government. I wondered what President Obama was thinking and if he now regretted his reticence to speak out about the Russian interference. I considered just how little impact Jeh Johnson and I had apparently had with the warning we'd issued a month before the election, and while I didn't know what effect the Russian interference had—and really couldn't know, because the IC was only assessing the world outside the US borders—I was disturbed and a little sickened to think the Russian efforts could have changed the outcome of the election. But the thought I kept coming back to was just how out of touch I was with the people who lived in Middle America. For the past several years, I'd watched as "unpredictable instability" around the world had prompted angry populations to rise up against their governments and societies. It led to al-Qaida, ISIS, and their ilk proliferating from Afghanistan to Southwest Asia and into North Africa and Europe. It led to civil wars in Libya and Syria and a global refugee crisis unlike anything the world had seen since the end of the Second World War, which my dad had helped end. Unpredictable instability brought pain, war, and suffering to the world. In the United States, it gave us Donald Trump.

I was far from being the only person who was shocked by the outcome, and as the Russians scrambled to stop their #DemocracyRIP social media campaign, President-elect Trump's circle seemed to have no strategy for shifting from campaign mode to administration-transition mode. Rather than working with the State Department, or even contacting it, Trump was taking calls from world leaders, apparently from whoever could get his personal cell phone number. Australian prime minister Malcolm Turnbull famously obtained it from professional golfer Greg Norman and was one of eight world leaders to call Trump with congratulations on the day his victory was announced. With no State Department involvement, no one briefed the president-elect on bilateral issues or existing agreements, and the United States has no official record of what was said during those conversations.

I wondered if our intelligence team was faring better than State. On election night, we'd deployed a team with each of the campaigns, ready to give whoever was president-elect his or her first President's Daily Brief—essentially the PDB prepared for President Obama. At the suggestion of the lead officer for candidate briefings, I'd handwritten nearly identical letters to both candidates. I assumed Secretary Clinton's was being shredded, as planned. The one that was delivered read:

> Dear President-elect Trump:
>
> First, I want to offer congratulations to you on your election.
>
> Second, on behalf of the Intelligence Community, I want to pledge to you our unswerving commitment to provide the best intelligence we can muster. We will rarely be able to completely eliminate uncertainty for you and the Vice President, but we can at least reduce it, and thus help you manage risk, in the face of many difficult decisions you will undoubtedly face.
>
> Finally, I hope you will support the basic writ of "truth to power" in which the Intelligence Community is expected to always "tell it like it is"—straight, objective, unpoliticized.
>
> Again, my congratulations.
> With great respect.
> Sincerely,
> Jim Clapper

I traveled from Oman to Kuwait and then to Jordan, where I had lunch with King Abdullah on Friday. The king tried to hide his pique that there had been no communication between Trump's team and his government. He ended the lunch early, and I watched wistfully as someone carried off my plate after I'd had only a couple of bites of a superb steak. The next day, I flew from Jordan to Israel, ending another trip to the Middle East with a meeting with Prime Minister Netanyahu. He seemed a different person, jubilant with the results of the election. He couldn't stop smiling and noted that he'd had a terrific conversation with the president-elect within hours of Trump's delivering his victory speech. I congratulated him, and he gave me another of his cigars.

When I returned to Washington, I focused primarily on what I needed to do before retiring—*this* time for good. Along with every other Senate-confirmed Obama appointee, I submitted a formal resignation letter, which was standard procedure for the transition between administrations. If a president-elect wished someone from a previous administration to remain in office, he'd reject the resignation and ask the official to stay on, as President-elect Obama had done with Secretary Gates. Still, despite the pro forma nature of the process, it did feel as if I'd taken a concrete step toward finally retiring, fifty-five years after I'd enlisted in the Marine Corps. I'd expected, if my former colleague Hillary Clinton had won the election, that she might ask me to stick around until she could get a new DNI confirmed. I didn't expect President-elect Trump to ask, and I don't think I'd have agreed to remain if he had.

The following morning I testified in what I believed—naïvely—was my final congressional hearing, with USD(I) Marcel Lettre, who'd replaced Mike Vickers, and Deputy Secretary of Defense Bob Work before the House Intelligence Committee. The topic of the hearing was officially "IC Support for DOD," but it became an opportunity for Chairman Devin Nunes and a few other committee members to take their parting shots. They all had their pet issues, but after six years and more of often politicized agendas at hearings, I was no longer concerned I'd slip into the trap of making a statement the press would spin into meaning something I hadn't intended. Besides, I couldn't see any member of Congress calling for my head after I'd resigned, a thought that pleased me privately. So, after Nunes and ranking member Adam Schiff made their opening statements and gave me the floor, I smiled—a rare occurrence for me on Capitol Hill—leaned into the microphone, thanked them, and then said, "I submitted my letter of resignation last night, which felt pretty good. I've got sixty-four days left, and I think I'd have a hard time with my wife for anything past that."

The hearing was unfocused and ranged widely from topics like analytic integrity to cybersecurity to threat assessments to deciding which overseas bases should house which DOD intelligence activities. Fifty minutes in, Schiff asked me about the Russian interference in the election and Russia's continued presence in eastern Ukraine and Syria, and what I thought would change under a Trump administration. I replied that the Russians were continuing their activity on all fronts, and that I couldn't speculate on what—if anything—would change. His follow-up questions all concerned Russian military activities, and he didn't bring up the election interference again. His final question was about how Putin would react if—given his cordial relationship with the new US president—he could no longer blame all his woes on the "American bogeyman." I thought that was a salient question, and I reaffirmed that Putin had indeed stayed in power in part by calling for Russian nationalism while painting the United States as bent on Russia's destruction. The discussion moved on.

About an hour and a half into the hearing, my legislative affairs officer slipped me a note. Apparently, it wasn't common knowledge that every political appointee had submitted pro forma resignations, and all the cable news channels and print media services that follow Washington politics were reporting "Clapper resigns!," saying I'd quit in protest over Donald Trump's winning the election. The story was trending on Twitter and was the top result on Google's aggregated news site. For once, I hadn't been tricked into making headlines. In the business, this is what we call an "unforced error." At the next opportunity, I interjected into the live feed and House record, "I do need to clarify about my statement about resignation; it's not effective until noon on 20 January 2017—not immediately—as is being reported in the media."

The media expected conflict between Obama administration officials and Trump's transition team, and so they saw it even when it wasn't there. I'd meant it in September when I'd told the IC and intelligence industry associations "It'll be okay," and continued to use that phrase after the election, both in internal IC and in public speeches, and my office was working hard to help Trump's national security transition team get up to speed. The president-elect had set up shop in Trump Tower in New York, and we arranged security to allow him to continue getting intelligence briefings there. He had designated Mike Flynn as his national security adviser, and without speaking about it directly, Mike and I put aside any animosity from his early exit from DIA to work toward a smooth transition of government. We had two phone conversations during the transition, both courteous and professional.

The media continued to see divisions that didn't exist, and when Admiral Mike Rogers was seen at Trump Tower, reportedly interviewing to replace me as DNI, the *Washington Post* published a story purporting that I had cosigned a letter to President Obama recommending that Mike be fired. That simply wasn't true, and ODNI public affairs director Brian Hale asked the *Post* to explain where the story had come from. The reporter, Ellen Nakashima, wouldn't name any sources, but cited a recommendation I'd sent to the White House that CYBERCOM be split off from NSA. We explained to the *Post* that my suggestion to split the organizations was intended to optimize IC and national security capabilities, was based on six and a half years of watching CYBERCOM grow its capabilities, and said nothing about firing Mike. The *Post* wasn't interested in this story without the conflict and wouldn't change their article. Despite the public narrative, we continued to work with the transition team, giving them access to IC leaders and facilities.

Regardless of our cooperation with the Trump transition team, we hadn't forgotten what Russia had done. The FBI and CIA were coming across new evidence of Russian activities relating to the election every day, and I was starting to see that the scope and scale of their effort was much bigger than Jeh or I had understood when we'd released our statement in October. In late November, Susan Rice asked the NSC staff to draft a menu of possible punitive measures the president could impose on Russia before leaving office. The resulting list spanned a spectrum that included increased sanctions, but I was particularly in favor of the suggestion to expel Russian spies and to close facilities in the United States that we knew were bases for espionage. Many FBI resources went into countering those efforts, and we could put those resources to better use if we shipped some of the counterintelligence threat back to Russia.

As we discussed those possibilities in the White House Situation

Room, the public dialogue about Russian interference was heating up. Seeming to fear it called the legitimacy of his election into question, the president-elect responded defensively whenever the subject was raised. In an interview with *Time* magazine on November 28, he countered a question on Russian activities with, "I don't believe they interfered. That became a laughing point, not a talking point, a laughing point." Asked who he thought had hacked the Democrats' email accounts and IT systems, he responded, "It could be Russia. And it could be China. And it could be some guy in his home in New Jersey."

We knew it was not someone in New Jersey, and I was fairly certain that President-elect Trump knew that as well. At an NSC meeting on Monday, December 5, President Obama told us he wanted CIA, FBI, and NSA to integrate all their relevant intelligence into a single report to pass on to the next administration and Congress. He also asked us to derive from it an unclassified document for public consumption with as much information from the classified version as possible. And critically, he wanted all of this done before January 20—the end of his administration.

After that meeting, John Brennan, Mike Rogers, Jim Comey, and I caucused privately. John had already volunteered to host a small group of analysts so they could share their findings, and we decided to expand the team to include almost thirty of the most seasoned people from the three agencies and from ODNI, working long hours through the ensuing holiday to produce as thorough a community assessment as possible.

On Friday, December 9, unnamed "officials briefed on the matter" leaked the effort to the press, saying the CIA and FBI had reached the conclusion that Russia had helped Trump win. The leak wasn't quite accurate, and certainly wasn't helpful, but the immediate response from President-elect Trump's transition team was even worse. Under the seal of "President Elect Donald J. Trump," the team published a press release that—with no preamble—began, "These are the same people that said Saddam Hussein had weapons of mass destruction. The election ended a long time ago in one of the biggest Electoral College victories in history. It's now time to move on and 'Make America Great Again.'" It was stunning. Based on rumors from anonymous sources, the president-elect had lashed out reflexively to delegitimize the Intelligence Community—the same IC that would be serving him in forty-two days, that was already giving him

President Obama's PDBs. The attack was disturbing, as was its demonstrably false assertion that his victory was one of the "biggest" ever.

On Monday, as I continued my personal farewell tour with the intelligence workforce, a young woman asked me, somewhat urgently, "What are we supposed to do now?" It took me a moment to get my head around the doubt and uncertainty underlying the question before I could respond, and then I told her and her colleagues the only thing I *could* say: "Keep doing the business of intelligence. Keep shoveling intelligence coal down in the engine room and let the people on the bridge worry about what direction we're headed, how fast we're going, and how to arrange the deck chairs. Keep our mission in front of us and stay true to the key tenets of intelligence work: support intelligence integration, speak straight, unbiased truth to power, and leave the business of policy making to the policy makers." I have no idea if those platitudes were helpful to her or anyone in the room, but it was about all I could muster that Monday morning.

Back in my office, I picked up the speech I had planned to deliver Wednesday night at a dinner in my honor, when I was scheduled to address INSA, the large intelligence industry association whose predecessor I'd been president of in the 1990s. My talk was—once again—built around the reassuring phrase, "It'll be okay." I called my speechwriter into the office, handed him the speech, and told him, "I don't think I can say this anymore."

On Wednesday night, I still opened with humor, borrowing a very old line to describe "the crucial partnership between the IC and industry" as being "kind of like the partnership between the taxidermist and the veterinarian—either way, you get your dog back." I added, "Bear with me. This is my last chance to use my well-worn one-liners." Then, instead of blowing smoke and assuring the crowd that everything would be okay, I told them about my conversation with that young intelligence officer Monday morning, and her question, "What are we supposed to do now?" I shared the answer I'd given her and added what I'd been thinking about since that conversation.

When I started out in the intelligence business—back when "intelligence automation" was acetate, grease pencil, and two corporals—I don't think the words "intelligence" and "integration" were ever used in the same sentence. But those other two principles I told her: "speak truth to power" and "let the policy makers make policy," have served me well for almost fifty-four years. And I believe we have to continue speaking truth to power, even—*or especially*—if the person in power doesn't want to hear the truth we have to tell him.

The applause cut me off so abruptly that I stepped back from the microphone; a few people even stood. It felt like a long time before they let me get back to my speech. Then I told them:

I believe everyone here knows, my connection to the business goes back even further, to when I was a kid, following my dad around to duty stations all over the world. So it's with mixed emotions that I'm stepping down as DNI—again, in thirty-seven days. There are things I *won't* miss about playing an active role in intelligence. That starts with the dysfunctional Congress, and it goes on to include the hyperventilation in the media. If they can't find something to hyperventilate about, they'll make up something like, "Clapper resigns in protest." And I won't miss the daily drudge of the job, of not having a whole day off in six and a half years, and never having a moment to myself.

I'll stop that list there, because at this point, I already feel like I'm attending my own wake—with a speaking role—which is *not* recommended when people are holding a wake for you.

I also have a list of things I will *most certainly* miss, in particular the remarkable people of the IC. We have the brightest, most inquisitive, most dedicated and patriotic workforce in government. After half a century, our people still have the ability to surprise me with their ingenuity, their brilliance, and their commitment to mission. And I will miss our mission. Those are the things I'll most miss: the people and the mission.

Finally, I said that "before I shuffle off the stage, since I've got one foot in assisted living already," I wanted to answer one frequently asked question:

Are we better? As in, are we better than we were before I started as DNI or before 9/11 changed the way we do business?

> Well, one upshot to achieving "intelligence geezerdom" is that I tend to look back even farther. I've got a lot more data points, and so, the question I ask myself is: Are we better now than we were when I was a young intelligence officer in 1963? The answer to that is a resounding yes. We're more efficient. We collect more, with more accesses and more tools at our disposal. Our technology is astounding, and we can put intelligence into the hands of deployed warfighters in real time, whereas we used to be days or weeks time-late.
>
> We are organized completely differently. We are a community; while fifty years ago, CIA and NSA might as well have been on two different planets. We, of course, haven't reached integration nirvana, but we've come a long way on that journey. And we've also, over the past few years, learned to embrace transparency. Well, "embrace" may be a strong word, but just a few years ago, transparency felt genetically antithetical to me, and it doesn't feel that way now.
>
> And the result of all that progress is that we're more effective at reducing risk for our national decision makers. Of course, policy makers have the option of accepting or rejecting the insight that intelligence gives them. If they reject it, they do so at their own peril, and unfortunately, at the peril of the nation, too. So, what do we do? We "keep on keeping on," doing the work of the intelligence business.

The president-elect seemed increasingly desperate to make the story of Russian interference go away, constantly denying there had been any impact on the election or any interference at all. On December 28, he said that it was "time for the country to move on to bigger and better things." President Obama didn't want to focus on the Russian issue during his final weeks in office, either, but he wasn't simply going to "move on." On December 29, he ordered new sanctions against Russia and declared thirty-five known Russian spies in the United States to be persona non grata and sent them home. He also closed the two Russian-owned facilities in Maryland and New York. I didn't think that response was commensurate with what they'd done to us, but I also knew we weren't prepared to take more drastic steps. We waited to see how Putin would respond, fully expecting a reciprocal retaliation.

The same day, as was confirmed when he later pled guilty to lying to the FBI about it, National Security Adviser-designate Mike Flynn called Russian ambassador Sergey Kislyak, assuring him not to worry about the sanctions and asking that Russia not retaliate. On the following day, Putin announced he would not expel anyone from Russia and would not respond in kind to the new US sanctions, saying he would wait to work with the next US presidential administration. Trump tweeted, "Great move on delay (by V. Putin)—I always knew he was very smart!"

New Year's Day fell on Sunday, and so Monday, January 2, was a scheduled government holiday. The IC assessment team did not take the day off, and neither did I, as the most highly classified version of the assessment was due to the president on Thursday. John, Mike, Jim, and I, along with our closest trusted senior staff members, gave the draft assessment a critical read. We agreed that after we briefed President Obama on Thursday, we would brief President-elect Trump on Friday and provide a still-classified but less sensitive version to Congress. Then, the team would have the weekend to redact the sensitive aspects of the classified version so that we could publish an unclassified assessment on Monday, January 9. We also agreed that the three versions of the assessment—including the version we published—would contain the same conclusions, word for word.

Our team of subject-matter experts cross-referenced independent sources across disciplines, each corroborating the others and each adding to the big picture, enriching what we knew about the scope and scale of Russia's efforts. I remember just how staggering the assessment felt the first time I read it through from start to finish, and just how specific our conclusions and evidence were. We showed unambiguously that Putin had ordered the campaign to influence the election, that the campaign was multifaceted, and that Russia had used cyber espionage against US political organizations and publicly disclosed the data they collected through WikiLeaks, DCLeaks, and the Guccifer 2.0 persona. We documented Russian cyber intrusions into state and local voter rolls. We described Russia's pervasive propaganda efforts through RT, Sputnik, and the social media trolls, and how the entire operation had begun with attempts to undermine US democracy and demean Secretary Clinton, then shifted to promoting Mr. Trump when Russia assessed he was a viable candidate who would serve their strategic goals. We added historical context to show just how much of an unprecedented escalation in directness, level of activity, and scope of effort all of this represented, and we assessed that the election operation signaled a "new normal in Russian influence efforts." The Russian government had done all of this at minimal cost and without significant damage to their own interests, and they had no real incentive to stop.

On Tuesday President-elect Trump attempted to undercut our assessment before its release, tweeting, "The 'intelligence' briefing on so-called 'Russian hacking' was delayed until Friday, perhaps more time needed to build a case. Very strange!" Of course, it had never been the plan to give him the assessment before it went to President Obama, but we chose not to respond to his tweet. On Wednesday, he tweeted, "Julian Assange said 'a 14 year old could have hacked Podesta'—why was DNC so careless? Also said Russians did not give him the info!" We again ignored the provocation, and I hoped the intelligence briefer who continued to present President's Daily Briefs to the president-elect wasn't being shot as the messenger.

I continued my Oval Office sessions with President Obama through all of this. On Tuesday, two days before the assessment was due to him, he was calm, patient, and supportive, never pressing me for details before the report was ready. That stood in stark contrast to Congress. Almost as soon as the president assigned us the task of studying the Russian interference on December 5, our oversight committees began demanding we give them updates on our progress. It's the only time I can recall ever giving Congress a flat no without making any attempt to compromise or deflect the contrived ire of their demands. We certainly didn't want the partisan congressional "guidance" that would have come as a result of briefing them, nor did we want anything to interfere with the team preparing the assessment, which leaks of their work certainly would have done. Even within the White House Situation Room, during the month it took to put the assessment together, we took extraordinary measures when discussing Russian interference, procedures comparable to those invoked during the endgame of the hunt for bin Laden.

One senator did find a way around our efforts to keep Congress out of our work until we'd briefed the president. John McCain informed my office in December that he wanted to hold a final hearing on "foreign cyber threats" before I retired. He said that the session would *not* be about the Russian interference, but instead would cover a broad look at cybersecurity. My office knew that even if that was genuinely his intent, the other senators on the committee would undoubtedly inquire about the assessment. McCain assured me he wouldn't let that happen but when, still dubious, my office continued to try to deflect the invitation, Senator McCain defaulted to his favorite persuasive technique and said that if I didn't agree to appear voluntarily, he'd subpoena me. For reasons that escape me now, we not only agreed to do the hearing, but scheduled it for Thursday morning—a morning I would normally brief the president in the Oval, and the very day that we would be delivering our assessment on Russian interference to him.

Preparing for that hearing was just about the last thing on my mind that week. Not only were the three directors and I poring over the IC assessment for any flaw, any reason why the president-elect, his team, Congress, or anyone else could call its conclusions into question, we were also settling on how we would actually present it. We'd decided in the interests of consistency that—no matter whom we were briefing—we'd use the same set of talking points. I would serve as the moderator, and we'd mark out specific cues for Mike, Jim, and John to amplify our talking points by briefing the NSA, FBI, and CIA equities in the assessment, in that specific order. Our mantra was "That's our story, and we're sticking to it." Of course, we couldn't have believed in that mantra if we weren't confident in the superb work the IC assessment team had done and the meticulous reviews we were continuing to put their work through.

We conducted a walkthrough of our presentation, and by Wednesday night, January 4, we were ready. We sent a copy of the assessment to the White House so that the president could read it before we met with him. Then—having seen on Twitter a preview of how the president-elect would characterize and attempt to dismiss the assessment and anticipating what would happen if he had a full weekend to tweet and talk about it before we released the public version—we made a difficult request of the overworked IC assessment team. We asked them to start working on the unclassified version immediately and to have it ready by Friday morning, instead of Monday, so that we could release the public assessment as soon as we finished briefing the president-elect that afternoon.

On Thursday morning, despite all my best efforts to avoid it, I found myself once again behind the witness table in the Senate Armed Services Committee hearing room. Before the hearing started, my staff had warned the committee staff that I would be traveling directly from the hearing room to the White House to brief the IC assessment to the president. Chairman McCain therefore knew that I was leaving the hearing at noon and that trying to extend the hearing past then risked an awkward scene. Also, while the assessment was complete and we no longer were concerned about congressional interference, we strongly wished to avoid discussing what was in it before we'd briefed the president and his successor.

After welcoming the senators who were new to the committee in the recently elected Congress and welcoming us as witnesses, McCain explained why we were gathered. In two sentences, he succinctly stated the difficulty our nation faced:

> This hearing is about the broad range of cybersecurity challenges confronting our nation—threats from countries like Russia, China, North Korea, and Iran—as well as non-state actors from terrorist groups to transnational criminal organizations. In recent years, we have seen a growing series of cyberattacks by multiple actors—attacks that have targeted our citizens, businesses, military, and government.

Having kept his promise that the hearing would broadly address "foreign cyber threats," McCain moved to the topic on everyone's mind, as I kept a poker face:

> But there is no escaping the fact that this committee meets today, for the first time in this new Congress, in the aftermath of an unprecedented attack on our democracy. At the president's direction, Director Clapper is leading a comprehensive review of Russian interference in our recent election with the goal of informing the American people as much as possible about what happened.

Continuing his opening remarks, Chairman McCain both relieved the most distinct point of anxiety among Republican legislators (and the president-elect's transition team), and at the same time deftly let us off the hook for the most controversial line of questioning we'd expected to face. "The goal of this review, as I understand it," he stated, "is not to question the outcome of the presidential election. Nor should it be." Then he explained what we would release the following day, saying we needed to move forward, "with full knowledge of the facts," and that, without previewing the assessment, "we know a lot already." He concluded, "Every American should be alarmed by Russia's attacks on our Nation. There is no national security interest more vital to the United States of America than the ability to hold free and fair elections without foreign interference. That is why Congress must set partisanship aside, follow the facts, and work together."

In fairness to Chairman McCain, over the next two and a half hours, we did occasionally discuss cyber-related topics other than Russian interference, and despite my having been strongly opposed to testifying that morning, his insistence on holding this hearing ended up doing us a huge favor. It served to introduce the scope of the assessment to the public, media, and Congress in a thoughtful manner that ran counter to the president-elect's tweets, and more important, the hearing gave us an opportunity to demonstrate that the IC assessment wasn't a politically motivated witch hunt, and that we hadn't conducted the assessment simply because President Obama didn't like the results of the election.

The discussion that followed was at times circumspect and often tense, but it afforded us an opportunity to discuss aspects of what had happened during the run-up to the election that our assessment did not cover. Chairman McCain returned several times to lambasting Julian Assange. At one point, he asked me directly, "Director Clapper, how would you describe Mr. Assange?" "Well," I replied, "he is holed up in the Ecuadorian embassy in London because he is under indictment, I believe by the Swedish government, for a sexual crime. He has—in the interests of ostensibly openness and transparency exposed [and] put people at risk by his doing that. So I do not think those of us in the intelligence community have a whole lot of respect for him." Mike simply said, "I would echo those comments."

In another exchange, Republican senator Dan Sullivan challenged me on the seemingly unforceful US response to the Chinese hacks of OPM's systems, asking, "But is that answer not part of the problem; that we are showing that we are not going to make it costly for them to come in and steal the files of twenty-two million Americans, including many intelligence officers?" I responded with a "truth to power" answer I suspect he didn't want to hear: "Well, as I say, people who live in glass houses need to think about throwing rocks because this was an act of espionage. And we and other nations conduct similar acts of espionage. So if we are going to punish each other for acts of espionage, that is a different policy issue."

A few minutes later Republican senator Lindsey Graham returned to the point, noting how similar the sanctions in response to Russia's actions were to those issued in response to China's. "Is there a difference between espionage and interfering in an election?" he asked me. "Yes," I responded. "Espionage implies, to me at least, a passive collection, and this was much more activist." He led me down a road that, for a change, I was comfortable walking. "So when it comes to espionage, we better be careful about throwing rocks. When it comes to interfering in our election, we better be ready to throw rocks. Do you agree with that?" "That is a good metaphor," I agreed. He concluded with a line he knew would be replayed on all the cable news networks: "I think what Obama did was throw a pebble. I am ready to throw a rock."

The hearing also gave me an opportunity to address a topic that had been on my mind since December 9, when the president-elect had first attacked the IC. Democratic senator Claire McCaskill broached it by asking if it was important "that we maintain the intelligence community as a foundational, apolitical bloc of our country." "I could not feel stronger about exactly that," I responded. "I think it is hugely important that the intelligence community conduct itself and be seen as independent, providing unvarnished, untainted, objective, accurate, and timely and relevant intelligence support to all policy makers, commanders, diplomats, et cetera."

She continued, "Do, in fact, members of the intelligence community engage in life-threatening and very dangerous missions every day, particularly as it relates to the war on terror?" "You only need to walk into the lobby of CIA and look at the stars on the wall or the front lobby of NSA [to see] the number of intelligence people that have paid the ultimate price in the service of their country," I replied. Then she got to the heart of what had been bothering me so much, expressing what I as DNI could not say:

> So let us talk about who benefits from a president-elect trash-ing the intelligence community. Who benefits from that, Di-rector Clapper? The American people? Them losing confidence in the intelligence community and the work of the intelligence community? Who actually is the benefactor of someone who is about to become commander in chief trashing the intelli-gence community?

I tried to be circumspect with my response: "I think there is an impor-tant distinction here between healthy skepticism, which policy makers, to include policy maker number one, should always have for intelligence, but I think there is a difference between skepticism and disparagement."

The hearing adjourned at 12:09, after Chairman McCain and I sparred—playfully, I think—each of us in "cranky old man" mode. Before gaveling the hearing to a close, he said, "Director Clapper, we will be call-ing you again." Breaching etiquette, I keyed my microphone back on to retort, "Really?"

My detail hustled me out of the hearing room and into the SUV. Just ahead of Mike Rogers's team, we raced down Pennsylvania Avenue to the White House. Mike and I ran in, meeting John Brennan and Jim Comey, and together the four of us discussed the IC assessment with the presi-dent, who was somber and appreciative. I've often wondered what would have happened—or more to the point, what *wouldn't* have happened—if President Obama hadn't tasked us specifically to gather all the intelli-gence reporting on the Russian interference into one report, or if we'd still been working in a culture in which the CIA, NSA, and FBI refused to share information with one another, as they'd been accused of doing in the summer of 2001.

Without that IC assessment, I don't know that all the subsequent con-gressional investigations would have been launched. The Senate Intelli-gence Committee started its investigation the day after we briefed them, followed shortly by the Senate judiciary, House intelligence, and House oversight and government reform committees. Likewise, I don't know if the FBI's investigation would have been so threatening as to provoke

President Trump to fire Jim Comey in May, or to prompt Attorney General Jeff Sessions to recuse himself from Russia-related matters and Deputy Attorney General Rod Rosenstein to appoint Robert Mueller as special counsel.

On Thursday night the team worked through the details of the still highly classified version for Congress, and the unclassified version we intended to publish Friday afternoon.

At 8:30 on Friday morning we were back on Capitol Hill, presenting our briefing to the "Gang of Eight": the party leaders in the House and Senate and the chairs and ranking members of the House and Senate intelligence committees. Our presentation was fast-paced and terse, as we had to leave by 9:30 to stay on schedule. I departed the Capitol with the impression that the leaders of both parties were taken aback, both by the extent of the Russian operation and by the thoroughness with which we'd documented the facts and evidence.

Jim, John, Mike, and I departed the Capitol on time, all of us and our personal security details in four separate, specially configured, up-armored SUVs, and sped across the Anacostia River to Andrews Air Force Base. John, Mike, and I boarded one plane, and Jim—who'd planned to remain in New York and meet with employees in FBI offices there after briefing the president-elect—boarded another. We landed at Newark International Airport around 11:30, where another four SUVs equipped with flashing lights were waiting on the tarmac to whisk us across the Hudson River to Manhattan and Trump Tower. With the media camped out in the lobby on the business side of the building, we took the residential entrance, which was fairly quiet, with only a few doormen and porters in the hallway, who all ducked aside as we passed. I briefly wondered if twenty or so government men in dark suits walking briskly through the residential hallway was an odd sight, or something to which they had already grown accustomed. Security officers held each elevator as we ascended to the fourteenth floor, crossed over to the business side, and ascended again. We transited a busy hallway, bustling with people I assumed were working on the transition, and finally reached the conference room where we were to brief the president-elect, a small and windowless space, which we were told had been secured as a SCIF—a Sensitive Compartmented Information Facility—by the Secret Service. Eight chairs were arranged around a table, with another row along a wall.

As the de facto leader of our four-man delegation, I posted myself by the door, and we waited for the president-elect. After about ten minutes, he walked in, smiling. When I extended my hand and introduced myself, he laughed and said, "I know who you are." He told me I had done "a great job" testifying the previous day, which seemed a diplomatic gesture, considering I hadn't been all that complimentary toward him during the hearing, and he concluded, "You looked good on TV." That final bit of flattery was a compliment I'm sure I've *never* heard before. I thanked him, while asserting that I actually have a face made for radio. He thanked me for the letter I'd sent along with his initial President's Daily Brief—the first of three times he brought up the letter during the meeting.

His pleasant, courteous attitude was a relief and set the tone for an affable briefing. President-elect Trump and Vice President-elect Pence sat at opposite ends of the table. I sat to Trump's immediate left with John Brennan beside me. Mike Rogers and Jim Comey sat across from us. National Security Adviser-designate Mike Flynn and White House chief of staff-designate Reince Priebus took the remaining two seats at the table to either side of Pence. This arrangement was much friendlier than if the four of us had been seated at one side of the table and Trump's team at the other, and as such felt more like a standard intelligence briefing than one of the tense negotiations for which Trump was famous. As we got settled, CIA director-nominee Mike Pompeo, Deputy National Security Adviser-designate K. T. McFarland, and Homeland Security Adviser-designate Tom Bossert took seats against the wall, along with Trump's PDB briefer, for whom the president-elect had high praise. After we started briefing, White House press secretary-designate Sean Spicer joined in, taking one of the wall seats.

We briefed virtually the same content we'd given the Gang of Eight that morning, with me as the lead presenter and Mike, Jim, and John delivering their amplifying parts on cue. While the material was the same, the whole session was more relaxed, and we took our time to explain terms and intelligence procedures with which we knew the group might not be familiar. The briefing remained professional, but conversational, too, and the president-elect and vice president-elect both interjected politely. Trump appropriately questioned some evidence and conclusions, and we answered his questions to his apparent satisfaction. Pence very astutely prompted us to clarify points on several occasions; I was impressed by the way he actively consumed the intelligence we were providing.

We were scheduled to spend an hour in Trump Tower, but the meeting lasted an hour and a half. By the end, I believe everyone in the room realized that the evidence—particularly from signals intelligence and cyber forensics—to attribute the influence operation to Vladimir Putin and the Russian government was overwhelming. The entire Trump team was happy to hear our assessment that the Russians had not successfully tampered with actual vote tallies. The only question they posed that we couldn't answer was whether the Russian influence operation had any effect on the outcome of the election. I told the president-elect that we had neither the authority nor capabilities to assess what impact—if any—the Russian operation had.

As we closed the briefing, Jim Comey took advantage of a pause in conversation to address the president-elect. We'd agreed that one of the two of us would bring up "one additional matter," a subject "best discussed on a one-on-one basis" with the president-elect. The additional matter was a dossier—a collection of seventeen "pseudo-intelligence" reports created by a private company—which I first learned about from John Brennan a week or so after we'd been tasked to conduct the IC assessment. I didn't know until after my tenure as DNI that the dossier had begun as opposition research against Mr. Trump during the Republican primary race and then, sponsored by the Democrats, had continued to expand during the general election campaign. The memos covered a wide range of topics all related to long-standing interactions between Trump, his associates, and the Russians. It further alleged that the Russian government had compromising material on the president-elect and his team, which it had not disclosed during the course of the election or since.

Some details in the report were salacious, but in our professional opinions, the more ominous accounts alleged ties between members of the Trump team and the Russian government. Because we had not corroborated any of the sources used to generate the dossier, we had not included it as part of our IC assessment. We knew that at least two congressional members and some of the media had copies of the dossier, and that it could be published—in whole or in part—at any moment. While we could neither confirm nor refute anything in the document, we felt what I expressed as a "duty to warn" the president-elect that it existed and that it potentially could be made public. I wondered at the time—and have often done so since—what the reaction would have been had we *not* warned the president-elect about the existence of the dossier, and he later learned we had known about it and chosen not to tell him.

We decided that it should be Jim to brief him about the matter, for two reasons: First, the FBI had initially uncovered the dossier in its earlier investigation into the Russian hacking of Clinton-campaign emails, and second, John and I were both retiring at noon on January 20, while Jim would continue on as FBI director for President Trump.

We all rose, and President-elect Trump thanked us. Reince Priebus asked him if he wanted anyone on his team to stay for the "additional matter," and the president-elect said no. So, leaving the two of them to talk, the rest of the party adjourned. Before we cleared the conference room, the Trump team had already begun drafting their press release about our meeting. I overheard their first point, that the US IC had assessed that the Russian interference did not change the outcome of the election—which was very different from our acknowledgment that we hadn't, and couldn't, assess its impact. We had to let it pass. In the hallway I took the opportunity to engage Tom Bossert, who in turn introduced me to the vice president-elect. I spoke with them briefly, suggesting that the new administration consider asking Nick Rasmussen to stay on as director of the National Counterterrorism Center, which it did.

In the car on the way back to Newark Airport, I called Brian Hale (who only requested to be described as "tanned and rested" if we mentioned him in this book) and told him to publish the unclassified IC assessment *immediately*. He replied that, just minutes before, he'd received the certified-as-unclassified version of the report as it was moved onto the ODNI system connected to the internet, and it was ready to go. Cutting the phone connection and sitting back, I felt just about as far from "tanned and rested" as one can get. My personal vision of dancing quietly off the stage while no one was paying attention had dissolved. I had less than fourteen days left on the job, and we still had hearings to get through with our oversight committees and each of the full houses of Congress within the next week. So far, I imagined—or hoped—that we appeared publicly to be like the proverbial duck gliding smoothly across the pond, but I could feel just how frantically we were kicking our legs beneath the surface. After we landed at Andrews, I called White House chief of staff

Denis McDonough to let him know that not only had we survived the briefing, but it had gone surprisingly well.

I got little rest over the weekend, both because I was preparing for the hearings and because I was running out of time to close on several issues that were important to the IC before the clock ran out on January 20. Early Monday morning I was on camera once again, this time under very different circumstances. Every four years, just ahead of Inauguration Day, our National Intelligence Council publishes its Global Trends report, an "unclassified strategic assessment of how key trends and uncertainties might shape the world over the next 20 years, to help senior US leaders think about and plan for the longer term." Global Trends represents years of work from our most strategically minded analysts, and I took a lot of pride in introducing the program of presentations planned for that day.

After advising the media and the spray of cameras, to chuckles, "If you're here to get the latest on the Russia hacks you're in the wrong place," I explained that "the Global Trends report does not represent the official, coordinated view of the US Intelligence Community; it does not represent the official view or policy of the US government, and it's not a prediction of the future." Instead it was, I told them, a framework for thinking about the world, designed to help each new administration. The report we published on January 9, 2017, was titled "Paradox of Progress," and it depicted a world at a crossroads, with "rising tensions within and between countries." It forecast:

> An ever-widening range of states, organizations, and empowered individuals will shape geopolitics. For better and worse, the emerging global landscape is drawing to a close an era of American dominance following the Cold War. So, too, perhaps is the rules-based international order that emerged after World War II. It will be much harder to cooperate internationally and govern in ways publics expect. Veto players will threaten to block collaboration at every turn, while information "echo chambers" will reinforce countless competing realities, undermining shared understandings of world events.
>
> Underlying this crisis in cooperation will be local, national, and international differences about the proper role of government across an array of issues ranging from the economy to

the environment, religion, security, and the rights of individuals. Debates over moral boundaries—to whom is owed what—will become more pronounced, while divergence in values and interests among states will threaten international security.

It will be tempting to impose order on this apparent chaos, but that ultimately would be too costly in the short run and would fail in the long. Dominating empowered, proliferating actors in multiple domains would require unacceptable resources in an era of slow growth, fiscal limits, and debt burdens. Doing so domestically would be the end of democracy, resulting in authoritarianism or instability or both.

The "paradox" was that, within this dark vision, there were unprecedented opportunities to reshape our world for the better, all dependent on how individuals, governments, and international groups renegotiated their expectations of and obligations to one another. The report raised profound questions, based on years of diligent research and engagement with novel thinkers around the globe. In any sane world, I would have spent weeks preparing for the speech that morning and would have framed many of my final public engagements as DNI around the milestone report. Given the events of the past year and my continuing responsibility to report on the Russian operation against our election, I almost felt caught in a microcosm of the dark world the report described. So, that Monday, I gave my introductory speech, thanked the team who'd created the report, and departed for a farewell town hall at DHS and then to prepare for additional Russia-interference briefings with Mike, Jim, and John.

On Tuesday morning we were back on Capitol Hill. At 10:00, we briefed the House Intelligence Committee in a classified, closed hearing, a gathering that turned partisan, personal, and nasty. In particular, three of the Republican lawmakers challenged our conclusion that the Russians actively supported Trump and seemed to resent that we had not involved them in the creation of the IC assessment or informed them as soon as we had any new information. Our explanations only served to stoke their anger. The briefing ran past schedule, and we hurried from the House briefing room south of the Capitol to a hearing room in an office building north of the Capitol for an open, televised hearing with the Senate

Intelligence Committee. We had about a twenty-minute break before the red lights went on above the cameras.

For the next two hours, as the American public, the Russian government, and the rest of the world watched, we answered questions about the Russian cyber and influence operation. The senators, and simultaneously the media, sought to parse our every word, Democrats looking for collusion between Trump's team and the Russians, Republicans for evidence of a conspiracy that the IC was attempting to undermine the president-elect. Senators on both sides pressed Jim Comey to reveal whether there were open FBI investigations looking into either of the presidential campaigns. The Democrats certainly remembered the letter Jim had sent to the Hill eleven days before the election about reopening its investigation into Clinton's emails. When Jim told Senator Angus King, "Especially in a public forum, we never confirm or deny a pending investigation," King voiced quiet exasperation, and the left-leaning media outlets were apoplectic.

When the red lights went off, we immediately moved with the Senate committee to their secure facility. Strangely, after answering questions about it for two hours in public, we then presented the IC assessment to the committee for the first time. By the time this session ended, we'd been testifying for seven straight hours. When I finally had the free time to check on world events, I found that all the contentiousness of the hearings and briefings had been completely overshadowed by other breaking news: BuzzFeed had published the now-infamous dossier on Trump, the one that Jim had warned the president-elect about five days earlier. In a classic case of "shoot the messenger," Trump publicly blamed us for the publication of the dossier—yet another indication to me that his administration would not appreciate anyone's speaking truth to power, particularly if the truth was politically inconvenient.

I woke Wednesday to find that Trump had tweeted another early-morning attack on us: "Intelligence agencies should never have allowed this fake news to 'leak' into the public. One last shot at me. Are we living in Nazi Germany?" I was floored by the analogy, and Jewish communities in the United States and abroad called for him to apologize and retract the statement.

That afternoon in my office, I watched the president-elect in a televised news conference, doubling down on his Nazi tweet, again alleging that US intelligence agencies had "allowed" the dossier to leak—as though we had any control over a document we'd discovered already "out in the wild." He continued, "I think it's a disgrace. And I say that, and I say that, and that's something that Nazi Germany would have done and did do." Not helping the situation, the *New York Times* quickly published a story apparently intended to clarify that he meant to refer to US intelligence as the Stasi, not the Gestapo.

As I was leaving the office for the drive to the NRO for a farewell town hall, I asked Stephanie Sherline to see if she could track down a phone number for Trump. Much to my surprise, several minutes later she told me the president-elect had agreed to speak with me later that afternoon. Connecting from the NRO, I thanked him for taking the call and said he'd gotten my attention when he'd referred to the IC as "Nazis." I explained to him that I wanted to defend the men and women of the Intelligence Community. I tried to appeal to his higher instincts and reiterated the points from my Election Day letter—that he was inheriting a national treasure and that the men and women of the IC wanted only to serve the nation and to make him successful as president. He thanked me and said that he valued the IC and the intelligence he'd been receiving. He then asked if I would put out a statement refuting what was in the dossier. The request felt very transactional—that he would play nice if I would do him a favor. I declined, saying that I couldn't refute or affirm what was in the dossier. He sounded disappointed.

On Thursday, Mike, Jim, John, and I briefed the entire Senate, and on Friday morning, the entire House. To accommodate the many of its 435 members who showed up, we gave the House presentation in an auditorium in the Capitol Visitor Center. After the briefing, the chair and ranking member of the Intelligence Committee—Devin Nunes and Adam Schiff—facilitated questions, with Republicans lined up at a microphone in the aisle on one side of the auditorium, and Democrats on the other. The questions were mostly partisan—from both sides—and we did our best to answer them within the scope of our IC assessment. When Adam Schiff recognized Congresswoman Debbie Wasserman Schultz, what followed was one of the more uncomfortable, dramatic, emotional displays I've witnessed on Capitol Hill. She ripped into Jim Comey over the hacking, the investigations, and the letter to the committees, channeling all of the frustration she'd felt since stepping down as DNC chair into a litany of allegations aimed at him. In the midst of so much chaos, partisanship, and controversy, her anguish was palpable. I truly admired Jim for responding calmly. I tried to think of something I could say to defuse the exchange, but I couldn't.

I traveled from the Capitol to NSA headquarters, where I held my final town hall with the workforce there, thanking them for their quiet service through all the controversies of the past few years and trying to reassure them about the future. That evening, when I arrived back at the office, Stephanie Sherline took a long look at me, and for the first time in six and a half years said, "You look tired."

On Monday morning, the final week of the Obama presidency, I attended an NSC meeting that was neither celebratory nor valedictory. We discussed a difficult national security matter the president needed input on and conveyed our thoughts and departmental positions to him. I spent the next few days focusing on writing performance evaluations and lining up awards and other forms of recognition for the people who'd worked with me the past few years, and who all so richly deserved them.

On Tuesday, I had lunch at the CIA. John then hosted a wonderful send-off with the staff in "the Bubble," CIA's auditorium, featuring a video with clips of me delivering all my well-worn one-liners and geezer jokes. That evening, I thanked the airlift operations team that had arranged my transportation all over the world for six years, including to North Korea. I pinned a medal on the uniform of the enlisted Air Force noncommissioned officer who'd coordinated much of that travel, although what he really deserved was retroactive hazardous-duty pay for his endless patience with me.

On Wednesday, I visited DIA for a farewell town hall there and then met with former senator Dan Coats, who had been named in the media as my likely successor as DNI. I'd first encountered Dan when he'd served as a member of the Senate Intelligence Committee. He understood intelligence oversight but wanted to know more about the day-to-day details of the job, and I didn't hold back. Dan is a very decent man whose belief in "truth to power" made him a solid choice to be DNI, and after our discussion, he took the job with his eyes wide open. Later I presented an award to Mike Dempsey, who had succeeded Robert Cardillo as deputy DNI for intelligence integration and who would serve as acting DNI after

Stephanie and I departed on Friday. That evening, I attended a final National Security Council meeting, at which we continued conducting business. The president thanked us all for our service and said he was proud of what we'd accomplished and that he'd miss us.

On Thursday, with Attorney General Lynch, after some seven years of staff work, I cosigned a directive that allowed for greater sharing of raw signals intelligence—the actual intercepts before they'd been processed—outside of NSA. It required quite a bit of compromise from the SIGINT professionals at NSA to accomplish, but it was another big step for intelligence integration. I met with the cross-agency team that had produced the IC assessment on Russian interference and thanked them for what they'd done for our nation, and at the request of the ODNI workforce, Stephanie and I set aside an hour before lunch to pose for pictures with the staff, the people who were so instrumental to any success we'd achieved in integrating intelligence. ODNI's public affairs team set up a red-carpet backdrop, and we ended up staying for two and a half hours. That evening, the leaders of the other sixteen IC components came to Liberty Crossing for one last meeting—a reception that included martini service. I thanked all of them for all that they had done, and for the work that was still ahead under the new administration.

Stephanie and I also hosted a mini reception for many of our protective-detail officers who had served us for the past six years. We both agreed that this was our most emotional farewell. These great men and women became part of our extended families, protecting us 24/7. They are wonderful people—professional, self-effacing, and dedicated—and always as respectful as possible of what little privacy we had.

On Friday morning, the twentieth of January, Sue and I had been invited to brunch at CIA deputy director David Cohen's home, with John Brennan and his wife. We spent the morning and early afternoon eating, drinking, and laughing, and at noon, noted that John, David, and I had all become private citizens. Early that afternoon, Deputy National Security Adviser Avril Haines and Homeland Security Adviser Lisa Monaco joined us. They'd been working at the White House on the morning of the inauguration, almost right up until noon. We never turned on the Cohens' TV.

For the first time since I started out as a scared second lieutenant in 1963, I left a job *not* thinking about what I would do next. I would turn seventy-six on March 14—eleven years past when most people retire—

never really having asked myself how long I wanted to work or when I'd stop, not until 2015 when Sue had become ill. In the years I was DNI, I'd never felt relieved of duty, not even knowing Stephanie O'Sullivan was at the helm, fully capable of handling everything. My personal security detail had been omnipresent, and I was always able to communicate with the national security structure. I had comms in the office. I had comms in the car. I had comms at home. If I traveled, a special comms team accompanied me. I was never out of touch and never able to completely relax. We have six years of vacation pictures in which I'm obviously not chilling out, because I was always aware of the emails and cables piling up. At noon on January 20, 2017, those obligations and all of that anxiety evaporated, much to my great relief.

On Saturday, with a good bit of help, I packed up the office, making sure I kept track of the jar of paperclips I'd received from President Obama, and all the other meaningful mementoes I'd accumulated on the job. Now that the DNI's office was no longer mine, with no one pushing to keep me on schedule, no calls from the White House and Congress to push me off schedule, no briefings, no papers to sign, no emails to catch up on and answer over the weekend, the place finally felt calm and quiet. By Sunday afternoon, as I stood and looked at the bare walls and empty shelves, it finally felt real that my fifty-five years of service was over. I didn't regret its ending.

Life as a retiree took some adjustment. My first trip through self-checkout at the grocery store had all the makings of vaudeville comedy, and the short-term protective-detail officer assigned to me seemed quite amused. I also had my grandson on speed dial for whenever I encountered IT difficulties. It's more than a little disconcerting to pivot from being a sought-after expert on national cybersecurity priorities to not being able to figure out where I'd saved a Word document before I closed the file. Some adjustments were pleasant, and cataract surgery was a life-changing event. Driving me home from Walter Reed, Sue asked why I was reading all the road signs aloud. "Because I can see them now!" I replied. She glanced at me sideways without saying anything else. Vacationing in Antigua, or just having morning coffee with Sue, I wondered what was so important that I hadn't found time to relax for so long.

I did relax, but after a break I continued making the rounds at colleges and universities, appealing to the next generation of US voters and potential intelligence officers about the virtues of public service. I felt such engagements were an "intelligence-geezer obligation." And I watched from the outside as the new administration struggled to govern while contending with the new president's aversion to inconvenient facts. On his first full day in office, he sent his new press secretary out to address the media coverage of the inauguration. All the papers and cable news networks had run side-by-side pictures shot from the top of the Washington Monument. One showed President Obama's inauguration in 2009, with crowds packed into the National Mall and spilling out into the streets and sidewalks, and the other showed President Trump's inauguration in 2017, which was visibly more sparsely attended. Contrary to all the images and data, Sean Spicer berated the media for their coverage, announcing, "This was the largest audience to ever witness an inauguration, period." Telling them the White House would hold them responsible for misrepresentations, he took no questions.

An hour and a half later, President Trump was on camera at CIA headquarters. When I'd heard the first place he would visit as president was the CIA, I naïvely wondered if my appeal to his higher instincts had somehow had impact. No. He took to the microphone and began rambling about the "dishonest media," the size of his inauguration crowd, and his belief that military and law enforcement people had voted for him en masse, lumping the CIA into those categories and saying, "Probably almost everybody in this room voted for me, but I will not ask you to raise your hands if you did. But I would guarantee a big portion, because we're all on the same wavelength, folks." He expressed his support of the IC with "I want to say that there is nobody that feels stronger about the intelligence community and the CIA than Donald Trump. There's nobody." He briefly interrupted himself to say, "The wall behind me is very, very special," and then resumed his self-aggrandizing diatribe. The problem was that the sacred wall he was standing before—with its 125 stars representing fallen CIA officers—is the CIA's equivalent of the Tomb of the Unknown Soldier, not a place for politics or boasting. I considered putting out a statement, but John Brennan expressed that he was "deeply saddened and angered" and that "Trump should be ashamed of himself," and I felt that covered it.

On Friday, January 27, a week after stepping down, I went to FBI headquarters for a wonderful farewell from the Bureau. Just before the ceremony, I met briefly with Jim Comey in his office, and he mentioned that earlier that day, he'd been invited to dinner at the White House with the president. My impression then was that he was uneasy about the invitation, and I hadn't seen much that had made Jim uneasy in the past. He said that he hoped to impress upon the president the importance of an independent FBI and an independent FBI director—that they couldn't and shouldn't be "buddies." I agreed, and I empathized with his difficult position. A few moments later, we were both onstage, and I told the FBI workforce that through all of the recent controversy, the Bureau—with their commitment to "fidelity, bravery, integrity"—remained a pillar of our democracy.

Throughout President Trump's first week in office, people on both sides of the aisle appeared shocked as he actually began fulfilling his campaign promises through a series of executive orders. The most questionable—legally and morally—appeared to be the travel ban he signed on Friday. The order indefinitely blocked Syrian refugees from entering the United States and suspended entry of anyone from Iran, Iraq, Libya, Somalia, Sudan, Syria, and Yemen for ninety days. The president stated that the executive order was being issued to prevent terrorism, but to many people, it echoed his call as a candidate for a "total and complete shutdown of Muslims entering the United States." More than sixty thousand visas were temporarily revoked, and hundreds of people were detained Friday after arriving at American airports, including US green card holders and permanent residents returning from travel overseas—people who lived in the United States who were prevented from returning home. With the same signature, President Trump also ceded leadership on the Syrian refugee crisis to Europe. We suddenly stopped helping those who were the true victims of the Islamic State, and of Assad's regime supported by Russia.

A national outcry followed over the weekend, with thousands of people protesting at airports where travelers were being detained without warrant or charges. People took to social media to protest, followed closely by a counterprotest in favor of detaining Muslims. I'd been a private citizen for a week and no longer had access to intelligence on what was happening, but I was well aware that Russian social media accounts had not been shut down and felt certain their activities on Facebook and Twitter were leading the charge in stoking anger between Americans with differing political viewpoints.

Meanwhile, President Trump—just like President-elect Trump—showed an aggressive indifference to getting to the bottom of the Russian interference in the election. He continued to deny that he or his campaign had any contacts with Russia, even as he fired Mike Flynn as national security adviser on February 13, officially for "misleading the vice president" about conversations he'd had with the Russian ambassador. Three days later Trump tweeted, "The Democrats had to come up with a story as to why they lost the election, and so badly (306), so they made up a story—RUSSIA. Fake news!" On February 26 he tweeted, "Russia talk is FAKE NEWS put out by the Dems, and played up by the media, in order to mask the big election defeat and the illegal leaks!"

Watching all of this, I knew it would be very difficult for anyone still in government to contradict the president, and I recalled how helpful it had been when Mike Hayden had appeared on television to say the things I could not say as DNI. I decided that speaking out was another obligation I had, and so I agreed to appear on *Meet the Press* on Sunday, March 5.

Early on Saturday, March 4—the day before my appearance—President Trump tweeted twice with a new conspiracy theory: "Terrible! Just found out that Obama had my 'wires tapped' in Trump Tower just before the victory. Nothing found. This is McCarthyism!" and "How low has President Obama gone to tapp [sic] my phones during the very sacred election process. This is Nixon/Watergate. Bad (or sick) guy!" So, of course, the first question Chuck Todd asked me the next day on the show was if I knew of a wiretap on Trump's offices. "For the part of the national security apparatus that I oversaw as DNI," I replied, "there was no such wiretap activity mounted against the president-elect at the time, or as a candidate, or against his campaign." I said I wouldn't necessarily know about law enforcement wiretaps, although I would know if a foreign-intelligence-related FISA warrant had been issued. I don't think Chuck Todd was expecting so straight an answer, so he pursued the line of questioning.

"And at this point, you can't confirm or deny whether that exists?"

"I can deny it."

"There is no FISA court order?"

"No, not to my knowledge."

"Of anything at Trump Tower?"

"No."

Chuck looked genuinely surprised and thought for a moment before replying, "Well, that's an important revelation at this point. Let me ask you this. Does intelligence exist that can definitively answer the following question, whether there were improper contacts between the Trump campaign and Russian officials?" This question couldn't be answered as easily, and I clarified that just because something had not been included as evidence in the IC assessment didn't mean it hadn't come to light since then. "There's a lot of smoke," Chuck observed, "but there hasn't been that smoking gun yet. At what point should the public start to wonder if this is all just smoke?" I answered, "Well, that's a good question. I don't know. I do think, though, it is in everyone's interest, in the current president's interests, in the Democrats' interests, in the Republicans' interest, in the country's interest, to get to the bottom of all this. Because it's such a distraction. And certainly, the Russians have to be chortling about the success of their efforts to sow dissension in this country."

That was the crucial point I most wanted to make—we needed to know the facts of what happened—because the Russians were going to attack us again, and the next time, either party or any United States institution could find itself their target. Allegations of collusion and the results of the election were secondary to the profound threat Russia posed—and poses—to our system.

On March 20—two weeks after my TV appearance—Jim Comey and Mike Rogers testified before the House Intelligence Committee. During the hearing, Jim confirmed that the FBI was investigating contacts between Trump associates and Russia during the election. He also said there was "no information" to support the president's claim that Trump Tower had been wiretapped. His testimony generated a lot of discomfiture in the White House, and six weeks later, on the eve of the next hearing at which Jim was scheduled to make an appearance, the president tried to preempt it with a series of tweets reading: "FBI Director Comey was the best thing that ever happened to Hillary Clinton in that he gave her a free pass for many bad deeds! The phony Trump/Russia story was an excuse used by the Democrats as justification for losing the election. Perhaps Trump just ran a great campaign?"

In the Senate Judiciary Committee hearing the next morning, Jim confirmed again that the FBI was investigating Russian interference and possible contacts with the Trump campaign, but went further, stating that Russia was continuing its interference in US politics. He referred to it as "the greatest threat of any nation on earth, given their intention and their ability." Democrats pushed him for an explanation about the letter concerning newly discovered Clinton emails that he'd sent to Congress on October 28, to which he somewhat famously replied, "It makes me mildly nauseous to think that we might have had some impact on the election, but honestly, it wouldn't change the decision." He explained that, because of everything that had led up to the discovery of new emails, he couldn't conceal the new information from Congress. "Everybody who disagrees with me has to come back to October 28 with me and stare at this and tell me what you would do."

I watched the hearing closely, for several reasons: because I admired Jim, considered him a friend, and wished him well, because I hadn't received an intelligence briefing in three and a half months and was interested in what was new, and because I was scheduled to testify five days later before a Senate judiciary subcommittee and wanted a preview of what I was in for. That hearing was originally scheduled for me, Susan Rice, and Sally Yates—the former acting attorney general whom President Trump had fired in January when she'd courageously announced her determination that the president's travel ban was unlawful and that the Justice Department would not defend it in court. The May 8 hearing would have been the first for each of us as private citizens, and we all had become controversial figures, although Susan and I had a head start on Sally.

Although Susan had the least to do with the Russian interference investigation, I expected that she would take most of the heat at the hearing—she always had, dating back to Benghazi. Her appearance at *this* hearing was highly anticipated because she'd acknowledged that as national security adviser, she'd requested "unmasking" of US persons who'd participated or been mentioned in valid foreign intelligence intercepts. When their real names were revealed, she learned that some of those individuals had been associated with the Trump campaign. The media—particularly RT and right-wing online "news" sites—implied that our government secrecy signaled an impropriety related to unmasking, and they conflated the implied impropriety with conspiracy theories about Susan and the Obama administration. Although I no longer had access to the intelligence, I felt certain that the Russian social media troll farm was helping to slander Susan—a favorite target of theirs. I knew for a fact that Susan had done nothing wrong, and that requesting an unmasking was sometimes critical to understanding the context of an intercepted conversation. During my tenure as DNI, I'd also requested unmaskings, to learn whom a foreign intelligence target was talking to or talking about. Susan wouldn't be able to discuss details of the classified intercepts during the hearing, but I knew she was looking forward to testifying to clear the air on the subject, and to clear her name.

Then, just four days before our scheduled testimony, the subcommittee's Democratic ranking member, Senator Sheldon Whitehouse, notified Susan that the Republicans had not coordinated with the Democrats on the committee when they'd invited her to testify, and he did not consent to her appearance, asking her to withdraw. Susan felt she had no choice and withdrew her name as a witness. Immediately the Republicans seized on another false narrative, asserting she'd withdrawn because she had something to hide. President Trump tweeted, "Susan Rice, the former National Security Advisor to President Obama, is refusing to testify before a Senate Subcommittee next week on allegations of unmasking Trump transition officials. Not good!" I was displeased with how Susan was being treated and felt I'd lost my only close ally at the witness table. I didn't know Sally as well. She had a reputation for being tough, but I worried the hearing was going to be ugly.

With my opening statement, I recapped the multifaceted Russian campaign and how we'd made our IC assessment. I reviewed the briefings we'd conducted and said that, four months later, "the conclusions and confidence levels reached at the time still stand." I talked about how the idea of unmasking was being misrepresented and misunderstood in the media, and I cited an ODNI transparency report that indicated that 1,934 unmaskings had occurred in 2016 from collections under Section 702 of the FISA Amendments Act. I explained that officials had to follow precise procedures for unmasking, and that unmasked names remained classified and very sensitive. By contrast, leaking those names—or any other classified material—was illegal and endangered national security. Next, I talked about counterintelligence investigations by the FBI, noting how acutely sensitive they are, and added that "during my tenure as DNI, it was my practice to defer to the FBI director—both Director Mueller and then subsequently Director Comey—on whether, when, and to what extent they would inform me about such investigations." I encouraged Congress to renew Section 702 before it expired at the end of 2017. Noting the sharp divisions and lingering anger in the country, I concluded by saying the Russians "must be congratulating themselves."

Over the next three hours, we covered familiar ground on the Russian interference and the IC assessment, the dossier, and the briefings, but we also heard Sally's riveting account of briefing the Trump White House counsel on Mike Flynn's actions that led to his firing as national security adviser. She said she'd met White House counsel Don McGahn on January 26, during the first week of the new administration, and warned him "that there were a number of press accounts of statements that had been made by the vice president and other high-ranking White House officials about General Flynn's conduct that we knew to be untrue." The Justice Department knew—and "the Russians knew—that General Flynn had misled the Vice President," and that created, "a situation where the national security advisor could be blackmailed by the Russians." She said that the FBI had interviewed Flynn on January 24, the Justice Department "got a readout from the FBI on the 25th," and she'd gone to McGahn on the twenty-sixth so that the White House could take appropriate action, noting, "You don't want your national security advisor compromised by the Russians." McGahn considered overnight and asked her to return for further discussion on Friday the twenty-seventh. She worked with the FBI over the weekend to document everything that had taken place and called McGahn on Monday, January 30, to inform him that the material "was available if he wanted to see it." In the hearing, Senator Whitehouse asked her if anyone from the White House ever reviewed what they'd prepared. "I don't know what happened after that," Sally responded, "because that was my last day." President Trump fired her that afternoon.

At one point as she recounted this story, Senator Graham stopped her, asking, "Okay and I don't mean to interrupt you, but this is important to me. How did the conversation between the Russian ambassador and Mr. Flynn make it to the Washington Post?" I answered for us, "That's a great question. All of us would like to know that."

For eighteen days after Sally Yates's conversation with Don McGahn, Mike Flynn stayed on as national security adviser, though both he and the White House knew that he'd been compromised by the Russians and that the FBI was investigating the compromise. President Trump finally— and reluctantly—fired Flynn on February 13. Jim Comey would later testify that the president met with him alone on February 14, telling him, "I hope you can see your way clear to letting this go, to letting Flynn go. He is a good guy. I hope you can let this go." Jim did not agree to drop the investigation. In December, after Flynn had pleaded guilty to misleading the FBI, President Trump tweeted, "I had to fire General Flynn because he lied to the Vice President and the FBI. He has pled guilty to those lies. It is a shame because his actions during the transition were lawful. There was nothing to hide!"

As I listened to Sally testify, I thought about what a shame it was that the Justice Department had lost someone so willing and capable of speaking truth to power. That impression was only strengthened as members of the committee grilled her on her decision not to defend the president's travel ban. Senator John Cornyn told her he found it enormously disappointing "that you would countermand the executive order of the president of the United States because you happen to disagree with it as a policy matter." "I appreciate that, senator," Sally shot back, "and let me make one thing clear. It is not purely as a policy matter. In fact, I'll remember my confirmation hearing, in an exchange that I had with you and others of your colleagues where you specifically asked me in that hearing that if the president asked me to do something that was unlawful or unconstitutional—and one of your colleagues said, or even just that would reflect poorly on the Department of Justice—would I say no? And I looked at this, I made a determination that I believed that it was unlawful. I also thought that it was inconsistent with principles of the Department of Justice and I said no. And that's what I promised you I would do and that's what I did." While I didn't know Sally well at the start of the hearing, I admired and respected the strength of character, convictions, and impeccable integrity she demonstrated, and I felt as if we bonded under fire as the hearing went on.

All of those conversations were interesting, but to me, there was one overriding reason we'd been called to testify. Midway through the hearing, I said, "I understand how critical leaks are and unmasking and all these ancillary issues. But to me, the transcendent issue here is the Russian interference in our election process, and what that means to the erosion of the fundamental fabric of our democracy, and that to me is a huge deal. And they're going to continue to do it. And why not? It proved successful." Then, near the end of the hearing—employing not very subtle sarcasm to introduce what I really wanted to say—I expressed why I was willing to testify publicly as a private citizen about what had happened: "Well, as much as I *love* congressional hearings, I think there is a useful purpose served, because I think the most important thing that needs to be done here, is to educate the electorate as to what the Russians' objective is, and the tactics and techniques, and procedures that they've employed and will continue to employ."

After the hearing, President Trump sat down with reporters from *Time* magazine to watch clips and critique Sally and me. He was quoted by *Time* as saying, "Watch them start to choke like dogs," and then, referring specifically to me, "Ah, he's choking. Ah, look." When a friend forwarded the story and I read Trump's comments, it occurred to me that if President Obama had said that I had "choked" at a congressional hearing, I'd have been devastated. President Trump's remarks just didn't bother me.

The thought I expressed at the end of the hearing—that we had to talk about what the Russians had done to us—was what led me to appear on *Meet the Press* in March and even—perhaps against my better judgment—to start writing a book around the same time. However, it took one more event to convince me that an occasional public appearance wasn't going to cut it, and that event happened the very next day after the hearing.

On Tuesday, May 9, my friend Jim Comey was talking to FBI employees in the Los Angeles field office when a nearby TV screen posted "breaking news"—he'd been fired as FBI director. No one had informed him. The same day, the White House put out a statement that the firing was on the recommendation of Sessions and Rosenstein, ostensibly because Jim had overreached with the investigation of Clinton's emails. Shortly after the announcement, according to a report in the *New York Times,* President Trump bragged to Russian officials in the Oval Office, "I just fired the head of the FBI. He was crazy, a real nut job. I faced great pressure because of Russia. That's taken off."

On Wednesday, White House deputy press secretary Sarah Sanders changed the story, saying the president had lost confidence in Comey because of his poor leadership at the FBI, "and frankly he'd been considering letting Director Comey go since the day he was elected." On Thursday, the president changed the story yet again, stating in an interview, "He's a showboat, he's a grandstander, the FBI has been in turmoil," and that the workforce had lost faith in Jim as a leader. Trump further said that he was going to fire Comey regardless of Sessions's and Rosenstein's recommendations. He went on: "And, in fact, when I decided to just do it, I said to myself, I said, 'You know, this Russia thing with Trump and Russia is a made-up story, it's an excuse by the Democrats for having lost an election that they should've won.'" Then, on Friday, Trump tweeted, "When James Clapper himself, and virtually everyone else with knowledge of the witch hunt, says there is no collusion, when does it end?" This was after tweeting on Tuesday, "Director Clapper reiterated what everybody, including the fake media already knows—there is 'no evidence' of collusion w/ Russia and Trump."

For me, this was the final straw. Jim Comey was a distinguished public servant, and his firing and the way it was handled were truly reprehensible. I think people could reasonably disagree with some of his decisions, but he'd always made them with the best interests of the nation in mind, and to say that FBI had lost faith in his leadership was a flat lie. I was angry at both the way President Trump and his White House had treated my friend and colleague and at the thought that our nation had lost yet another leader with the courage to speak truth to power. And then the president asserted that I had exonerated him of collusion when, in fact, I'd made it very clear that the Intelligence Community simply could not corroborate allegations of collusion by the time we'd completed our report in January.

On Friday, the same day the president posted that second tweet naming me, I went on MSNBC to refute the words that he had attributed to me. "My practice during the six and a half years that I was at the DNI," I told Andrea Mitchell, "was always to defer to the director of the FBI—be it Director Bob Mueller or Director James Comey—on whether, when, and what to tell me about a counterintelligence investigation. So it is not surprising or abnormal that I would not have known about the investigation, or even more importantly, the content of that investigation. So, I don't know if there was collusion or not, I don't know if there is evidence of collusion or not, nor should I have in this particular context." Andrea started to ask a question, but I wasn't finished. "And if I may make one more point, what we were focused on and certainly what I was focused on in the madcap environment of the end of my time as DNI was the Intelligence Community assessment that we put together on Russian interference in our election, which by the way is the issue we really ought to be focusing on as a nation." On the issue of collusion, I told her, "There was no evidence that rose to that level at that time that found its way into the Intelligence Community assessment, which we had pretty high confidence in. That's not to say there wasn't evidence, but not that met that threshold."

On Sunday, May 14, I told Jake Tapper on CNN, "I think in many ways our institutions are under assault both externally—and that's the big news here is the Russian interference in our election system—and I think as well our institutions are under assault internally." Jake asked, "Internally from the president?" And I responded, "Exactly." I explained, "The Founding Fathers, in their genius, created a system of three coequal branches of government and a built-in system of checks and balances, and I feel as though that's under assault and is eroding."

Looking at the recording of that interview, I again appeared tired. This time, I wasn't tired from working around the clock for months on end. I was tired because my journey of seventy-six years had led me to a place that should be home, and I'd found that the foundation of that home was beginning to crumble and the pillars that supported its roof were shaking. In the period of just a few months, our president had attacked Congress that wouldn't pass legislation at his will, the judiciary that dared to rule against his travel ban, the "dishonest media," the "Nazi" Intelligence Community, the FBI investigating his campaign, and anyone who said no to him. Beyond that, he had disparaged minority Americans and mocked those with disabilities. At the close of his first week in office, the *Economist* Intelligence Unit updated its Democracy Index to indicate that the United States no longer qualified as a full-fledged democracy. For the first time, because of an "erosion of public trust in political institutions," our democratic status was listed as "flawed."

Since then, President Trump's motto, "America First," has meant tearing up agreements that the United States had made with other nations and not meeting obligations we'd incurred before he took office. He marginalized NATO, pulled out of the Paris Climate Accord, said he wouldn't honor the North American Free Trade Agreement, abandoned the Trans-Pacific Partnership, and decertified the Joint Comprehensive Plan of Action to prevent Iran from acquiring a nuclear weapon. I don't see how North Korea or any other nation would trust the United States to live up to any new deal we tried to make. We have ceded leadership on global issues to China, Germany, and Russia.

I also looked tired in that interview because I knew who was behind all of this. In a 2005 Russian "state of the nation" speech, Vladimir Putin had said: "Above all, we should acknowledge that the collapse of the Soviet Union was the major geopolitical disaster of the century. As for the Russian nation, it became a genuine drama. Tens of millions of our co-citizens and copatriots found themselves outside Russian territory. More-over, the epidemic of disintegration infected Russia itself." He blamed the United States for that disaster and wanted nothing more than for Russia to regain glory at our expense. By May 2017, when Jim Comey was fired and I began appearing on the talk shows, we'd learned that the Russian operation had been even more expansive than the IC had assessed in January. We knew now that the Russians had thousands of Twitter accounts and tens of thousands of bots that posted more than a million tweets. They posted more than a thousand videos on YouTube with days of streaming content. Facebook has said Russian content reached 126 million of its American users—an astonishing number, considering that only 139 million Americans voted.

As the leader of the Intelligence Community, I testified that the IC did not attempt to assess whether the Russian influence campaign impacted the results of the election. As a private citizen, I had no doubt they influenced at least some voters. Looking at the savvy ways the Russians targeted specific voter groups—for instance, buying advertisements on Facebook promoting Clinton's support of the Black Lives Matter movement and ensuring those ads ran only on the pages of white conservative voters in swing states; at how they created lies that helped Trump and hurt Clinton and promoted these falsehoods through social media and state-sponsored channels to the point that the traditional US media were unwittingly spreading Russian propaganda; and at how they ran a multi-faceted campaign and sustained it at a high level from early in 2015 until Election Day in 2016 . . . of course the Russian efforts affected the outcome. Surprising even themselves, they swung the election to a Trump win. To conclude otherwise stretches logic, common sense, and credulity to the breaking point. Less than eighty thousand votes in three key states swung the election. I have no doubt that more votes than that were influenced by this massive effort by the Russians.

As the investigations have advanced, the specter of collusion has dominated the discussion. When I left office on January 20, I'd seen no smoking-gun evidence that the Russian government and the Trump campaign were in substantive coordination of their efforts. I didn't learn about the June 9, 2016, meeting between candidate Trump's closest advisers and representatives of the Russian government—purportedly to discuss "dirt on Hillary" and sanctions against wealthy Russians—until I was firmly retired. But what I did see as DNI—something brought home for me as I relived the election while preparing this book—is that the Russians and the campaign seemed to employ strikingly parallel messaging in social media posts and public statements, effectively complementing each other to great effect, with no attempt to hide it.

That combined effort appeared to go well beyond candidate Trump's calling on a foreign power to find thirty thousand missing emails belonging to his political opponent and publish them, or his praise for WikiLeaks—which Trump's CIA director later aptly characterized as a non–nation state hostile intelligence service—for publishing materials Russian intelligence had stolen. On a routine basis, whenever the campaign published an allegation that hurt Clinton, the Russians would repeat, amplify, and embellish that claim; and when the Russians promulgated a conspiracy theory about her, Trump would repeat it at campaign rallies and on Twitter. Whether secretly coordinated or not, whether there was actual collusion or not, this parallelism constituted a putative team effort by the Russian government and the Trump campaign to undermine truth and to cause much of the American public to question if facts were even knowable. And it didn't end with the election.

The possibility that Trump's campaign worked or coordinated any political tactics with the Russian government—directly or indirectly—is unquestionably of crucial importance. But in my mind, far more concerning than any specter of collusion is the aggressive indifference of President Trump's administration to viewing Russia as a threat and its abject failure to do anything about this existential menace to our nation and our way of life. Repeatedly, the president has spoken about Iran's violating the "spirit" of the Joint Comprehensive Plan of Action—the agreement that prevents it from attaining a nuclear weapon—and he announced in October 2017 that he was decertifying the deal. Yet Russia has built, repeatedly tested, and deployed cruise missiles capable of carrying nuclear warheads in violation of the Intermediate-Range Nuclear Forces (INF) Treaty. Those violations are a serious threat to global security, and Putin's March 2018 speech in which he described "invincible" nuclear weapons—messaging aimed at both domestic and foreign audiences—further illustrates the profound animosity he has for the United States, the only adversary these weapons are intended for. Russia has continued to occupy large parts of Ukraine and to murder civilians in Syria. It has worked against American interests in Afghanistan and helped North Korea avoid sanctions. And it has continued to attack American institutions and to drive social divisions deeper, on social media and state-sponsored broadcasts. Whether that involves assailing the credibility of the press, the FBI, and the US Intelligence Community or promoting the violent rise of neo-Nazis, the Russians have been there, often finding their propaganda effectively supported by the US president. And they've done these things with impunity. In July 2017, Congress voted to impose sanctions against Russia in response to election interference. The sanctions bill passed the House 419–3 and the Senate 98–2. Knowing any veto would be easily overridden, Trump allowed it to become law, and then the administration simply chose not to enforce the sanctions.

And there's something that bothers me even more. On Sunday, January 22, 2017—just two days after the inauguration—NBC's Chuck Todd confronted Counselor to the President Kellyanne Conway on *Meet the Press*, asking her about Sean Spicer's blatant and obvious lie that "this was the largest audience to ever witness an inauguration, period." She responded, "Don't be so overly dramatic about it, Chuck. You're saying that it's a falsehood, and they're giving, Sean Spicer, our press secretary, gave alternative facts."

"Alternative facts." I just can't square "alternative facts" with my life experience. My parents taught me that one faced life's truths head-on. Professionally, my dad approached his work without slant or politics, and I don't recall his ever changing facts to make his bosses happy. I never heard the phrase "truth to power" from him, but I saw how he lived and worked. For fifty-three years, I tried hard to speak truth—sometimes very uncomfortable truth—to people making crucial decisions for our national security. Telling General Bill Livsey that I couldn't provide him with "unambiguous" warning of a North Korean invasion was a difficult truth to deliver. Telling Wayne Downing that it was wrong to hold Terry Schwalier accountable for Air Force institutional failings was another. When I made mistakes—mistakenly finding WMD sites in Iraq or misunderstanding Senator Wyden's question in testimony—they were honest mistakes.

I don't believe our democracy can function for long on lies, particularly when inconvenient and difficult facts spoken by the practitioners of truth are dismissed as "fake news." I know that the Intelligence Community cannot serve our nation if facts are negotiable. Just in the past few years, I've seen our country become so polarized because people live in separate realities in which everyone has his or her own set of facts—some of which are lies knowingly distributed by a foreign adversary. This was not something I could idly stand by and watch happen to the country I love.

I've often thought about General George Patton's quote "The time to take counsel of your fears is before you make an important battle decision. That's the time to listen to every fear you can imagine. When you have collected all the facts and fears and made your decision, turn off all your fears and go ahead." Applying Patton's battlefield wisdom to the profession of intelligence, we provide facts to decision makers more broadly—whether they sit in the Oval Office or are hunkered down in an oval foxhole—to reduce uncertainty, risk, and, yes, fear. That's why intelligence is vital; that's what we do and why we do it.

As I left government service, I had my own decision to make. I thought hard about all my concerns—my "fears"—about the idea of writing a book. I had not planned to write anything, in spite of the urging of many friends and colleagues who thought I should, if for no other reason than to chronicle living through fifty years of the history of American intelligence. But after experiencing the election, the unprecedented Russian interference in our political process, and the behavior by and impact of the Trump administration, I changed my mind. I think the catalyst was the stark, visceral realization of seeing the fundamental pillars of our country being undermined both by the Russians and by the president. This shook me, since it was these very attributes—our form of government, our deference to the rule of law, our rich mix of ethnicities and nationalities, and our freedoms, including especially a free and independent press, and freedom of religious practice—that all seemed under siege, no longer universally respected and protected as assumed "givens."

My parents instilled respect for these unique attributes of America throughout my formative years. My dad, who served faithfully for twenty-eight years in the Army during World War II, the Korean conflict, and Vietnam, was a living example to me of the importance of actively defending and protecting this country and what it stands for. And as I've described, I followed in his footsteps, serving thirty-four years in the military, sixteen years as a civilian in government, and six years in industry—virtually all in the profession of intelligence. I always considered this a noble calling, a sacred public trust, because, simply stated, I believe in this country. Part of this instilled ethos was profound respect for the president as commander in chief; I served in that spirit every president from John Kennedy through Barack Obama. So, speaking critically of our current president is counterinstinctive and difficult for me to do, but I feel it is my duty.

We have elected someone as president of the United States whose first instincts are to twist and distort truth to his advantage, to generate financial benefit to himself and his family, and, in so doing, to demean the values this country has traditionally stood for. He has set a new low bar for ethics and morality. He has caused damage to our societal and political fabric that will be difficult and will require time to repair. And, close to my heart, he has besmirched the Intelligence Community and the FBI—pillars of our country—and deliberately incited many Americans to lose faith and confidence in them. While he does this, he pointedly refuses to acknowledge the profound threat posed by Russia, inexplicably trusting the denials by Putin about their meddling in our political process over the considered judgments by his own Intelligence Community.

The Russians are astutely and persistently exploiting this divisiveness with every controversial issue they can identify, and regrettably, we are a very inviting target for them as they target both sides of every issue. They exploit Black Lives Matter by pretending to be hateful white people online, and they incite anger among targeted groups of whites by playing to negative black stereotypes; they engender fear of Muslims among Christians and vice versa; they stoke fear on both sides of the gun control debate; and so on. To be clear, the Russians are our primary existential threat. All those nuclear weapons they have or are developing are intended for only one adversary: the United States. They have been at war with us in the information realm for some time, and the apathy displayed by many Americans toward this profound menace is very disturbing. President Trump abets this apathy by his willful and skillful deflections. What we need him to do is to recognize this threat for what it is and to galvanize us in a coordinated national response. Only he can provide this leadership.

My hope is that this book will, in some measure, help people regain awareness. That's also the reason I decided to appear regularly on CNN, so that I could continue to speak "truth to power"—in this case, to the American people. In the letter I wrote to President Obama in the spring of 2010 when he was considering whether to send my nomination as DNI to the Senate, I said: "I do not like publicity. I've spent the last week cringing every time I saw my name in the paper, or my face on the tube. I think it is part of the unwritten code of professional intelligence officers to stay out of the media." That seems like a very long time ago, in a very different, more innocent environment.

I often encounter strangers in airliners, airports, and other public places who, upon recognizing me, convey gratitude for my speaking up and out, and giving them a voice. They do so in a way that doesn't sound like the reflexive cliché "Thanks for your service." I certainly don't make the pretentious claim that I am carrying the torch of truth, but in some ways, that seems to be what many people implicitly expect of me and others—such as John Brennan and Jim Comey—who are staunch advocates for our values. That's not to suggest that everyone I've encountered is uniformly supportive; some have angrily confronted me, questioning my loyalty and patriotism for speaking out.

It is, at this point, impossible to know whether we will restore our balance and national conscience. We have a reassuring history of recovery from similar national traumas, most prominently the Civil War and the Vietnam War. Our institutions were battered, and our national fabric severely stressed to the breaking point. But we recovered from both and, over time, emerged the better for it.

Acknowledgments

I have many people to thank, starting with many friends and colleagues who urged me to write a book, though I think the greatest credit goes to my collaborator and friend Trey Brown. Trey served with great distinction as my speechwriter during my final three years as DNI. We quickly mind-melded on speeches he wrote for me—a rare chemistry, something that happens once a career, if ever. Several of our speeches were published in *Vital Speeches of the Day*, and Trey was recognized with the internationally prestigious Cicero Award for "Why Black Lives Matter to US Intelligence," a speech I gave at two historically black colleges. After I stepped down as DNI, Trey and I had several deep conversations about whether to take on this project, and I realized that I would never be able to do it solo, so we forged our partnership. As we had with our speeches, we developed a battle rhythm on drafting the book, and suddenly the manuscript was done. If it wasn't for Trey, I'd still be struggling with the first chapter.

I also need to thank four friends and colleagues who volunteered to wire-brush the manuscript—Stephanie O'Sullivan, my former deputy; Bob Litt, my former general counsel; Shawn Turner, my public affairs director; and Trey's wife, Amy, whose "outsider" perspective was always spot-on. They provided invaluable critiques and suggestions. I want to thank Gail Ross for being my Sherpa through the world of publishing and for connecting me with Viking. As well, I want to thank Viking, which took a big gamble based on only a short proposal for the book, and specifically Rick Kot for his confidence in us, Jane Cavolina and Rick for their brilliant edits, Diego Núñez for marrying the text with pictures and graphics, and Bruce Giffords for shepherding this book through the production process on a daunting schedule.

The responsibility for any and all errors of commission or omission is entirely mine, and finally, the views expressed here are entirely mine and do not in any way reflect positions and policies of the US government generally, or the Intelligence Community specifically.

Glossary of Abbreviations

AFMIC	Armed Forces Medical Intelligence Center
AFTAC	Air Force Technical Applications Center
AQAP	al-Qaida in the Arabian Peninsula
AWACS	Airborne Warning and Control System
BND	Federal Intelligence Service (German intelligence agency)
CBJB	Congressional Budget Justification Book
CERN	European Organization for Nuclear Research
CIA	Central Intelligence Agency
CR	continuing resolution
CYBERCOM	US Cyber Command
DARPA	Defense Advanced Research Projects Agency
DCI	director of central intelligence (led IC before DNI established; is also CIA director)
DHS	Department of Homeland Security
DIA	Defense Intelligence Agency
DMA	Defense Mapping Agency
DMZ	Demilitarized Zone (between North and South Korea)
DNC	Democratic National Committee
DNI	director of national intelligence
DOD	Department of Defense
DPRK	Democratic People's Republic of Korea (North Korea)
EKIA	enemy killed in action
FBI	Federal Bureau of Investigation
FISA	Foreign Intelligence Surveillance Act
FSB	Federal Security Service (Russia)

GCHQ	Government Communications Headquarters (UK signals intelligence agency)
GDIP	General Defense Intelligence Program ("Gee-Dip")
GEOINT	geospatial intelligence
GOP	Grand Old Party (alternate name for Republican Party)
GRU	Main Intelligence Directorate (Soviet, now Russian military intelligence agency)
HF	high frequency (radio)
HUMINT	human intelligence
IAEA	International Atomic Energy Agency
IARPA	Intelligence Advanced Research Projects Activity
IC	Intelligence Community
ICBM	intercontinental ballistic missile
IC ITE	IC Information Technology Enterprise—"eyesight"
IED	improvised explosive device
IG	inspector general
INF	Intermediate-Range Nuclear Forces Treaty
IRTPA	Intelligence Reform and Terrorism Prevention Act of 2004
ISIL	Islamic State of Iraq and the Levant (a.k.a. ISIS)
ISIS	Islamic State in Iraq and Syria (a.k.a. ISIL)
JCS	Joint Chiefs of Staff
JWICS	Joint Worldwide Intelligence Communications System
KGB	Committee for State Security (primary Soviet security agency)
LGBTA	lesbian, gay, bisexual, transgender, and allies
LX	Liberty Crossing
MAC	Military Airlift Command
MIP	Military Intelligence Program
MSIC	Missile and Space Intelligence Center
NATO	North Atlantic Treaty Organization
NCPC	National Counterproliferation Center
NCSC	National Counterintelligence and Security Center
NCTC	National Counterterrorism Center
NGA	National Geospatial-Intelligence Agency
NIC	National Intelligence Council
NIE	National Intelligence Estimate
NIM	national intelligence manager

NIMA	National Imagery and Mapping Agency
NIP	National Intelligence Program
NPIC	National Photographic Interpretation Center
NRO	National Reconnaissance Office
NSA	National Security Agency
NSC	National Security Council (chaired by president)
OCO	overseas contingency operations (additional funding line for combat support)
ODNI	Office of the Director of National Intelligence
ONCIX	Office of the National Counterintelligence Executive
OPM	Office of Personnel Management
OSD	Office of the Secretary of Defense
OSI	Office of Special Investigations (Air Force)
PACOM	US Pacific Command
PC	Principals Committee (chaired by national security adviser)
PDB	President's Daily Brief
PDDNI	principal deputy director of national intelligence
PLA	People's Liberation Army (Chinese army)
PLC	Platoon Leaders Course
POW/MIA	prisoner of war/missing in action
RGB	Reconnaissance General Bureau (North Korean intelligence agency)
RNC	Republican National Committee
ROK	Republic of Korea (South Korea)
ROTC	Reserve Officer Training Corps
RPG	rocket-propelled grenade
RT	Russia Today
SAC	Strategic Air Command
SAM	surface-to-air missile
SASC	Senate Armed Services Committee
SCIF	sensitive compartmented information facility
SIGINT	signals intelligence
STRATCOM	US Strategic Command
TAC	Tactical Air Command
TAO	Tailored Access Operations
TARP	Troubled Asset Relief Program
TLAM	Tomahawk Land Attack Missile

TNT	tunnel neutralization team
UGA	University of Georgia
USD(I)	undersecretary of defense for intelligence
WMD	weapons of mass destruction
WTF	WikiLeaks Task Force (CIA)

Index